AF607951

THE MYSTICAL SCIENCE OF THE SOUL

Medieval Cognition in Bernardino de Laredo's Recollection Method

JESSICA A. BOON

The Mystical Science of the Soul

Medieval Cognition in Bernardino de Laredo's Recollection Method

UNIVERSITY OF TORONTO PRESS
Toronto Buffalo London

Toronto Buffalo London
www.utppublishing.com

ISBN 978-1-4426-4428-1

Library and Archives Canada Cataloguing in Publication

Boon, Jessica A., 1976–
The mystical science of the soul : medieval cognition in Bernardino de Laredo's recollection method / Jessica A. Boon.

Includes bibliographical references and index.
ISBN 978-1-4426-4428-1

1. Laredo, Bernardino de, 1482–1545? – Influence. 2. Mysticism – Spain – Castile – History – To 1500. 3. Cognition – History – To 1500. 4. Human body – Religious aspects. 5. Science, Medieval – Spain – Castile. 6. Spirituality – Spain – Castile – History – To 1500. 7. Recollection (Theology). 8. Theological anthropology. I. Title.

BV5077.S7B65 2012 248.2'2094630902 C2012-903672-2

This book has been published with the help of a grant from the Program for Cultural Cooperation between Spain's Ministry of Culture and United States Universities.

University of Toronto Press acknowledges the financial assistance to its publishing program of the Canada Council for the Arts and the Ontario Arts Council.

University of Toronto Press acknowledges the financial support of the Government of Canada through the Canada Book Fund for its publishing activities.

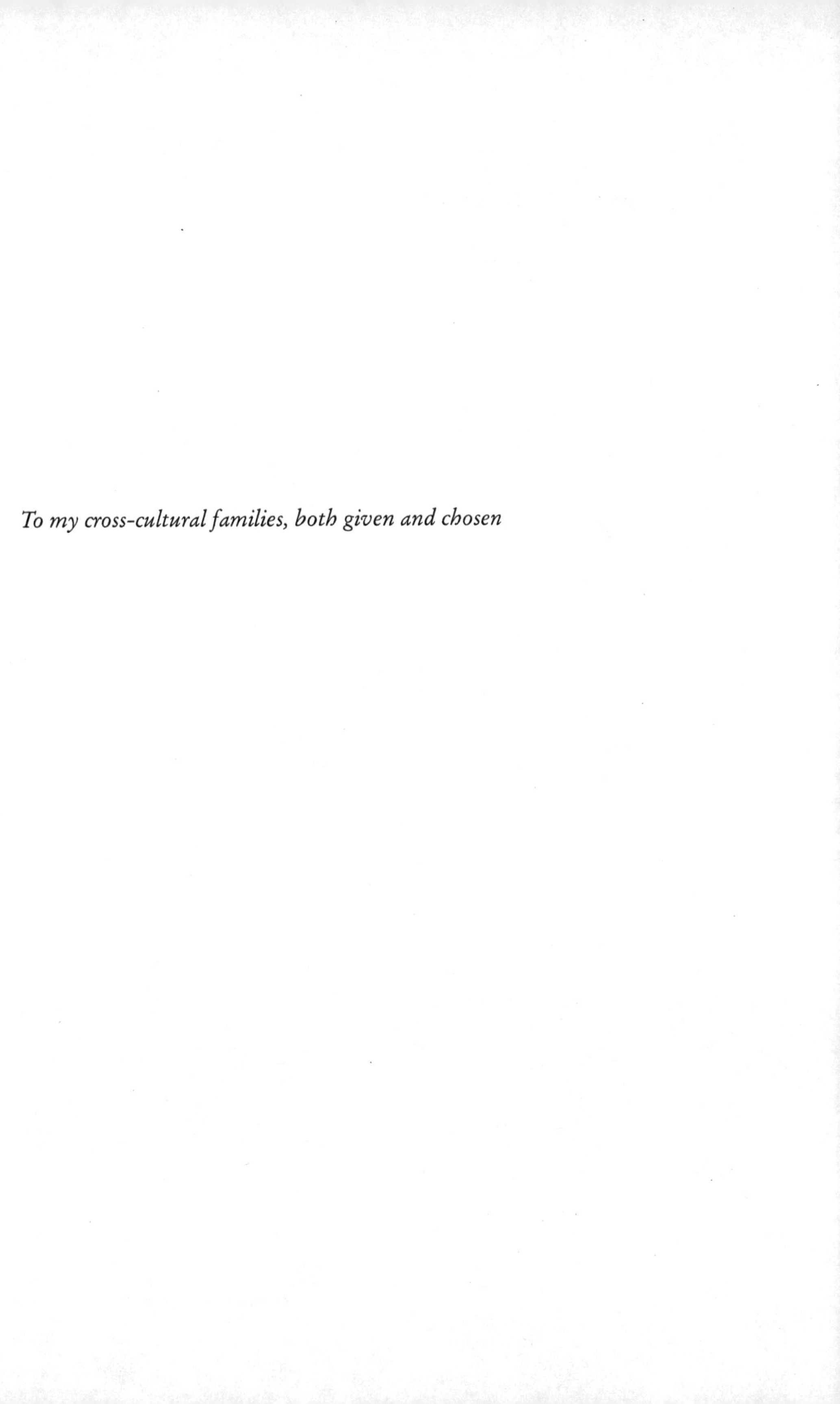

To my cross-cultural families, both given and chosen

My work on mystic writings ... comes from many a sojourn in these remote corners of the past that reveal to the historian the infinitude of a local singularity.

Michel de Certeau

Being spiritual does not entail being nonphysical.

Robert Pasnau

Contents

Illustrations

Acknowledgments

No project that spans a decade and requires the acquisition of knowledge in numerous disciplines can come to fruition without the aid of countless people. This book, begun in the department of Religious Studies at the University of Pennsylvania, has benefited not only from the extraordinary expertise and generosity of E. Ann Matter and Ronald E. Surtz, but also from the model of interdisciplinary work provided by Ann in particular and the medievalist community at the University of Pennsylvania in general that taught me to follow the questions primary sources prompted me to ask. This monograph is a remarkably different project than its original conception as a result of the recent cognitive turn in medieval studies. However, the ethical need to cross disciplines if the source material required it – to become a historian of science in order to accurately analyse the mystical treatise of a prominent apothecary – is an instinct initially instilled in me by my graduate training.

I have accrued many debts in the course of researching and writing this book, debts owed on both sides of the Atlantic and at my three institutions of employment: the University Writing Program at Duke University, Perkins School of Theology at Southern Methodist University, and the Department of Religious Studies at the University of North Carolina at Chapel Hill. Two of my research assistants – Meredith Minister and Josh Masterson – gave invaluable comments on drafts of the manuscript and helped edit the work in its final stages. Deep appreciation is also due to other readers of the manuscript or of previously published articles that are incorporated in it: Catherine Adamson, Jodi Bilinkoff, Erica Gelser, E. Ann Matter, Quincy Newell, Pamela Patton, Lisa Siraganian, Ronald Surtz, Elizabeth Williamson, the history/religious studies writing group Disaster Euphoria, and various anonymous reviewers of the articles and the book manuscript. The staff in the Rare Books and Manuscripts room of the Biblioteca Nacional de Madrid have been unfailingly helpful during my yearly visits, while the Interlibrary Loan staff of Duke's Perkins Library and Perkins's Bridwell Library (especially Sally Hoover) have met the many challenges I set them with aplomb. Duane Harbin and his IT assistants at Perkins scanned reams of photocopied articles to reduce my research from several overweight suitcases to a file full of PDFs on my computer. Julia Perratore provided much-needed assistance with last-minute tasks related to the final manuscript and obtaining images, while Sarah Bloesch took infinite pains in proofreading the bibliography and in counting source texts in a book written in a language she does not know. The index cost was underwritten by a grant from the McLester Fund (UNC, Religious Studies). Others who offered their insights into this project or early access to their forthcoming books and articles include Marla Carlson, María M. Carrión, Laura Delbrugge, Michelle Karnes, Laureano Rodriguez Leleañez, Josefina C. López, James Melvin, Felipe Pereda, Sara Poor, and Cynthia Robinson.

Various conference forums allowed me to present aspects of this work, including the 2003 Society for Spanish and Portuguese Historical Studies annual meeting, the 2004 American Academy of Religion annual meeting, the 2007 Sixteenth Century Society conference, the 2003 and 2008 meetings of the International Medieval Congress in Kalamazoo, Michigan, the 2010 Annual Meeting of the Renaissance Society of America, and the 2010 Centro de Ciencias Humanas y Sociales (CSIC, Madrid) conference on 'Alumbrados y disidencia religiosa en el mundo ibérico.' More specifically, small portions (and the basic insight) of parts of chapter 1, the final section of chapter 2, and certain paragraphs of chapter 5 appeared in 'The Agony of the Virgin: The Swoons and Crucifixion of Mary in Sixteenth Century Castilian Passion Treatises,' *Sixteenth Century Journal* 38, no. 1 (2007): 3–26. The first half of chapter 2 and some paragraphs in chapter 5 appeared in 'A Mystic in the Age of the Inquisition: Bernardino de Laredo's *Converso* Environment and Christological Spirituality,' *Medieval Encounters* 12, no. 2 (2006): 133–52. Chapter 3 is a slightly expanded version of 'Medical Bodies, Mystical Bodies: Medieval Physiological Theory in the Recollection Mysticism of Bernardino de Laredo,' *Viator* 39, no. 2 (2008): 245–68. My thanks to these journals for permission to reprint this work.

It is customary to thank only one's academic influences in book acknowledgments. This project has taught me, however, that a balanced life leads to better scholarly work; those friends who made life and laughter possible are thus key to this book, starting with my early compatriots from Yale and the University of Pennsylvania. While more people than I can name have accompanied me in my perpetual quest for dance venues, I wish to mention those who provided much-needed distraction from my book revisions at junctures in my professional life when balance was lacking: Catherine Adamson, Sarah Bloesch, Ethan Fingerman, Jessica Nelson, and Teri Walker. My grandparents James and Mary Boggs and my uncle Terry lent a sense of home to holidays in Texas. In addition, this project would not have been possible without the forbearance of my dear friends in Madrid, who taught me nearly all the Spanish I know. More people would reach fluency if such good cheer and late-night laughter were incorporated into language curricula on a regular basis. Tina Travecedo Sierra and Miky Casado were particularly patient with my grammatical trajectory; their continuing hospitality makes Madrid my second home.

Last but not least, I have the great good fortune to come from a family of readers and academics. My father, James, has a profound love of linguistic play and cultural complexity that he passed on to me. His mantra 'Never assume!' echoed throughout my childhood and continues to do so in my work to this day. My mother, Olivian, approaches books as both an intellectual and a material puzzle, a puzzle she delights in transforming in order to transmit the text to those cognitively unable (or not yet ready) to receive it in its original form. Working alongside her during the summers of high school and college provided me with the readiness to grasp that both authors and readers can address themselves to texts in far different ways than I do. My sister, Tili Boon Cuillé, was my childhood idol – growing into being the best of friends and each other's closest academic reader has been a joy and a gift. I cannot remember a single semester since I entered college when she did not rescue me from the depths of stress by injecting laughter, energy, and carefully crafted sentences into my life and my writing. I sometimes suspect she knows me better than I know myself.

I dedicate this book to the family who got me started and to the homes I found along the way.

THE MYSTICAL SCIENCE OF THE SOUL

Introduction: Passion Spirituality and Cognitive Studies

> And wouldn't the poor sinner merit that the pupils of the eyes of the veins that are inside the entrails of my soul be beautiful vessels in which could be collected the sacred blood that ran down from the nail in the feet of my loving Lord, [down] the wood of the cross without stopping until it reached the ground …
>
> Bernardino de Laredo (1482–1540?),[1]
> *Subida del Monte Sión* (1535, revised 1538)[2]

Bernardino de Laredo's directive that 'the pupils of the eyes of the veins' found in the 'entrails' of the devotee's soul should become containers for Christ's blood might well strike the modern reader as both physiologically and theologically incomprehensible. How could souls have entrails complete with veins, or veins have eyes? Even if they did, how could Renaissance Castilian readers turn their souls' organs into reliquaries for first-century bodily fluid? Surely this phrasing is simply an elaborate rhetorical gesture, a forerunner to the baroque flourishes of Counter-Reformation piety that saturated southern Europe after the 1563 Council of Trent. In his *Subida del Monte Sión* (*Ascent of Mount Zion*),[3] sometimes categorized as a *recogimiento* (recollection) mystical treatise, sometimes as a method of mental prayer, Laredo mapped three stages of preparation for mystical union: self-knowledge or self-annihilation; Passion spirituality; and recollection, that is, 'transformation of the self into God through love.'[4] By combining previously distinct genres in a vernacular treatise,[5] he extended both spiritual and mystical techniques to a wide audience of male and female members of religious orders, and potentially to a lay audience.[6] Laredo's *Subida* was a foundational text in the uniquely Spanish *recogimiento* tradition formulated in the 1520s and 1530s, particularly for his deployment of the apophatic phrase *no pensar nada* (literally, 'not thinking nothing') to describe quiet unitive prayer.[7] Yet scholars have concluded that his most famous reader, Teresa of Avila,[8] quickly surpassed Laredo in both prose style and mystical method. Easy enough to dismiss the teacher in favour of the stellar pupil; easy enough to dismiss that odd and over-burdened phrasing concerning Jesus's lifeblood in the soul's entrails as tangential to the essence of Laredo's mystical theology.

An intellectual history constructed on these grounds, however, occludes the fact that Laredo was a lay friar and apothecary at a reform Franciscan house outside of Seville,[9] that his other published books were the first pharmaceutical treatises to appear in the Castilian vernacular,[10] and that he was lauded by royalty and local gentry alike for his spectacular medical cures.[11] Laredo's *mystical* treatise displayed his intimate familiarity with medieval *scientific* notions in the Galenic tradition, ranging between explanations of the four elements (earth, water, air, fire), meditations on the digestive and arterial systems, and references to the reigning optical theories, all topics he also addressed in his medical writings. It is the argument of this book that descriptions such as the 'eyes of the soul's entrails' were not simply a stylistic flourish, since Laredo, far more than any of his peers involved in the Observant Franciscan reform of the Spanish church in the early sixteenth century,[12] would have attached actual physiological implications to such a phrase.[13] I contend that Laredo articulated a notion of 'embodied soul' based on his scientific view of cognition, a theory of soul that then served as a unifying basis for the different types of meditation included in his treatise. By presuming an 'embodied soul,' a term scholars usually reserve for studies of neo-Platonic authors, world religions, and seventeenth-century medicine rather than the history of Christian mysticism,[14] Laredo re-patterned existing theological debates over the respective roles of the body versus the soul during the mystical experience of union with an incorporeal divine.

Laredo's cognitively adept mystical method helped inaugurate the Golden Age of Spanish mysticism, and it depended on a deep engagement with medieval Galenic medicine and physiology, monastic assumptions about the roles of memory in conceptual thinking, and even scholastic theories of optics. His version of *recogimiento* found in the 1538 revision of the *Subida* directly influenced Teresa of Avila and John of the Cross, the usual stars of Spanish mystical history.[15] It had a far broader influence as well, for the *Subida* appeared in five editions in several areas of Spain within a century,[16] and is cited among the first books shipped to the New

World.[17] Nor did this new phase in Renaissance mysticism meet with much resistance: Laredo was the only major Castilian mystic of the sixteenth century who was never tried by the Inquisition for a judaizing heresy, nor ever had his treatise expurgated or banned by the famous 1559 Index of Prohibited Works and its subsequent updates. I argue that far from being the mere footnote to Teresa studies that has been his sole trace in American scholarship,[18] Laredo should be considered a key figure of sixteenth-century religious and intellectual history. His vocational training in medieval Galenic medicine (Dioscorides, Avicenna, Mesué, Arnau de Villanova, Joannitius) and his spiritual autodidacticism in a broad array of twelfth- to fifteenth-century religious texts (Gregory the Great, Richard of Saint Victor, Hugh of Balma, Bonaventure, Heinrich Herp, Ludolph of Saxony, Angela of Foligno) enables us to examine for the first time the profound impact of medieval scientific and religious discourses on the Golden Age of Spanish Christianity.

In his *Subida*, Laredo proposed a method of mystical prayer permeated by the prevailing medical constructions of epistemology and physiology, in which the mystic's body becomes complicit in the torture of Christ on the cross. Physiological suffering thus proves to be central to union with the Trinity. Unfortunately, the terminology of 'ascent' (*subida*) so often paired with transcending the body in medieval thought has misled scholars to emphasize only those aspects of Laredo's method that promoted contemplation as separate from embodied devotion:[19] they consistently examine the third, presumably disembodied stage of recollection alone, dismissing the stages of self-knowledge and Passion spirituality as preliminary.[20] I suggest that Laredo's focus on the medical body and its cognitive functions led him to foreground the violence inherent in the suffering bodies of Christ and the devotee as foundational to the discovery of God *within* the soul's 'entrails.' My rereading of the *Subida* counters all previous scholarly discussion of his method as articulating a union through the soul's faculty of the understanding (in the 1535 version of the *Subida*, depending on Victorine intellectual union) and through the faculty of the will (in the 1538 edition, depending on texts of negative theology that identify 'unknowing' with the verb 'love').[21] Laredo's embodied approach is particularly intriguing in the midst of a treatise deploying language from his favourite medieval sources on asceticism and apophatic theology, sources normally considered to reject the body in favour of abstract contemplation.[22] His elevation of Passion meditation is thus central rather than preliminary to his mystical praxis; this requires that we reread the final abstract stage of recollection mysticism (and the phrase *no pensar nada*) with attention to its roots in the physicality of the believer.

The premier scholar of *recogimiento*, Melquíades Andrés, powerfully defines the final stage as 'the transformation of the soul into God' through the 're-collecting' or 'reducing'[23] of the powers of the soul (memory, understanding, will) normally focused outward towards creation, in order to direct them internally towards a God found at the centre of the soul.[24] I argue instead that if Laredo's medieval medical training is taken into account, the internal trajectory of external senses that Andrés identifies as unique to *recogimiento* (and therefore Spanish Golden Age) mysticism turns out to be a common Galenic theory of epistemology modelled on the brain's correlation of sensory data received in its front ventricle, which then flows to middle and rear ventricles where it is assessed by judgment, recombined by imagination and fantasy, and eventually stored in the memory (the 'cell theory' of the brain; see discussion below). Scientifically speaking, then, Spanish *recogimiento* is a logical consequence of medieval and Renaissance theories of cognition rather than a unique mystical method.

Given the scientific plausibility of the three stages of recollection, Andrés's list of words that *recogimiento* authors used for the location of God in the soul is noteworthy.[25] God is found at the soul's *centro*, or its *fondo* (heart, bottom, most intimate depths). More provocatively, God is at the soul's *cima* – which in sixteenth-century usage referred to the highest part of man[26] – not just as *sinderesis* (the apex of the soul's powers, a term beloved by scholastic theologians) but also in terms of organs, that is, the brain connected to the heart.[27] Laredo, a physician before he was a mystic, used all these words interchangeably with the term *entrañas*, or entrails, as the seat of God in the soul. In other words, no analysis of his process of *no pensar nada* can be effective without considering its historical scientific context, for *pensar* (thinking) consists of a physiological epistemology that cannot be negated spiritually if it is not yet understood cognitively. Laredo's interweaving of medieval religious and scientific discourses led him to chart a mystic way in which the embodied soul seeks union with a God located not above in heaven but internal to itself, as its entrails.

Ultimately, I propose that considering internalization *as* embodiment is a critical methodological shift in understanding mystical methods in general, and especially for probing recollection mysticism in depth.[28] The inner man as opposed to the outer man is a Pauline and Lutheran commonplace that is too frequently taken out of context, leading historians of the Renaissance in general, and of Spanish Renaissance religion in particular, to value references to internal (or mental) methods of spirituality as an improvement over external (or bodily) rituals.[29] This book takes its cue from the recent 'cognitive turn' in medieval studies that complicates studies of the body in religion by focusing on the embodied aspects of cognition, claiming a continuum between body and soul rather than a hierarchy.[30] I argue that medieval theories of cognition made the divorce of the body from the soul impossible for a Galenic doctor, even one who spoke of the body and the world with contempt, and by implication impossible for his Castilian audience.[31] Without serious consideration of Laredo's reliance on an embodied soul rather than on a body–soul dualism, therefore, no proper assessment of the unitive stage of *recogimiento*, much less its corollaries in the writings of Teresa of Avila and John of the Cross, can be made.

What 'Matters' in Medieval Religion:[32] From Body–Soul Dualism to Passion Spirituality

If an unprecedented intersection of medieval scientific and spiritual discourses led to Laredo's reconfiguration of the soul as embodied, it is worth taking the time to trace the assumptions among scholars that have allowed his embodied view of soul to be overlooked. Spanish scholarship on the history of Castilian mysticism frequently takes at face value the common rhetoric in the moral treatises of the Middle Ages that denigrated the body as the source of evil (*contemptus mundi*, contempt for the world). In these types of intellectual histories, also common among scholars of early Protestantism, the story goes as follows:

While Christianity is set apart from its family of monotheistic religions by the creedal belief that the divine took on a human body for thirty-three years, the early encounter of Christian authors with neo-Platonic thought led to a theological emphasis on the abstract nature of God and a strong body–soul dualism among the leaders of the church. Plato, in his Socratic dialogues, posited that the objects of human knowledge were ideal Forms, which as abstract concepts are 'real,' while any particular instantiation of them in a concrete object only partially participates in the conceptual category.[33] 'Plato separates the sensible from the thinkable ... [E]ternal objects and necessary truths comprise reality and the real objects of thought are not found in the physical world, nor can they be extracted from it. Knowledge comes out of the mind itself.'[34] Plato originally articulated his theory of ideal Forms in order to support an anthropology that described all human souls as possessing full knowledge until they were joined with a body, at which point they forgot the Forms. Born ignorant of the 'real,' the body–soul complex learns throughout its life by slowly remembering the ideals that were known in full before birth.[35] In such a system, any information that comes through the senses from the world is necessarily less 'real' or 'true' than abstract concepts in the mind or soul.

Neo-Platonism's rejection of any fundamental role for the world or the body in epistemology, as seen in the works of Philo and Plotinus,[36] provided one of the intellectual underpinnings for the work of Augustine, the most influential early Western Christian thinker to address the question of anthropology. While Augustine's anti-Pelagian theory of original sin may now be considered the strongest articulation of his understanding of bodily abjection, in the Middle Ages it was Augustine's definition of the Trinity and the concomitant doctrine of exemplarism – the human soul alone is the *imago Dei*, as demonstrated by its trinity of powers: memory, understanding, and will — that most effectively erased the body from any positive role in religious experience.[37] Scholars who depend on Augustine's famous hierarchization of the three forms of visions (corporeal, spiritual, and intellectual) tend to negate the value of any but an 'incorporeal' form of a vision of God, that is, an infusion of non-visual knowledge.[38] Several recent works rebuke interpretations emphasizing Augustine's valuation of soul over body by elaborating on the critical role of embodiment in various of his works; at least one scholar also designates the later appropriation of an abstract rather than embodied Augustine ('hyper-Augustinian' modes) as a particularly Protestant rereading.[39]

The Western Augustine was not the only influential thinker who (apparently) rejected the body as a source for knowledge. In a neo-Platonic Eastern text that had marked influence on the development of scholastic and mystical theology in the West after its ninth-century translation into Latin,[40] the sixth-century Syrian monk Pseudo-Dionysius the Areopagite advised his readers to '[l]eave behind everything that is perceived and understood' and furthermore, lauded Moses, who 'breaks ... away from what sees and is seen ... renouncing all that the mind may conceive, wrapped entirely in the intangible and invisible, he belongs completely to him who is beyond everything.'[41] His *Mystical Theology* was a primer for apophatic, or negative theology, a technique that rejects all verbal descriptions of God as insufficient to describe God's infinite nature; it became a key text with the rise of the universities,[42] while many monastics attached to the influential Victorine school wrote commentaries on it in the twelfth and thirteenth centuries.[43] (Apophatic theology remains a primary topic of scholarship on Golden Age mysticism.)[44] Following the principle that abstract thought was the most appropriate method by which to gain knowledge of, even union with, an infinite God, medieval theologians frequently advocated a tripartite method of contemplation in which the devotee attempted to strip away the body and its senses in his or her contemplative practice by following a sequence often named the 'purgative,' 'illuminative,' and 'unitive' stages.[45]

The difficulty of this traditional narrative that places abstract contemplation as the pinnacle of Christian religious expression, however, is that during the late Middle Ages, religious authors and the devotees they taught dedicated far more of their vocal and mental prayer to the least abstract of meditation methods: meditation on the Passion. Whether gazing at a crucifix adorned with a gruesome body, meditating on the 5,475 wounds extrapolated from a popular visionary text as the extreme of Christ's torture,[46] visualizing deep kisses to Christ's side wound,[47] or receiving the stigmata,[48] the most common spiritual techniques and the most valorized miracles in the Middle Ages emphasized achieving absolute identification between the wounded divine body and the grieving devotee's body. Although Sarah Beckwith proposes the terms 'Christocentric piety' or 'crucifixion piety' (with a preference for the latter term) for these types of devotions,[49] neither fully captures the medieval focus on Christ during the entirety of his last days from Palm Sunday through the Easter resurrection. I prefer the term 'Passion-centred devotions' recommended by Richard Kieckhefer,[50] or more simply, Passion spirituality, a category including devotional rituals, meditative practices, and mystical methods alike.

The 'best-selling'[51] spiritual guides promoted meditation involving imaginative visualization of Christ's life in order to transform medieval devotees into spectators to the historical events of Christ's life. The authors of these *Vita Christi* (Life of Christ) treatises instructed their readers to imagine being present at the scenes narrated in the Gospels, all the way from envisioning themselves as tickling the toes of the infant at the inn to standing with John and Mary at the foot of the cross. Some of the early texts provided a rather bare-bones narrative of the events of Jesus's life,[52] while others recited quantities of specific details or entire scenes followed by extensive reflection on the theological or ethical implications of the interpolated scenarios.[53] Ewert Cousins has articulated the connection between imaginative visualization and mystical practices.

> In this type of consciousness, one recalls a significant event in the past, enters into its drama and draws from it spiritual energy, eventually moving beyond the event towards union with God … In this form of prayer, one imagines the

> physical setting of the event – the place, the persons, the circumstances ... However one does not remain a detached spectator, but enters into the event as an actor in the drama, singing with the angels and worshipping the infant with the shepherd ... It is important to recognize 'the mysticism of the historical event' as a distinctive form of mystical consciousness ... In a generic sense, it belongs to that form of consciousness whereby we remember a past event, of our own lives or of our collective history. But it is more than merely recalling, for it makes us present to the event and the event present to us ... In and through our immersion in the event, we can discern its meaning.[54]

According to Cousins, one 'enters' into the 'historical event' in order to move beyond it to find meaning. While he begins to articulate the way external history can lead to mystical experience, he overlooks that which was most central to medieval (and especially Franciscan) configurations of this history: the role of the (suffering) body.

Treatises on the life and death of Christ configured the primary content of daily meditation for monks, mendicants, nuns, and the laity as both highly visual and highly participatory. Regardless of the length of the narrative, medieval writers consistently enhanced the technique of imaginative visualization by paying particular attention to the bodily torture inflicted on the Godman between his capture in Gethsemane and his Crucifixion. Authors often envisioned how Jesus could have been stretched to fit a cross that was too big for him, or debated whether the Crucifixion itself took place while the cross was on the ground or already upright.[55] Likewise, the human body of the devotee was made a part of the spectacle, as meditators were directed to imagine themselves close enough to the route to Calvary to be splattered with drops of Jesus's blood during one of his seven falls with the cross. As medievalist Esther Cohen succinctly states, '[T]he new Christocentric religiosity of the later Middle Ages [was] centered on pain.'[56] More broadly, recent scholarship has proposed that '[t]he era between 1300 and 1700 witnessed something like a *theological pain contest*' (emphasis in original).[57]

Ergo, the most typical form of Christian devotion in medieval Europe (often used by those seeking mystical experience) involved sight and violent action rather than abstract, passive contemplation. Since the 1990s, historians, art historians, and scholars of English literature have reconfigured the traditional narratives of the Middle Ages to centre on the dominance of Passion spirituality among persons of all levels of education and participation in the church during the high and late Middle Ages.[58] The human body was a starting point for accessing knowledge of a God willing to take on flesh, yet by pairing this focus on the divine flesh with grim references to the rotting corpse of a body to which each devotee was enslaved, many theologians at the time – and scholars of mysticism today – disparaged beginners who could do no more than rely on their imagination and external bodily senses to think about an infinite, omnipotent (and invisible) divine. Although the medieval trend came late to Castile, a critical yet often-overlooked chapter in Spanish Renaissance spirituality was the dramatic increase in the publication of Passion texts in the last quarter of the fifteenth century under the Catholic Monarchs, Ferdinand and Isabella. Despite the predominance of Passion spirituality in the records of the late Middle Ages and even into the early modern period, scholars mapping the history of Christian mysticism on the European continent have rarely considered Passion-centred devotion to be an appropriate object of study within their discipline,[59] frequently assuming treatises following the purgative–illuminative–unitive sequence to be the apogee of mystical contemplation.[60] As I delineate in the next section, the study of Christian mysticism, particularly as it is currently articulated in Spain, continues to denote body–soul dualism as foundational to the parameters of the object of study.

Body–Soul Dualism in the History of Christian Mysticism

Many influential historians of mysticism, well-versed in the medieval theological preference for apophatic theology and contemplation, have concluded that abstract linguistic techniques such as the negating of God-descriptors central to apophatic theology were the highest expression of mystical experience available in the Middle Ages. Ever since William James generated his influential four-fold definition of mysticism (ineffability, noetic content, transiency, passivity) by identifying the abstract elements of certain types of Christian mysticism, including that of John of the Cross, with similarly intellectual elements in other religious traditions,[61] theorists of mysticism have advocated a hierarchy of abstract or speculative contemplation over embodied practice. This in effect has given pride of place in histories of medieval mystical practice to an emphasis on the abstract that was in reality an attitude primarily characteristic of medieval scholastic theologians, and not even all of them.

For example, Bernard McGinn's multi-volume series *The Presence of God* (1991–2005), covering influential mystics in depth from early Christianity through the late Middle Ages, is the premier overview of the premodern Christian mystical tradition available today. McGinn's definition of mysticism in the first volume continues to be the reigning definition in the historical study of Christian mysticism: '[T]he mystical element in Christianity is that part of its belief and practices that concerns the preparation for, the consciousness of, and the reaction to what can be described as the immediate or direct presence of God.'[62] In an appendix to the first volume, McGinn reviews the development of theological, philosophical, and comparativist theories of mysticism from the end of the nineteenth century through the 1980s.[63] Categorizing the scholars who promote an essentialist or universalist view of mysticism versus a historically contingent methodology, McGinn's summary is useful in demonstrating that both theologians and religious studies scholars may fall in either camp. He does not, however, examine the methodologies for the history of Christian thought emerging from other disciplines, such as history or literature, and therefore his survey of the field does not categorize or assess the various ways of addressing the body's role in mysticism that have emerged from attention to vernacular and women's writings or from cultural studies in general ever since the 1980s, despite his dependence on such studies in individual chapters and in later volumes of the series. Elsewhere, McGinn's rereading of women's visionary experiences as biblically rooted visualizations, while valuing the theological import of the women's writings, removes these (possibly) embodied experiences from the purview of mysticism as a category.[64]

Although McGinn's 1991 methodological overview dates quite early in the proliferation of cultural studies and certainly appears many years before the cognitive turn, it signals a tension concerning the role of the body in mysticism that continues throughout the series. In the third volume, for example, McGinn emphasizes that the body and its senses are in some way a problem to be surpassed in the pursuit of a bodiless union. In particular, he relegates Ewert Cousins's proposal of a Franciscan genre of 'mysticism of the historical event' to a purely preparatory role:

> I have no difficulty in seeing a 'mysticism of the historical event' as one form of Christian mysticism, and Francis (both the real Francis and the hagiographical model) as playing an important role in its evolution. I would suggest, however, that such intense pictorial realizations of the events of Christ's life should be seen as belonging more to the preparation for a direct and often non-pictorial consciousness of identification with Christ, both human and divine, at the summit of the mystical path, than as constituting its core.[65]

While McGinn analyses medieval Christian mystical thought with extensive attention to historical and social context, it is nevertheless clear that he creates a hierarchy of mystical experience that relegates 'pictorial consciousness' to the beginning stages of the mystical process. Images, dependent on the senses, can be useful before beginning the mystical path, indeed may be involved in the first (purgative, illuminative) stages. But the unitive stage, the 'summit,' is non-pictorial and therefore cannot be achieved by the imaginative visualization that was key to the Passion-centred devotions that dominated the late medieval religious panorama.[66]

Similar approaches plague the study of Renaissance mysticism in Castile, especially among Spanish-language scholars, and I argue that such privileging of intellectual or abstract forms of mysticism stems from an implicit hierarchy between soul and body. The first mystical treatises written in Castilian were published in 1500, far later than the trend in the rest of Europe (including Catalonia), where vernacular works of mysticism from the pens of both men and women were in circulation as early as the thirteenth century.[67] The foundations for a mystical genre indigenous to Castile were finally laid in the second quarter of the sixteenth century, when Bernardino de Laredo, Francisco de Osuna (1492–1540), and Bernabé de Palma (1469–1532) wrote their formative guides to recollection mysticism, a form of mystical ascent with roots in a method of prayer called *recogimiento* that had been practised in their Observant Franciscan communities for the previous forty years.[68] Andrés, the premier scholar of Golden Age mysticism, considers *recogimiento* the core practice of all major mystics from the 1520s to the 1650s in Castile. In his influential definition of the genre in a massive volume, *Los recogidos* (The Recollected, 1976), he claims, 'The complete way [of recollection] embraces three parts: self-knowledge or annihilation; following or imitation of Christ as man and as God; transformation of the soul into God by means of love. *The present history will focus especially on this last part*' (my emphasis).[69] (It is notable that Laredo is the only author in the 150-year trajectory outlined by Andrés to actually present the method in this particular sequence.) Despite the fact that Andrés himself acknowledges that many recollection authors required devotees to meditate on the Passion every morning even after reaching the heights of contemplation,[70] scholars since Andrés copy not only his definition but also his dismissal of the first two stages in favour of a focus on the third.[71]

Eulogio Pacho's 2008 survey of Spanish spirituality from 1450 to 1650 is the first since Andrés's 1976 work to attempt a full synthesis of Golden Age mysticism and also the first to systematically critique Andrés. Pacho challenges Andrés's evaluation that *recogimiento* is the element that makes Golden Age Spanish mysticism unique.[72] While his critique is perceptive, he does not propose a new method for approaching the period, nor does he go beyond rehearsing the standard biographies and analyses of individual mystics. Pacho also agrees with Andrés on some pivotal points. For one, he does not challenge the canon that relegates visionaries such as Juana de la Cruz to a few pages in the historical context section. In addition, he contrasts the general usage of *recogimiento* to denote fervent devotion with its technical definition as an experience that surpasses the senses and the body in favour of a purely abstract experience. '[*R*]*ecogimiento* acquires a technical connotation when it is applied exclusively to a type of contemplation that absorbs the capacities and powers totally in the experience of God present in the deepest depths of the soul.'[73] Rather than discuss *recogimiento* as the starting point for a century-and-a-half tradition, as did Andrés, Pacho argues that the method must be understood as a middle era directly influenced by fifteenth-century spirituality.[74] While his point is accurate, he focuses mainly on the Iberian background, thereby missing the dramatic increase in Passion spirituality characteristic of medieval Europe in general that was heavily influential in sixteenth-century Castile.[75] Finally, he isolates the historical context in self-contained chapters, leaving it out of the sections dedicated to leading mystical authors and thereby failing to recognize the specific elements of social and intellectual history influencing the composition of these primary sources. Pacho's work, while magisterial in its range and pungent in its critique of former scholars, does not ultimately replace earlier scholarship with a new methodological vision or new insight into specific mystics.

The principal rationale among scholars of Spanish Renaissance mysticism for analysing mystical union in the soul alone, without the body, is that the Augustinian triad of the soul's powers of memory, understanding, and will were considered the primary locus for union with God. In this view, the Renaissance rediscovered Plato in the wake of the scholastic emphasis on Aristotle, and thus the neo-Platonism of Augustine is assumed to have returned to ascendency in the sixteenth century.[76] As a result, the uniquely Castilian 'heresy' of the *alumbrados* (Illuminists), identified in 1525 by inquisitors as a rejection of church ritual and a corporeal hell in favour of private mental prayer and mystical experience, appears to have been a natural extension of the neo-Platonic tendencies of the era, not to mention attractive to recent converts from Judaism in the wake of the 1492 Expulsion.[77] Attention to this heresy dominates scholarly analysis of Castilian Christian experience from the 1520s on (see chapter 1). The impact of assuming a neo-Platonic distinction between soul and body on studies of *recogimiento* is quite clear; most of the scholarly debate over Laredo's drastic revision of his third stage, considered until now the central problem of Laredo studies, concerns whether he shifted his technique from reaching a union through understanding (Victorine) to doing so through the will (apophatic theology).

For that matter, English-language scholarship on Golden Age mysticism also regularly inflects the discussion towards the soul without body, or towards abstract methods of contemplation.[78] Colin Thompson, a specialist on John of the Cross, puts the emphasis on soul rather than body when he asserts in the prologue to the recent interdisciplinary collection *A New Companion to Hispanic Mysticism*: 'At the heart of mystical experience is the journey of the soul to union with the divine.'[79] Even the interdisciplinary work of cultural historians who focus principally on the body nevertheless cannot quite integrate the body into mysticism itself, no matter where else they find it. For example, in her discussion of body as the site for the inscription of Iberian alterity, focusing on lyric poetry, medical treatises, and the monstrous, Jean Dangler equates mysticism with apophatic theology alone, thus presuming a fundamental disparity between a linguistic method of spirituality versus medical discourse about the body.[80] None of these studies of mystical texts or types of devotional practice take into account the important work of Robert Folger, who has explored the intersection of medical cognition and mnemotechnique in Spanish Golden Age secular literature,[81] an intersection that I argue has an impact on Golden Age religious literature as well.

These unproblematized assumptions about the hierarchy between body and soul elide the cognitive continuum between them that I will examine in the next section. Yet historians of mysticism, and of Spanish mysticism in particular, repeatedly portray Passion meditation, newly popular in Castile after the Reconquest of the Muslims and Expulsion of the Jews in 1492, as a form of spirituality categorically separate from mystical contemplation owing to its emphasis on the body and the senses.[82] This insistence on the soul (and its three faculties of memory, understanding, and will) as the sole locus for mystical union with God is at odds with the fact that medieval Christians did not believe the afterlife (and its possible beatific vision of God) to be incorporeal, as Caroline Walker Bynum has demonstrated in her analysis of scholastic discussions concerning the reincarnated body.[83] As she argues, if humans are embodied in such rich detail in the afterlife, then surely mystical union in this life must include some of the same elements, indeed, must take the body into account!

Bynum and those who follow her contextual, critical methodology have directed intensive attention to the question of the body as the instrument with which the mystic yearns for (desires) mystical union, thus placing particular emphasis on the body as gender or the site of the erotic.[84] I take a different tack, drawing on the turn to cognitive studies that marks the last decade of medieval, but not early modern hispanist, studies. In this book, I show that the contemporary assumption that mystical practice is at its best when abstract flies in the face of medieval and Renaissance scientific reality, the epistemology that underpinned many of the theological developments in the era. As will be seen in the next section, the neo-Aristotelian and Galenic framework of medieval thought defined epistemology as a progressive abstraction from sensory data to conceptual thought that takes place in a bodily organ, the brain. Although locating God at the centre of the soul is relatively common in medieval mystical treatises, the cognitive turn in medieval studies can help recognize that the inward turn ('interiority') to find God posited by *recogimiento* follows the same process as the inward turn required for all thought that begins from the Aristotelian collection of sensory data. If abstract thought develops from the workings of the body, however, then the body cannot be worthless in comparison to mental functioning. Rather, the mind and soul *depend* on the body. Historians of mysticism must begin to account for the fact that, according to medieval and Renaissance science, without the body, there is no abstract thought – and thereby, no final conceptual stage of mystical union.

The Medical Evidence: Cognitive Studies and the History of Mysticism

Any study that explores a medieval or Renaissance mystical technique must assess it in its context of the intersection between scientific knowledge and theological systems, a narrative that begins with Greek and Roman philosophy and medicine. Aristotle's theory that thought is initiated by data received from the five external senses had long-lasting impact outside of philosophic circles because of its appeal to the leading physicians of the ancient and medieval eras.[85] Pivotally, Galen (second century CE), whose texts on medicine and physiology formed the core of medieval scientific knowledge as understood by theologians and physicians alike, agreed with many of Aristotle's theories. Working from the basics of humoral theory (elements: earth, water, air, and fire; qualities: hot, cold, dry, and wet; humors: blood, phlegm, black bile, and yellow bile), Galen elaborated and extended these Aristotelian presuppositions into a full-fledged scientific system.[86] What follows is a brief outline of the cognitive sequence – from the collection of sense data through to abstract thought – that was at the basis of all scientific inquiry in the Middle Ages,

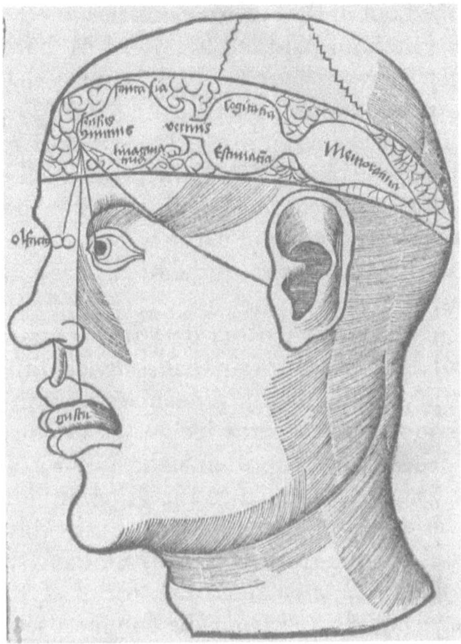

Fig 0.1 Phrenological head showing the outer and inner senses. Hieronymus Brunschwig (ca 1450–ca 1512), *Liber de arte distillandi de compositis* (Book of the Art of Distillation of Compound Bodies) (Strasbourg, 1512), fol. 284r. Probably derived from an illustration in the 1506 edition of Albert the Great, *Philosophia naturalis*. Credit: Science Museum Library/SSPL.

in large part owing to the systemization of Galen's thought brought about by eleventh-century Arabic medico-theologians such as Avicenna and Alhazen. The intent of this outline is to highlight how knowledge of the body's role in the production of mental thought immediately reframes the typical queries scholars bring to their assessment of mystical methods that sought to train the reader into a devotee capable of experiencing God.

Discussions of cognition in the Middle Ages invariably identified the sense of vision as the pattern for the production of knowledge, so this medical survey must begin with the two competing theories of optics available to theorists (whether scientists or theologians). Authors such as Plato and Augustine posited extramission as the manner by which visual information was collected.[87] According to the theory of extramission, 'visual rays' streamed out of the eyes towards the object and then bounced back with the information. Alhazen, followed by Latin natural theologians such as Roger Bacon in the thirteenth century, suggested the theory of intromission instead, which held that the form (*species*) of the object radiated out through space until it reached the eye and imprinted the optic nerve with the form of the object.[88] Regardless of which visual theory they promoted, all scientists who studied cognition assumed that the visual information was sent along the optic nerve to the *sensus communis* (common sense), a ventricle in the front of the brain that collated information from all the senses.

Yet what happened with the sensory data after it was collected? Islamic scientists proposed a map of the brain that assigned different functions to each cell, or ventricle, of the brain; Avicenna's version proved the most influential on Western medical knowledge (see Figure 0.1).[89] It is noteworthy that the term 'faculty' so often associated with the three powers of the soul was a term also applied to the different 'inner senses' in the brain and to the functions of specific parts of the body.[90] In addition to the *sensus communis* in one front ventricle, another front ventricle held the sensory imagination that retained the 'form' of what the common sense put together. Data flowed from the common sense to the sensory imagination, and then on to the two middle ventricles. One middle ventricle held the cognitive imagination, believed to construct fantasies by amalgamating and dividing the forms provided by the *sensus communis*. The other middle ventricle was the source for the 'estimative faculty' (sometimes called reason) that added judgment to the information collated from the *sensus communis*. (The most common medieval justification for judgment as a distinct faculty was that the form of the wolf ends up instilling fear even though the sensory data does not include any reason to fear a wolf more than a dog.)[91] Finally, the rear ventricle was entirely dedicated to memory, that is, a repository of images of the forms created by the front and middle ventricles' processing of sensory data. It is noteworthy that these images were not stored as language, but rather as if they were images stamped on wax, as the oft-repeated metaphor by Plato and Aristotle put it.[92]

As not only a scientist but also an Islamic theologian, Avicenna was concerned with more than mere physiology. Considering the sequence described in the previous paragraph, he elucidated the progressive 'dematerialization' of data absorbed by the external senses as it travelled across the ventricles of the brain, suggesting that cognition was the progressive stripping of accidents from the essential form of whatever was received through the senses, thereby producing abstract concepts that could be thought by the higher, rational soul in its ascent towards God.[93] Likewise, Latin commentators examined how 'reason can move from sensation to grasp what is beyond sensation,' thus producing a theory of cognition.[94] In sum, medieval epistemology was a process begun externally to the individual that moved sequentially through the external senses to the nerves, reaching each ventricle of the brain in turn, each of which processed the information in its inner sense. The result was stored in the memory as an image (either a bodily image, or a visual image of printed words) until it was needed for further conceptual thought.

The role of the visual sense in this cognitive process was not only related to the initial collection of sense data, however. Carruthers's landmark work on the centrality of memory for monastic meditation (rather than our modern valuation of imagination) demonstrates the pivotal role of memory – at once a physiological location and a power of the soul – for understanding the body–soul continuum recognized by medieval thinkers. She suggests that the Aristotelian 'thinking with an image' (and since images are based on sight, thinking with an image composed of bodily forms) was foundational to monastic methods of meditation. 'The emphasis upon the need for human beings to "see" their thoughts in their minds as organized schemata of images, or "pictures," and then to use these for further thinking, is a striking and continuous feature of medieval monastic rhetoric.'[95] Whereas modern academics privilege linguistic and abstract modes of thought, often leaving visual learners in university classrooms bewildered by our verbiage, Carruthers argues strongly that in the Middle Ages the most adept thinkers were consistently those who placed visualization and imagery at the core of their thought process. Her work thus problematizes any binary dualism between abstract thought on the one hand and visual information on the other, instead demonstrating the intrinsic reliance of memory (an Augustinian power of the soul) on imagery drawn from the visual sense that is stored in the memory as a cognitive location in the brain.

Building on Carruthers's insights and carefully reconsidering the writings of scholastic theologians, more recent scholarship has found that there was no such thing in the late Middle Ages as a simple duality of body versus soul, sensory data versus abstract concepts. Based on the confluence in twelfth-century Cistercian writings of, on the one hand, an Augustinian system that assigned memory, understanding, and will to the soul, and on the other hand, Arabic scientific treatises that located the memory in the anterior ventricle of the brain,[96] Janet Coleman argues that the dual location of memory in the soul and the body led to a reconceptualization of soul itself.

> What is significant for the twelfth century is the neo-Platonist emphasis on the separation between sense and reason, lower and higher mind. By contrast, what was required for a more sophisticated understanding of the memory was an anthropology in which memory could lead on progressively and continuously to higher mind and therefore, a theory that linked rather than divorced sense and interpretation in a continuum. In other words, what was required was another look at Aristotle where the soul is the form of the body.[97]

In other words, the co-influence of Galenic science and Aristotelian logic in the high and late Middle Ages led to an implicit rejection of neo-Platonic and Augustinian duality in favour of a continuum between the body, the sensitive or appetitive soul, and the rational soul. The sensitive soul, also called the five inner senses,[98] was foundational to an epistemology that described a progressive abstraction from sensory data to conceptual thought that was understood to take place in a bodily organ, the brain.

Over the last decade, scholars have begun to recognize that modern conceptions of epistemology have consistently obscured or obliterated the continuum between body and soul found in these medieval cognitive models, thereby overlooking their influence on theological propositions and mystical possibilities.[99] Western texts based on Arabic scientific theory that we now disciplinarily categorize within the history of science, such as Roger Bacon's development of Alhazen's optical theory of intromission, or Bartholomaeus Anglicus's scientific encyclopedia, *On the Nature of Things* (*De proprietatibus rerum*, 1220s), were in fact written with an eye to their relevance for Christian theological concerns.[100] Likewise, the scientific discussions of the brain and visuality found in Bacon and Anglicus were in turn central to the theories of cognition developed by Albert the Great, Aquinas, Scotus, Ockham, and others.[101] The scientific-theological epistemologies they elaborated in medieval university classrooms were disseminated to the clerical hierarchy, and through them to audiences across Europe in popular collections of sermon exempla.[102]

The influence of translations of Avicenna's *Canon* on university theologians in Paris confirms that scholasticism depended on an epistemology that was not merely conceptual but also physiological.[103] For example, Aquinas's theory of hylemorphism was grounded in the Aristotelian and Avicennean insistence on the cognitive continuum between body and soul.

Aquinas argued that 'the soul is the form for the body' (hylemorphism);[104] that is, there is an unbreakable connection between body and soul because neither can function nor be affected independently from the other.[105] As Bynum states, 'What self is (including what body is) will be packed into soul; body will be the expression of that soul in matter.'[106] Donald Mowbray emphasizes that according to this theory, all physical sensations (in medieval terminology, the 'passions') that affect the body will ultimately affect the soul, and vice versa.[107] He summarizes this point by saying that the medieval soul had 'a natural tendency towards embodiment,'[108] and that '[t]he soul only sensed things as a consequence of its relationship to the body.'[109] Nor was this idea only articulated by medieval thinkers and repeated by modern medievalists. Juan Luis Vives (1493–1540), an Iberian contemporary of Laredo famous for his philosophical dialogues, stated that 'the spiritual is understood by starting with the corporeal.'[110]

These various combinations of science and theology influenced lay and vernacular understandings of theological anthropology beyond a simple dualism between the sinning body and a valuation of the soul as the *imago Dei*. These Galenic-Avicennean physiological and cognitive models reigned in full force until the second half of the sixteenth century and after, until Vesalius's rejection of the theory of the inner senses, the anti-Galenic model of Paracelsus, and new directions in the art of memory beginning with Descartes shifted the broad-based societal understanding of how thought operates and soul exists.[111] Until that time, however, Galenic science dominated theological paradigms to such an extent that Renaissance developments in theology and mysticism cannot be understood apart from their roots in Galenic physiology and monastic-scholastic epistemology.[112]

Cognitive Theory in Mystical Texts: Laredo as Case Study

If the medical body is returned to the equation – taken seriously as an intrinsic element of the quest for mystical union with a Christian God because of its centrality in human epistemology – the types of questions that must be put to medieval and early modern mystical texts are startlingly distinct from the traditional ones. The most basic question of categorization of medieval mystical texts has been, for centuries, whether the method advocates union with God by means of the faculty of the understanding, or by the faculty of the will.[113] Yet what of the third faculty or power of the soul, the memory, in these histories of mysticism? If, as Carruthers argues, memory is the creative motor of thinking, and if, according to the history of medieval medicine, the memory is located in the brain on a physiological continuum with the bodily senses, the pressing question of understanding versus will is actually better cast as a final question rather than an opening one. In sum, the initial questions posed by a historian of mysticism concerning the practices of a particular mystic ought instead to first encompass the bodily epistemology by which the human could think itself into a state in which God might chose to interact with him or her.

My project recasts these questions in general, and for the history of Spanish spirituality in particular, in two ways, and thus is divided into two parts. Broadly speaking, hierarchizing the non-pictorial over the imagistic as McGinn and Andrés do is a valuation of abstract thought over visuality, and consequently over the senses and indeed the body as a whole. In response to this pervasive scholarly assumption, the first part of this book explores how embodied devotion in general and Passion spirituality in particular have been set apart from mystical topics in the study of Castilian religion during an age marked by the Inquisition's pursuit of heretics (especially those converted from Judaism). This part is therefore particularly useful for scholars of Renaissance and Golden Age Spain. In chapter 1, I reconsider the influential Observant Franciscan reform of the Spanish church (1420s–1510s), highlighting the many ways that the reform emphasized questions of the body in religious devotion, in addition to the movement's famed emphasis on mental prayer. I then examine popular spiritual texts, religious art, and visionary experience to illuminate the constant emphasis on embodiment that I argue led naturally to the development of the Holy Week processions of flagellants and the accompanying sculptures that have been the hallmark of Spanish Christianity from the 1520s through the present day.

In chapter 2, I turn to Laredo as an individual: an individual in a particular historical context that not only expected a religious emphasis on the body but indeed legislated it through the medium of the Inquisition. Remarkably little is known about Laredo's life, but I offer a reconstruction of his heritage and *converso* environment that makes his novel status as the only major sixteenth-century mystic to avoid Inquisitorial pressure or censorship all the more intriguing. I suggest that it was Laredo's careful insistence on his comfort with the embodied spirituality of the era that helped him (and his text) navigate the vagaries of Inquisitorial suspicion. His elevation of Passion meditation to the central technique of a tripartite treatise that otherwise depends on resources in apophatic theology and intellectual mysticism, however, sets his method apart from the two other authors of the first half of the century who discuss the Passion to any extent, García de Cisneros and Francisco de Osuna.

Ultimately, Laredo's insertion of a narrative meditation on the Passion into the midst of a treatise on unitive contemplation was not solely a rhetorical response to an Inquisitorial age, but rather proposed a version of 'interiorizing spirituality' that follows naturally from a scientific epistemology. This is the argument of the book's second part; it is intended not only for scholars of Spanish mysticism but also for medievalists and early modernists interested in integrating cognitive studies into the historical study of mysticism. Consideration of Laredo's deployment of medicine, mnemotechnique, and optics throughout his mystical text helps highlight the scientific underpinning of his theory of the embodied soul in the first two stages of his method, a necessary step before any clarity can be reached about *no pensar nada* in the last stage of transformation by love. I should note here that the interdisciplinary efforts of this book require me to depend on valuable primary source research in various branches of medieval science. I do not offer new research in Galenic medicine or optical theories but rather apply the innovative conclusions of these separate fields in an effort to shed light on the intellectual context of early Golden Age mystical methodology.

Chapter 3's reading of the *Subida* in light of Laredo's scientific training reveals a constant refrain of medical information in the context of the training of a novice mystic. Laredo structured a week of meditation on self-knowledge around an original poem concerning the dust from which we are made and to which we will return, playing on the fact that the Castilian word for the Galenic element earth (of earth, water, air, and fire) is 'dust.' Dust/earth then becomes the dominant metaphor for the *nonada* (no-nothingness, changed to *nada* in the 1538 edition) of the annihilated self.[114] Laredo also introduced sophisticated medical language referring to the body, a body he diagnosed using the medical language of elements, primary and secondary humors, qualities, innate heat, and radical moisture. This passage comes just before the stage on Passion meditation, a stage that Laredo also imbued with details drawn from medical familiarity with blood as well as with the number of bones and nerves in the body that could be injured during torture. The product of Laredo's medical approach to self-knowledge was a form of spirituality that was fully dependent on the mystic's body and the created world.

In chapter 4, an examination of the central role of mnemotechnique in monastic understandings of cognition shows that Laredo anchored his rhetoric, often considered by modern readers as aimless or meandering, in memory devices that inscribed abstract ideas in concrete pictures and spaces. Not only was memory physiologically located in the rear brain ventricle, but memory devices depended on the visualization of physical aspects of material objects.[115] As Mary Carruthers has proven, image and location were central to all levels of thinking in medieval and Renaissance cognitive theory; they were elements not to be transcended in the quest for union with God but rather to be redirected towards a God found at the centre of the soul. In this chapter, I analyse Laredo's most extensive memory devices: seven elements of the riding equipment needed to ride a horse up the mystical ascent; a jewelled fortress surrounding a meadow of candles; and a fountain that is at the same time three rivers that are themselves an ocean. This chapter reveals memory devices as at once visual, locative, agile, and playful, requiring an awareness of space and place that leads to associative play on the mnemonic image. When a Renaissance doctor and mystic deploys these medieval monastic meditative devices, readers must consider the spatiality of his metaphors and analogies in order to understand the impact of embodied cognition on the framing of the mystical ascent and the definition of the divine. Assessing the efficacy of a mystical technique according to the cognitive standards of its era, rather than continuing our dependence on historical (or contemporary) theological views concerning the value of abstract contemplation over and above embodied practices, will thus become an essential evaluative tool available to historians of mysticism.

In chapter 5, I consider the particularities of vision and the related medieval definitions of epistemology, arguing that theological and medical discourses that used the physics of optics to explain epistemology provided scientific theories in which tactile connections between an object and its viewer led to a possible identity between an icon of Christ and a devotee. I posit that Laredo inscribed external bodily meditation on the interior heart and entrails of the contemplative by drawing on scientific understandings of how visual messages underpin all epistemological constructs, including violent mnemonic devices; violence and pain were theological as well as medical constructs in the era. Therefore, visual models of cognition underlying the Renaissance scientific view of the world, combined with the spiritual value of envisioned violence, led Laredo to create a locative Passion spirituality that suggests the devotee can turn his or her body *into* the Holy Land. In this view, the viscera of the believer become the site of Christ's torture, such that Passion meditation was far from being a 'beginner' technique, as so many medieval theologians and modern scholars have described it. Instead, it was the cognitive crux by which to experience the divine. Ultimately, Laredo's medical approach to recollection mysticism elucidates for his readers that the transformation of the soul into God first occurs by means of a cognitive transformation of the soul into the tortured Christ. Once the soul transforms itself into its God by discovering its identity with the wounded Christ at the centre of the soul, then the final stage of recollection aids the divinized soul in conforming to its bleeding centre.

I conclude by tracing the continuities of the first two stages of self-knowledge and Passion meditation with the third stage of recollection privileged by all previous scholarship. Those continuities include Laredo's continued emphasis on the embodied soul, deployment of medical and cognitive details from the scientific tradition, and the pervasiveness of Passion meditation throughout a level supposedly configured solely by apophatic theology. I then offer a brief glance at the traces of the medical and cognitive body in Laredo's well-known Carmelite audience, Teresa of Avila and John of the Cross.

In sum, a historically contextualized and scientifically accurate reading of Laredo's method of mystical prayer proves that not only do body and soul go hand in hand towards mystical union, but that in fact the critical step towards transformation into God takes place in and on the body *before* the third stage that has been the focus of all previous studies of *recogimiento*. Assessment of Laredo's integration of the physiological body into a mystical route to intellectual union with God thus offers the opportunity to reconsider some normative categories in modern scholarship of mysticism, including the common narrative of 'ascent' to a union between God and soul in a spiritual realm beyond the flesh.[116] Laredo's extravagant description of an embodied soul that catches Christ's dripping blood in the eyes of its entrails is not a ridiculous example of purple prose, but rather articulates an experience of mystical union that is deeply embodied and fully reliant on the scientific and theological epistemologies of its day.[117]

PART ONE

Rereading the Historical Context

1 Renaissance Castilian Spirituality: An Embodied Christianity

It is imperative that the various ways that body was central to the spiritual landscape of early modern Castile be accounted for in any history of Spanish Christian thought. This chapter will reassess Renaissance Castilian spirituality, offering a corrective to the traditional view relayed by historians of Spanish mysticism that the era hierarchized soul over body, incorporeal spirituality over lay ritual and embodied meditation. It will become evident that the bodies of Christ and the believer were key concerns in the early decades following the religious unification of Castile, that is, the age of Cisneros's reform of the Spanish church in 1495–1517 and the aftermath of openness and innovation that lasted from his death until the Tridentine crackdown in the 1560s. In such a context, Bernardino de Laredo's 1535 proposal of an 'embodied soul' would not have struck his readers as entirely extraordinary, for bodies were everywhere, and never as detached from soul as traditional historiography would have us believe.

For more than two decades, medievalists who study northern Europe or the British Isles have considered the primary characteristic of the late Middle Ages to be its 'somatic spirituality,' in other words, meditation on and identification with the humanity rather than the divinity of Christ, especially as regards his suffering and death.[1] Very recently, several scholars have indicated that the creative theological impact of somatic spirituality and its accompanying Passion-centred devotions peaked in the fourteenth century, suggesting that by the fifteenth century Passion spirituality in England had ossified and been detached from high theological endeavours, while in Germany authors had begun doubting the validity of accounts of Christ's bodily suffering that went beyond the Gospel narratives.[2] This sequence is quite different in Spain. Cynthia Robinson makes the provocative argument that fifteenth-century Castile was unique not for drawing back from this trend but rather for not yet having welcomed it; she suggests that the need to convert Jews and Muslims prevented fourteenth- and fifteenth-century Christians from embracing forms of spirituality that would have disgusted their fellow monotheists.[3] Her project, centred on the fifteenth century, does not address the shift that occurred once political domination over the Muslims and the religious disappearance of the Jews were finalized in 1492. Post-Reconquest Castile saw a dramatic increase in the popularity of treatises and religious art depicting various extremes of gore and mental pain in the context of Passion-centred devotions, as I will delineate in this chapter.[4]

Given the unprecedented explosion in the composition and publication of texts exploring Jesus's humanity in the early sixteenth century, it is curious that scholars of sixteenth-century Castilian spirituality ignore the impact of this medieval somatic trend and instead highlight only Erasmianism, the uniquely Spanish *alumbrado*, or Illuminist, heresy, and the third stage of recollection mysticism as the central elements of early sixteenth-century Spanish spirituality.[5] These new movements are consistently presented as devotional practices intended to transcend the body in favour of an incorporeal spirituality or internalizing mysticism.[6] As a result, the Spanish sixteenth century appears as a purely spiritual, purely intellectual Golden Age, showing little continuity with the wider panorama of late medieval devotional trends. I argue, in contrast, that Renaissance Castilian religious experience took a primary cue from the late medieval emphasis on somatic spirituality.[7] Laredo's scientific view of the human body, a topic I turn to in chapter 3, will thus prove to be a particular instance of a broader trend towards somatism, a key development in post-*convivencia* Spanish spirituality that has received little attention to date.

Histories of Spanish mysticism spotlight the 1520s as the first era of original, vernacular Christian mysticism in Castile. Melquíades Andrés even claims the authors of this age – Francisco de Osuna, Bernardino de Laredo, and Bernabé de Palma – to be 'major mystics' whose innovative leaps made them the giants upon whose shoulders rested the works of the 'minor mystics' Teresa of Avila and John of the Cross![8] In addition to the evident difficulty that this assumption presents in negating the importance of visionary texts written or preached by women in the second half of the fifteenth century and early decades of the sixteenth (María de Santo Domingo, Juana de la Cruz, etc.), it also presumes texts such as *Carro de dos vidas* (Cart of Two Lives, 1500) or *Ejercitatorio de vida espiritual* (Book of Exercises for the Spiritual Life, 1500) that reorganize medieval mystical material to be of less importance than 'original' works, a highly modern rather than medieval view of creativity.[9] To correct such oversights (if ignoring the sustained contributions of an entire gender can be categorized with the gentle word 'oversight') is not the purview of this book. Although I do not focus on a woman's text in this monograph, my project of recuperating the value of embodiment for abstract contemplation is intended in part to strike down the distinctions between 'true' and 'problematic' mystical experience that so often serve as a rationale for leaving women visionaries out of the field of study of Renaissance Castilian mysticism. This trend is particularly prevalent in Spanish-language scholarship that ignores the recuperation of various Renaissance female visionaries and *beatas* (uncloistered religious women)[10] so persuasively surveyed by Ronald Surtz and Angela Muñoz Fernández.[11] Embodiment is a key element consistently overlooked in scholarship on the organized, prescriptive mystical methods of recollection that mark the 1520s as the originating epoch for Golden Age mysticism, that is, as the transitional stage between various trends in late medieval Iberian devotion that did not produce innovative guides to mystical prayer, and the later sixteenth century that was nourished by precisely such texts.[12]

The near-absolute absence of questions of body (unless the mystic was a female visionary) from the historiography of Spanish Golden Age mysticism is a result of Protestant-inflected scholarship that, even when detached from a Protestant theological context, continues to define religions around belief rather than practice, an assumption that leads easily to deriding the late medieval era in general and early sixteenth-century Spanish spirituality in particular as characterized by 'empty' ritual. The study of religions as an academic project first came about in Protestant universities in the nineteenth century, and the field as a whole has struggled ever since to propose a definition of religion that fully takes into account the many orthopraxic religious systems found throughout the world, ranging from Mahayana Buddhism to Catholicism.[13] In the case of sixteenth-century Spain, whose history is addressed relatively rarely by religious studies scholars, the challenge lies in the presumption that the Reformation in northern Europe not only drastically shifted religious discourse but also set the framework for religious debates throughout the century, even on the Catholic side.[14] Traditional histories of Christianity highlight the Protestant Reformation as the first successful movement to reform the 'excesses' of late medieval devotion, in other words, a supposed overemphasis on ritual, indulgences, and purgatory. Yet such histories elide the fact that an internal reform of the Catholic Church in Spain had been in process for a century before Luther composed the theses that led to schism.

This reform, led by Observant Franciscans, formed the backdrop to the rapid changes in Renaissance spirituality after the religious unification of the peninsula in 1492 and is a highlight of Iberian particularity within the larger narrative of European Christianity.

Let us consider the fundamental views of body that would necessarily underlie a reform led by Luther, an Augustinian monk, in contrast to one undertaken by a group of Observant Franciscans. The Augustinian order was rooted in the neo-Platonic duality between body and soul, and Luther's key theological insight is based on his experience of continual, overwhelming, bodily sin. It was natural for him to critique forms of spirituality that appeared external and bodily, such as indulgences or a focus on the mass, as well as late medieval nominalism that seemed to emphasize human capacity to achieve good actions.[15] His disdain both spotlighted the body and denigrated it. On the other hand, Francis of Assisi's experiences had made the body of the believer and the body of Christ central to spirituality in the orders he founded. Francis's initial mission was configured around a vision that occurred during prayer in front of a crucifix in Saint Damian in Assisi. Francis heard Christ speaking through the crucifix; the physical sculpture of Christ conveyed auditory information to him.[16] A culminating sign of Francis's acceptance by God was a vision he received on Mount La Verna of a seraph opening its wings to reveal the crucified Christ. During the vision, Francis received the stigmata, according to his contemporary biographers.[17] In the Franciscan view, then, Christ's body (physically present through sculpture or received as a mental representation) and the believer's body (at times physically impacted by the divine) both had intrinsic value as sources of profound spiritual experience. The Franciscan role in Castilian spirituality, pivotal from the height of the Reconquest of the peninsula throughout the Golden Age, is a clear signal that the role of body is likewise key to this era.

My rereading of the history of spiritual reform on the peninsula proposes that it provided a positive valuation of embodiment rather than disdaining externality. This chapter is thus intended to counteract the easy generalizations so frequently applied to this era, an example of which can be found in a recent study. Yirmiyahu Yovel critiques scholarship on New Christians (*conversos*) and their spirituality in the fifteenth and sixteenth century as simplistically ascribing either a full crypto-Judaism or a full Catholicism to any given individual, a stance he considers misleading because the interstitial nature of a dual identification made *conversos* always 'the other within.' In the course of this nuanced argument, Yovel claims the following quite baldly: 'Spanish Catholicism at the end of the Middle

Ages was predominantly formalistic and external. It was based on external ritual, church power, coercive scholasticism, and rigid hierarchy; and it suffered from extreme clerical abuses.'[18] This statement, made without citation, is characteristic of scholarship on the Golden Age[19] and rests on two profoundly problematic assumptions. For one, it implicitly characterizes all that is external or ritualistic as meaningless, thus dismissing the core religious framework for the vast majority of Catholics of this era as not 'really' religious. Second, perhaps less obviously, the author apparently considers this statement a full and sufficient depiction of standard Catholic practice of the period. Catholicism appears as an unchanging monolith of perpetual ritualism, and thus the only elements worthy of scholarly attention are examples of shifts towards interiority. In other words, all that is ritual is presumed timeless and unchanging, while any new direction must of necessity be towards the spiritual, the mental, the internal. In the first section of this chapter, I counteract this pervasive assumption by arguing that the Spanish Franciscan reform of the fifteenth century elaborated an emphasis on mental prayer *in the context of* an increased attention to ritual and external devotion. Interiority did not supplant exteriority in a fortunate shift towards what 'really' matters,[20] but rather, the predominant attitude towards what counted as greater piety and devotional attention was at one and the same time mental and embodied – for indeed, neither the soul nor the body could be attended to or surpassed without the other.[21]

Based on this new vision of Castilian Franciscan reform as promoting increased internal *and* external observance, the rest of the chapter examines the changes in Castilian spirituality inaugurated under the Catholic Monarchs, Isabella, Ferdinand, and Charles V. Attention to a range of new developments previously noted by scholars from diverse fields such as literary studies (Passion poetry and plays in the era of Isabella's reign), art history (immense altarpieces called *retablos* and private devotional sculpture commissioned from the 1480s on), and the history of Spanish religion (apparitions of the Virgin in the late fifteenth century; female visionaries in the early sixteenth) allows us to construct a broad yet complex vista of what it meant to be Catholic in the early Golden Age. I argue that the principal spiritual developments of the turn of the sixteenth century were highly embodied, yet cannot be dismissed as non-theological or emptily ritualistic.

Rather, these various trends, all primarily concerned with the bodies of Christ and Mary, enable us to recognize that these two bodies, one male, one female, were central to post-Reconquest spirituality, a fact that in turn leads us to the realization that the suffering bodies of both Jesus and Mary were critical to the discourse of Castilian Christianity. The dual attention to embodiment and mental prayer, proven through these various devotional genres as the core of Castilian Franciscan reform, provides a new way to consider the religious developments of Laredo's productive decades, the 1520s and 1530s. In other words, both embodied Holy Week confraternal processions and the anti-ritualistic *alumbrado* heresy were key novelties of these two decades, and cannot be effectively analysed separately from one another.

Re-embodying Iberian Franciscan Reform

The introduction of the mendicant movements into Spain coincided with the first and most extensive thrust of the Reconquest. Both the Dominicans (founded by the Castilian native Domingo de Guzmán) and the Franciscans started proselytizing among the Muslims in Spain in the first decade of the spread of their orders (1210s) while also setting up convents in newly conquered towns as the Reconquest spread south. Eventually, the Dominicans gained prominence in the province of Aragon, while the Franciscans dominated Castile.[22] In response to the close connections formed between Spanish mendicants and the ruling powers of Castile and Andalusia throughout the thirteenth and fourteenth centuries, in the 1420s rural Castilian Franciscans began to criticize the extreme wealth of certain convents, setting up examples of poverty and humility in direct contrast to the courtly Franciscans and their focus on university education.[23] Pedro de Villacreces (ca 1362–1422) was a leading voice in the reform.[24] He rejected the life of a student at the University of Salamanca to retire to the 'desert' (in Arlanza, a lonely part of the Castilian *meseta*) in imitation of the first Franciscan hermitages.[25] He and his followers founded a number of retreat houses, *casas de retiro*, throughout the southern part of Castile that were still central to Franciscan spirituality a century later. These included La Salceda, home to Francisco de Osuna and source of some of the *alumbrado* heretics, and San Francisco del Monte del Villaverde, home to Laredo.[26] In his writings, the Villacrecian writer Lope de Salinas y Salazar[27] enumerated the major concerns of the reform houses: poverty of body and spirit, obedience, chastity, humility, simplicity, and prayer.[28] Careful attention to this list of Franciscan reforms indicates equal concern for both body and soul rather than the privileging of one over the other.

For the reformers, 'poverty of body and spirit' included not only the typical restrictions on gluttony and private ownership of goods, but also control of the soul's faculties of memory, understanding, and will.[29] The pursuit of simplicity required remaining content with reading the breviary and other 'simple' spiritual works rather than pursuing liberal arts and scholastic forms of education, a choice that leaned towards the 'bodiliness' of vocal prayer as outlined in the breviary rather than the 'intellectual' work of theology.[30] Indeed, Salinas y Salazar described humility as consisting of falling to one's knees in sorrow for one's many sins (a literal embodiment of a mental attitude) and obedience as accepting the prelate's mandate of physical penitence and discipline.[31] Interestingly, while proud of being 'untutored and illiterate' (*idiota y sin letras*) because university education was understood as a distraction,[32] this new breed of Observant Franciscans nevertheless insisted on their high level of Christian culture. After all, they argued, they read the Bible aloud on a three-year cycle, knew their Church Fathers, and were word-perfect in all rituals.[33] This list indicates that education was intimately linked with ritual rather than defined solely in relation to training in scholastic theology. Their critique of Catholicism in general, and Conventual Franciscans specifically, proved to be aimed at a trend towards over-intellectualizing.

The Observant Franciscan rejection of pure intellect can be seen clearly in the concern over the category of prayer, for reformers urged the pursuit of both vocal and private prayer. Salinas y Salazar directed his readers to dedicate at least an hour at a time to the task of prayer, to prepare themselves for prayer by seeking humility, and to spend at least an hour and a half concentrating on the line 'Miserere mei, Deus.'[34] These admonitions suggest that mental prayer was a primary element added by the reformers to the typical patterns of monastic liturgy; the new practice was possibly a forerunner of the type of prayer termed *recogimiento* that emerged from the *casas de retiro* sometime in the 1480s and would later form the basis for *recogimiento* mysticism from the 1520s on (see chapter 2). Yet although scholarly descriptions of this movement privilege interiority,[35] it was not the only element of the reformers' practice: Villacrecian emphasis on mental prayer was accompanied by an equal increase in emphasis on bodily devotions, including vocal prayer and participation in rituals. A key aspect to the daily devotions in the *casas de retiro*, in addition to singing the monastic hours, was the nightly performance of several stations of the Eucharist and sequences of prayers to specific images.[36] The leader of each house also had the option to add to the daily liturgies an additional half-hour chant of the 'Passion of Saint Anselm,' a probable reference to a sung version of Pseudo-Anselm's *Dialogus beatae Mariae et Anselmi de passione domini*.[37] In sum, on any given day, the newly reformed Observant friar would not only withdraw to contemplate his misery internally for an hour[38] but would also process from image to shrine around the church. The increase in religiosity posited by the reformers thus involved greater interiority through private prayer *and* greater exteriority in movement throughout the ritual space. (This 'development' is more likely a renewal; Saenger argues that on the wider European scene, private or silent prayer only became distinct from public or oral prayer in the middle of the fourteenth century.)[39]

The increased emphasis on rituals related to images was not a development internal to the Franciscan order alone, however. Rather, it most likely took its cue from the growing importance of devotional figures for private devotion in late medieval Castile. Felipe Pereda argues persuasively that during the fifteenth century the cult of images left the Castilian church grounds and was relocated firmly in private space.

> The development of a culture of religious images in the fifteenth century is one of the most extraordinary events in the evolution of late medieval and early modern spirituality. Images moved from altars to the interiors of houses, from churches to monastic cells, and devotional practices began to concede ever more importance to the figurative element, as much to the products of imagination as to the paintings or sculptures which inspired them.[40]

So many devotees had small crucifixes or images of the Virgin Mary in their own homes that during the early years of the Inquisition, owning a private devotional image was taken as a primary marker of faith.[41] Although medievalists repeatedly characterize Books of Hours (private guides to prayer following the monastic hours, usually concentrating on prayers to the Virgin) as the primary method of lay access to devotion, a view that limits the 'laity' to the literate and wealthy,[42] in Spain, the Inquisition trials of *conversos* examined by Pereda indicate a widespread use of private sacred images by the laity (see Figure 1.1). Thus, the visual sense and the corporeality of the bodies of Jesus and Mary played a greater role than literacy did in the flourishing of lay devotion after the religious unification in 1492. In turn, it is probable that the popular and Inquisitorial emphasis on faith mediated by private religious images was formative for the increasing public deployment of sculpted altarpieces (*retablos*) with three-dimensional scenes of the lives of Christ and Mary, as well as free-standing religious sculpture in cathedrals.[43] The relation of the altarpieces to Passion meditation will be remarked upon later in this chapter; for now, it is sufficient to conclude that visual images, especially those in three dimensions and therefore clearly embodied as well as symbolic, were key to spiritual practices in post-Reconquest Castile.

Fig 1.1 Friar carrying a book and a crucifix. Placed at head of part 3, chapter 1 of Laredo's *Subida del Monte Sión* (Seville: Jacobo Cromburger, 1535), fol. 150r. Credit: Biblioteca Nacional de España, Madrid.

While the frequent disappearance or reuse of small religious images in later centuries has made it difficult for art historians to document the sacralization of domestic space in Renaissance Castile,[44] it is possible to verify the growing attention to religious images through consideration of a complementary trend. Throughout the fifteenth and sixteenth centuries, apparitions, possibly inspired by local religious images, centred attention on nearly forgotten crucifixes or images of the Virgin.[45] Peasants and children, especially females, claimed God's direct intervention in the revival of local devotional rituals concerning the sacred images. William Christian Jr remarks that these visions never achieved the widespread impact that the experiences of a Teresa of Avila or John of the Cross did. Nevertheless, the impact of private visions on the public's increased attention to local devotion brought statuary and shrines into the forefront of the Castilian religious landscape (not to mention into the forefront of the local economy, thanks to the influx of pilgrims).

My suggestion is that these elements combine to indicate a devotional shift over the course of the fifteenth century. There was a concomitant elevation in private prayer (the *recogimiento* prayer developed in *casas de retiro*, or the prayers muttered by devotees at newly miraculous shrines) and embodied devotion (walking the stations after compline, or attention to physical images in the home or in nearby shrines). In addition, emphasis on the devotee's body during ritual performance was on the rise at the same time as an increased attention to the physicality of Christ and Mary in crucifixes and Marian statues. In these new forms of embodied devotion, however, as the quotation from Pereda above indicates, the 'figurative' element that was the marker of Christian faithfulness could consist of either actual or imagined figures; that is, devotional focus could be directed towards either sculptures in shrines or towards imaginative meditation on the events of Christ's life. It is to the imagined figures that we must turn, for it is the ever-increasing emphasis on imaginative visualization of the events of Holy Week from the 1480s on, I argue, that sowed the seeds that sprouted as the extremely physical approach to devotion found in the penitential confraternal processions for Holy Week in the 1520s and onward. While this new trend in Passion-centred devotions in Castile might simply seem to be a belated rendition of the late medieval turn to 'somatic spirituality,' nowhere else in Europe did somatic spiritual practices result in what would be the most colourful and visible aspect of Spanish spirituality from early modern through contemporary times: processions during Holy Week, or *Semana Santa*, of flagellants carrying floats with immense statues of Jesus and Mary. The next sections of this chapter will examine the increased Castilian attention to the physicality of Jesus and Mary in early sixteenth-century texts that narrated how to visualize their suffering, a development, I posit, that in turn provided the momentum for the establishment of *Semana Santa* rituals and the visual impact of processional sculpture.

Guides to Passion Meditation in the Cisnerian Era

Although Villacreces and his followers focused their reforming critique on their own religious order, their pattern of religious life gained attention in other venues. In 1495, just three years after removing the political threat of the Granadan polity and the religious challenge of the Jews, the Spanish monarchs charged the newly appointed Archbishop of Toledo, Francisco Jiménez de Cisneros, with the reform of not only of his own Observant Franciscan Order but also of the Spanish church as a whole.[46] While his best-known initiatives were the Polyglot Bible and the innovative theology curriculum at the newly established Universidad de Alcalá,[47] several other projects provided a new openness and accessibility to spiritual methods that led to a surge in lay and female devotion.[48] Not content with importing scholastic methods alone, Cisneros commissioned a press at Alcalá to publish the first translations of various spiritual and mystical writers, including Gregory the Great, Angela of Foligno, Ludolph of Saxony, and Catherine of Siena.[49] In addition to increasing the range of spiritual works available to literate Spaniards, Cisneros also supported popular devotion to local mystics, including María de Santo Domingo (the Beata de Piedrahita) and Juana de la Cruz (abbess of Santa María de Cubas), whose visions he accepted as prophecy.[50] It is well known that the openness of the highest ecclesial official in Spain to innovative forms of spirituality provided opportunities for new voices and new attitudes in the life of the church; it has been less frequently noted that a large percentage of the new works printed after the introduction of the printing press to Castile in 1474 were focused on meditations on the life, and especially the Passion, of Jesus.[51] Both Isabella and Cisneros provided extensive publication support for this genre, newly available in the vernacular everywhere from the secular court to the libraries of the mendicant retreat houses. Nevertheless, the impact of this genre on the flowering of Renaissance Christian practice in Castile has been undervalued in scholarship on Spanish religion.[52]

Several scholars suggest that the texts promoted by Isabella and Cisneros were a rather 'austere' version of the medieval tradition of meditation on the Passion.[53] Pairing this attribution of austerity with a presumed turn to interiority has resulted in the history of the Spanish Renaissance Christianity being written consistently without the body (unless that body happens to be that of a female devotee). However, my own work on post-Isabelline Passion treatises indicates the quick development of interest in highly emotional, violent, and embodied meditations, as we will see below. In order to examine the progressive elaboration of these techniques that resulted in the unique Castilian Passion genre called the 'Passion of Two,' it is necessary to start with the essentials: the consistent framing of medieval Passion meditation techniques around the three foci of pain, dialogue, and compassion.

Devotional focus on the humanity of Christ began to increase in most of Europe in the twelfth century,[54] centring on the devotee's imagined presence as spectator at the events of Jesus's death: kissing the feet of the child in the crib, travelling alongside the Magi,[55] and ultimately wincing with every witnessed blow to Christ's body during his final days on earth. The power of this type of devotion is to remove the mundane world of the devotee from centre stage. The meditator instead deliberately transports him- or herself to another realm, one which is thoroughly of this world in the enumeration of details about birth, hunger, thirst, and pain, yet which is fundamentally separate from normal human experience because of the ultimate and divine significance attached to each and every moment. In the most popular medieval texts, known as *Vita Christi* (Life of Christ) treatises, the visualizations guide the meditator concerning doctrine, morals, and the level of intensity of devotion he or she must strive for in response to the intensity of the sacrifice of Christ.[56]

The medieval Latin tradition directed attention to the entirety of Christ's life, including his childhood and his teachings, yet it was the sufferings of Christ on the way to and upon the cross that were most extensively extrapolated in the Latin 'best-sellers.'[57] Ludolph of Saxony's *Vita Christi* (the lengthiest and latest of the genre and the most influential in the Spanish Golden Age as a result of Isabella's commissioning its translation in 1502) devotes a full quarter of its attention to the Passion and rehearses, even quotes verbatim, earlier works. It can serve as an overview of the entire medieval trend. The Crucifixion scene is always particularly dramatic: the nail holes were made without regard for the size of the man, so after nailing through the nerves and bones of Jesus's right hand, they had to wrench his body towards the other side of the cross with such force that he ended up 'stretched like a skin for parchment' on the cross, to the point that his bones could be counted.[58] Ludolph interprets the visualization of the wounds in each of Jesus's limbs as teaching believers to dedicate their hands to charity, their feet to following the commandments, and so on.[59] The goal was to find moral and spiritual concordances in the devotee's life that would allow him or her to imitate not the physicality but the meaning behind Christ's sacrifice. In other words, the medieval genre brought about an explosion of attention to the physical in order to aid the spiritual growth of the believer.

In addition to the shock value of the torture itself, *Vita Christi* texts expanded the role of almost every participant in Christ's life and death, from Jesus and Mary to the supporting disciples, female followers, the judges that sentence him to death, and so on, primarily by including extensive dialogue that highlights the participants' emotional reactions to the events. Of particular interest, meriting its own genre, was Mary's lament at the foot of the cross (*Planctus Mariae*). Authors such as Pseudo-Bernard in the twelfth-century *Quis dabit* took these brief laments as opportunities to recite violence done to Christ through the point of view of the spectator who was most grieved by the events.[60] Pseudo-Bernard has Mary say to the reader: 'I was indeed in Jerusalem ... And when I looked at him, struck by fists, beaten with blows, crowned with thorns, spat upon and made the reproach of all men, all my innards were stirred, my spirit failed, there was in me neither sense, nor voice, nor sound.'[61] Mary's reactions were articulated at such length in order to serve as a model for the devotee's own sorrow.

Beyond the utility ascribed to Mary as role model, continual compassive attention to Mary's grief led some devotees to posit that she had had a quasi-divine role in Christian soteriology. They perceived a parallel between her response to Gabriel at the Annunciation and her presence at the foot of the cross, even calling her 'co-redeemer' for having assented to the key moments of Jesus's incarnation and sacrifice.[62] If performed perfectly, a compassive response to the suffering God could result in the divinization of the ideal devotee. Ultimately, the gestures, physical surroundings, and violence that accumulated in the formulas for meditating on the events of Holy Week served to orient the believers' attention firmly towards the embodied divine, as well as to elaborate on the divine actions of the ideal human, Mary.[63]

Although a few Marian laments survive from the high Middle Ages in Castile and a fairly coherent tradition of Passion spirituality emerged from medieval Catalonia,[64] the first sustained development of Passion-centred devotions in Castile was linked directly with the leading voices of religious reform. Castilian ventures in *Vita Christi* poetry, all written for Isabella's court, began to appear within a decade of the introduction of printing, corresponding exactly with the first step in the Catholic Monarchs' program for religious unity on the peninsula, the Reconquest of Granada.[65] It is therefore worth highlighting that all but two of these poems focus on the Passion alone instead of on the entire life of Christ.[66] While some of these new texts reflect details drawn from Pseudo-Bonaventure or from Ludolph, others seem simply to follow the general intentions of the technique by elaborating on the events in original ways.[67] For example, Diego de San Pedro's lengthy *La pasión trobada* (The Versified Passion), possibly the most widely disseminated work on the Passion in the Golden Age, focuses mainly on the conversations of Jesus with his followers, his accusers, and with God, in accordance with the Latin imaginative tradition of extra details concerning the dialogues.[68] San Pedro also follows the medieval tradition discussed earlier in his description of the nailing of Christ and in his insertion of a Marian lament at the foot of the cross.[69] Recited at court and transmitted in both compilations and in pamphlets, it is clear that meditation on the death of Christ was a leading element of the official reform movement.

The tradition of court-sponsored Passion poetry directly influenced the first Castilian Passion plays (a type of *auto sacramentale*) produced under Cisneros.[70] For example, a quarter of the verses in Alonso del Campo's *Auto de la passion* (1499) are from two of Diego de San Pedro's religious poems.[71] Some of the *autos sacramentales* were performed at court, while others were performed in cathedrals and churches during feast day processions such as Corpus Christi.[72] The attention to the strong affective component provided by visual interaction with a historical narrative would have disseminated a high valuation of this tradition of imaginative meditation throughout Castile.

Although scholars term these vernacular Passion texts 'austere' in comparison to the Latin tradition, a closer look indicates that it is an austerity or restraint in terms of added scenarios rather than a bodily austerity. Ishikawa claims that in contrast to the 'dramatic, anecdotal' versions of the Passion found in vernacular texts elsewhere in Europe from the previous century, these new Castilian texts all rely on a 'sequential, chronological format with only occasional minor digressions … simple, straightforward language that would make the works easy to read aloud,' and all 'employ a measured pace to convey a sense of inevitability and truth.'[73] For example, Ishikawa includes the first prose vernacular Passion text, Andrés de Li's *Thesoro de la passion* (Treasure of the Passion, 1494), under the category of restrained Isabelline texts.[74] The restraint is seen in such scenes as the nailing to the cross, for Li's four chapters on the nailing of each extremity do not attend to the violence done to each hand and foot. Rather, Li examines the symbolism of each detail, proposing analyses such as the possibility that Christ's left foot is always shown in front of the right in Crucifixion scenes because the left foot stands for the devotee's evil desires, which must be conquered before he or she can concentrate on more virtuous ones.[75]

Yet this 'austere' characterization only truly applies to the earliest texts in Renaissance Castile, those laying the foundation for a practice rather than extending a known tradition, because as we will see, the urge to provide doctrinal rationale for added details disappears in the post-Isabelline treatises. As the Castilian tradition of somatic spirituality developed its unique slant on the *Vita Christi* tradition, becoming what could be termed a *Passio Christi* genre, authors introduced a pivotal new element: focus on the Son's devotion was broadened into a focus on the Passion of the Son *and* the Mother. I argue that not only was early sixteenth-century spirituality marked by attention to the bleeding body of a male divine, it was also centred on the pain and agony of the ideal woman.

The Evolution of Passion Spirituality in Early Sixteenth-Century Castile

The influence of this late medieval focus on Christ's embodiment (and Mary's divinity) on Renaissance Castilian spirituality must be understood in light of the delayed peninsular diffusion of the Latin 'best-sellers.' Although there is at least one possible manuscript translation of Pseudo-Bonaventure's *Meditationes Vitae Christi* from the fifteenth century, Cynthia Robinson has not found any evidence that it was as widely known as previously supposed, and rejects the thesis that it may have been influential on fifteenth-century devotions in Castile at all.[76] Keith Whinnom likewise argues that Ludolph's *Vita Christi* was not available, even in Latin, any earlier than the 1490s.[77] For that matter, the Latin prose meditations on Christ's humanity were not the only format of Passion meditation to have a belated impact on Castilian spirituality. Rosary meditation, a popularized, versified version of the *Vita Christi* relating the joys and sorrows experienced by Mary in response to the events of Jesus's life and death, had swept Europe for a century before the first Castilian translation appeared in the 1490s.[78]

When the new translations of the *Vita Christi* did begin to influence peninsular spirituality, they addressed the prevailing concerns of the Villacrecian reform. Note the emphasis on Christian knowledge gained without a university education that a Castilian Observant Franciscan would have found in the Carthusian *Vita Christi* of Ludolph: 'As it were, the memory of His Passion makes all unlearned men very wise and turns the unschooled and simple into masters – not masters of science, which breeds arrogance, but masters of love, which is edifying.'[79] This interest in unschooled forms of bodily devotion coincides strongly with trends specific to fifteenth-century Castile, yet the surge in sixteenth-century Passion meditation texts has been little noticed, despite the fact that the Christocentric Franciscan order led Spanish church reform.

The novelty of the *Vita Christi* genre in the vernacular on the peninsula is made clear by Li's statement that he composed his *Thesoro de la passion* in response to his publisher's complaint that, of all the many books he had published and seen in other publishing houses, he had never held a prose meditation on the Passion composed in Castilian.[80] Since the tradition of the *Vita Christi* entered Castilian spirituality primarily as works about the Passion alone, not about Christ's birth or teachings, I posit that a crucial difference exists between the development of somatic spirituality throughout Europe, which coexisted with forms of meditation that took into account Christ's body while alive, and the peninsular somatic spirituality (more appropriately termed *Passio Christi*), which paid attention only to the bodies of Mother and Son during his march towards death. In particular, the Castilian genre appears to be distinct from the *imitatio Christi* tradition with which it is often confounded, for Kempis's pre-eminent work on the imitation of Christ focused on his virtues while alive.[81] In other words, the new texts in Castilian inaugurated not just a general emphasis on the humanity of Christ in peninsular spirituality but a specifically somatic ideation that attended to his torture and death above all.

Unlike the translations of Latin *Vitae Christi* in circulation in Castilian from around 1500 onward, texts by Spaniards do not include extensive prologues that justify the technique of meditation, or lengthy discussions of doctrine and practice inserted between the scenes of Jesus's life and death. As I have argued elsewhere, these new vernacular works are distinctive for devoting half of every chapter to considering Mary's actions and emotions during Holy Week, extending the technique of imaginative visualization primarily in terms of ascribing the torture of the Passion to Mary's experience, not just her son's.[82] While Marian devotion had always been a keynote of Passion-centred devotions, as discussed above in relation to her lament, this element in Passion spirituality was magnified as a result of its reception by Castilian Christians, who had already put the Virgin Mary at the forefront of Catholic practice since early in the Reconquest. In medieval Spain, the Virgin led battles, protected shrines, rescued captives, and inspired kings; in the early sixteenth century, the Virgin suffered mentally and physically.[83]

In order to examine the manner in which the two bodies and their catastrophic suffering were central to the Castilian extension of medieval somatic spirituality, let us turn to two representative Passion treatises, both with Latin titles but vernacular content and exceedingly popular in their time:[84] *Fasciculus myrrhe* (1511),[85] and *Passio duorum* (1526; attributed to Francisco de Tenerio with revisions by Luis de Escobar).[86] The two works are remarkably similar in the chronological framing of their narratives, for both describe the events from Palm Sunday through Good Friday. Both treatises were originally circulated anonymously, a custom especially prevalent among Franciscan authors as evidence of humility.[87] I suggest that these two works provide further proof of the pivotal role that the reform Franciscan focus on the humanity of Christ played in the Spanish Renaissance. *Fasciculus myrrhe* is closer in tone to the austere Isabelline poetry and plays discussed earlier, while *Passio duorum*, the more influential work, marks a clear shift in terms of its strong emphasis on body, especially the bodies of Mother and Son.

The 1511 *Fasciculus myrrhe*, while still somewhat restrained, brings the devotee into the midst of the story in direct relation to the embodied mental agony of the Virgin. The anonymous author tells the reader, addressed directly as 'devota anima' (devout soul),[88] that meditating with emotional affect on the events of Holy Week is an important aid.[89] In order to demonstrate the way visualizing is a step beyond other types of meditation, the author gives samples of interactions between Christ and other people, especially Mary. Although highly charged and emotional, these scenes are provided as third-person dialogues, limiting the affective response of the devotee in favour of the visualization:

> The Virgin, hearing the blows of the hammer ... cried out, saying, 'Woe is me, my son and my joy, with what cruelty you are treated by these evil men. It would be better that these blows hit my body and head: so at least I could fulfill my desire to die with you, my life and all my good, fulfilled.' So, you soul, go there and accompany that sad mother and put yourself next to her and keep other people away so that they do not annoy her, and having compassion for her, console her and cry with her and the other women and do not desert them.[90]

Fasciculus myrrhe's process of imaginative visualization ascribes intense experiences to the various historical and divine figures in the narrative, then suggests ways that the devotee insert him- or herself into the scenario in response to the emotion. In effect, visualizing interactions between other people leads directly to a participatory form of devotion. The participation is often linked with responding to the corporeality of the actants in the dramatic scenario. Mary faints dead away on numerous occasions,[91] an embodied form of emotional distress, and the reader is directed to imagine with what difficulty she struggles to get up after each fall.[92] At many points, the author tells the reader to enter the scene in order to cry with Mary and the other women, begging the reader not to desert the Virgin.[93] The devotee thus develops a sense that it is possible to participate in the scene: to at once imitate and aid the Virgin by weeping physical tears, walking along with the participants, and even supporting her emotionally (and perhaps to keep her from falling down once again).

Given the conjunction of third-person narration of events and directives to the soul to enter the scene and participate physically, the author of the *Fasciculus myrrhe* ultimately does not elaborate on what the reader is supposed to be thinking, much less mentally praying, in response to the imagined scene. In this respect, Tenerio's *Passio duorum*, appearing around a decade later, shows a marked stylistic contrast to *Fasciculus myrrhe*.[94]

The narrator addresses Christ, Mary, and other participants in the drama directly with 'O Lord, you ...' and gives suggestions at the end of each chapter for the appropriate response on the part of the reader. The treatise's 'apostrophe and *exclamatio*' style has prompted one scholar to read the work not as a narrative but as an extended prayer.[95] Mary remains present as an interlocutor for the soul even when she is not part of the narrative itself, for Tenerio consistently directs the soul to imagine what Mary's reaction would have been to the events between Gethsemane and her first sight of Jesus carrying the cross.[96] For example, the chapter on the nailing of Christ's feet to the cross ends with a passage in which the pronoun shifts mark an important change.

> O my Jesus who loves me so ... What are my good works so that for me, a sinner, you show yourself to your mother in the way she sees you, for you cannot sustain yourself with your feet because they are twisted and pinned down, nor can you help yourself with your hands, and you cannot hope for repose until death. O cruel killers, the law bans cooking the lamb in the sheep's milk, yet here you cook the sheep and lamb together, him in her presence and her in his. O spotless lamb spit-roasted on the Cross: you are boiled entirely in your mother. O soul, choose as you will how to celebrate the Easter of the lamb, for if you want him grilled, look at the Cross, if you want him stewed, look at his mother.[97] You will see that all is used up – his blood, her tears – and that this sacrifice has no comparison with any other in terms of being profitable for the world, agreeable to the Father, costly for the Son, painful to the Mother.[98]

Rather than creating an affecting scene between two characters separate from the reader, as in the *Fasciculus myrrhe*, the author of *Passio duorum* puts the visual aspects (twisted on the cross) in the mouth of the reader as an element of the reader's direct entreaty to Christ. The author himself then enters into the narrative by directing the soul to 'look' at the participants on several levels, either at the dead, grilled body on the cross or at Mary's compassionate, stewed-in-tears reaction to the event. The devotees imagine themselves as spectators analysing the visual data entering their senses, integrating their own corporality into the scene.

In addition, the *Passio duorum* is remarkable for assimilating Mary directly into the physicality of the Crucifixion. Medieval versions of the scene at the foot of the cross had traditionally emphasized Mary's participation by exaggerating the wording of her lament. However, in Tenerio's version of the 1520s, Longinus must reach over the Virgin's head in order to thrust the spear into Christ's side, a description that imagines Mary's body as physically intruding into the core events of the Crucifixion.[99] Similar emphasis on the body marks Tenerio's description of Mary's compassion as co-participation, for Mary herself feels the pain of the nails *before* they had actually been driven into Christ's hands and feet.[100] Tenerio emphasizes the motif of Mary's body, and even Mary's pain, that had been begun by the earlier *Fasciculus·myrrhe*. It is evident from both these texts that Castilian Passion-centred devotions forefronted the physicality of the twisted, pained bodies of Jesus and Mary, sometimes even finding a place for the reader's body in conjunction with the bodies of the Mother and the Son.

Given the publication of the second of these exemplary Passion meditation guides in 1526, this review of the progressively greater trend towards violence in the Castilian tradition around the Passion brings us from the Cisnerian era to the transitional era of *recogimiento*, the *alumbrado* heresy, and the beginnings of the *Semana Santa* processions in Seville. And, in fact, beyond, since the *Passio duorum* was widely distributed in the libraries of the New World,[101] and translated into Tagalog in the mid-seventeenth century to accompany *via crucis* (stations of the cross) processions in the furthest outpost of Spanish political and cultural control.[102] The emphasis on the humanity of Christ that began with brief poems presented at the court of Ferdinand and Isabella thus ultimately spread throughout the Spanish empire in the form of full-length treatises that spotlighted the mental and physical pain of both Mother and Son.

Envisioning the Passion

As is now evident, bodies, both of the devotee and of Christ and Mary, were highly valorized in the spiritual genres promoted during the Cisnerian era. It is not only the prescriptive guides to embodied, even bloodthirsty, meditation that allow us to affirm this fact; the visual impact of the Passion meditation techniques outlined above cannot be fully understood without attention to other contemporaneous valuations of the visual sense. During the Cisnerian era (and beyond), visionaries enjoyed a measure of popular authority, while religious art in the form of three-dimensional sculpted *retablos* began to dominate cathedral decoration.

The most stunning example of the role of body in the visual experience of God is the series of *sermones* given over a period of thirteen years by Juana de la Cruz (1481–1534), which were heard not only by the nuns of her Castilian convent but also by such auditors as Cisneros and Emperor

Charles V.[103] Juana is said to have gone into rapture publicly, lying stiff and apparently dead in front of her audience, a loss of consciousness that was nevertheless accompanied by a deep voice issuing from her voicebox. This voice identified itself as Christ (or as the Holy Spirit, or as Juana's guardian angel) and proceeded to narrate the constant festive meals, plays, and dances occurring at every moment in heaven, events that Juana was 'seeing' while in her trance. Her visionary experiences, collected in a book called *El Conhorte*, forefront the bodies of Christ, Mary, the saints, and angels in a remarkably human manner as they hold court, eat enormous dinners, dance and sit on each other's laps, and parade around in fancy gowns (when they are not half nude and caressing each other).[104] A Christian public that listened entranced to an abbess describing feasts whose main delicacies included plates of pastries issuing forth from the nail wounds on Jesus's hands and excellent liquor pouring out of his side wound was surely a public for whom embodied devotion was acceptable, perhaps even essential.[105] Note however that Juana's body, transformed into a vehicle for the voice of Christ, did not entirely disappear, since Christ narrated what an enraptured Juana was seeing; thus the female body, or at least the female gaze and voice, is critical in conveying the celebration of embodiment occurring in heaven.

In addition to the key part played by Juana's senses in the visionary experience, Christ's body, specifically Christ's wounded body, is central to the articulation of her theology, as I argue elsewhere.[106] While many devout might have imagined Christ's resurrected body as 'glorious,' its full healing proving his divinity,[107] in Juana's visions, Jesus at the head of the dinner table surrounded by his angels is still stigmatic and bleeding, although often his body switches back and forth between being bloody and untouched.[108] Later in the century, as artistic versions of the Trinity became more popular, artists such as El Greco depicted God the Father as a powerful man with a white beard cradling Jesus, whose wounded body was formed in a classical *pietà* pose.[109] In one sermon, Juana presaged this trend, describing Jesus's stigmatic body nestled in the breast of the Trinity.[110] For this female visionary, what I term Christ's 'perpetually passionate body' proves the individuality of salvation, as Christ experiences yet another iteration of bodily death for each and every soul saved from purgatory.[111]

In the end, it is not surprising that the manuscript recording Juana's sermons and her dictated autobiography were not published in her era;[112] rather more intriguing is the fact that she was allowed to speak publicly to such a wide audience in the first place. Archbishop Cisneros was known for fomenting innovative forms of spirituality, whether original published texts or the spiritual leadership of women, and indeed supported Juana's authority specifically.[113] Yet I would argue that Juana's attention to Christ's bleeding body serves to ground her spectacular proposals concerning Jesus's participation in highly embodied heavenly festivities within the newly popular Passion-centred devotions discussed in this chapter. In addition, her authority within her convent depended on regular visions of the Virgin Mary, who was understood to periodically participate in the life of the convent by coming into its grounds to bless the crops or lead rituals.[114] In other words, while visually stimulating and corporeally startling, Juana's sermons may not have been as theologically disquieting as modern readers find them, given the embodiedness of devotion common to the Spanish Renaissance.

As important as these renditions of imagined and envisioned bodies were for the era, however, it is equally critical to realize that they did not stand alone as imagined bodies. Rather, they were disseminated at the same time as a visual, tactile, and even three-dimensional articulation of Passion spirituality took centre (visual) stage. From the 1480s through the 1520s, art historians document a rise in the number and sumptuousness of *retablos*, altarpieces that presented a narrative of the life of Christ with an emphasis on the Marian elements; both the physical *retablos* and their textual equivalents such as Padilla's poem for the Isabelline court, *Retablo de la vida de Cristo* (Altarpiece of the Life of Christ) date to the last quarter of the fifteenth century in Seville.[115] Nor did Passion texts affect the visual iconography of altarpieces under Isabel (and Cisneros) only. For example, a number of scenes in the most elaborate *retablo* ever built, the *retablo mayor* in Seville's cathedral, match woodcuts in Passion meditation treatises from the same era.[116] This *retablo* was finished just in time for Charles V's marriage in 1526 in Seville.[117] It is worth noting that not only did Laredo frequently enter Seville from his retreat house in an outlying village in attendance to royalty as a physician, but that his fellow recollection mystic Francisco de Osuna and the famous Passion preacher Juan de Avila also lived in Seville in the late 1520s.[118] Whether these three mystical teachers preached in the cathedral in front of the *retablo* or in less formal settings to an audience who would also have attended mass at the cathedral, the *retablo* emphasis on the sculpted bodies of Christ and Mary would have been a constant theme and therefore a crucial backdrop to the Andalusian development of *recogimiento* as a mystical praxis. As grandiose as the *retablo* was, however, in its depiction of many moments from Christ's life with a strong scattering from the life of Mary, some of the most fully articulated and emotional scenes in the upper register would have been barely visible to the faithful. The poetic and prose Passion meditation texts, the Passion sermons of Juan de Avila, or the Passion meditations in *recogimiento* texts may have been reinforced by the presence of a *Vita Christi* altarpiece, yet the texts in turn served the laity as a fuller explanation of Passion devotion than that provided by distant glimpses of images high up on a cathedral wall.

The extraordinary efflorescence of attention to the dying body of Christ traced in this chapter – in poetry, plays, meditation guides, visionary sermons, and altarpieces – was a critical element of the Cisnerian reform and the decades immediately following. Both the imagined and actual figures of a bleeding Christ and of Mary's reaction to his suffering and death were key to published texts and to religious practice throughout this era. The trends towards increased lay participation and innovation in the religious arena did not end with Cisneros's death in 1517, however. It was in the 1520s that the religious festivals and public processions of the confraternities associated with Seville's *Semana Santa* had their first tentative beginnings.

The Origins of *Semana Santa*

Laredo composed the Passion narrative found in part 2 of the *Subida* during the same decade as the *via crucis* became an integral part of Sevillian public religious life. It cannot be a coincidence that the beginning of lay fascination with a physical, visual, and emotive celebration of the Passion events featured in *Semana Santa* corresponds to the same decade in which Andalusian Franciscans began publishing the first prescriptive guides to a mystic way that include Passion meditation as a major theme. However, *Semana Santa* is usually analysed separately from mystical trends, as the apparent overlap between orthodox *recogimiento* and the heretical *alumbrado* technique of *dejamiento* (letting go) has led scholars to associate *recogimiento* purely with mental prayer. I suggest that Laredo's method, written with an awareness of the beginnings of Holy Week processions, may have reconfigured the processional practices but never un-embodied them.

In 1521, the same year that Laredo's first medical treatise was printed, a local noble, Don Fadrique Enríquez de Ribera, the Marqués de Tarifa, returned to Seville from a pilgrimage to Jerusalem and planned a public *via crucis* by mapping stations of the cross onto the streets of his hometown. The local Spanish Franciscan reformers had probably fuelled his interest in pilgrimage in the first place, as they financed several monasteries in the Holy Land. The Catholic Monarchs who appointed the Franciscan Cisneros to lead the reform also clearly supported pilgrimage, given the pope's concession of the title of 'King of Jerusalem' to Ferdinand and his successors in 1510.[119] In 1524, Pope Clement VII issued a bull granting Jubilee status to any of Tarifa's family or servants who completed the Sevillian *via crucis*,[120] followed by a 1529 bull that provided Jubilee indulgences to any person of faith who offered a vocal prayer (Pater Noster, Ave Maria) in front of a Marian image, a cross, or a saint's relic.[121] By mid-century, seven of the twelve Sevillian penitential confraternities were participating in the public processions through seven stations during *Semana Santa*;[122] the number of penitential organizations grew to twenty-six by 1579.[123] From that time until the present, Spanish Christianity, both on its home ground and throughout its empire, has been distinctive among Christian traditions for its celebration of *Semana Santa*. Nevertheless, the origins of this practice have been shrouded in obscurity; the few details provided in this section are all that historians have definitively adduced.

In my view, the relatively unfruitful search for a document trail overlooks the historical context of the confraternities: the contemporary phenomenon of Passion meditation in poetry, drama, and prose guides. I argue that the *Semana Santa* processions should be considered another variant among the many that contributed to the rise of Passion-centred devotions in Castile. They are also a key backdrop to the development of *recogimiento*, at least as influential on the new systematization of mystical prayer as the struggle to define *recogimiento* as distinct from the *dejamiento* practice of the *alumbrados*. Here I examine *Semana Santa* processions in the context of other Passion-centred devotions, a discussion that sets the stage for a re-evaluation of the *dejamiento/recogimiento* debate given their different attitudes towards embodied spirituality.

The particularities of Golden Age Castilian lay devotional processions are a consequence of medieval religious trends. Sánchez Herrero characterizes Sevillian religious practice as ludic: 'Medieval Christianity was festive, even more so in Seville.'[124] During the fifteenth century, the Sevillian celebration of the festival of Corpus Christi was particularly spectacular, as plazas throughout the city were converted into theatrical arenas. Headed by the religious talisman of the host in its silver chest, the processions included frames or floats pushed through the street, with people dressed as Mary, Jesus, or saints standing in various scenarios (*pasos*). Accompanied by giant puppets and dance troupes performing towards the rear of the parade,[125] the processions moved from plaza to plaza, where plays or jousts were performed in the open spaces.[126] Romero Abao analyses this ritual as part of a late medieval Sevillian trend to create 'sacralized space' in addition to the 'sacred space' of the cathedrals.[127]

Not all Sevillian processions were so festive, though all increased devotion by sacralizing public arenas. In her work on the processional sculpture of the Sevillian confraternities, Susan Verdi Webster differentiates between three types of Golden Age confraternities: penitential (dedicated to various aspects of the Passion, processions during Holy Week), sacramental (dedicated to the Eucharist, processions during the feast of Corpus Christi), and devotional (dedicated to specific saints, most often the Virgin Mary).[128] Penitential processions, while not regularly scheduled in the fifteenth century, had occurred at various intervals in response to periods of plague and famine, usually as avocations to the Virgen de la Antigua.[129] The first Sevillian brotherhood, the *Vera Cruz* (True Cross) associated with the Franciscan Order,[130] was established sometime in the late fourteenth century and converted to a penitential focus in 1448.[131] Its 'rule' was first written in 1501 and reached its final official version in 1538,[132] providing extensive information concerning both private and public commitments by members of Sevillian confraternities in the earliest decades of the development of the processional tradition. It will be the basis for what follows.[133]

Most research into confraternities focuses on their members, yet there was a distinct contrast between the devotional experience of the confraternity members and that of the spectators to the public ritual.[134] The 1538 rule describes the processional ritual for Maundy Thursday that had developed in the previous fifteen years (see Figure 1.2). Two levels were available to both men and women.[135] Members 'of light' paid high dues and acted as aides to the other level, while members 'of blood' gave low monetary contributions but performed the highest-profile acts of the confraternity as flagellants in the Holy Thursday processions.[136] The leading scholar of Andalusian confraternities, José Sánchez Herrero, summarizes the processions as follows, noting that the confraternity distributed cat'o'nine tails and proper raiment to all members who did not have their own, as well as to any non-member who chose to pay a small fee to join the procession:

> A black flag with a coloured cross was carried by the majordomo who led the procession. Next, two by two in a line, [came] those practising discipline, with two members of light interspersed after every four or five [members of blood]. At the end a cleric [dressed] in his 'black shirt' carried 'a great

Fig 1.2 Francisco de Goya, *Procession of Flagellants* (1812–19). Royal Academy of San Fernando, Madrid. Credit: Archivo Oronoz.

> crucified [Jesus] on the cross,' accompanied by confraternity members that were marked out by wearing the black habit and [carrying] battleaxes. Friars from the Convent of San Francisco accompanied the procession. Cantors were never included, instead [came] 'four trumpets playing sorrowfully.' They visited five stations: the Convent of San Francisco, the cathedral, the church of El Salvador, the church of Santa María Magdalena, and the church of San Pablo.[137]

For the participants, then, whether lay, monastic, or clerical, it was their own bodies, symbolically clothed but physically maltreated, that formed the nucleus of the experience. They would have experienced the day as one involving movement through space, physical duress, symbols and markers of excessive violence, and an excess of auditory and visual grief and pain. Nor were the processions a unique event, but rather their incorporation into the liturgical calendar ensured that, unlike the flagellant movement of fifteenth-century Italy, the embodied praxis was a regular feature of life rather than a single moment of excessive self-discipline.[138]

Fig 1.3 Gasper de Becerra, *Cristo yacente* (ca 1560), detail of side wound as reliquary. Convento Descalzas Reales, Madrid. Credit: Archivo Oronoz.

For observers, on the other hand, the primary visual focus during *Semana Santa* would have been the ritual dress and portable sculptures of Jesus and Mary carried from station to station by the penitential confraternities (see Figure 1.3).[139] Although the spectators did not necessarily move through space or suffer blows as did the confraternity members, the Renaissance theory of cognition would have made the observers' experience identical to that of the flagellants rather than distinct from it (see chapter 5).

The processions provided a companion focus to the visual meditation of the Passion recommended by the new publications of vernacular (often Franciscan) spiritual treatises. Sánchez Herrero includes both processions and imaginative visualization as equal preoccupations for confraternity members, yet he cites no documentary evidence confirming that members of confraternities meditated regularly, nor does the rule of the *Vera Cruz* confraternity (upon which he bases his comments) include any mention of private meditation:

> I understand a Holy Week or Passion confraternity as an association of the faithful, in the majority of the cases exclusively laity, which join two further elements: in the first place the contemplation of the Passion and death of Christ, and in the second place the imitation of the suffering of Christ in his Passion and death by means of a public penitence which took the concrete form of auto-flagellation ... brought to a head in the undertaking of a procession or a station of penitence on one of the days of Holy Week.[140]

I suggest that the importance of Passion meditation for the inhabitants of Golden Age Seville is more easily determined by examining written texts on the Passion and their use by Sevillians than by reviewing archival evidence of confraternal practice. Laredo's use of Passion meditation as a mystical technique intentionally replaces the practice of pilgrimage to Jerusalem or the mapping of Jerusalem to city streets as we will see in chapter 2, yet historians of confraternities have not assessed this type of evidence. Nor have historians of *recogimiento* considered the possible implications of these common practices for the embodied experience of *recogimiento* authors, much less for their audiences.

Conclusion: Finding the Body among the First Generation of Castilian Mystics and Heretics[141]

This chapter has reconfigured traditional overviews of Spanish Renaissance spirituality to indicate the predominance of Passion-centred devotions in post-Reconquest Castile.[142] As portrayals of this era generally focus on *alumbrados*, Erasmianism, and Lutherans,[143] it is necessary to reframe these three topics as relatively minor elements in the larger panorama of Castilian religious practice in the first half of the sixteenth century. To properly assess Laredo's unique contribution to sixteenth-century spirituality, one that draws on medieval European mystical trends in general as well as on the distinctive developments of Renaissance Castilian spirituality in particular, we must revisit the problematic manner in which 1520s religion is presented in modern scholarship as exclusively concerned with the anti-body approaches of Erasmianism and the *alumbrados*.[144] The debate over Erasmianism and its rejection of much of late medieval spirituality engaged a tiny proportion of the public, primarily theologians and ecclesial officials who had intellectual concerns with the bodily excess of medieval ritual. Scholarship identifying Erasmianism as a primary topic in Renaissance Castilian spirituality presumes that the spirituality of the vast majority of devotees was fully traditional, as do those scholars who limit discussion of Castilian religion between the Reconquest of Granada through the Tridentine era to the topics of Erasmianism and the tiny sects of Lutherans discovered in the 1550s in Seville.[145] In this concluding section, I propose that a more illuminating view of the era highlights the widespread dispute among Franciscans and their followers, both male and female, over the best method to access mystical experience: orthodox *recogimiento*, or the heterodox Illuminism of the *alumbrados*.

Despite extensive analysis, scholars are still unable to attribute a coherent heresy to the Franciscan entourage prosecuted as *alumbrados*, and most believe the heresy of Illuminism to have been an invention of the inquisitors.[146] The Inquisition had been established in 1482 in order to examine charges of judaizing (backsliding) among Jewish converts to Christianity, a task that continued as its main priority after the Expulsion of the Jews in 1492 and subsequent mass conversion. Thirty years after the Expulsion, however, not many converts retained Jewish customs, and so the Inquisition began examining the heresies found among Christians that might particularly attract *conversos*, or New Christians. Most modern definitions of the *alumbrado* heresy draw on Inquisitor Alonso Manrique's 1525 edict to ascribe four common beliefs to the earliest generation of *alumbrados*: refusal to believe in hell, rejection of church rituals, iconoclasm, and the spiritual practice of *dejamiento*.[147] The first three points would evidently have concerned church authorities given the contemporaneous Protestant rejection of traditional rituals and the periodic iconoclastic violence in the north of Europe, yet Illuminism is generally considered a heresy particular to Spain because of the fourth point, the mystical prayer of *dejamiento*. Accused *alumbrados* such as Francisco Ortíz saw no heterodoxy in their prayer format, claiming to have learned their method for achieving union from the *recogido* Francisco de Osuna's lessons at La Salceda, in turn instructing *beatas* such as Francisca Hernández.[148] Nevertheless, Osuna and other early recollection authors hastily distanced themselves from the taint of Illuminism by insisting on the difference between the methods of mystical prayer attributed to each group: *dejamiento* was an attitude of 'letting go' or 'abandonment' (potentially quietistic), while *recogimiento* was a 're-collecting' of the powers of the soul away from the exterior towards an internal focus on God.[149]

The debate over these two techniques was central to a number of Inquisition trials in the 1520s and 1530s, including the prosecutions of Ortíz and Juan de Avila,[150] and almost every major mystic of the entire sixteenth century fell foul of Inquisitorial suspicion of Illuminism,[151] yet it has long been a puzzle to scholars as to how best to distinguish between the two.[152] Most rely on the following distinction: if both methods aim at union with God, then *dejamiento* is marked by a passive expectation of God overtaking the soul and causing a permanent union, while *recogimiento* is a practice that actively prepares for God's periodic action on the soul.[153] This set of distinctions is insufficient, however.[154] In particular, the permanent consequences of *dejamiento* may well distinguish its goal from that of *recogimiento* but do not serve to differentiate the two as process.[155] Inquisitors accused *alumbrados* of believing that once overtaken by God, they no longer needed church ritual to access divine power. If God dictated all their actions, all actions were therefore divinely mandated, regardless of whether those actions or friendships appeared inappropriate or even scandalous to an outside world.[156] Ultimately, scholars examining the consequences – what *alumbrados* were accused of believing and doing *as a result of* union through *dejamiento* – explain only the moral behaviour of *alumbrados* as heretical instead of addressing the actual methods of mystical prayer.

Even though the *alumbrado* heresy remains mysterious, *recogimiento* has received a very specific definition; an analysis of this definition helps elucidate the confusion in scholarship between the two practices. The type of prayer termed *recogimiento* had been practised in the *casas de retiro*, or *recolección* (retreat houses) of the reform Observant Franciscans in Castile for forty years before its systematization into a mystical method. Although no records remain that detail the specifics of this practice, Andrés argues that the key changes in the 1520s were its systematization as the stages of self-knowledge, Passion spirituality, and recollection, and its publication in a form available to laity as well as friars. Andrés consistently pairs the definition of *recogimiento* with the claim that the recollection mystics are of especial interest because of their concomitant focus on both body and soul,[157] yet his magisterial book undermines his own insight by focusing on the third stage, and the third stage alone, in detail. He articulates this final stage as a 'reducing,'[158] re-centring, or re-collecting of the powers of the soul usually focused externally inwards to the essential centre of the soul.[159] Recollection of the powers of the soul – memory, understanding, and will – is accomplished by quieting the senses; in Osuna's phrase, by making the physical and spiritual senses 'deaf and mute' (*sorda y muda*).[160] Full recollection leads the soul to discover that God exists at its own centre, at which point the self is transformed into God by means of love (the function of the will), a process Andrés also terms 'deification.'[161]

In addition to analysing only the final stage of *recogimiento*, which has a reductive effect, Andrés insists on the contrast between *recogimiento* and *dejamiento*,[162] even suggesting that Franciscans had condemned attitudes similar to *dejamiento* in the 1480s and at the 1524 Franciscan council in Toledo.[163] It is thus startling that the precise terms Andrés uses to name the core practice of *recogimiento* – 'quiet,' 'deification,' and 'transformation into God through love' – were shortly thereafter identified by the prominent scholar of *alumbrados*, Antonio Márquez, as the essential heretical elements of *dejamiento*. Accusations no. 9 and no. 32 in the Toledo edict ('That God's love in man *is* God'; 'God is our heart')[164] are, in Marquéz's view, a 'method' for union, since once received, God's love guides all actions and thoughts in the *alumbrado*. Setting himself against other scholars who have pointed to similar yet fully orthodox phrases in Peter Lombard, Jean Gerson, and Bernard of Clairvaux, Márquez harshly critiques this view: 'If man's love of God is God, [God's] transcendence is abolished, man is deified, Christianity is inverted.'[165] The absolute equivalence of transformation into God through love with heresy by one scholar and with the source of all that is best in orthodox Spanish mysticism by another scholar indicates an unresolved paradox in the framing of questions concerning 1520s religion in Castile.[166]

The overlap, or even absolute identification, between the two methods produced by the pivotal definitions of Andrés and Marquéz has resulted in what I believe to be a profound mis-characterization of *recogimiento*. Subsequent scholarship has consistently considered 1520s mystical prayer to be accomplished by an incorporeal soul, opposing mental prayer to the bodiliness of ritual and vocal prayer, as well as to discursive meditation on the death of Christ's body.[167] Since both *dejamiento* and *recogimiento* are 'mental' prayer – that is, not vocal – they are assumed to be abstract rather than bodily. Pairing this assumption with the accusations that *alumbrados* despised external rituals and the embodiment entailed by them,[168] modern scholars of Spanish religion make a simplistic distinction between *recogimiento* authors who recognized the need to continue bodily practices *in addition to* the mental prayer that transforms the self into God, and *dejamiento* practitioners who abandoned external practices.[169] The mental prayer of *recogimiento* is presumed to be entirely separate from any type of embodied devotions, even if complemented by them, as can be seen in Osuna's mnemonic, 'Let your body follow Jesus and your soul his divinity,' which requires devotees to conform their bodies to Christ's 'exterior virtues' while their souls seek union.[170]

There is a more effective way to distinguish between the two methods, if the role of embodiment in Renaissance Castilian spirituality is taken into account. As this chapter has shown, *recogimiento* as a method generated by Observant Franciscans in *casas de retiro* is not a purely mental practice, but rather is permanently imbricated with the physicality and visuality of the devotee. Laredo's reliance on a *Passio Christi* meditation at the heart of his *recogimiento* treatise, while at the same time distancing himself from *dejamiento* and from the *via crucis*'s re-creation of the external sites 'where the mysteries of the Passion occurred,' is a key example of precisely how interwoven *recogimiento*, *dejamiento*, and Passion spirituality were in the 1520s. Overlooking this fact has hampered scholars in their quest to define *recogimiento*, on the one hand, and to distinguish it from *dejamiento*, on the other.

The second part of this book will consider the scientifically somatic aspects of Laredo's mystical method, thus highlighting the naturalness of a Passion meditation technique rooted in medical assumptions about human cognition. Ultimately, I argue, the primary distinction between *dejamiento* and *recogimiento* is not whether external rituals do or do not accompany the particular process of mental prayer, nor whether the union is presumed to be permanent or periodic. Rather, *recogimiento* draws heavily on scientific epistemology as the basis for a practical approach to seeking union with a God found at the centre of the soul, while *dejamiento*'s rejection of the body is a negation of all that is human, including basic 'truths' of Renaissance cognitive processes. First, however, Laredo's own historical circumstances, particularly his navigation of a *converso* environment and his unprecedented insistence on Passion devotion in contradistinction to all his mystical contemporaries, will round out Part One's reconsideration of Spanish spirituality as integrally embodied.

2 Navigating an Inquisitorial Culture

While Inquisition trial transcripts have provided modern historians with an unparalleled record of daily religious life in sixteenth-century Spain,[1] the lives of those who did not run afoul of the inquisitors remain obscure. The archives of many convents were lost during the nineteenth-century 'exclaustration,' or closure of the monasteries, making it particularly challenging to find data concerning those housed in religious orders.[2] As a result, it is not possible to provide a traditional biography of Bernardino de Laredo, despite his dual fame as author of the first Castilian pharmaceutical treatises and as one of the primary mystical authors to influence Teresa of Avila. The undisputed facts of Laredo's life are few and far between. Marcos de Lisboa's 1570 chronicle of the Franciscan Order provides the earliest known historical data on Laredo, summing him up as a doctor, lay friar, and author in a mere two sentences. He is noted for being a specialist in the 'science of charity,' fusing his two vocations into one.[3] In his 1587 *De ordine seraphicae religionis* (Of the Blessed Religious Orders), Francisco Gonzaga devoted most of the paragraph on the convent of 'S. Francisci de Monte' to the first biography of its only well-known friar, Bernardinus à Laredo.[4] According to Gonzaga, Laredo was a lay friar and a doctor who, despite his 'simplicity' and 'humility,' composed the books *Ascensus montis Sion*, *Modus faciendi*, and *Metaphora medicine*. As a result of Laredo's success in treating his patient King John III of Portugal,[5] the province was granted a yearly supply of spices and other supplies from India, a grant later confirmed in perpetuity by Philip II (1556–98). Finally, Gonzaga described Laredo's character in glowing terms and links the miraculous cure of an epileptic nun with Laredo's use of a special cross against the devil's work. In other words, Laredo's books were worth listing by title, but the events of his life worth recording for posterity were his reward for finding a medical cure and his effective use of prayer to produce a medical miracle. These few facts are repeated nearly verbatim in later chronicles, including in Lucas Wadding's well-known account of the Franciscan Order, the 1625 *Annales minorum* (Annals of the Friars Minor).[6]

The version that has provided most of the detail rehearsed in modern scholarship is found in the 1662 vernacular *Historia de la Santa Provincia de Los Angeles* (History of the Blessed Province of Los Angeles). Andrés de Guadalupe expanded the known version of Laredo's life from one paragraph to a seven-chapter hagiography that also includes selections from his writings.[7] Despite the efforts by the editor of the modern facsimile edition of Guadalupe's text to valorize it as the best of the Franciscan chronicles of its time,[8] however, it is hard to disagree with Fidèle de Ros's critique in his 1948 monograph on Laredo: although Guadalupe's chronicle is more organized and less pretentious than other such works, it is nevertheless littered with errors, hagiographic commonplaces, and generalities.[9] Ros suggests that only the specific dates and details that serve no apparent hagiographic or apologetic purpose (concerning Laredo's youth, for example) might count as accurate historical information.[10] As I describe elsewhere, Guadalupe's assertions concerning the dates of Laredo's life,[11] his *hidalgo* (noble) status,[12] and his education at the University of Seville,[13] frequently repeated by modern scholars, are either factually wrong or impossible to prove.[14]

Only the following facts can be asserted with a reasonable degree of certainty.[15] Laredo lived in Seville or its environs for most of his life, began working as a doctor around 1507, and professed as a lay or tertiary Franciscan around 1510. At some point these two ventures became one, for Laredo joined one of the *casas de recollectos* founded by the Villacrecian reformers, San Francisco del Monte (in Villaverde, a small town outside Seville) as apothecary to its twenty inhabitants.[16] He published two pharmaceutical treatises, *Metaphora medicine* (1522) and *Modus faciendi* (1527), as well as two editions of the *Subida del Monte Sión* (1535, 1538). Clues to his professional interactions (assessed below) emerge from the addendum to his mystical treatise, in which he provides a list of patients he cured with prayer rather than pharmaceuticals,[17] and from a few brief documents in Seville's archives, including his publisher's last will and testament naming Laredo as his executor.[18] Beyond these bare details, the only possible 'biography' of this nearly forgotten mystic hinges on Laredo's participation, either documented or extrapolated within reason, in various aspects of Castilian religious, social, and medical history. Grassroots reform, trends in popular religion that reached their apex among Franciscans, and controversy over heresy and sacramental practices were the keynotes of the early decades of the sixteenth century, as reviewed in the previous chapter. Yet none of these circumstances of the Franciscan-led internal reform of the Spanish Catholic church took place apart from the reign of the Inquisition.

It is perhaps surprising that the same country and era would implement an extensive juridical tool for curbing heterodoxy (the Inquisition) while at the same time fostering the development of early modern mysticism, as seen in the works of Ignatius of Loyola, Teresa of Avila, and John of the Cross. Less astonishing is that these two extremes, while coexisting, did not do so peacefully. Most sixteenth-century Castilian mystics either appeared before the Inquisitorial courts or had their writings proscribed by inquisitors in the Spanish *Indice de libros prohibidos* (Index of Prohibited Books), updated at regular intervals after 1559.[19] While it is true that mystics posed a potential problem for inquisitors because of their originality and individuality in the practice of Christian devotion, most of the mystics who were denounced during the Inquisition received official scrutiny based on their status as *conversos*, or New Christians – that is, as the descendants of converted Jews. This fact has generated a subcategory of scholarship that seeks to prove the *converso* genealogy of particular (and particularly famous) mystics, either by locating documented evidence as proof of the mystic's family background,[20] or by demonstrating the ways that Jewish belief can be adduced from the best-known mystical treatises of the Golden Age.[21] This approach in turn draws on the debate within modern scholarship over the religious affiliation of the *conversos* in general: whether converts retained covert links to their religious heritage (the theory of the crypto-Jews), or whether they converted fully, without any carryover of practice or belief.

In this chapter, I propose a different approach to the question of religious commitment in the age of the Inquisition. Laredo is unique among sixteenth-century Castilian mystics for neither coming before the Inquisition nor having his *Subida del Monte Sión* banned or expurgated by the Index.[22] These facts are remarkable, and scholars have attempted to elucidate them by proffering the explanation that Laredo took care not to cite from authors later banned. This claim is easily proven false. Ángel Alcalá, for example, states that Laredo was too prudent to rely on such authors as Heinrich Herp, later banned in the 1559 Index. Yet the 1538 revision of the *Subida* was based in large part on Laredo's encounter with Herp's work, which he cites sixteen times.[23] The fact of Laredo's avoidance of Inquisitorial scrutiny has yet to be explained, and indeed, is all the more remarkable given the evidence I present in the first half of this chapter that Laredo's life choices would have led his fellow residents of Seville to identify him with the New Christian community. Rather than use Laredo's connection with New Christians as reason to seek evidence of Jewish belief or Kabbalistic influence, I suggest that awareness of Laredo's problematic social status returns us to the question of how he, among all mystics of the sixteenth century, managed to negotiate the difficult task of appearing sufficiently orthodox so as to avoid Inquisitorial suspicion, much less condemnation.

In the preface to the *Subida*, Laredo provides a schema for one week of meditation that seems to indicate that entire second part of the book will be an exercise in meditating on the Passion from Gethsemane through to the Resurrection. Yet he spends only a quarter of part 2 narrating the Passion, while the rest of it is taken up with extensive excursions into such doctrinal topics as Trinitarian theology, Mariology, and angelology.[24] I argue that Laredo wrote the preface to his work in a deliberately misleading fashion, not simply emphasizing but *over*-emphasizing how much of his text was dedicated to Passion meditation. Nevertheless, his focus on the Passion was unique among the first generation of recollection mystics, as we will see in the second half of this chapter by examining a forerunner of recollection, García de Cisneros, and the best-known voice of recollection, Francisco de Osuna. While the theme of the second part of this book is that there were strong scientific and epistemological reasons to forefront the Passion in an interiorizing spirituality, in this chapter I explore the key fact that the centrality of the Passion in Laredo's *recogimiento* technique would have been presumed to be of no interest to a covert Jew. Laredo's development of a Passion-centred recollection mysticism, unique both in terms of medieval mystical precedent and in terms of his contemporaries' *recogimiento* methods, ultimately enabled him to insist on his fully Christian status.

When framing the *Subida*, Laredo had recourse to several rhetorical and political strategies for emphasizing his full commitment to Christianity, the most important of which was the embodied Christianity outlined in chapter 1. This fact has escaped the notice of previous scholars who identify shifts away from embodiment as key to the era; I posit that it was precisely Laredo's emphasis on the physical goriness of Christ's Passion in an age of ever-greater attention to the body of Christ and that of the devotee that allowed him to write an interiorizing mystical method without attracting official remark. The rhetorical and political framing of the *Subida* served the double purpose of clarifying his status as Christian over against Jew, despite his association with the *converso* community that was presumed to be always disposed towards Jewish practice, and as mystic over against heretic, despite the ways his treatise is unique in the history of Western Christian mystical methods. Ultimately, these rhetorical strategies aimed at his contemporaries not only led inquisitors to accept the unique mystical method of a possible *converso* as orthodox, they have also *mis*led modern scholars into perfunctorily dismissing the centrality of the body to Laredo's scientifically sound mystical technique.

Guilt by Association: The 'Converso Problem'[25] in the Sixteenth Century

Perhaps the most controversial issue at hand for all ranks of Spanish society in the fifteenth and sixteenth centuries was the status of converts from Judaism to Christianity. In what had formerly been a pluri-religious society, the interstitial category of *converso* was born in the wake of widespread pogroms in 1391, grew as a result of violent outbreaks against Jews in 1449 and 1471, and became the primary category of 'other' in Iberia after the expulsion of the remaining Jews in 1492.[26] The *conversos* had not only disassociated themselves from a religion that exposed them to attack or property loss but had also joined the official religion of the peninsula, a move that allowed them access to the advantages accorded to the majority – that is, greater freedom to practise a variety of trades, not to mention politics on a local and national level. The obvious practical benefits of conversion were of great concern to both Jews and 'Old Christians' at the time, giving rise to a rejection of the New Christians by Jews on the one hand (as heretics or apostates),[27] and by Old Christians on the other (as false converts seeking security and social status).[28] Over time, these concerns were extended to the descendants of converts, which resulted not only in the establishment of the Inquisition to seek out and quash heterodoxy among New Christians but also in the expulsion of the Jews in 1492 in order to prevent them from luring *conversos* back to Judaism.[29]

The social upheaval that the Catholic Monarchs had tried to address by the Edict of Expulsion, however, was not resolved by the conversions and exile of the Jews or even by the wholesale examination of *converso* belief and practice undertaken by the Inquisition in its first four decades. Instead, even as the Inquisition turned its attention to other forms of heterodoxy by 1520, discrimination based on the notion of 'pure blood' (*limpieza de sangre*) was legalized in progressively more strata of Iberian society. Attempts to bar *conversos* from public office had had varying success since the early fifteenth century,[30] while many religious orders or their schools adopted rules prohibiting the entrance of *conversos* in the late 1400s.[31] The passing of *limpieza* statutes gained traction in the first decades of the sixteenth century: the cathedral of Seville was one of the earliest churches to bar *conversos* from clerical positions (1515),[32] while the 1525 *limpieza* statute of the Franciscan Order specified, among other points, that the General of the Order could not have had Jewish blood in his family for the previous four generations.[33] As the number of religious, educational, and governmental institutions passing laws limiting *converso* participation multiplied, the '*converso* problem' became one of public perception, for it was potentially fatal for the reputation and livelihood of a family and its descendants to receive even the imputation of being New Christians. Over the course of the sixteenth century, it became so easy for individuals to start rumours about their enemies' heritage (thereby stripping a family of its access to education, professional advancement, and governmental positions) that increasing numbers of Old Christians turned to the courts to request official validation of their genealogies.[34]

The question of the 'true' religious affiliation of these converts and their descendants was not only a prominent polemic prior to the establishment of the Inquisition and throughout its existence but has also been of primary concern in modern scholarship.[35] The debate has been conducted most frequently as one of extremes – either all *conversos* were actually crypto-Jews seeking ways to remain in touch with their religious past (according to Yitzhak Baer and Heim Beinart), or all *conversos*, but especially their descendants, were fully and unproblematically Christian (Benzion Netanyahu and Norman Roth).[36] Recently, however, historians of both Jewish and Christian practice on the peninsula have argued that *converso* faith and practice was in no way a monolithic construct. For example, Gretchen Starr-LeBeau marshals evidence from the 1480s Inquisition trials in Guadalupe to prove that *conversos* participated in daily Christian life on a continuum similar to that of Old Christians. That is to say, on any given Sunday, both New and Old Christians might be found anywhere from attending mass to frequenting the local tavern.[37] Focusing on the evidence of daily life and practice found in Inquisition documents, her study indicates grey areas in the extremist portrait of crypto-Jews versus perfect Christians. Likewise, David Gitlitz provides a 'taxonomy' of four varieties of *converso* response after the 1492 conversions (fully Christian, fully crypto-Jewish, syncretic, and sceptical).[38]

However, despite Starr-LeBeau's accurate observation that examining New Christians only in continuum with Jews does not allow us to explore their interactions with Old Christians, and despite Gitlitz's recognition of the range of belief among the *converso* population in the first decades of the early modern period, both Starr-LeBeau's and Gitlitz's books focus on the techniques that judaizing New Christians used to recover Jewish practices.[39] Thus, even scholars who call for awareness of the complexity of *converso* religious belief and practice still reserve the thrust of their arguments for a New Christian spirituality that was crypto-Jewish, rather than considering those New Christians who identified themselves as fully Christian while living spiritual lives in a world that doubted their fitness as citizens and as religious persons. Inversely, Yirmiyahu Yovel argues for an understanding of *converso* religion as neither crypto-Judaism nor orthopraxic (what Yovel terms 'ordinary') Christianity, but rather a 'new, spiritual Christianity.'[40] '[T]he Christian variety [of Marrano religion] dissented from Catholic orthodoxy by shaping itself as a "religion of the interior," and discovering new religious territories inside the believer's subjectivity.'[41] In other words, in Yovel's view, the sincere Christians of *converso* heritage were nevertheless not sincere about Catholicism as it was being practised by Castilian Renaissance Christians.

As a result of these two trends in existing scholarship, evidence from those New Christians who embraced existing Iberian Christian trends and did *not* run afoul of the Inquisition has not been taken into sufficient account. Texts such as Laredo's *Subida*, produced post-Expulsion for the Christian faithful both old and new – rather than those produced by Old Christians for Old Christians, or by New Christians for Old Christians worried about judaizing[42] – allow us to explore a different set of questions than those posed by the camps of Baer, Netanyahu, and even by mediating scholars such as Starr-LeBeau, Gitlitz, and Yovel. Such documents enable us to investigate how New Christians navigated the complex circumstance of adhering to Christianity in a society that consistently, vocally, and often abusively made religious genealogy (conceived along the lines of racial heritage)[43] the touchstone for the possibility of faith.

As I delineate in the next section, my research indicates that Laredo may have been from New Christian stock. Given the concerted effort of many of Laredo's contemporaries to distance themselves from any suspicion of being a *converso*, however, it is more relevant that Laredo appears to have moved comfortably in what I term a '*converso* environment,' based on his choice to follow a *converso* career in medicine, his acceptance of *converso* patients, and his interaction with *converso* theologians. An environment conducive to gaining Inquisitorial attention is particularly apt for assessing the history of Sevillian spirituality for several reasons. It is evident from Geraldine McKendrick's exploration of the publisher Juan de Varela and his role in Seville's *converso* community (to which he had no proven genealogical ties but for which he became the spokesperson during the *comunero* riots of 1521[44]) that frequent association with *conversos* could link an individual inextricably to the *converso* community.[45] In addition, given the interconnections between Franciscans, *conversos*, Illuminist heretics, and recollected mystics that were the focus of a number of Inquisition trials in Seville between 1525 and 1535,[46] it would have been impossible for any individual to function in close connection with the *converso* community as a Franciscan and as a mystic without inviting Inquisitorial questions concerning orthodox belief and practice. Although I provide in the next section the first viable reconstruction of Laredo's familial circumstances as a probable *converso*, I consider the subsequent reconstruction of his network of *conversos* in his professions as more effective proof that Laredo would have needed to insist on his commitment to the norms of Spanish Christianity in order to balance his suspicious (in the eyes of the Inquisition) life circumstances.

Converso Status or a '*Converso* Environment'?

Several preliminary historical considerations are worth noting. Not only was Laredo a Jewish last name during the fifteenth century in the northern town of that name, but *conversos* who moved to other parts of Spain in order to hide their heritage often took the name of their former town as their patronym.[47] Bernardino, while not a common first name, is not only found in the lists of Sevillian *conversos* but is tellingly associated with *conversos* in the church.[48] Most importantly, one key fact does exist concerning Laredo's extended family. Laredo's only mention of a family member is found in the personal correspondence he redacted to form the 'Extravagante' published at the end of each edition of the *Subida*. Although he removed the names and locations of his correspondents, he included a general description of the recipient to give context to the content of the letters (for example, 'response to a friar, not old, concerned about questions of virtue').[49] Laredo's seventh letter is entitled: 'Sent to a nun, kin to or niece of the author, the day of her profession and taking of the veil.'[50] The only further information on this relation of Laredo's comes from Guadalupe, who quotes the entire letter in his chronicle or hagiography,[51] identifying its recipient as Sor Catalina, a nun in the monastery of Santa Inés in Seville. This institution was founded in 1374 for forty nuns and may have housed around fifty in the mid-1500s,[52] yet no direct confirmation of

Guadalupe's information survives, as only three records relating to professions before 1550 still exist in the convent archives.[53]

Thanks to Juan Gil's publication in 2000–3 of extensive genealogies of New Christian families in fifteenth- and sixteenth-century Seville, it is possible to examine the *converso* heritage of a large proportion of the city's inhabitants. Gil traces the names of reconciled *conversos* and their families as well as the names of descendants of executed *conversos* in municipal economic documents (such as wills, trade agreements, and so on),[54] briefly summarizing the documents relating to each *converso* and enumerating interconnections through marriage, trade, or inheritance between individuals whose relative insignificance would otherwise leave them outside of the scope of modern research. The volumes likewise provide the necessary information to reconstruct a *converso* environment: by cross-checking the names of all known acquaintances of an individual against the genealogies, it is possible to estimate his or her level of interaction with *conversos* and consequent vulnerability to rumour concerning problematic heritage. In the case of Laredo, judicious use of Gil's work provides both a probable *converso* family line and a convincing case for Laredo's tranquil interaction with a *converso* social circle.

Gil's entry on the patronym Laredo is headed by the caveat that 'despite their absence from the lists of the rehabilitated, there are Laredos (the judges and accountants) which seem to me to be *conversos*.'[55] Of the three individuals listed, Gil gives extended genealogies for the family of Gaspar de Laredo, married to a woman who is indicated as having her own entry as a *converso* elsewhere in the volume, as well as for the spouses and children of Gaspar's brother Francisco de Laredo and his sister Iseo de Belmañia. The information on Gaspar's sister Iseo de Belmañia, identified as the wife of Pedro Riquel and living in the parish of Santa Catalina, is drawn from her 1552 will, in which she mentions, but leaves no inheritance to, her daughter Ana Tenorio, a nun in the monastery of Santa Inés.[56] It seems quite improbable that there would have been two nuns with the same rare last name (Laredo) but from two entirely unrelated families professing at the same monastery, especially given the likelihood that Ana Tenorio, faced with the choice of taking another name at her profession, may well have picked the name of her home parish in order to become the Sor Catalina listed by Guadalupe. The possibility that she was Bernardino's niece and that Gaspar, Francisco, and Iseo were either Bernardino's siblings or his close relations thus seems evident.[57]

Another piece of the puzzle concerning Laredo's heritage emerges through a close examination of the interconnections between the *converso* families enumerated in Gil's work. The richest source for determining Laredo's circle of acquaintances is found in an addendum to the 'Josephina,' a tractate on the life of Joseph appended at the end of the *Subida*, in which he lists the patients who were cured of disease or had avoided medical danger by praying a mass that he had prescribed.[58] Unlike the anonymity he wished for his correspondents in the other appendix, the letters in the 'Extravagante,' Laredo took great care in this section to provide sufficient information (full name, employment, parish of residence) in order to identify the exact person to whom he was referring.[59] One person on this list is named Juan de Espinosa, a merchant of Seville, who in the 1535 edition is further identified as living in the parish of 'La Madalena.'[60] Gil gives the genealogy of an Espinosa family, 'very active merchants' believed to be *conversos*,[61] listing a Francisco de Espinosa (d. 1528) with a son Juan de Espinosa. Notable among Francisco de Espinosa's numerous siblings are his sisters Francisca de Espinosa, of the parish of Madalena, and Doña Juana de Espinosa, the wife of Francisco de Laredo, judge, of the parish of Santa Catalina. Thus, if the connection to Ana Tenorio that I adduce is accurate, Bernardino would have known his patient, the merchant Juan de Espinosa of the parish of Magdalena, as the nephew of his brother Francisco's wife.[62] The accumulated proof sums up as follows: one of Laredo's patients, a probable *converso*, came from a family of presumed *converso* origins that shared Laredo's last name, were alive in the same decades as Laredo, and had a member of the family living in the same monastery that a relative of Laredo had entered. I argue that this family of presumed *conversos* was kin to Bernardino.

As suggestive as this evidence is, without certain proof it is also necessary to turn to Laredo's social circumstances in order to determine whether a reputation due a probable *converso* heritage would have been further aggravated by interaction with a *converso* social circle. Laredo exercised his twin professions of medicine and mysticism in primarily *converso* settings, yet either, much less both, could have led to a presumption of New Christian heritage. The profession of medicine was so closely linked with the *converso* population that subsequent to 1492 many Old Christians refused to enter it so as to not live under a cloud of suspicion about their origins.[63] For that matter, the Inquisition had not only focused on *converso* doctors in particular during the early years, but had in fact defined *converso* status through attention to the physiology and racial heredity of Jewish blood.[64] Of the patients named explicitly by Laredo in the 'Josephina,' nearly half have *converso* origins, indicating that Laredo exercised a *converso* profession freely among the *converso* population of the province of Seville.[65] In addition, Laredo evidently had New Christian friends, as he is on record as being executor of the estate of his publisher, Juan Cromburger, a man of German origins whose family intermarried regularly with *conversos*.[66]

Laredo did not limit his interaction with the *converso* community to his medical practice, however, as his only explicit references to contemporary theologians and ecclesiastics in the pages of the *Subida* are to New Christians. Laredo petitioned several theologians to review his work before committing either edition of the *Subida* to print,[67] and was also careful to ensure approval in the highest circles of Castilian ecclesiastics by at once dedicating his work to the existing archbishop of Seville and indicating at least passing acquaintance with the previous archbishop.[68] All four theologians and archbishops named by Laredo were high-ranking members of the Sevillian Inquisition, making them the primary mediators of who was Christian and who was heretic in Seville in the 1520s and 1530s.[69] Archbishop Manrique, for example, consolidated his reputation in part through publishing the first formal definition of the *alumbrado* heresy.[70] More importantly, these four theologians and bishops were themselves *conversos*, each with a historical record of protecting *conversos* (though not necessarily *alumbrados*) from the full threat of the Inquisition in which they exercised power.[71] Converso participation at the highest levels of church hierarchy was an artefact of the extensive intermarriages between Old and New Christians throughout the fifteenth century, before *limpieza* statutes became commonplace. Laredo thus seems to have intentionally positioned himself to receive the seal of orthodoxy for his mystical method by the Christian establishment as mediated by *conversos*, and *conversos* alone. This fact in no way detracts from the power of Laredo's work as a prescriptive method for achieving union with the Christian God – indeed, it makes a strong argument for further studies to catalogue the political manoeuvring to which certain New Christians resorted to in order to live out their Christianity while being constantly subject to suspicion.[72]

It is safe to assume that Laredo's strategic appeal to theologians and ecclesiastics known to be favourable to *conversos* enabled him to avoid attracting Inquisitorial attention during his lifetime. Such tactics, however, do not explain the astonishing fact that his *Subida* was never questioned by the compilers of the Indexes of Prohibited Books between 1559 and 1790, despite the generalized suspicion directed towards all spiritual works in the vernacular, including those written by Laredo's fellow recollection mystics.[73] Laredo's choice of rhetoric in certain portions of his mystical treatise cannot be properly evaluated if we overlook the simple fact that before his work was even considered for publication, he would have needed to prove his orthodoxy as a Christian in order to counteract a presumption of racially based heretical tendencies.

Laredo thus made intentional political use of his mystical interest in Passion meditation as a way to reinforce his ability to write as a Christian mystic, despite his *converso* environment. This rhetorical move is found in the preface to his treatise, where Laredo states merely that he will provide a week of meditations on the Passion in the second stage of his treatise, allowing his readers to assume that the second stage of his method includes only the narrative of the Passion. In fact, if one were to believe his prefatory discussion of the structure of his *Subida* (found in the 'Notable'), the first part on self-knowledge would contain three weekly meditations, the second part would present the Passion of Jesus, and the third part on recollection would provide a week of meditations on biblical quotations, first from the Old Testament and then from the New.[74] In reality, part 1 treats two weeks only, part 2 devotes at most a fourth of its chapters to the Passion, and no days are assigned to any of the chapters in part 3, nor is either the 1535 or the 1538 version of part 3 structured around biblical quotations.[75] In other words, Laredo's prefatory description of part 2 is based on only the nineteen chapters out of sixty-five in the 1535 edition that actually narrate the events of Holy Week. In the remaining chapters, Laredo addresses the doctrines concerning the Trinity, angels, and Mary. By highlighting the Passion narrative and the Passion narrative alone among the many complex concepts under consideration in the second stage of his treatise, Laredo uses his introduction to consciously direct the attention of his readers (be they *converso* theologians, the general public, or modern scholars) to his focus on the Passion. Since Laredo issued this preface with both editions of his book, we can be relatively sure that its disjunction with the contents of his text was intentional rather than a result of hasty editing.

By suggesting in the prefatory material that the narrative itself parallels the popular medieval and new Castilian treatises on the technique of Passion meditation, Laredo implies a traditionalism that serves to mask the originality of part 2 of his *Subida*. Given his choice to highlight his Passion narrative, it is intriguing that Laredo does not acknowledge his medieval precedents explicitly, for he never mentions the name of the highly popular 1502 translation of Ludolph's *Vita Christi* anywhere in part 2, despite having cited the work in the 'Josephina' addended to both editions of the *Subida*.[76] Nor does he refer to the *Passio Christi* treatises produced in abundance by his immediate predecessors. Furthermore, in the nineteen chapters dedicated to recounting Holy Week, Laredo does not give equal weight to each scene, as was the custom. Instead, he passes over many of the events mentioned in the prefatory schema quite quickly, such as the fall with the cross,[77] while spending entire chapters on details such as the rope around Christ's neck, or the medical and theological bases for the possibility of Christ actually having sweated blood in Gethsemane.[78]

I do not wish to suggest that Laredo's interest in Passion meditation was entirely political. Rather, his reformulation of the technique is fundamental for his prescriptive method for reaching mystical union. I think it is clear, however, that as a Franciscan mystic who associated with *conversos*, Laredo was fully aware of the difficulty of being allowed a voice by his fellow citizens and by the Inquisition. In the age of the Inquisition, for authors like Laredo, the option to speak – indeed, to publish – as a *Christian* depended on using rhetorical devices to emphasize *non-Jewishness*. The emphasis on the somatic nature of God, the need to accept a past (not future) Messiah figure,[79] the contrast with the blood taboo in Judaism, the memory of centuries of persecution during Holy Week as the accused 'killers of Christ' – these elements would all have combined to make the Crucifixion particularly problematic to one whose immediate background included Jewish beliefs and practices.[80] Although he negotiated his right to publish during his lifetime by appealing to *converso* theologians for approval, only by out-Christianing the Old Christians on the specific subject of Christ's humanity did Laredo manage to publish a treatise on mystical union that could survive repeated Inquisitorial review of vernacular religious writings over the centuries. The remainder of this chapter examines Laredo's distinctive method of Passion meditation in light of his unique elevation of this traditional element of embodied devotion as the focal point of a tripartite mystical method.

Passion Spirituality and Renaissance Mysticism

Laredo's Passion technique reflects Castilian Franciscan insistence on embodiment more completely than other mystical writings of the era do, even those by writers who were Franciscan. This emphasis initially stemmed from his scientific appreciation of the body, as we will see in chapter 3, but ultimately served to establish his credentials as fully Christian when they might otherwise have been in doubt, given his constant interaction with a *converso* environment. Laredo's fellow Castilian mystics provide no direct precedent for his choice to present Passion spirituality as the second level of a tripartite method, especially one that he (in the 1538 version) designates with the terminology of purgative, illuminative, and unitive.[81] Indeed, only two incorporate Passion meditation to any great extent. Since one such version is found in one of the first vernacular works to appear in Castile and the other is by Laredo's closest contemporary, the differences between their methods and Laredo's illuminate the unexpectedly embodied interiority of his rendition of the Passion.

As discussed in the introduction, Andrés's classical definition of *recogimiento* renders it as a tripartite method progressing from the stage of self-knowledge to Passion spirituality to the 'true' mystical stage of recollection. Strangely, even a surface reading of the foundational texts of *recogimiento* mysticism immediately reveals fundamental problems with Andrés's definition. If we look to the other two figures in the triumvirate of *recogimiento* founders, Francisco de Osuna and Bernabé de Palma, we see that Osuna's vision of recollection in the *Abecedarios espirituales* (Spiritual Alphabets, 1528–40) places Passion meditation as the first step of the tripartite way, not the second, while Palma in his recollection guide *Via spiritus* (Way of the Spirit, 1532) rarely mentions Christ, and then only in terms of his divinity.[82] Nor do immediate Castilian antecedents among the 'classical' Spanish Renaissance mystics provide any precedent for Laredo's interest in Passion-centred devotion. For example, Gómez García in his *Carro de dos vidas* (Cart of Two Lives, 1500) mentions the Passion only in terms of the miracles that occurred at the same time, thus avoiding the question of the human, much less the suffering, Jesus in both the sections on the contemplative life and on the active life.[83] For that matter, Alonso de Madrid in his ascetic *Arte para servir a Dios* (Art for Serving God, 1521), often cited as an immediate precursor to the first generation of recollection mystics, makes no mention of the Passion at all. The only mystical writers included in the traditional canon of Renaissance mysticism (a canon that does not include visionaries before Teresa of Avila)[84] to highlight the humanity of Christ to any extent were García de Cisneros (1456–1510), who offered Passion spirituality as a valid alternative to the tripartite mystical methods found in his Latin sources, and Francisco de Osuna (1492–1540), who included the Passion in *recogimiento* in a manner framed in direct opposition to the early Golden Age Franciscan Passion treatises discussed in chapter 1.

García de Cisneros, abbot of Montserrat and relative of the reforming Archbishop Cisneros discussed in chapter 1, wrote his *Ejercitatorio de la vida espiritual* (*Book of Exercises of the Spiritual Life*, 1500; banned in the 1583 Index) as a book of spiritual exercises to aid in the reform of his abbey. A 'florilegio'[85] of spiritual writings from across Europe, this work streamlines medieval resources into a methodical approach to the daily search for God, a process extended by its most famous reader, Ignatius of Loyola.[86] The first three books of the *Ejercitatorio* follow the traditional medieval scheme of the purgative way, the illuminative way, and the unitive way.[87] Here, the unitive stage produces a 'loving union with God' reached by 'inward recollection of yourself from outward things to things which are within.'[88] There is no mention of the humanity of Christ in relation to mystical union, while the purgative stage includes a mere paragraph of narrative concerning the events of Gethsemane alone before moving on to a topical (rather than chronological) consideration of Christ's suffering.[89] Rather than ignore the humanity of Christ entirely (as had many medieval contemplatives and his contemporary Goméz García), separate the subject into non-contemplative treatises (as had Bonaventure),[90] or slot the Passion directly into one of the stages of a tripartite ascent (as would Osuna and Laredo), however, García de Cisneros appends a final section on the humanity of Christ and the Eucharist that is fully as long as the tripartite method. His work is thus the only Castilian exemplar published before the *Subida* that recommends meditation on the violence done to Christ's body while at the same time valorizing the highly abstract, contemplative union traditional in the *via unitiva*.[91] I argue that García de Cisneros's final section reveals his ultimate discomfort with incorporating both genres in the same mystical text; his text serves both as necessary context for and an intriguing contrast to Laredo's comfortable integration of meditation on Christ's bleeding body into his scientifically accurate method for union.

The abbot begins part 4 of the *Ejercitatorio* by discussing the preferential status of the contemplative life over the active life.[92] In contrast to the medieval authors of tripartite contemplative texts who so often considered meditation on Jesus's life to be a beginning or an external practice, one that might fit in well with the active life or as the first step towards embracing the contemplative life, Cisneros depends on sources that promoted stages of meditation on the humanity of Christ as a contemplative rather than an active practice. Quoting an author he had made required reading for his monks as a part of his reform effort,[93] he details three consecutive stages for meditation on the life of Christ, thereby imposing the structure of a contemplative tripartite ascent onto a *Vita Christi*. In the first type of meditation, the devotee models his actions after those of the disciples, imagining Christ's beauty, his actions, his healing, or his miracles.[94] In the second, the devotee treats Christ as both God and human, primarily considering the great pain the Son suffered. Christ's pain is expanded in order for the devotee to fully recognize the divine sacrifice made in those moments.

> Knowledge of his humanity is easier for us, as it is more imprinted on our mind than knowledge of [his] divinity which is much more distant from [our mind] ... [I]f you could consider and contemplate one and the other, that is, the divinity and humanity, a great devotion would be born in you, [also] love, confidence, fear, and reverence.[95]

In other words, contemplation of the dual human and divine nature is achieved by considering the actions and events of the human side of Christ rather than by ignoring them.

Yet it is the final stage of meditation on the *Vita Christi* that underscores the role of Christ's humanity in the devotee's experience of union with the divine. Here, García (or his source) proposes an ascent to union in which meditation on Christ is the motivating force of the entire ascent.

> The third [kind of] contemplation is raising oneself to spiritual affection by means of the humanity of Christ and looking at this Lord with the eyes of the mind in a mirror and by comparison, and in such a way you will come by knowledge of the humanity to knowledge and love of the divinity (with the help of God). And by such looking and union and transformation by the mind, man begins in some fashion to be made one spirit with God and to pass outside of himself and to look at this very Truth and be made ready for union and a yoking together with God ... And so then this is the highest level of contemplation in this journey until we reach the essential vision of God.[96]

Christ's life forms the focus of the first stage, his death and sacrifice is the second stage of an ascent to 'the vision of the Essence of God,' and his humanity is still present in the final stage as the mechanism by which to look at the Lord 'with the eyes of the mind.' After this retrieval of the *Vita Christi* for the purposes of contemplatives, not beginners only, Cisneros then turns to Passion meditation in particular.

Although the immediate chapters after this tripartite distinction teach 'beginner' meditation on the narrative of Christ's life,[97] recommend frequent reception of the Eucharist,[98] and advocate an imitation of Christ's virtues demonstrated during the Passion scenes,[99] Cisneros amplifies the possibilities of the Passion as more than a subject for beginners or pure externality. He quotes, without citation, a formula common in the medieval *Vita* tractates, including Ludolph of Saxony's *Vita Christi*:[100]

> Concerning the Passion of the Lord, the contemplative man may contemplate as follows: First, he may meditate so that he may imitate it; second that he may be moved to compassion; third that he may wonder; fourthly, that he may rejoice; fifthly, that he may make resolutions [for the future]; sixthly, that he may find rest.[101]

García de Cisneros then expands this list into a description of several pages. Although he assigns imitation of the Passion as the first of six stages, he then builds the next five stages with attention to the first by remaining focused on Christ's suffering. The culmination, 'resting in God,' is a version of Passion meditation designed to produce union in the manner of medieval renditions of bridal mysticism.[102]

> And the closer he draws to Him [through Passion meditation], the more he swoons away and melts through most devoted love ... and thus the union of love and devotion increases jointly, until the Bride is wholly absorbed by that burning fire of love in the passion of her Beloved.[103]

Thus, through meditating on the Passion, the devotee at Cisneros's monastery develops feelings of intense love, but this emotion does not end his continual consideration of Christ crucified. In Cisneros's alternative to a tripartite method, then, the Passion, and the Passion alone, is portrayed as the key to all levels of the ascent to a union of love with God.

García de Cisneros's second mystical method therefore seems to contradict the tripartite way described in the first half of his treatise. In fact, the *Ejercitatorio* presents two tripartite ascents to union, one almost entirely separate from the late medieval devotional attention to the humanity of Christ, the other revolving solely around a consideration of Christ (in terms of his human life, his human and divine Passion, and as the divine towards whom all thoughts of union with the Beloved must be directed). In both cases, the goal of loving union with God is the same, but the methods for the ascent itself present stark contrasts. Yet in the end, it is not clear that García de Cisneros values these two methods equally.[104] For example, the last sentence of the tripartite Passion meditation suddenly undermines the level of union achieved: 'And this third degree of the contemplation of the life of the Lord belongs to those who are adepts and who are drawing nigh to perfection.'[105] The unitive level was traditionally associated with the 'perfect,' whereas the purgative was for beginners and the illuminative for the proficient, so that the last stage of the method of the Passion seems to rank lower than its unitive language (quoted above) would suggest. García de Cisneros thus at once valorized the role of the life and especially the Passion of Christ, yet was not able to comfortably integrate it into the traditional format for contemplative treatises. It remained for the Spanish recollection mystics, Osuna and Laredo, to attempt the ultimate merging of the tripartite contemplative treatise with meditation on the humanity of Christ.

A closer look at the other premier *recogimiento* mystic, Francisco de Osuna, clarifies that the difference between his method and that of Laredo is not simply the placement of Passion meditation as the first or second stage.[106] In his *Primer abecedario* (First Spiritual Alphabet, 1528), Osuna, while relegating Passion meditation to the first level, in fact dedicates much more space to meditations on a diverse series of topics about the humanity of Christ than does Laredo. Yet no narrative of the events of Holy Week appears until the penultimate chapter. Thus the similarities assumed in modern scholarship between the methods of recollection as organized by Laredo and Osuna are not borne out by the works themselves. Osuna treats Passion meditation as a preliminary practice before entering full-fledged mystical prayer, in contrast to Laredo's emphasis on it. And while Laredo's insistence on embodied spirituality likely validated his text in the eyes of the Inquisition, allowing his work to survive uncensored, one of Osuna's books was banned and his Passion treatise was expurgated.[107]

Osuna was a leading voice in the Observant Franciscan movement of the 1520s, a popular teacher in retreat houses such as La Salceda who would eventually move up the ranks to be appointed to high positions overseeing Franciscans in the Indies and elsewhere. His oral teachings on the method of recollection in the *casas de retiro* or *recollectos* (retreat houses) were based on three 'spiritual alphabets,' mnemonic sets of couplets that begin with each letter of the alphabet and are designed to lead the devotee through a series of meditations. His teachings were initially popularized and circulated without his approval, which in the wake of the *alumbrado* trials put him in danger of Inquisitorial investigation,[108] and he therefore hurried to publish an official version of his three alphabets. These three volumes are traditionally equated with the three stages of recollection mysticism that Laredo unites into one volume.[109] The discontinuity of the series, in which the third volume was published first and the second last, seems to be the result of chance, for Osuna worked on the official versions of all three of the original set at the same time, happening to finish the third one before the other two.[110] Osuna's division of the alphabets into separate works had a critical effect in the dissemination of his thought, however, as it was the *Tercer abecedario* alone that reached extensive and enduring recognition.[111] What is of interest for this chapter, however, is not the eventual influence of Osuna's work, but rather the role it filled in the panorama of primarily Franciscan spirituality of the first three decades of the Golden Age.

Osuna in fact deliberately set out to write a treatise on Passion spirituality that did not follow in the footsteps of his fellow Franciscans of the *Fasciculus myrrhe* and the *Passio duorum* (see chapter 1).[112] As he explains in his prologue:

> After having thought a great deal about the Passion, I began to read the popular vernacular books that treated it, to see if the Christian people were familiar with the things that I had felt on the subject. And as I saw that all the books spoke about it in a very human manner as though it was the passion of just any martyr, I determined to write a unique offering to God.[113]

Osuna indicates direct familiarity with the genre of vernacular Passion treatises that had been recently developed by his fellow friars, yet interprets the available *Vita* and Passion treatises as reductive of Christ's role. He proposes in their stead a vernacular treatise in which he will treat much more than just the narrative of the Gospels, giving extra attention to the doctrine that humanity's salvation could only be accomplished by a figure both divine and human. He adds immediately that his interest is not primarily in the divinity of Christ.[114] A glance at the contents of the work indicates that in addition to several chapters on the 'causes of the Passion' or the reason for the Godman's sacrifice, Osuna follows themes such as Christ's blood, tears, or limbs as the topics of entire chapters.[115]

In other words, the twenty-three letters of the *Primer abecedario* are not primarily devoted to a chronological consideration of the Passion, in contrast to the usual structure of the vernacular poetic and prose Passions written in late fifteenth- and early sixteenth-century Castile. Osuna's version has more parallels with García de Cisnero's work discussed above, since Cisneros surrounded his Passion narrative with advice and definitions. However, Osuna's interest in such elements as Christ's blood or Christ's tears also draws on the popular manifestations of devotion that became more and more widespread in southern Spain as the century progressed; for example, the confraternities in evidence during his several-year stay in Seville were frequently devoted to a particular image related to Holy Week, such as the five wounds of Christ.[116]

Osuna gives an explicit rationale for the form of his Passion account, found in letter Z on 'zeal for the Passion.'[117] He works out a version of the Passion from Gethsemane to 'the garden of the tomb' that synthesizes the events of the four Gospels into one vernacular whole.[118] This version is intended for those who 'wish to see the case as it occurred, not clothed in glosses, and who wish to see the naked truth without the cosmetic adornment of human composition.'[119] Osuna here sets himself counter to the late medieval technique of dwelling on imagined details that were not discussed in, but also not contradicted by, the biblical accounts. For example, in letter Z he does not portray the sufferings of Christ with any more detail than the simple statement that Christ was crucified next to two thieves.[120] Elsewhere he had, of course, devoted two letters to Jesus's blood and the wounds that allowed his blood to flow, but he carefully separates this type of imaginative meditation from his narration of the events of Christ's Passion.

Osuna proposes a form of devotion to the humanity of Christ that presents the Passion as spectacle, yet by limiting its chronological retelling to the end of his work, he problematizes the role of the Passion as historical event in the spiritual life of the meditator. The structure of the *Primer abecedario* deliberately reinforces the traditional notion that participatory meditation on the humanity of Christ is meant for beginners. Osuna rescues the Gospel narrative of Christ's sacrifice for humanity from the 'make-up' of wild detail that the vivid imaginations of late medieval believers had used to dress up the scriptural tale. In narrating this sequence in the penultimate chapter, he could be assumed to be relegating it to last place. I would argue instead that he places his stripping of the popular devotion to the bare bones of its earliest and scripturally authoritative version at the end of the *Primer abecedario* as a necessary transition to the *Segundo abecedario*, where visual meditation has no place in the exercises on self-disgust and the pursuit of virtue.

Osuna himself supports this reading, for he devotes the last letter (Tilde) to the necessary, and higher, corollary to the meditations proposed in the previous twenty-two letters: '[C]ontemplation of the Passion should serve you like the moon does the night and the imitation of it should serve you like the sun does the day.'[121] Thus not only do the extensive visual meditations of letters A–Y drop out in the Gospel concordance of letter Z, but the last and highest stage is defined as imitation by works, a necessary step in Osuna's view for the reader to be able to prove how devout his or her internal meditations are.[122] The appearance of numerous editions of

Thomas à Kempis's *Imitatio Christi* (*Imitation of Christ*) in the first decades of the printing age in Spain,[123] a work that lauds the virtues learned from Christ's sacrifice but gives no extended meditation on the bloody Passion sequence, therefore correlates well with Osuna's placement of the Passion as the first rather than central stage of his version of *recogimiento*.

García de Cisneros's proposal of Passion mysticism as entirely distinct from the medieval tripartite unitive methods and Osuna's presentation of Passion meditation as preliminary to an abstract goal beyond visual meditation are the only examples in Laredo's era of mystical methods that in some part acknowledge the overall extent of Castilian embodied spirituality. I suggest that it is impossible to realize the coherent rationale underlying Laredo's tripartite mystical method if, following McGinn's definition of mysticism or Andrés's definition of recollection (see introduction), we dismiss the second stage of Laredo's method as preliminary simply because it includes a focus on the narrative of Christ's death. In my reading, Laredo is unique in the history of mysticism through the sixteenth century for his resolution of the perennial disjunction between the popular (yet overly external) spirituality concerning the suffering Christ and the abstract (and requiring extensive education) methods of mystical contemplation. Of course, we do have many records of mystical experience that seem to have been a direct result of meditation on the Passion from such figures as Angela of Foligno, Julian of Norwich, Heinrich Suso, and others. In terms of prescriptive guides to meditation in which the author does not attempt to derive authority from his or her personal experiences, however, Laredo's *Subida* is the only treatise of which I am aware that designates Passion meditation as the central stage of a unitive method.

Conclusion: Passion Meditation as Interiorization

Laredo's choice to highlight Passion spirituality in contradistinction to his mystical contemporaries and predecessors raises the question as to why Andrés took Laredo's text as the basis for the general schematic of *recogimiento*. More importantly, it forces a consideration of how embodied Passion-centred devotional practices could be central to a leading text in a genre usually defined as a process of interiorization away from empty external rituals in Golden Age religion. Let us look briefly at the details of Laredo's method, to which the entire chapter 5 of this book is also dedicated, in order to assess the particularities of a method proposed by a mystic navigating the Inquisitorial culture of suspicion towards those immersed in a *converso* environment.

Laredo set his visualization technique in apparent opposition to the beginnings of the tradition of public Holy Week processions by confraternities that followed a *via crucis* mapped onto the streets of Seville. In order to create a contrast to the drama and externality of a physical re-creation of the route to Calvary, Laredo asks his readers not simply to substitute a mental journey to Palestine, but rather to imagine their own bodies *as* the Holy Land: 'And you will be the Holy Land if you know how to enclose yourself and be joyful.'[124] He recommends that devotees, rather than envisioning themselves as travellers, envision the Passion transcribed onto their own souls and bodies. The mystic should imagine his or her heart as the column to which Jesus is tied under torture, receiving the tail end of the blows of the whip.[125] Alternatively, Laredo recommends that the mystic's heart become the material base of the cross, inundated with the blood dripping from Christ's wounds.[126] Laredo's focus on the heart, often a synonym for the soul, as the physical site of the torture and crucifixion of Christ is thus at once both thoroughly bodily and thoroughly interior.

Laredo's internalizing Passion meditation technique should be of great interest to historians of Christianity as an example of a mystical guide that crosses historically conceived categories of meditation versus contemplation. That Laredo's treatise has not received the treatment it is due by historians of mysticism, however, seems to be the result of an uncomplicated acceptance of Laredo's intentionally inaccurate presentation of his tripartite way in his preface, in which he asserts parallels to traditional external forms of Passion devotion in order to prove to the Inquisition that he fully embraced the embodied Catholic spirituality of his era. In the end, scholarly attention to the *converso* status of only those individuals attracted to crypto-Judaism has limited our ability to read between the lines and identify the social pressures surrounding the publication of works in the age of the Inquisition, a limitation that has led modern scholars to issue readings of mystical techniques that reproduce the assumptions of the Golden Age inquisitors.

Note that the two Passion works by Laredo's contemporaries suffered at the hands at the *Indice de libros prohibidos*, for passages were expurgated from Osuna's Passion treatise in 1640 while García de Cisneros's work was banned in 1583, possibly because it was circulating in an anonymous vernacular edition.[127] Laredo's recollection method, long considered one of the foundations for all that is central to Golden Age mysticism, proves distinct from other methods generally considered 'mystical' precisely by drawing profoundly on the dominant aspects of Renaissance Castilian spirituality that centred on the suffering of Jesus and Mary and on the embodied devotional response of believers. His work, informed by a range of spiritual and mystical genres from the Middle Ages and drawing on the Castilian development of the 'passion of two,' synthesizes his sources by focusing on the embodiment of interiority.

I suggest that Laredo's mystical method integrates the outer and inner persons in a manner distinctly different from that generally attributed to *conversos* but cognitively appropriate for any scientist. Consideration of Laredo's Passion spirituality thus problematizes simplistic assumptions that *converso* heritage automatically leads to an embracing of Catholicism-with-a-difference, for the scientific rationale explored in the second part of this book proves more essential than any supposed discomfort, handed down from Jewish ancestors, with external ritual. It thus becomes necessary to take seriously the category of the New Christian who embraced Christianity in all its specifically Castilian aspects, since elements of social context such as medical training could affect the ways in which a *converso* paid attention to a physicality that other *conversos* avoided. Scholarly acceptance of mystical union as necessarily abstract and linguistic has made peripheral the bodily devotion that is actually core to Laredo's mystical method, proposed in a time of Franciscan dominance, quietistic heresies, and Inquisitorial oversight. While Yovel argues that the religious constructs of *conversos* are neither fully Christian nor fully Jewish, being always 'other,' Laredo's historical circumstances were determined instead by the intersection of bodily spirituality fomented by his own Franciscan Order and his own interests in the human body arising from his medical profession. These twin influences provided the fodder with which he would construct a method of mystical ascent to a Christian, not a *converso*, God found at the core of the embodied soul.

It is to the body of the human, a *nonada* (no-nothingness) in relation to God, yet made out of elements and pulsing with blood, that we must turn as we begin our reconsideration of Laredo's tripartite mystical method of recollection. For Franciscans of this time period, the body of the devotee and of God was seen in the riveting sculptures of Jesus's suffering, felt during the penitential flogging through the streets, emphasized in the Eucharistic mass over against the *alumbrados*, and experienced as the medium for torture and control in the eyes of the Inquisition. For Laredo, that same body is not just the focus of devotions or the manner by which devotions are enacted. The human body is explained and described by a medical system of thought, one that applies not only to every Renaissance human but also to the God made man.

PART TWO

A Scientific Close Reading

3 Medical Bodies, Mystical Bodies

Of late, scholars have produced any number of excellent studies on the role of 'body' in late medieval religion, bringing to light aspects of ritual, popular religion, and cult about which we were previously unaware.[1] Yet historians of Christian mysticism, although attentive to the role of body in relation to such matters as visionary experience and to the role of gender in mysticism, have rarely taken into consideration the medieval or Renaissance body as a scientific reality according to the physiological models prevalent in those eras.[2] Whether the body was denied or exalted en route to mystical union, mystics, as did physicians and theologians,[3] would have understood human bodies as composed primarily of the element earth, along with small amounts of water, air, and fire. Bodies were affected by the qualities of heat, cold, wetness, and dryness, and were filled with the fluids of blood, bile of varying colours, and phlegm. Flesh was created out of blood, and blood was produced when food was consumed under optimal conditions of the four qualities.[4] While not all laypersons (in the scientific sense) would have understood such details as the 10:1 ratio of elements (earth is ten times heavier than water, which is ten times heavier than air, and so on),[5] or entered into the abstruse debates concerning how the 'vital heat' of the body was passed from parents to child,[6] the basic building blocks of medical reality would have been as well known as DNA is today among non-biologists. Thus, when medieval and Renaissance mystics focus on the body in their guides to the mystical ascent, it is not just a body that needs to be fed (or starved), not just an illness-prone body that can aid in *imitatio Christi*, not just a body that senses gluttony and sexual desire and therefore needs to be controlled and negated, not just the opposite of soul. It is also an elemental body, one with a high proportion of earth. It is a body that is a delicate balance of moisture and heat, and if the balance is disrupted, old age and death are the inevitable consequences. It is a body in which blood is the reigning fluid, and every effort must be made to regulate the effects of heat and cold, wetness and dryness to make sure more blood is produced. If so, if the elemental body turns out to be one half of the body–soul dichotomy, what effect does physiological reality have on mystical methods intended to unite the mystic with God?[7]

In order to understand the religious and medical landscape that influenced Laredo's twin mastery of the professions of physician and mystical author, we must recognize that the tension between medical knowledge and religious vocation that many modern people experience was not conceivable in the medieval and Renaissance world, for the spirit and the body were intimately linked in natural philosophy as well as in Christian theology.[8] The intersection of medicine and religion is evidenced by the decree of the Fourth Lateran Council (1215) that doctors ought to 'first and foremost admonish the sick to attend to the health of their souls,'[9] with a warning to doctors to discontinue treatment of any person who refused the sacrament of confession. Many of the laity not only treated priests and physicians with equal respect[10] but also called on monks as well as doctors for physical cures, not just prayers.[11] The Italian doctor Michele Savonarola (1385–1466) distinguished between diseases caused by nature that could be cured by physicians and those caused by God that must be cured by prayer,[12] while Alfonso Chirino, a doctor from Salamanca who wrote a popular early fifteenth-century medical text, *Menor daño de la medicina* (Least Harmful Medicine), argued that the preservation of good health was necessary to fulfil the second half of the commandment to love your neighbour as you love yourself.[13]

In the twelfth and thirteenth centuries, theologians were offering theories about the physical constituents of the world.[14] Both theologians and physicians identified Adam and Eve and the Fall as the source of the potential for illness in the originally perfect human body.[15] In addition, the rise of the universities in the twelfth and thirteenth centuries was sparked in part by the translation into Latin of Aristotelian philosophy, a broad system that addressed subjects now studied separately, such as metaphysics, political philosophy, and science (natural philosophy). At the same time, Arabic compilations of Galen's medical theories, which relied on Aristotelian theories, were being translated into Latin, as were commentaries on Galenic texts by leading Muslim medico-theologians such as Avicenna. As a result, the Aristotelian medieval universities trained theologians who had recourse to medical evidence to support doctrinal understanding,[16] and trained physicians who prescribed prayers and often shared healing roles with local priests.[17] By the fourteenth century, not only were medical textbooks written with the scholastic methods of argument (the *quaestio*) found in theology, they also often relied on religious analogies, a kind of interdisciplinarity known as *diglosia*.[18] Iberian authors such as Arnau de Villanova (1235–1311) and Bernardino de Laredo drew on both types of scholasticism, medical and theological, to address more popular issues such as apocalypticism and mysticism.[19]

Laredo's deep familiarity with the body as an object of scientific inquiry initially infiltrates his mystical treatise during the first stage of the tripartite treatise, self-knowledge. The first half of part 1, the first of two weeks of exercises, is a series of meditations on a poem asking questions of humankind such as 'Who are you?' and 'Where are you going?', to which the answers describe human origins and death as muddy 'earth' or dust.

Monday[20]	O man! Who are you? – I am earth [dust],[21] and indeed very unclean [contemptible].[22]
Tuesday	Where are you from? – Let him respond: From the sandy earth.
Wednesday	By what path have you come? – Across the rugged[23] earth.
Thursday	Where are you? – In the dangerous world.
Friday	Where are you going? – To the fearful earth.
Saturday[24]	What are you carrying? – A great load of muddy earth. And let the man tell himself: So put on some mud [i.e., humiliate yourself],[25] since you have more than enough earth.

The questions in the poem are taken directly from the sequence posed about the origin of the soul in the well-known spiritual treatise, Pseudo-Augustine's *De salute anime*.[26] Laredo therefore appears to situate the opening of his mystical treatise, written primarily for fellow mendicants, firmly in the medieval tradition of *contemptus mundi*, or rejection of the world.[27] However, he substitutes new answers to the original questions, answers that emphasize the earth as the origin and destination of all humanity.[28] In Castilian, the word *tierra* means both 'earth' and 'dust';

Laredo goes beyond the dust and ashes of Genesis and Job to brings the role of the scientific element earth in medicine and natural philosophy (*physica*) to bear on the mystic's self-knowledge.[29]

Laredo recapitulates the medieval notion of the formation of the physical world from combinations of the four basic elements, a notion that led many to equate the human body with the element earth.[30] Thus, the earth he is referring to is not only the earth we see around us as soil and dirt on a daily basis, or even the earth or dust into which our bodies will crumble after our deaths. It is instead the medical reality of our bodies as composed almost entirely of the element earth that allows Laredo to argue for our permanent state of corporeal abjection. Humans, while alive, are always and entirely mere dusty earth.[31] While Caroline Walker Bynum and others point in particular to women reclaiming a denigrated body as the locus of contact with the suffering divine, it must be kept in mind that Spanish Franciscans of both genders displayed great interest in nature in general and the body in particular as a result of their founder's formative experiences, as we saw in previous chapters.[32] As a lay Franciscan working as an apothecary at a Franciscan retreat house, Laredo's mystical discourse begins from a scientific awareness of the healthy body.

A reading of the *Subida del Monte Sión* in light of his medical background reveals that Laredo's approach to *recogimiento* was profoundly affected by his awareness of the human body and the physical world. In about half of the daily meditations on dust,[33] Laredo uses a definition of dust as dry earth in order to introduce more sophisticated medical language referring to the body, including terminology concerning the elements, primary and secondary humors, qualities, innate heat, and radical moisture. Although these terms were available to medieval theologians and preachers, as demonstrated by Caroline Walker Bynum and Joseph Ziegler,[34] their puzzling appearance in a treatise guiding the mystical ascent of the soul poses the central question of this chapter. Coming just before the stage on Passion meditation, a stage that Laredo imbues with details drawn from medical familiarity with blood, not to mention details on the bones and nerves in the body that could be injured during torture,[35] the result of Laredo's medical approach is a form of spirituality that is *a result of* the body and the world rather than a rejection of it.

In this chapter I examine the medical discourses in parts 1 and 2 of the *Subida del Monte Sión* as proof of Laredo's dependence on the particularities of human bodies for the didactic sequence proposed by his mystical method. After briefly situating Laredo's awareness of the common medieval spiritual discourse of contempt for the human body (*contemptus mundi*), I then outline in full the medical background and physiological information that provided Laredo with the tools to construct his mystical dissection of the believer's body.

The Spiritual Language of *Contemptus* Mundi

In the course of the six days devoted to each pair of poetic questions and answers, Laredo paints in vivid terms how humans even while alive are dust, ashes, and putrefying corpses;[36] how bodies function as prisons in which humans reside before suffering capital punishment;[37] and the biblical understanding that humans are ashes and to ashes will return.[38] He returns several times to the scientific fact that mud is formed of dirt mixed with water, linking it to the story of the creation of Adam out of mud to ensure that his readers take his remarks literally.[39] This point was not unique to Laredo. As Cohen points out, 'At some point [in the Middle Ages], the metaphor must have lost its transcendent meaning and become a synonym: earth and clay were almost synonymous with human matter; fire and water, with pain.'[40] According to Laredo, complete awareness of one's own nature and destiny as human enables the devotee to fully appreciate the magnitude of a Creator God who created the earth and dust, and also created the person who will fall to dust at the end of his allotted span. Once devotees accept that the self is worth nothing, they can begin to praise the glory and infinite goodness of the Creator of the world.[41]

Despite several indications that he might use the misery of human existence to frame a consideration of God, a frequent approach in medieval treatises, in the end Laredo does not expand on God in any particular detail in this first week, preferring to retain his reader in an extended meditation on the *nonada* (no-nothingness) of the self.[42] On first reading, Laredo's meditations on the dust poem appear to follow the familiar contours of the discourse in spirituality, so common throughout late medieval and early modern Europe, that denied the body because of its 'miserable' origins. A brief survey of treatises from the *contemptus mundi* tradition and the topic as incorporated into essential Franciscan treatises will clarify Laredo's familiarity with the spiritual discourse of bodily denial,[43] a discourse the rest of this chapter will prove he significantly alters by putting the physiology of the body front and centre during the process of denial.

Some medieval spiritual treatises were intended to re-orient entirely the devotee's valuing of human life and possibilities. Pope Innocent III's famous work from the late twelfth century, *De miseria humanae conditionis* (*On the Misery of the Human Condition*), widely popular in vernacular translation from its first dissemination and available in Spanish by the early fifteenth century,[44] is split into three parts that treat the horrific nature of birth, life, and death. Once convinced that all stages of human life are pure misery, the reader would presumably recognize the glory of God and focus his or her devotion on the divine, who offers salvation from the 'human condition.' One example will suffice:

> Man was formed of dust, slime, and ashes; what is even more vile, of the filthiest seed. He was conceived from the itch of the flesh, in the heat of passion and the stench of lust, and worse yet, with the stain of sin. He was born to toil, dread, and trouble; and more wretched still, was born only to die ... He will become fuel for those fires which are forever hot and burn forever bright; food for the worm which forever nibbles and digests; a mass of rottenness which will forever stink and reek.[45]

Innocent's focus on the human body is intended to negate its worth from the moment of birth through to death itself. Although the terms Innocent III uses are powerfully evocative of corporeality, they reflect generalizations about the cycle of life and death rather than a detailed physiology. Those sections of part 1 of the *Subida* in which Laredo does not use medical terminology have a very similar tone to that of Innocent's work: 'Our being, made of corruptible things and living in corrupt subjection and ending in corruption ... [is a] dungheap.'[46] Innocent's work, and later treatises modelled on it, thus provided the basic approach to spiritual self-annihilation that Laredo uses in the early chapters of his mystical treatise. Yet Innocent is so dismissive of the body that all concrete details of the body's composition are missing; it is therefore worth delving deeper into the immediate context of late medieval Franciscanism to determine which elements of Laredo's stage of self-knowledge are a result of his training as a lay member of the Franciscan Order, given its focus on bodily devotion.

One of the most influential Franciscan treatises in the late Middle Ages was the basic handbook for those newly entering Franciscan monasteries. The *De exterioris et interioris hominis compositione* (translated into Castilian under the title *Forma de los novicios*, 'Form for Novices') was attributed to Bonaventure but actually composed by David of Augsburg.[47] In this treatise, available in Spain by the late fifteenth century,[48] the author guides the novice through the various attitudes he must either develop or avoid. After part 1's regulations for matters like sleep, choir, prayer, and meals[49] comes part 2's discussion of corporeal control, especially the sources of vice and ways for regulating it.[50] In part 3, Augsburg addresses love of God, love of neighbour, and the place of visions and prayer in the spiritual life, following this with a lengthy discourse on the attainment of the reform Franciscan virtues of humanity, patience, obedience, poverty, and *mesura* (desiring only a modest amount).[51] In the final, unstructured section of part 1 of the *Subida*, Laredo echoes the concerns of Augsburg's novice handbook by providing recommendations on 'corporeal harshness,' such as limits on food and wine and the ideal forms for vigils and abstinence.[52] Yet they are not Laredo's first concern, for he does not find them interesting enough to provide a weekly schema for their meditation, as he does with the dust poem.[53] Instead, the chapters in the *Subida* that parallel David of Augsburg's work serve to remind the reader of the structural framework in place in monastic life for the achievement of self-awareness and self-annihilation, while avoiding any suggestion that corporeal penitence is a subject worthy of creative meditation. It is the parts of the body, not the body as a whole and capable of being subjected to harsh treatment, that are of greater concern to Laredo.

Bonaventure, the premier Franciscan theologian and mystic, was, not surprisingly, a primary source of inspiration for many Observant Franciscans in the Castilian Villacrecian reform. Although Fidèle de Ros suggests that Bonaventure was at best a minor source for Laredo, since he references him less frequently than he does Richard of Saint Victor, Heinrich Herp, or even Gregory the Great,[54] Laredo's Franciscan context may have allowed him to refer to Bonaventurian ideas without need for explicit citation.[55] One particular treatise by Bonaventure is intriguing in relation to Laredo's poetic musings on soul and dust. Bonaventure's *De perfectione vitae ad sorores* (Of the Perfection of Life, for Nuns), a short work written for a Clarisan sister, was often included in collected works.[56] In a section on humility that follows a Passion meditation, Bonaventure connects a series of questions on the soul's origins with Genesis 3:19:

> The third path on which you ought to travel, if you want to arrive at perfect humility, is that of considering the fundamental aspects of your being. Which you do, O dearest Mother, when you examine *where you come from* and *where you are going*. Consider, then, *where you have come from*, and you will learn what has been done with the dough of perdition and dust and mud from the earth ... Consider also the second thing, *where you are going*, and you will see that you are going to corruption and will be converted into ash, because *you are dust and to dust you will return.*[57] (my emphasis)

Bonaventure thus provides a crucial link between the Genesis quotation on the origins of humans as dust and the questions posed by Pseudo-Augustine's *De salute anime* that Laredo later uses in his dust poem, interspersed with medical considerations of *tierra*.[58]

The late medieval tradition of *contemptus mundi* clearly required the inclusion of a stage of self-awareness in Laredo's prescriptive mystical guide, all the more so given his immediate context of the Observant Franciscan reform and its emphasis on poverty of body and spirit.[59] Yet his meditations on the questions and answers in his original poem on dust bring a different type of text into dialogue with the Christian tradition of body-denying spirituality, a shift all the more evident as Laredo's attention to the elemental body is not paralleled by any of the early sixteenth-century Spanish authors classically designated as mystical.[60] Laredo fully renders the mystic's body in all its medical detail in order to downgrade each corporeal aspect, thus expecting that the mystic become more aware of his or her physical body as a means of fully recognizing its physiological nothingness. The side effect of such a technique, however, is that the body does not disappear immediately. Rather, it takes centre stage so that the believer can take full note of every thing that it contains, then realize how the sum of its parts adds up to ... *nonada*.

I posit that Laredo creates a cataphatic theology of the body in order to fulfil more effectively the negation of body that was part of the *contemptus mundi* tradition. As Denys Turner elegantly states in the preface to his discussion of the *via negativa* in medieval thought:

> The cataphatic is, we might say, the verbose element in theology, it is the Christian mind deploying all the resources of language in the effort to express something about God, and in that straining to speak, theology uses as many voices as it can. It is the cataphatic in theology which causes its metaphor-ridden character, causes it to borrow vocabularies by analogy from many another discourse, whether of science, literature, art, sex, politics ... or whatever ... For in its cataphatic mode, theology is, we might say, a kind of verbal riot, an anarchy of discourse in which anything goes.[61]

In Laredo's scientifically accurate method of mystical prayer, the believer's body, created by God according to the medieval world view, provides a cataphatic discourse of blood and flesh, elements and moistures, which points back to its creator. The medical fragmentation of one half of the body–soul dichotomy does not elide it, however, but rather points to embodiment as the starting point for recollection mysticism, even in a technique later translated into the language of negative theology in the 1538 revision. Given that Laredo's insistence on physiology extends to Christ as well as to the devotee, the embodiment of the divine paves the way for the embodiment of the highest element of the human, the soul.

Laredo's Medical Education

An overview of Laredo's education and career as an apothecary and/or physician will contextualize the medical theory that he later brings to his mystical guide. Unfortunately, once again only a broad outline is possible, as there are no more verifiable details about Laredo's education than there are for his life in general. Scholars usually rely on Andrés de Guadalupe's claim in his hagiography that Laredo studied 'Latinity' in Seville and then attended the University of Seville.[62] While it is a viable theory that Laredo went to the local cathedral school, the 'estudio de San Miguel,'[63] it is impossible that he could have attended medical school at the University of Seville, as the medical faculty was appointed only two years before Laredo published his first medical book in which he cites his many years of medical practice. Without certain proof, we must extrapolate on the basis of reasonable assumptions. According to Luis García Ballester, the late *maestro* of the history of medieval Spanish medicine, there were two paths for medical education on the peninsula in the late Middle Ages and the Golden Age: attending a university, or training under an individual member of the medical profession.[64] Looking to Laredo's citations in his medical publications, we see that his sources range from the ancient Greek Dioscorides to the late antique Galen, to the Arabs Mesue and Avicenna, to the Christian Arnau de Villanova – precisely the authors assigned in the medical curriculum for the University of Salamanca.[65] These authors were also, however, required background for *all* doctors and apothecaries, regardless of university or private training, according to the 1477 legislation of the Catholic Monarchs introducing kingdom-wide proficiency examinations for all members of health professions.[66] Regardless of whether he trained locally or at the university, Laredo most likely read for his exams through the *Articella* (in circulation in manuscript and print at the time), a compendium of Hippocratic and Galenic treatises that included all of the requisite medical authors mentioned above.[67]

It is thus to his Galenic context and to Laredo's specific teachings rather than to a university curriculum that we must turn to ascertain Laredo's view of the body. A well-known doctor or apothecary who treated royal, noble, and bourgeois patients,[68] at some point (whether before or after his professional success is unclear) Laredo took up residence at San Francisco del Monte, a small *casa de recollectos* outside of Seville.[69] Since he insists on his status as a *lego*, or lay friar, he probably served as the community's apothecary, with the freedom to continue treating the laity of Seville and to write his medical and spiritual treatises. Laredo's pharmaceutical writings, *Metaphora medicine* and *Modus faciendi*, provide a portrait of a Renaissance-trained Galenist.[70] For example, his second pharmaceutical treatise, the *Modus faciendi*, begins with a description of the elements and humors in the tradition of Arabic textbooks.[71] In fact, Laredo's vernacular writings reflect the popularity of medical treatises among Spanish laity that Michael Solomon has traced throughout the sixteenth century.[72] Vernacular medical writings initially gained attention as part of the democratization of knowledge spurred by the printing press, and later because of shifts in medical and pharmaceutical understanding produced by contact with the New World.[73]

In the late fifteenth and early sixteenth centuries, Iberian medical humanists revived interest in Galen by issuing Spanish and Latin translations of works by one of Galen's primary sources, the Greek Dioscorides.[74] 'Modern' (or 'reform') Galenism, based on deduction and eventually experimentation, came to replace the scholastic Galenism that had stayed strictly within the framework Galen had originally set down.[75] Ballester terms Laredo's second and more popular medical treatise, the *Modus faciendi*, 'the first work written in Castilian which addressed pharmaceutical technique with the rigour of Galenism.'[76] Included in the 'rigour of Galenism' is the idea that Galen sought to inspire others to search for facts rather than create disciples who followed his ideas slavishly.[77] As such, Laredo's medical works, which mainly transcribe and organize pharmaceutical recipes from Arabic and Latin works into Castilian, follow the spirit of Galen rather than the medieval scholastic tradition, providing only five treatments directly from Galen while recommending (and contradicting) far more from an extensive range of more up-to-date authors, including ninety-five from the Arabic author Mesue and perhaps thirty-four original to Laredo.[78]

In all his published works, Laredo echoes the scholastic *diglosia* between medicine and theology in a number of ways. In the first chapter of *Modus faciendi*, he traces the medical profession's roots back to God. Galen had described his analysis of anatomy as a form of meditation on God;[79] Laredo in turn provides what can best be described as an early malpractice defence, citing from Ecclesiastes that God has appointed the time of death; thus doctors either do God's work in preventing a patient from dying too early or cannot prevent the death that God had planned.[80] He evidently expected his audience of apothecaries to be receptive to his combination of spirituality and medicine, since he includes a Latin hymn to Joseph after the preface and a vernacular (despite the Latin title) *Laus Deo Marie et Joseph* at the end of *Modus faciendi.*[81] And in the 1536 reissue of his first treatise, *Metaphora medicine*, his publishers printed a classic Calvary scene on the reverse of frontispiece (see Figure 3.1).[82] Laredo's religious audience must also have displayed some interest in the intersection of medicine and faith, since at the end of the 'Extravagante' letters in the *Subida*, he appends a list of his medical successes owing to prescriptions of cycles of masses.[83]

Given Laredo's Galenism, it is not possible to understand his semantic range or his implicit assumptions about the workings of body and soul without a thorough grounding in the fundamentals of medieval and Renaissance theories of the body that were available in medical textbooks (manuscript and print) and then mirrored in Laredo's writings, both pharmaceutical and mystical. While scholars such as Jean Dangler have gestured to the intersection of mystical and scientific discourses in Iberia, the medical information adduced relates primarily to the biology of gender and sexual intercourse, not Galenic physiology.[84] The next section of this chapter therefore offers modern scholars who may be unfamiliar with Galenic theories a review of medieval medical views of the human body, a critical step towards the goal of parsing the medical mystical body that would lead Laredo to the notion of an embodied soul.

The Body in Galenic Medicine

Two of the most influential Galenic works to reach the West were the introductory textbook, the *Isagogue*, by Joannitius or Hunain ibn Ishaq (809–77), and the *summa* of Galen's thought collected by Avicenna (980–1037) in his *Canon*, both of which became key texts at the universities of medieval and early modern Europe. I will draw primarily from these two works, both of which Laredo cites in his pharmaceutical treatises,[85] to delineate the framework of Laredo's medical thought, turning occasionally to details from the books often bound with them in compendia in the *Articella*, a likely textbook in Laredo's training. By considering the fundamental physiological information at the core of medical knowledge, it will then be possible to properly assess whether, in his meditations on the dust poem, Laredo functions as a physician describing the elements or as a spiritual teacher importing a convenient metaphor.

Fig 3.1 Crucifixion scene with Mary and Joseph. Reverse of frontispiece to Laredo's pharmaceutical treatise *Metaphora medicine*, originally published 1522 (Seville: Juan de Varela, 1536). Credit: Biblioteca Nacional de España, Madrid.

First, let us consider the definition of health itself in Galenic medicine. As Nancy Siraisi explains in her overview of Renaissance medicine: 'Basic constituents of the human body, like deadly sins and cardinal virtues, formed part of a conventional set. This was the list of things natural, which were, in turn, one of a group of three categories: the naturals, the non-naturals,[86] and the contra-naturals.'[87] The naturals included the components of the human body, and thus the physiological understanding that underlies discussion of body for both theologians and physicians.

> The list of things natural ... usually included elements, complexions ... humors, members, virtues, operations, and *spiritus*. The things natural thus joined together alleged material components imperceptible to sense (the elements of earth, air, fire, and water in the human body), and *spiritus*, which was supposedly a substance manufactured in the heart from inspired air and

> transmitted through the body via the arteries); physically perceptible bodily parts (humors, that is bodily fluids, and members, that is, parts of the body); and activities or functions (virtues and operations).[88]

Although the matrix of the four elements – earth, water, air, and fire – was foundational to an understanding of the world from both a medical and a theological standpoint, the practising physician did not spend time working with the actual four elements, as he could not influence them directly. Instead, physicians focused on the circumstances that produced the fluids and temperatures of the body, in order to preserve life. The medical view was that life itself was the result of an 'innate' or 'vital' heat that kept the body balanced between the extremes of hot and cold, wet and dry (the qualities). In fact, most doctors, including various important Iberian authorities, explained ageing and death as the result of the drying out of the 'radical moisture,' or 'radical fluid' (*humidum radicale*) of the body, a divine moisture first infused into Adam and then handed down through semen.[89]

Given the foundation of heat and moisture that ensured health, medieval and Renaissance doctors were interested in maintaining the balance of the specific forms of moisture found in the body, that is to say, the four humors (blood, phlegm, yellow/red bile, black bile).[90] Avicenna traced the origins of bodily humors to the food humans consume,[91] claiming that which humor the food becomes is dependent upon how the environment (the body) is affected by the four qualities (hot, cold, dry, moist). In the most balanced situation between hot and cold, moist and dry, the 'best' humor, blood, is produced.[92] If the qualities are not in balance, then the food ends up as one of the other humors.[93] It is noteworthy that phlegm is 'unmatured' blood that simply needs more heat to be transformed into blood, while the two kinds of bile, once produced, remain as they are.[94]

The relationship of phlegm to blood indicates the importance of blood in this sequence. Avicenna, and many doctors after him, including Laredo, identified blood itself as the life-giving 'radical moisture.'[95] Physicians believed that blood, the most productive of the four humors, travelled throughout the body and eventually become part of the 'substance' of an organ or member.

> Food entering the body undergoes a first digestion or purification in the stomach and a second in the liver; the product, venous blood, is then conveyed to the several members and transformed into their substance in a third digestion. We can distinguish four different *humiditates* in this transformation. There is first the blood contained in the veins, on its way to the mem-

> bers; second, that which is contained within each member but which has not yet begun to be assimilated to the body in the third digestion; third, that which is in process of assimilation; and finally, that which has been completely assimilated, made part of the substance of the member.[96]

Each of the *humiditates*, or moistures, had a different name and was considered a secondary humor, sub-categories under the primary humor (or general layman's category) of 'blood';[97] together they constituted the radical moisture.[98] In summary, for Renaissance physicians, the primary focus of their craft was not the elements of earth, water, air, and fire but was instead the sequence that produces healthy bodies: food composed of elements is changed into the humors that affect health, at which point the most important of the humors, blood, can then become flesh. This was the sequence that they were hired to keep in balance – no wonder that bloodletting was a primary tool of the Galenic physician![99]

One final point about medieval and early modern medical theories of the body is worth noting, in part because it is the only major physiological concept from which Laredo draws terminology without providing a full explanation. According to the *Isagoge*, the processes of generation of humors and organs described above all related to the 'natural energy' derived from food that had its source at the liver.[100] Two other forms of energy, however, were present in the body. Spiritual energy, derived from the heart, resulted in 'indignation, victory, domination, astuteness, and anxiety.'[101] Animal energy, seated in the brain, resulted in imagination, reason, memory, and the interpretations of the five senses.[102] It is evident that despite the fact that the four elements were considered the basic building blocks of material bodies according to both theology and medicine, the definition of 'human' was different for each profession. Theologians identified the soul as the location of the powers of memory, understanding, and will, a different source than that identified by physicians, who posited that it was the body's animal energy that gave rise to memory and reason.[103] Likewise, theologians considered the heart as the centre of the human that makes each person unique, while doctors located that function in the brain.[104] Laredo's tendency to consider the memory as somatic (see chapter 4) is thus traceable to his medical background, one that gave him language and metaphors with which to propose a God at the centre of an embodied soul.

The Medical Body in the Stage of Self-Knowledge

Laredo's first project in the *Subida* is a series of meditations that lead to greater self-awareness, a necessary step that allows the believer to recognize the relative glories of God. He uses the dust poem to achieve this goal. The meditations on the questions and answers of his poem do not at first reading convey a coherent argument or meditative sequence, one after the other, as one might expect from a guide meant to lead the reader step by step up the mount of contemplation. However, I contend that the entire physiological system discussed above in purely medical detail provides the underlying structure for Laredo's reflections on how to achieve spiritual self-knowledge. In his analysis of the influential Catalan author Arnau de Villanova (1235–1311) as a 'theologizing physician,' Joseph Ziegler differentiates between two 'levels of medical language,' high and low.

> A religious text ... of high-level medical language includes medical terms and concepts which originate specifically in academic medical discourse, and betrays knowledge that is particularly expressive of a medical background ... A text which uses low-level medical language will contain banal medical terms such as references to organs of the body, to the senses and to diseases, or allusions to the humoral theory; they do not signify any specific medical knowledge and training and could have originated in biblical, philosophical or theological sources ... [T]here may be texts that qualitatively use low-level medical language, yet these terms saturate the text to such an extent that the quantity acquires a qualitative value ... Furthermore, the context in which medical language appears should not be ignored. Thus there is a difference between Thomas Aquinas talking about the ensoulment of the fetus ... and his use of medical language in a debate over a strictly metaphysical question. The latter case would be more striking and could serve as evidence for the 'medicinalization' of theology.[105]

Laredo is well aware of his audience, since he always directly links sophisticated 'high-level medical terminology' to spiritual questions, never allowing physiology to overtake the sense of the mystical text for those unfamiliar with such concepts. At the same time, Laredo goes to great lengths to explain certain more basic physiological truths ('low-level medical language') in the interests of co-opting them as effective metaphors for theological truths. It is worth noting that he explicates all the essential scientific terminology in the first section of the first part of his mystical treatise, thus indicating that the medical model is his point of departure for promoting self-knowledge.[106] Laredo's reliance on medicine as a way of thinking through concepts that seem far removed from medical ideas does not end there, however. He later makes the workings of the cardiovascular system central to a point about Christ's Passion in part 2 of the *Subida*. (Even in the final stage of recollection, he continues referring to Galenic humoral theory; see the conclusion.) In this section, I will include the ideas in Laredo's spiritual meditations in part 1 (with an excursus into part 2) in the order in which they make *medical* sense, that is, the way the elements make up the body, the heat and moisture that lead to the development of humors, with further attention to the most important humor, blood.

Laredo mentions in the preface and then in the first lines of meditation on the dust poem that the human body is composed of earth and water, a medical belief. 'It is necessary in this body, which is [made] of corruptible things and lives in corrupt subjection and ends in putrefaction, that we ground the imagery (*fantasia*) of our dungheaps, of my bestial body, of mud made of water and earth.'[107] Although he seems to be echoing Innocent III's language of *contemptus mundi* with his references to the 'bestial body' and his next comment provides a proof text for the fact that God created humans from mud, a mixture of water and dirt,[108] Laredo nevertheless reverts to medical terminology, pointing out that the elements earth and air are coupled in the human body because the air causes the earth to dry out to being nearly non-existent, or nothing. This scientific fact allows him to expand on the theological position that the dry dust – ash[109] – is the source and end of human life, and why human bodies do not matter much, for they are 'nothing, and made of nothing.'[110] As we saw above, this point is taken from the *contemptus mundi* spiritual tradition, yet Laredo gives it a medical slant by discussing the actual base elements that make up corporeality.

Laredo does not simply refer to this common theory of physiology in passing, however, for he makes earth and water key components of his apparently non-medical analogies in all of part 1. Throughout the *Subida*, he provides brief analogies taken from a variety of professional realms to illustrate his theological points about human nature, Christ's nature, God's divinity, and so on. In the chapters leading up to his introduction of the dust poem, having already defined humans to be made of earth and water, Laredo suggests that the readers base their journey into self-awareness on the fact that bricks are also made of the elements mud and water; that is, humans are no better than a fire-baked brick.[111] A few chapters later, he renders the stage of self-knowledge as the foundation for the rest of the mystical process, a foundation dug as a ditch (out of mud) into which a sort of cement made out of *limo* and sand is poured.[112] Since he had earlier defined the combination of earth and water that makes the mud of humans to be *limo*, it is evident that the elements of the human body are the foundation for the journey towards God. Laredo's use of these particular details of medical knowledge is different from his reference to terms such as 'innate heat' and 'radical moisture,' because the linking of earth and body would have been known to his mendicant audience through theological study. Thus he is able to justify his reliance on medicine in part through providing a framework for it that would be familiar to his readers, allowing him to fill in more advanced knowledge as an addition to this comfortable base.

By clarifying the role of earth as a scientific element at the very beginning of the treatise, Laredo then has the freedom to allude to it periodically without having to re-describe the entire scientific background. For example, in the last portion of part 1 (theoretically a week of rules for corporeal penitence, but in reality unstructured),[113] he discusses Adam and original sin in order to emphasize the nothingness of the perpetually stained body. It is possible to interpret this point purely along the lines of the Villacrecian emphasis on restraint of both body and spirit, yet the first line of the chapter insists that the earth out of which Adam was created was particularly pure, and thus the original creation was likewise pure.[114] Coming after the extended play on earth as element, it is impossible to read this line as referencing only the spiritual meaning of the Genesis story. Rather, the purity of Adam came from the pure element earth, as well as from his construction from the actual substance of mud. The dust poem in its theological and medical aspects continues to echo throughout the chapter: Laredo describes original sin as causing the body and soul to end up 'completely drenched in several kinds of mud,'[115] using the term for mud (*cieno*) that he had defined in the prefatory material as a mix of earth and water.

Once the wordplay on the dust and ashes of human bodies as the element earth is established, Laredo feels able to make physiology fundamental to self-knowledge. In his most thorough physiological meditation (Friday: 'Where are you going? To the fearful earth'), there is a complete description of the four humors as resulting from 'radical moisture' and ending up as organs of the body.[116] He begins with the Genesis 3:19 verse on 'remembering that man is dust and must return to ash,' connecting it to theological discussions of the resurrection of the body.[117] Quickly turning again to a medical framework, in the course of the meditation Laredo spends an entire page on the process of the generation of the body from elements. The example is a flower whose pollen is harvested by bees and turned into honey, honey that in turn is eaten by a person. The elements in the honey become the organs of the body, while the qualities of the honey in turn affect the proportion and balance of humors in the person who ingests it.

> In addition, these four elements ... and their qualities are already mine in my humors, which, when coming in the radical moisture, already stop being humors and pass into the particular members [i.e., limbs or organs], in order within the [members] to always conserve themselves well, seeking perpetuity.[118]

It is worth pausing to consider that medical detail concerning the humors would not have been a foreign discourse in Inquisitorial Spain. As Gracia Guillén points out, the blood purity statutes enforced in varying degrees from the middle of the fifteenth century on through the reign of Emperor Charles V (and beyond) relied in part on a rendition of Jew versus Christian that depicted them as different in terms of humors, complexions, and heredity.[119] For this reason, Spanish authors of religious treatises could describe Christ accurately, not metaphorically, as a 'doctor,' for he had brought physiological aid to a 'weak' race' when preaching to his fellow Jews.[120]

In Tuesday's meditation ('Where are you from? From the sandy earth'), Laredo explicates high-level medical terminology in order to use the nothingness of the human condition to emphasize the greatness of God.[121] He describes the innate heat that produces life as a gift originally from God, passed on from parent to child. Critiquing those 'presumptuous youths' who assume that their bodies are their own and that only the (loosely translated) 'vital spirit' comes from God,[122] Laredo points out that both 'vital spirit' and 'natural heat' (innate heat) come from God.[123] Indeed, the body, pointedly made out of 'putrefaction' and 'horrendousness,'[124] cannot exist as living without God's gifts of heat and spirit.[125] Thus, Laredo situates the medical concept that heat is that which causes the body to function (and without which its 'radical moisture' desiccates, leading to death) in a context that reflects this medical reality back to God's creation of the world.[126] The treatment of medical detail that modern scholars might expect to be irrelevant in a treatise on abstract contemplation is instead incorporated in full in the mystical prayer of the embodied soul.

By tracing the minutiae of the process of creation and the maintenance of the elements through the organs and the temperaments, Laredo emphasizes the composition of the body. Rather than identifying the body as miserable and ignoring it, as in the *contemptus mundi* tradition, he instead focuses the reader's attention on the scientific details of the production of flesh and blood, a move that at once paints the body in vivid terms but also renders it suspect because of its composition from the inconsequential, even invisible elements that move from plants to animals to humans. In this natural merry-go-round of conservation, Laredo proves the insignificance of humans who are made of the same elements as all created entities.

Medicine in Support of Christology

By the end of the first week of meditations, Laredo has made full use of the way that the elements are incorporated into the physical body and even explored the basic building blocks of heat and moisture that lead to life. The most striking of his extended physiological meditations, however, he saves for another part of his *Subida*. After all, most of his audience would know of the importance of blood for life, even if the term 'vital heat' or the process by which the four elements are turned into flesh was not common knowledge, so Laredo does not bother to bring in his scientific background concerning blood to emphasize self-knowledge as treated in part 1. Instead, he saves the information for a moment when the general knowledge that blood was an essential humor in the human body would be most theologically effective. His discussion of blood physiology occurs during his meditations on Holy Week and marks the first time he brings his medical knowledge to bear on the human nature of Christ.

Laredo presents an interpretation of the Gospel reference to the bloody sweat of Christ at Gethsemane, translated into Spanish as *casi gotas de sangre* (almost drops of blood), which he then retranslates as *gotas de casi sangre* (drops of almost-blood).[127] First, Laredo makes reference again to 'vital spirit' and 'innate heat,' the terms related to the gift of life that make the human body function, saying that the fervour of emotion experienced in Gethsemene caused Jesus's innate heat to increase.[128] Although several medieval authors had attempted explanations that took into account Jesus's scientific body,[129] Laredo is the only author of whom I am aware who provides a fully Avicennian explanation. He carefully explains the four types of blood in the same manner he does in his pharmaceutical textbooks,[130] specifying that only one of the four is actually termed 'blood,' plain and simple. 'Blood' is found only in the heart and veins, and it is not the most pure form of the humor. The liquid that passes from the veins to spread through the pores in order to be 'converted into flesh' is a more pure and perfect form, and is called *rórida humidad* (dewy moisture).[131] When the second form gets a bit heavier in the process of conversion, it is named 'gluten.' As it becomes fully flesh, it is called *cambio* (change).[132] Laredo makes this extended digression into medical detail in part 2 in order to support a theological argument: Christ could have sweated blood because he was not actually sweating 'blood' (which cannot leave the veins), but rather, *rórida humidad*, the most pure and perfect liquid in the human body.

Oddly, Laredo follows this point with the much more typical spiritual suggestion that Christ is the only person to ever have sweated *rórida humidad*, because he suffered more severe emotional agony than anyone before or since. From a modern point of view, it is easy to wonder why Laredo felt it useful to clarify (for a full folio) what kind of blood the sweat was, if the explanation that it was Christ's mental agony that caused him to perspire so intensely is a purely Christological and traditional one. But Laredo's statement about Christ's mental pain is not an unscientific one, nor even an untheological one.[133] Mowbray has offered a cogent argument that it was scholastic theologians, not physicians, who first developed a medical terminology in the Middle Ages for pain, in the interest of differentiating between the types of pain (*dolor*) that Christ would have suffered.[134] This point will be discussed in greater depth in chapter 5; here it is sufficient to note that corporeal and therefore medical topics had a greater connection to emotions and mental states than is customarily supposed in modern conceptions of cognition. As early as Augustine, theologians had associated pain more closely with the soul than with the body, thus allowing pain to be linked with emotions such as grief or fear.[135] Eventually, mental agony and grief would be described as one element of the many types of pain afflicting Christ, as disturbing, if not more, as the gaping wounds inflicted by his torturers.[136] For Laredo, consideration of Jesus's body leads automatically to consideration of Jesus's emotions during the perspiration, for body and soul were not separate, not even in the realm of pain.

Ultimately, Laredo's use of medical information in the *Subida* serves to place not the generalized body of Christ but rather the entrails, veins, and pores of Christ front and centre.[137] Laredo did not invoke his scientific background concerning blood to emphasize the role of self-knowledge on the way to God but instead deploys his knowledge of blood physiology to emphasize the human nature of Christ. This emphasis on Christ's medical humanity is also evident in another passage from Laredo's Passion meditation that echoes the Castilian 'passion of two' tradition, but with a medical slant:

> With the Son of God in the wounded arms of his ... Mother, both bodies torn to bits, what pain would have made her more faint? ... [T]o see the sacred head deeply penetrated with spines ... the mouth a bit open like one who lost his life ... To see the fallen arms, the dislocated bones ... the veins evacuated

> [of blood], the nerves contracted? ... What greater affliction than to look at the dislocated legs or at both feet pierced with one nail which enters the heart of [Mary's] soul.[138]

At this point, the same scientific awareness that allows Laredo to devalue the human body as being simply like the rest of the elemental creation is now subverted to enable humans to understand the divine humanity. The fact that human physiology can convey theological truths about the Godman leads to an important reconsideration of Laredo's use of human physiology in the mystical stage of self-knowledge.

Conclusion: Annihilating the Mystical Body

Given Laredo's careful inclusion of all the introductory medical terminology concerning the human body into part 1 of the *Subida*, it is necessary to acknowledge that he does follow theological rather than medical thinking on some topics. For one, he maintains Aquinas's theory of hylemorphism (the soul provides the form for the body) over against the full intermixing of body and soul promoted by scientists such as Galen and Arnau de Villanova.[139] As a result, Laredo supports the scholastic rationale that the dead body decomposes into the earth, water, air, and fire that made it, clarifying that those elements will be purified by fire from their intermixed existence as 'elementation,' and that the resurrected body will be re-composed of the purified original elements at the end of time.[140] He therefore balances the more medically grounded portions of his work with arguments that fit into a theological system, although the connection between body and soul adduced by proponents of hylemorphism indicates that the body is never left out of the equation. In addition, some tension is reflected in the fact that Laredo uses, but does not properly define, the terms 'innate heat' and 'vital spirit' in conjunction with each other (see above). These deviations from medical specificity may have allowed him to avoid the troublesome conundrum that the theological world view located human powers and capacities in the soul or heart, while the medical view located them in the brain.[141]

These moments when Laredo subsumes his medical knowledge in order to privilege theology do not detract from the impact of sustained low-level and periodic high-level medical language throughout the *Subida*, however. As we will see in chapters 4 and 5, theological views are themselves bodily, since cognition was understood physiologically. I argue that Laredo peppers the *Subida* with medical terminology in order to demonstrate the intentions of natural philosophy: talking about human physiology is talking about created physiology. That is to say, to cite the body in the course of a spiritual treatise is always at once to reference the creator of the body, God; to speak of humans as dust while alive (and not dust only before life and after death) is to reference a reality that God set up. Grounding the first set of meditations in medical terminology enables the development of the reader's self-knowledge by concentrating on the body as muddy dungheap, yet this technique does not limit the reader to self-loathing. Rather, a focus on the medical body is the necessary filter to help readers achieve self-knowledge through awareness of the minute details that order physical life. Once body and creation have been properly parsed, believers can discern that God is to be found in the (medical) entrails of their embodied souls.

Laredo, engaged thoroughly in the world through his role as doctor and apothecary, could not simply dismiss the reality in which mystics find themselves. Rather than carping on the vanity of worldly goods and trying to disengage his readers from attention to existence in order to focus them on God, as did the *contemptus mundi* tradition, Laredo instead presents reality not just in the broad strokes of the difficulties of pain and strife but also in the details of corporeal composition. Laredo directs his readers to look at their own bodies – to be aware of the fluids that course through them, the heat that sustains them, the flesh that results from the digestion of food. This is the body that the reader needs to recognize, the actual flesh and blood (and *rórida humidad*) that God has provided. It is a complex concept that Laredo is trying to convey – that the nothingness that is human medical reality needs always to be refracted back to God.

In the end, Laredo's discussion of mud, filth, and humors serves not so much to eliminate the body from mysticism as to make it the starting point for thinking about God.[142] It is not possible to proceed towards union with God without a comprehensive understanding of what it means to be fully and physiologically human. Given the orthodox two-nature Christology in place since the Council of Chalcedon, it is quite logical that human corporeality is a part of the ascent to God, not simply a vice-ridden interference. To understand the body on the basis of elements and humors is to understand the fluids and physiological processes that Christ once shared with humans. Likewise, for modern scholars, to understand the medieval or Renaissance body denied or celebrated in various mystical methods is to understand the body fragmented into its constituent elements and humors, not just a body wholly despised or wholly subverted. For Laredo, this deployment of scientific training in the pursuit of mystical self-knowledge does not end with the flesh and bones (and nerves and veins) of the body shared by humans and Christ. Human cognitive processes are equally pivotal to his method of prayer as human physiology. The fulcrum role of memory as at once the fifth ventricle of the human brain, involved in processing data from the five senses, and as the first of the three powers of the soul is the subject to which we turn in the next chapter. The specific topic of optics (a branch of physics related to medicine) as well as the cognitive value of physical pain in relation to an embodied epistemological process will be the subject of the final chapter.

4 Mnemotechnical Mysticism

Research in medieval epistemology has shown that Aquinas, followed by other scholastic theologians, 'insisted more completely than the Arabic commentators on the "embodiment" of all kinds of human knowledge,'[1] and reflected a familiarity with the scientific theory that mapped the five inner senses to brain ventricles. The intersection of the history of science with the study of medieval religion that produced the cognitive turn in medieval studies, however, has yet to yield any full-length treatments of mystical treatises[2] and has had no impact on studies of Spanish mysticism or devotional experience.[3] This absolute disciplinary divide must be rectified in order to fully engage Laredo's assumptions concerning the 'embodied soul.' The cognitive theories of Galen and Avicenna were known to the Castilian medical community through the texts collected in editions of the *Articella*, a popular textbook for physicians,[4] and familiar to the educated elite through the various Castilian editions of Bartholomeus Anglicus's encyclopedia, *De proprietatibus rerum* (On the Nature of Things), which described, among other scientific details, the brain ventricles as the basis for cognition.[5] The broad outlines of this theory were presented in the introduction; let us consider Laredo's own rendition of it in greater detail.

Laredo provides a version of the cell theory of the brain in his second pharmaceutical treatise, the *Modus faciendi.* Differing from commentaries on Avicenna but in line with both Joannitius and Anglicus, Laredo identifies three faculties of the mind and divides them into three locations, ignoring the typical description of double cells in the front and middle of the brain.

> In the front [ventricle] is the fantasy or *virtu imaginativa*, from which we take [information from] sight and the other senses. [W]hat it is that we

> imagine is decided in the middle ventricle, and we see whether it is good or bad and choose which we want, and this is the free will that causes us shame or merit depending on what we decide. Next is the operation of the posterior cell or ventricle, and there is the useful memory where is conserved or kept that which it is made responsible for. [I]n this fashion, that which comes to the [faculty of] thought or fantasy is imagined with the virtue of the front part of the brain and is decided with the part in the middle and is remembered another day or after many years in the posterior part or cell. *Item*, all the nerves begin in the brain ... which provide sensation to any part of the body, and principally the seven pairs of nerves that form the senses begin there, i.e., vision, hearing, taste, touch, and smell, and along with them the virtues, i.e., imaginative, digestive, and memorative [virtues], and these 'common senses' make up both the rational and the sensitive 'animal' (or animated) virtue.[6]

In contrast to Galen's perception, imagination, reason, and memory, Avicenna's common sense, sensory and cognitive imaginations, estimation, and memory, or Joannitius's imagination, cogitation/reason, and memory,[7] Laredo proposes the terminology of imagination, digestion, and memory.[8] By detailing the brain as the physiological root for the nerves carrying the information from all the senses, Laredo associates all sensory information with the brain even if he does not use the standard terminology of *sensus communis*. This follows in the tradition of theological popularizations of medical knowledge, such as Peter of Limoges's well-known medieval treatise of preaching exempla based on optical theory. (Limoges had used 'imagination' and 'common sense' as synonyms, indicating that for the purposes of the average educated preacher, the existence of one implied the other, whether or not they were understood to be separated into two different front ventricles.)[9]

It is noteworthy that Laredo chose to pass over the Avicennean cognitive imagination in the middle ventricle and concentrate instead on what Avicenna termed the estimative faculty, or judgment. In the first part of the quotation above, Laredo renames judgment as the *libre alvedrio*, or 'free will,' which enables us to 'determine whether what we imagine is good or bad and choose the one we want,' thus giving a physiological location for a theological debate.[10] This is particularly important for an author who would go on to formulate a mystical method, as it indicates that not only did Laredo assume the cognitive continuum between body and soul advocated by medical science, but in fact supposed that the brain ventricles housed elements such as the free will that some medieval theologians associated with soul alone. For that matter, in the second part of the quotation, he refers to judgment as 'digestion' – a figurative term drawn from a fully bodily process that other medical authors used as a simple and convenient metaphor.[11]

The one section of the brain that Laredo does not modify from any of these dominant models is the memory ventricle. Avicenna suggests that it is the 'desire to remember' (*recordatio*, Aristotle's 'reminiscence') that distinguishes humans from animals, because it leads to rational estimation and thence to reason.[12] In other words, for Laredo as for all Galenic physicians, memory is at once the end point of the physiological sequence for processing sensory data and also the spark that produces rational thought. Laredo's familiarity with the medieval cell theory of the brain, a theory shared by all sixteenth-century Spanish theologians and scientists until its repudiation by Francisco Suárez in 1621,[13] must be taken into account when considering his understanding of the soul and its three faculties. As an inner sense located in a brain ventricle but also a faculty of the soul, memory is the fulcrum connecting the physical body and the soul's highest levels. While scholars of mysticism have tended to concentrate their analyses on which faculty, the will or the understanding, is most appropriate for experiencing union with God, historians of ideas such as Mary Carruthers and Frances Yates offer a potent corrective to the imbalance produced by focusing on two of the three faculties. Since medieval theories of cognition identified the memory as the ventricle of the brain in which all information and higher-order concepts were stored as visual images of the original sensory input, memory devices known formally as mnemotechniques were not simply handy rubrics for monastic meditators. Rather, deployment of mnemonic devices activated the physiological sequence of perception and cognition in the devotee's brain in order for theological meditation or unitive experience to occur. It is my argument that Laredo, extensively trained in medical science but equally extensively an autodidact in the monastic writings that relied heavily on mnemotechnique, designed his treatise to activate the reader's memory. This critical fact enables a reinterpretation of the method of recollection mysticism as a technique that does not simplistically rely on a sequential body-negating ascent to abstract union with God.

One of the reasons historians of religion and historians of mysticism have consistently undervalued the role Laredo played in the development of Renaissance Castilian spirituality is because they have judged his treatise as unstructured and even meandering.[14] I propose instead that while Laredo's seeming disorganization is a problem for modern readers, it was not for his contemporaries. Our scholarly approach to books, starting at the beginning and reading through chapters in order to gain information, only to move on to another book after finishing the first, places conceptual limits on our ability to comprehend a text that was intended to induce a periodic mode of contemplation. Laredo's systematic use of the full range of medieval memory devices is best understood as a method for instigating creative appropriation of his method in ways that went beyond his text rather than as an obstacle that might cause the reader's attention to wander.[15] It is precisely the wandering – yet wandering with the building blocks supplied by effective memory devices – that allowed readers to move beyond Laredo's text into a continual contemplative mode that might lead to mystical union. (It is suggestive that a modern scholar deems *recogimiento*, withdrawal from the world, as an essential circumstance for proper concentration on the memory arts.)[16] Laredo's medieval understanding of cognitive processes, resulting from both his medical practice and his voracious reading of medieval spiritual treatises that deployed mnemonic devices, led him to prescribe a method of mystical prayer that does not seem well-structured to post-Enlightenment rational thinkers,[17] yet it is not to us that he is speaking. Instead, he was forming and releasing his readers' inventiveness within the cognitive constructs of their era in order to facilitate their search for a God who was always already at the core of their being.

My argument depends on the somatic nature of memory in medieval theory. Physicians believed specific combinations of humors or extra weight in certain parts of the body had a direct result on how effectively memory, a faculty of the soul, worked.[18] For example, memory as a part of the Galenic physiological body is more or less efficacious depending on the dryness or moisture of the person. According to Avicenna (drawing on Aristotle's *De memoria*), the humors affect the memory, as do the complexions. Dry complexions are better at remembering, while wet complexions are better at learning new things.[19] The physiological 'theory of localization,' or 'the idea that memory originates in a particular location of the brain,'[20] was based on many medical cases of memory loss sustained after a blow to the back of the head. Based on this principle, physicians (not to mention quacks) often prescribed salves and ointments to be applied to the exterior skull in order to stimulate memory.[21] Authors of mnemotechnical treatises likewise associated the memory with bodily functions; an early treatise of the genre by Quintilian claims, according to one modern scholar, that the memory was 'a stomach-like receptacle for the food and drink of the mind.'[22]

For that matter, the storage of images in the memory was not itself abstract or linguistic, as we might assume it today. Plato and Aristotle portrayed the memory ventricle receiving the image as though it were stamped much the way a seal moulds warm wax, a model subsequently deployed by Thomas Aquinas and other medieval theologians.[23] Similar theories describe images as inscribed on the memory like writing on a wax tablet; writing as 'incision' was a deeply physical act.[24] According to one scholar of early modern mnemotechnical treatises, 'The art of memory ... thrives in a borderland somewhere between physical and intellectual perception: it is intended to create bridges, modes of communication, and reciprocal translatability between body and psyche.'[25] I argue that in addition to displaying the medical body as key to self-knowledge, Laredo drew heavily on monastic mnemotechnique, recognizing its utility on the basis of an epistemology grounded in medieval cognitive theory. He does in fact make reference to the theory of the inner senses in his mystical treatise, not just in his pharmaceutical treatise. In the 1535 edition of the *Subida*, he mentions the classic example concerning the role of the estimative faculty in distinguishing a wolf from a dog as part of a disquisition on the role of imagination in which he cites Richard of Saint Victor.[26] This chapter thus explores the cognitive body that is a component of the medical body discussed in chapter 3.

The first two parts of Laredo's *Subida* are littered with mnemonic devices. For example, he follows the initial week of meditations on self-knowledge organized by the dust poem with a striking image or emblem intended to guide the second week. He explains that a gentlemen seeking to equip his horse for an important journey must pay attention to a variety of details, the sum of which are a useful mnemonic for keeping in mind the different types of virtues that are necessary in the pursuit of self-knowledge in the first stage of self-knowledge. A bridle includes reins, while a saddle comes with stirrups attached by leather straps, not to mention the saddlebags that hold food. Once the horse is set up, the rider adds spurs to his own costume. The simple job of getting ready for a canter through the country turns out to involve a complex web of devices.

In addition, putting the equipment on the horse involves a routine of attention to detail, very likely in the same sequence each time to make sure no piece of equipment is overlooked or untested. What order the rider chooses to attend to his kit, however, might well vary per person. For this reason – attention to detail in a sequence, but a flexible sequence – the equipment for riding a horse turns out to be a useful mnemonic device for organizing religious meditation.[27] Laredo maps his second week of meditation on self-knowledge to this emblem:

Monday	bridle	guarding the tongue
Tuesday	reins	infused love/charity (knotted together)
Wednesday	saddle	resting in prayer
Thursday	saddletrees	external and internal recollection
Friday	leather stirrup straps	obedience, charity (provide control)
Saturday	stirrups	patience and humility (steady the ride)
Sunday	spurs	filial love, fear (stimulus towards the goal)[28]

This chapter explores Laredo's use of memory devices as the internal structure for the first two mystical stages of his method. I analyse the emblem of the riding equipment found in part 1 of the *Subida* to ascertain what elements of mnemotechnique provided Laredo with the most theological and mystical utility, then apply that model in order to dissect the two mnemonic devices found in the portions of part 2 that bookend the Passion meditation. These two mnemonic devices, a bejewelled castle surrounding a field of candles and a complex fountain metaphor, prove central to developing both theological sophistication and mystical cognition in the course of recollected union. In the following chapter, I will show that the violence inherent in the Passion will render it the most powerful mnemonic image available to Laredo in his context of Passion-centred Renaissance Castilian devotion.

Ultimately, it will become clear why Laredo's mnemonic image of riding equipment during stage one of his tripartite way includes one element, Wednesday's mystical saddle, that symbolizes *recogimiento*, even though scholars usually assume *recogimiento* is the purview of the unitive stage alone. The recollected saddle indicates that the goal of the ascent is always already present, reflecting Laredo's theological belief that the God with whom the mystic will unite is found at the centre of the soul, in its entrails, not infinitely distant across a mystical abyss.

Mnemotechnique as 'Locational Memory'[29]

It is a false cognate to equate the medieval monastic *memoria* with what we today term 'memorization,' a rote practice that stores facts in order to reproduce them accurately at a later date.[30] Rather, as Carruthers has persuasively argued, memory was the faculty underlying creative thinking, for it is only with a memory full of information and ideas from others that one can begin cogitating; classical and medieval authors understood original thinking to be the result of associating known ideas and facts with other known ideas or facts in novel ways. The attention that medieval thinkers gave to the art of *memoria* led them to develop techniques for improving the retentive memory in order to improve the quality of their thinking. This *mnemotecnica*, famously articulated in (Pseudo) Cicero's *Rhetorica ad Herennium*,[31] thereafter affected medical, theological, and monastic assumptions about cognition.[32]

The most famous of these mnemonic devices, first discussed in detail by Frances A. Yates in her well-known *Art of Memory*, is the memory room. A person interested in memorizing a speech or sermon imagines a building (a church, monastery, or castle, for example) with many rooms. Each line or idea of the sermon is associated with some object that evokes it, and each object occupies a place in a specific room. In order to recall the speech in sequence, the author progresses mentally through the building, looking at each object in order. Carruthers, in her seminal *Craft of Thought*, terms this technique 'locational memory,'[33] suggesting that 'place is required for the mental task of recollection,'[34] and that a 'locational structure' is the basis for 'inventive thinking.'[35] In this view, thinking is never abstracted from place or space; the location creates the *possibility* for thought. Carruthers claims even more strongly that 'memory-places are not significant as "ideas" themselves, but as the forms or moulds upon which, out of other pieces of memory, ideas are constructed.'[36] These 'other pieces of memory' were of course believed to be incised on the memory like words on a wax tablet, so that the memory place is the 'mould' for constructing ideas on the basis of somatically retained memories.

As Carruthers points out in a corrective to Yates, it is important to remember that this mnemotechnique actually incorporates a great deal of flexibility.[37] To tailor a speech or sermon to a different audience, the author need only walk through the rooms in a different order and the elements of the sermon end up recombined. (In other words, the mind is furnished with knowledge, but the impact of the interior decoration depends on the tour guide's route.)[38] This idea of moving through and experiencing a story, while most obvious in narrative images, is also applicable to single images, metaphors, emblems, or other static symbols; the most important element of this flexibility is the flow of movement – the eye moving from element to element – around an image, be it a furnished palace, an emblem, a map, or some other image. Termed *ductus*, this movement is 'the way that a composition guides a person to its various goals.'[39] Memory technique does not simply involve imagining a static place or a picture but instead relies on the movement of the eye as it examines different parts of the emblem, or even on imagined movement through physical space as the speaker walks through an architectural structure. 'Composition begins with clearly and deliberately locating oneself in a place, which may be an actual location but is most importantly conceived as a mental position, both a habitation for the mind and a direction.'[40] Some mnemonic devices even included elements known as *imagines agentes* (active agents) – individuals imagined within the device who moved around, guiding the thinker through it.[41]

Not all mnemonic devices were purely visual, at least not in the modern sense of the term. In contrast to the frequent assertion that allegory differs from mnemotechnique because it induces readers to determine the author's meaning rather than create their own,[42] Carruthers posits that many apparently literary devices, including metaphor, punning, rhyming, and irony, were intended to be memorable for their cleverness, while also producing creative new ideas by enticing the reader to further the punning joke or add yet more symbolic levels to the metaphor. The associative play or allegory produced by an author would never be useful to the reader's progress unless it was personalized and connected to his or her own 'associational web.'[43] In addition to using these literary forms of associative wordplay, monastic emphasis on memorization of Scripture promulgated reading and reflecting through following 'hooks' given in the text, that is, associative play on common words (or words that sound alike) found in various different texts of the Bible.[44] Although these types of literary memory devices seem to be purely verbal, according to medieval theories of cognition they were not stored in the memory as linguistic units but instead as (incised) pictures of words on a page or on a wax tablet.[45] Carruthers's insight points to the necessity of reading Laredo, an autodidact thoroughly familiar with medieval monastic treatises, for the mnemonic impact of the many word pictures and allegories he utilizes.

An often-overlooked shift occurred in the intent of mnemotechnique in the late Middle Ages from its origins as an aid to rhetoricians to remember their orations (Cicero, Quintilian),[46] and its use by monks in the early and high medieval periods as a practice for forming the self.[47] Mnemotechnical treatises, formerly written by rhetoricians, were attached to preaching manuals in the late Middle Ages; at this point, mnemonic devices were developed to enable the audience, not the preacher, to remember the sermon. This shift is demonstrated in the first known treatise on mnemonics to appear on the peninsula, the *Ars praedicandi* (Art of Preaching, late fourteenth century) of Francesc Eiximenis, which focused on the utility of mnemonics for the congregation.[48] Likewise, a Latin treatise produced in Laredo's own era, an *Arte predicandi* followed by an *Arte memorandi* (Art of Memory) at the end of Pedro Sánchez Ciruelo's *Expositio libri missalis* (Exposition of the Missal, 1528), emphasizes that too many parts and sections in a sermon makes it difficult for any but the most learned in the audience to follow, so that moral instruction for an unlearned audience should come at the very end of the sermon, since that is the moment when the 'rude populace' begins to pay attention.[49]

The progression of mnemotechnique from an oratorical trick to a didactic method recast it as an effective tool for one of the first prescriptive guides to *recogimiento*, as we shall see below, yet scholars have not previously assessed the impact of mnemonic devices as an element of mystical prayer intended to achieve the capacity for mystical union. While Carruthers's seminal scholarship is bounded by the chronological time limits typically assigned to the Middle Ages, treatises teaching mnemotechnical practice achieved fresh popularity towards the end of the fifteenth century and therefore influenced the education of Castilian religious authors publishing the first wave of vernacular spiritual treatises from the 1480s on.[50] Most scholars who study mnemotechnical usage in Iberia begin with the thirteenth-century Catalan Ramon Llull's innovative usage of mnemonics to discover parallels between the three monotheistic religions,[51] then jump to Ignatius of Loyola's deployment of mnemotechnique in the 'composition of place' in his *Ejercicios espirituales* (Spiritual Exercises, 1535).[52] Ignatius proposes that meditation is most effective when the different senses are taken one by one:

> The first prelude is the composition, which is here to see with the sight of the imagination the length, breadth, and depth of Hell ... The first Point will be to see with the sight of the imagination the great fires, and the souls as in bodies of fire ... The second, to hear with the ears wailings, howlings, cries, blasphemies against Christ our Lord and against all His Saints ... The third, to smell with the smell smoke, sulphur, dregs and putrid things ... The fourth, to taste with the taste bitter things, like tears, sadness, and the worm of conscience ... The fifth, to touch with the touch; that is to say, how the fires touch and burn the souls.[53]

Ignatius's meditation on hell incorporates the physical senses in order to construct a sense of place in which the memory can wander, yet note in the quotation that only some of the senses are affected physiologically: hearing and smell are described with elements that normally impact the auditory and olfactory senses, but the other senses are addressed metaphorically. Traditionally, the history of Iberian mnemotechnique then skips a half-century from Ignatius's 1535 work to the vernacular memory treatises written to catechize the Nahuatl in the New World,[54] and to the effect of mnemonic devices, especially emblems, on Teresa of Avila's image of the 'interior castle' and John of the Cross's sketch of Monte Carmelo.[55] I suggest that Bernardino de Laredo's *Subida* represents a key stage in this history, not only as a primary source for both Teresa and John but because his reliance on the full range of mnemonic devices, both images and words, makes him a fulcrum for the impact of medieval monastic mnemonics on the Golden Age.[56]

Various clues confirm that mnemotechnique was known and practised on the peninsula during Laredo's primary writing years, the 1520s and 1530s. Juan Luis Vives (1492–1540), a famous Spanish humanist, indicated familiarity with mnemotechnique, even proposing that proper care for the body was essential to a fully functioning memory.[57] In addition, the Latin genre of emblem treatises, originating in the Italian and Northern Renaissance and focusing on a specific type of mnemonic device, became popular in Spain as well;[58] widespread use of emblems in Castile has been linked to the influence of medieval vice and virtue treatises on the new vernacular works of the early sixteenth century, as well as to the bestiaries used by encyclopedists and theologians alike.[59] Nor was mnemotechnique unfamiliar to physicians of Laredo's era, for Juan de Aguilera, a Salamancan doctor and astronomer, wrote an *Ars memorativa* intended to aid practising physicians (and philosophers) in 1536.[60]

The premier scholar of Castilian emblems and memory arts, Fernando R. de la Flor, suggests that the interest in *ars memorativa* was entirely contemporary with the Spanish Franciscan reform.[61] Interest in mnemotechnical devices among Laredo's Franciscan contemporaries is certainly apparent, given Francisco de Osuna's choice of the 'spiritual alphabet' as the organizing principle for all his *recogimiento* treatises.[62] Osuna's role as a teacher in *casas de recollectos* such as La Salceda led him to organize his method in an easily memorable format. Flor also mentions that the *retablos* (altarpieces) that grew ever grander during the Renaissance were themselves a form of memory art.[63] In fact, he suggests that the core practices of Christian devotional life in this period, such as the stations of the cross or praying before images and altars, match Quintilian's emphasis on movement, visuality, and repetition.[64] One could easily add to this list the multiple masses for the dead, pilgrimages,[65] and praying the rosary, not to mention the *Semana Santa* penitential processions, with their bright costumes imprinted with emblems and their stately marching throughout the city in standardized routes that turned the city itself into a memory device.[66]

Laredo, however, was likely most familiar with classical mnemotechnique through his voracious reading of medieval spiritual texts, including those by Richard of Saint Victor.[67] In part 3 of the 1535 *Subida* edition, Laredo draws extensively on Richard's *Twelve Patriarchs*, an elaborate allegorical device associating the numerous children of Rachel and Leah with the multiple spiritual talents needed to achieve mystical union, and on Richard's *Mystical Ark*, in which the ark of the tabernacle functions as an architectural mnemonic device. Although Laredo radically revised part 3 in the 1538 version of the *Subida*, adding sources from the high medieval negative theology tradition that many scholars take to be a rejection of the Victorine model, he did not eliminate the mnemonic devices from the stages of self-knowledge or Passion spirituality (nor his references to Richard in the stage on recollection).[68] Laredo's continuing dependence on mnemotechnique, regardless of apparent changes in the mystical union because of revisions to part 3 of the *Subida*, proves that the monastic usage of mnemonic devices that Carruthers explores as central to the medieval mindset was equally central to this Spanish Renaissance mystical method. This fact is not only critical to an assessment of *recogimiento* treatises, but in view of Laredo's mnemotechnical dependence also indicates the problematic nature of the scholarly tendency to divorce Renaissance Castilian spirituality from the broader panorama of European cultural and religious trends.

Laredo's Mnemotechnics

According to Carruthers's expanded definition of mnemotechnique to include both visual images and associative wordplay, the first two stages of the *Subida* are replete with mnemotechnical devices ('comparison ... figure, or example'),[69] and it is the accumulation of such devices that suggests that the horse with its riding equipment is more than just a literary emblem or ornament. Several brief yet striking examples occur periodically:

1. In one of the meditations on the riding equipment, Laredo details the utility he finds in an image of a cross seven lengths long (one length for each day of meditation). At the end of each arm of the cross is etched a triangle, with a letter marked at each point of each triangle.

He suggests composing a phrase for meditation in which every word begins with that letter of the alphabet.[70]

2. Laredo repeatedly structures his work through lists. In addition to the various weeks of meditation, Laredo defines recollection itself as the final three of seventeen stages (steps on a ladder) towards union with God,[71] and often designates the number six to subdivide portions of any topics that do not have a location in the overall weekly scheme.[72]
3. The *Subida* is also filled with brief metaphorical topoi, often drawn from artisanal production of pottery (indicating a connection with and knowledge of local crafts, perhaps owing to an interest in storing pharmaceuticals) or from military metaphors that periodically extend the scenario initiated in part 1 by the image of the gentleman rider with his riding equipment.[73] These metaphors could be read as parables, yet equally well as mnemonic storytelling devices to appeal to a lay audience.[74]

The variety of mnemonic devices that Laredo considers useful clarifies the previously overlooked fact that the stage of self-knowledge is structured around the mnemonic devices of the dust poem and the emblem of the riding equipment. In turn, the stage of Passion spirituality draws its form and content from three primary mnemonic devices. Throughout the first twelve chapters of part 2 (on the Nativity), Laredo uses an aquatic metaphor of a fountain that becomes three rivers while emptying into a single sea, to which he returns after the extended Passion meditation (itself a mnemonic device) but with variants involving ships and oceans: half of stage 2 is organized based on aquatic or nautical images.[75] In addition, in an extensive section towards the end of part 2, Laredo recommends visualizing a castle with jewelled walls and multiple towers whose walls encircle a field full of candles of varying heights. The candles represent various aspects of doctrine about Christ, human nature, angels, the virtues, the apostles, the New Testament, and so on.[76]

The presence of such memory devices in parts 1 and 2 of the *Subida* is not simply a compositional fact. Carruthers clarifies the result of mnemotechnique:

> Thus one 'sees' one's reading, and one 'walks' through it, not just to store it away conveniently and safely, in order to be able to reconstruct it as it was, but also in order to meditate on it, digest it, and interpret it, and make it fully useful, ethically and compositionally. A reader is constantly in motion, all senses continually in play, slowing down and speeding up.[77]

Laredo's images are well adapted for the necessary visual and playful aspects of effective mnemonic devices. Whether etching letters on a cross, following a military canter, moving as a river flows, or viewing the walls of the celestial castle, the reader is intimately involved in the production and construction of his or her daily meditation.[78] It is my argument that both the first and second stages of Laredo's mystical method are dependent on mnemotechinque not as a device for remembering a method but as a way to create a cognitive sequence leading towards mystical union. A closer look at the specific device of the riding equipment that structures Part One's second week of meditation will help determine the various ways mnemotechnique advances the goal of Laredo's mystical method and discovers God at the locational centre of the human, the entrails.

The device of the riding kit allows Laredo to interweave several disparate topics that medieval authors typically had separated into different genres, such as treatises of virtue and vice on the one hand and treatises on contemplation on the other. As described earlier, Laredo's mnemonic device of riding equipment for the ascent of the mount of contemplation includes the following tools: Monday's bridle represents five ways to guard the tongue from speaking badly of others, and Tuesday's reins are love and charity knotted together. Wednesday's 'mystical saddle' signifies resting in prayer, and attached to it are Thursday's double layer of saddlebags that signify the internal and external forms of recollected prayer. Friday's straps for the stirrups are obedience and charity, Saturday's stirrups are patience and humility, and finally, Sunday's spurs are the twin attitudes towards God of filial fear and love.[79] This list of the 'virtues' needed to attain self-knowledge in the first stage leading towards mystical union thus contains a surprising conjunction of the medieval list of seven virtues (as well as ways to avoid a few of the seven vices) with ideas core to the Franciscan reform movement in Castile. In the wake of the 1215 Lateran Council's interest in local reform, a number of authors had issued treatises enumerating vices, including general categories of vice, the seven deadly sins, and the five sins of the tongue, as well as virtues, including the theological virtues, cardinal virtues, and the beatitudes.[80] While the tenor of these books reflects a concern for the prevalence of vice and the fundamentally sinful nature of humans, the authors also adduce the possibility of developing virtue by hard work and great spiritual care – thus they tend to be somewhat optimistic about spiritual development over a lifetime. Such an approach sharply contrasts with the need to annihilate the self in order to transcend the self and reach mystical union with God, as per Laredo's stage of self-knowledge. This contrast may explain why Laredo integrates elements from other sets of virtues into the mnemonic device. Some of the 'virtues' included were those promoted by Franciscans (with renewed emphasis by the Villacrecian Observant movement), such as obedience and humility,[81] or were specific to the concerns of recollection mysticism, especially Wednesday's incorporation of *recogimiento*, the goal, into the beginning stage of the overall technique, as we will see later.[82]

Laredo could have accomplished the goal of uniting the genres of vice and virtue treatises with meditative or contemplative treatises simply by assigning seven topics for seven days of meditation, but he elected instead to organize them around a visual image. I suggest that this choice was deliberate, because it is the image itself that allows him to prove certain points about the seven topics at hand that otherwise might have been difficult to convey. Analysis of the riding kit reveals how a visual image is useful as a cognitive tool. For one, mental visualization of the different pieces of the image leads to the likelihood of the image itself being in movement, setting the stage for the possibility that one specific memory device will interconnect with other devices, just as the details within the one visual image are connected. Second, the interconnections between the visual elements allow aspects of meditation on any one element to provide vocabulary and theology for any other meditation physically attached to it; thus visuality activates transference of ideas. Finally, the image itself can at once hierarchize elements of a list by representing some as large or central, yet subvert the hierarchy by overlapping two visual elements onto the same space or by emphasizing the physical connections between the peripheral, and therefore apparently minor, elements with the centre.

Laredo's mnemonic device in the second week of meditation on self-knowledge is not meant merely to ensure accurate remembrance of seven topics but also to organize and inflect the mode of understanding of those seven themes. Likewise, the fact that the chosen mnemonic device is based on an aid to travel – there is no point in saddling up a horse only to stay in one place – means that Laredo's presentation of traditional and recollected virtues has energy, a sense of movement towards a goal outside itself, up the mount of contemplation. Although the riding equipment seems to freeze disparate topics in permanent relation to each other once it is mapped onto the horse's body, as a collectivity the pieces of the kit sweep the reader along. The flow of the mind's eye around the mnemonic image is extended by the image itself cantering on a journey, expanding the potential of the mnemonic device for recollective practice by making it mobile. Laredo highlights this point by means of another wordplay, noting that in contrast to the restful saddle, the term for stirrup straps is *acciones*, a term that he equates with constant action.[83] Such movement implies an engagement not only with the spatiality of the mnemonic device itself but also with the space through which the device moves.

Most importantly, the physical connections between the pieces of riding equipment force a certain kind of movement, or *ductus*, between the elements of the mental image that in turn creates visual interconnections between certain virtues that might not occur naturally to the meditator in the abstract. For example, since two reins are always knotted together, Laredo provides an extended reflection in Tuesday's meditation on why love and infused charity are connected in God, and thus must be connected in the soul ascending to that God. Later in the text, Laredo relies on the fact that the reins connect across several of the other days' riding equipment, and therefore he can return comfortably to the subject of love and charity during meditations on other virtues.

> And this love with which the living God wants to love himself, because it is the cause of his goodness – the soul feels [this love] in quiet contemplation. [Contemplation] is the charity of God in God, and the effect of wanting to love God is feeling that [such love] is love of God in God. And, thus, such a soul says that the beloved and the love and the lover in God are one pure thing, not more [than one] ... And the charity that knows itself and demands itself in men is not God's ... [but rather,] God infuses [this charity] in [their] hearts by his great benign nature, so that he ignites them with it. Because living fire is lit, and because from this spark – or let it be called inflammation – such living cinders jump out that they set fire where they fall, and if they fall on a naked one, the fire distilled from it is felt in the heart. And thus God wants to dress the soul as He does Himself, because He knots in the soul itself the knot of the two reins, so that he who possesses love already has charity, nor will charity be had without this same love, since they are one thing, knotted with only one knot, and together in one rein which guides without being able to fail.[84]

The very physicality of the image, which might seem to impose constraints on the reflection, actually provides avenues for creativity. Not only do the reins connect different riding tools and therefore different virtues, but the specific ideas in the meditation can also be revisited on different days. In a discussion of human (rather than infused) charity during Friday's stirrup straps of obedience and charity, Laredo reiterates Tuesday's analogy of living cinders (human charity is catching fire with love for others).[85] Ultimately, the meditations are connected through the emblem not only because they attach to the saddle but also topically through the analogy of 'living fire.' As well as linking major topics the image also enables the results of one day's meditation to influence the theological framework for another day's topic. These mnemonic interconnections serve another purpose as well: the quotation above has many parallels with the disputed *alumbrado* phrasing that 'God's love in man is God.' Laredo's repetition of the language of fire in more than one meditation serves the useful function of 'reining in' potentially heretical Illuminist language from Tuesday by connecting it to the cardinal virtues of love and charity on Friday.

In addition to making use of the interconnections between separate elements implicit in the physical particulars of riding equipment, Laredo relies on the size and function of the different elements to unite the medieval list of Christian virtues and the technique of recollection mysticism, thus rooting recollection mysticism in the standard practices of the church. At first, the emphasis of the second week seems to be on the avoidance of vice and the pursuit of virtue, since the meditations are bookended by 'avoiding the sins of the tongue' on Monday and by the virtues patience, humility, obedience, and charity later in the week. However, the details of the equine image allow Laredo to place the spotlight on recollected prayer instead of the virtues, using the largest and most striking piece of any riding kit, the saddle. Wednesday's meditation on the mystical saddle and its directions for 'repose in prayer' not only fall in the middle of the sequence of daily meditation, but are visually vital to the mnemotechnical image.[86]

The mystical saddle is front and centre in the image while also providing various key functions for the journey up the mount of contemplation, such as being the resting place for the seeking soul. With a mnemonic pun, Laredo indicates that the mystical saddle is for placing yourself/sitting (*assentar/sentar*), or for sitting/resting (*estar posado/reposado*).[87] He returns to the wordplay in the same chapter to articulate the role of memory in contemplation, critiquing the diabolically inspired tendency to jump 'magpie-like' from thought to thought, since such prayer means that the devotees are sitting without an effective seat or achieving repose.[88] They ought instead use the faculty of the memory to find a way to stop and settle down, the faculty of the understanding to order the brain to halt, and the faculty of the will to quiet the self. In addition, in contrast to the repose offered by Wednesday's saddle at the centre of the image, the other days' Christian virtues are associated with the elements of the image that guide the horse that is taking the soul on its journey: the reins of love and charity give direction, the stirrups of obedience and charity give balance, and the bridle on the sins of the tongue gives control. Thus, while the image of the riding equipment initially seems simply to be a handy mnemonic for organizing a week of meditation on each of the separate elements required to make the mystical ascent of the soul, the fact that all these separate topics are envisioned in relation to one image provides a totalizing context that at once unites them in one physical object and makes the interplay between them the critical balance to the journey.

Laredo clarifies the centrality of Wednesday's mystical saddle of recollection by using the next meditation to connect recollection mysticism to medieval Christian, especially Franciscan, virtues. On Thursday, he equates exterior and interior recollection with the outer and inner saddlebags. The exterior practice may reflect the typical ritual of daily Christian life and the vocal prayer of Villacrecian Franciscan practice,[89] though it could equally well be the performance of Christian virtue since he names poverty, self-contempt, charity, and humility specifically.[90] Describing the exterior saddlebag as covering the interior, richly decorated saddlebag of recollected private prayer, protecting it from dust,[91] Laredo argues for a hierarchy of recollection over virtue. Yet he makes sure to indicate that the image of the double saddlebags is accurate, because the exterior and interior practices are physically layered onto the same location. After using the outer saddlebag, the rider 'turns to the saddle and takes the decorated saddlebag … [and] finds himself where he was before, without having to search further.'[92] Thus external virtuous practice and internal mystical recollection are not sequential, but overlay each other in such a way that close proximity somehow becomes mutuality or equivalence. Not only does this approach reflect Laredo's Villacrecian roots in increased emphasis on both external ritual and private prayer, it also indicates that the goal of his mystical method, recollection, never exists without external practices nor is it only available to those who reach the third stage of the mystical technique.

Once we interpret the riding equipment as a mnemonic device providing the critical crossovers and fluidity meant to aid readers in creative appropriation of the daily meditations, the functionality Laredo assigns to the device becomes a call for us to explore the ways Laredo's other mnemonic suggestions place parameters on (or extend the possibilities of) the meditations for mystical ascent. For example, the dust poem that structured the first week of meditations in part 1 is evidently a memory device, one that Laredo himself extends by overlapping biblical phrases such as 'dust to dust' with the medical view of the human body as primarily composed of the element earth. Indeed, as we saw in chapter 3, his discussion of *limo* is related to creating a 'foundation' for the journey to God, an architectural image reminiscent of mnemotechnique.[93] By structuring the stage on self-knowledge using two mnemonic devices, a poem and an emblem, Laredo implicitly makes the point that effective meditation depends on effective deployment of the faculty of memory. Inserting this argument in the midst of a stage meant to enable self-knowledge in order to transcend the self, the consequence is that memory, like the medical body, is the core of the human that paradoxically needs to be deployed in order to be surpassed.

Yet full supersession never takes place. Although most scholars assume the body disappears during the third stage of recollection, such an assumption depends on ignoring the cognitive relevance of the memory faculty as a physiological location for any mystical technique that deploys the will or the understanding in the pursuit of union with God. Laredo's medical understanding of cognition led him to incorporate mnemonic devices in the pursuit of recollection union, as analysis of the memory devices present throughout stage two – water metaphors, and a castle surrounding a meadow filled with candles – will prove. An examination of the more typical trope, the castle, followed by discussion of the innovative yet paradoxical water metaphors highlights the significance of movement in space for the locational memory that Laredo is activating in his readers. I propose that Laredo had a theological purpose underlying his structural use of mnemotechnique: the two devices analysed in the next section both define the God found at the centre of the soul and define humans as the (cognitive) *imago Dei.*

Constructing Doctrine

As we have seen, partitioning a week of meditation by associating each day with a different element of a mnemotechnical image enables Laredo to emphasize interconnections between virtues, which would otherwise seem to be valued hierarchically in a progression from one to seven. Towards the end of part 2 of the *Subida*, Laredo introduces a type of medieval memory device popular from the thirteenth century on with authors of vernacular *ars memorativa*, based on buildings with which a literate laity might be most familiar.[94] Laredo describes a walled, bejewelled fortress with twelve towers,[95] a typical architectural mnemonic device found in authorities such as Gregory the Great and both Hugh and Richard of Saint Victor,[96] but provides an original twist by extending the architectural trope to include a field of candles bounded by the walls of the city. (Notably, Laredo had begun describing health versus illness in his *Modus faciendi* with a comparison of a human life to a burning candle that eventually dies out.)[97] In addition to using a single visual image with enough elements to connect numerous disparate points (the towers and their decorations all have separate significations, yet are interconnected), Laredo also maps disparate theological ideas onto the single fundamental image of the candle. Drawing attention to the size and number of candles, as well as to the different materials that make up a candle (wax, wick, and so on), he deploys the memory device to reflect theologically on a range of subjects from angelology to Mariology to anthropology. By hinging diverse theological topics on one image, Laredo schematizes the essential unity of all theology in a monotheistic system.

Not only does this architectural trope reveal aspects of Laredo's theological orientation,[98] it also serves to problematize an assumption implicit in Carruthers's understanding of visual images as mnemonic devices. Although Carruthers acknowledges the multiple levels of potential meaning within one word (in puns or ekphrasis, for example) as a form of memory wordplay, she does not analyse the multiple potential meanings within one visual memory aid. As previously noted, her extension of Yates's description of the memory palace brought to medievalists' attention the flexibility inherent in walking different routes through one palace. However, Carruthers continues to assume that each object in the memory palace or building corresponds to one specific idea, such that each sign has a single significance and that creativity only results from forming different patterns of signs.[99] However, Laredo's most stereotypical memory device, a walled city, presents a version of a device in which the sign–signifier relation is itself flexible, for I argue that each sign can be read and reread on multiple levels in what might be considered a form of visual wordplay. Laredo's extension of medieval mnemotechnique will prove critical not only to understanding the technique of recollection mysticism but also to tracing the development and extension of medieval forms of thought as they inform early modern theology, for Laredo's mnemonic device is intended to reveal God at work in the soul.

Laredo suggests imagining the self in the middle of a field whose boundaries are marked off in a remarkable manner. Over the course of several chapters, he maps out the city of God (the heavenly city, or Jerusalem) as a gemstone setting surrounding a central field of candles.[100] Relying on the tradition that Revelation 21 was a visual rendition of the city of God, as discussed in Gregory's *Homiliae in Ezechielem* (Homilies on Ezekiel), for example,[101] Laredo describes a field enclosed by a square crystal wall. In each corner, there are three towers made of precious jewels and hung with four golden shields. In the middle of the field (next to the meditating soul, one assumes) is a single paschal candle made of the purest wax and a perfect wick, glowing with a flame that never flickers, whose light reflects in the gems on the wall.[102] No other medieval or Renaissance religious author associates the candle image with an architectural structure in the production of a mnemonic device, as far as I am aware. Laredo identifies this single lit candle as Christ, though notably the Christ of the Trinity, not Christ in his humanity.

> [T]he wax is the most holy body of Christ; the wick, his most felicitous soul, and from his perfectly lit light you can ... raise your understanding to the holy Trinity as a single, most pure substance. In this way the paternal Person is contemplated in the essence of the light, and let the soul raise [itself] up to the Son by the glow, and you can lift your spirit to the Holy Spirit by the light's clarity.[103]

The image of the Trinity as wax, wick, and candle was common in the late Middle Ages, deployed, for example, by Langland in the key English medieval text *Piers Plowman*, yet here Laredo applies the image to Christ specifically.[104] Since candles were often mentioned as an analogy in scientific discussions of optics,[105] it may be that Laredo was familiar with the candle as a typical mnemonic device rather than with its specific theological use.

Although the candle itself does not seem to have any structural affinity with the walled city, Laredo quickly modulates the mnemonic to define the light from the candle flame as the Trinity, a light so bright that it is reflected in the crystal walls of the city, the gems on the wall, and even off the gold of the shields. The light passes through and 'reverberates' from one glowing aspect of ornamentation to the next, yet this process in no way diminishes the original light source.[106]

> Let us consider the lit candle, whose purity, perfection, and greatness give off from itself such great light and clarity that it [the light] wants to pass through the wall and to lance itself into the crystal [wall] ... The most alive resplendence, which is already both within and without each of the precious stones, moves reciprocally and passes into the animated crystal, and the clarity of the crystal reverberates in each of the stones; and the stones and the crystal throw their reverberations to the shields ... and the gold on the stones and crystal receives radiant resplendence and they do not even for a moment cease to reciprocate, that is to say, to pass and turn to pass again this same resplendence amongst themselves.[107]

Laredo then equates the decorative aspects of the building with various details of religious significance (the crystal wall = virginity; various gems = the beatified; twelve towers = the twelve apostles; four shields = the four evangelists; many gold shields = the many merits of the church). He relies on the notion of the reverberating light to indicate that the merits of the church are communicated or passed between the blessed and the saints.[108] The sense of *ductus*, or movement around the image, previously provided by the sightline along the reins that pulled the mind's eye around the equine emblem, is here produced by the translucently reverberating reflection of the Trinitarian flame as it burns forever on the candlewick of Christ. Thus the space of the architectural image is literally illuminated by God, since it is the light from the Trinity that allows the devotee to note the different physical details of the building. Laredo's deployment of locational memory is therefore not about remembering the elements of a meditation in a specific order, but rather sets the devotee's mind in the proper mode to be guided by God through a doctrinal sequence.

In later chapters, Laredo continues to provide information about the construction of the walled city, with specific attention to the largest of the twelve towers that is closest to the candle. In a square city inset with twelve towers no one tower should be closest to the centre, but Carruthers emphasizes that architectural mnemonic devices rarely map out accurately, as a mental three-dimensional image can be shifted and recombined in a way that a two-dimensional schema cannot be.[109] Laredo renders the tallest tower more fully than the others: its gates are made of sapphire and emerald (one provides hope and the other cures illnesses, an interesting conflation of spiritual and medical concerns).[110] The tall tower's jewelled gate is identified as the Virgin Mary, an unremarkable play on the typical medieval trope of Mary as the gate to God.[111] Yet not only is the gate Mary, but so is the entire tower, following the many one-line litanies popular from the eighth century onwards that call Mary a 'tower of refuge.'[112] Laredo refers to the tallest tower as the 'spouse of the Son of God'[113] and more fully: 'this tower of Zion, this homage to God, our fortress, my very great Lady, our universal queen of all that is not God, is the principal tower of the sovereign city.'[114]

The components of the building do not simply exist to remind the reader of the topic of Mariology; the quality of the construction of the building is itself a detail in the mnemonic device meant to stimulate reflection on Mary's ideal nature in comparison to all other humans.[115] Specifically, Mary as tower is made from the finest of jewels, those that most effectively reflect light from the candle of Christ.

> The more precious and clear the jewel and the closer to the candle it is, the more it glows brightly and the more it reverberates with much greater clarity than all the others ... And the glory and all the clarity that she has, all her reverberations and all her resplendence, she takes from the candle from which all get [those things].[116]

The excitement of this meditation lies in the dynamic tension produced by the light reverberating incessantly between the virginal bejewelled tower and the pure Jesus wick. Identifying Mary with the tallest tower allows Laredo to bring in a new theological subject, but the most significant element is provided by the *ductus* of moving light that indicates the essential relationship of Mariology to Christology. As was seen in chapter 1, Mary and Christ were equal partners in the Renaissance Castilian devotional engagement with the events of Holy Week. Although Mary's role in this architectural image does not associate her with violence as in the 'passion of two' tradition, it does prove that Christology and Mariology went hand in hand in all theological arenas, not just the tortured ones.

In the following chapters, Laredo persists in using the multiple levels of his mnemonic device to emphasize the implicit unity of all theological subjects, continually modulating the candle image as the key mnemonic object in sequential meditations. He imagines placing four progressively shorter pairs of candles on each side of the single candle, then duplicates this set of nine candles endlessly until the entire field is full, making the point that the original candle loses none of its light in comparison, just as God's greatness is not diminished by the nine hierarchies of angels.[117] Among the nine ranks of candles, there prove to be yet more candles dotted about the meadow, representing the saved or beatified in heaven.[118] Finally, he contrasts the purity of these candles with candles made of poor quality wax and a wick dipped in vinegar and salt, an evocative image for 'miserable souls, who are cold, bitter, and dried out in mortal sin,'[119] that is to say, made bitter in vinegar and dried out with salt.[120] This image of nine candles, or even multiple ranks of nine, may have been meant to remind his reader of the mass cycles common in sixteenth-century Spain, the so-called superstitious masses that comprised a sequence of masses recited to the Trinity, Christ, Mary, the beatified, and specific saints, accompanied at each point with a predetermined number of candles.[121] It is also worth noting that in the late Middle Ages in Seville, the Purification of Mary feast was known as the *candelaria*, and thus there might have been an implicit Marian association with any image based on ranks of candles.[122] In the *Subida*, Laredo draws on these ritualistic aspects of Catholic devotion practices for theological purposes, for he equates the different aspects of the field of candles with a variety of theological topics, such as the question of angelic nature and capacity to respond to God, the nature of the blessed and how they overcome sin to enter into heaven and be of similar composition to the angels, and the nature of sinful humans who must become self-aware in order to overcome their degradation.[123] These various analogies of candlelight and waxy composition reveal new insight into the body–soul complex that is always a key element of Christian theology because of the incarnation of the divine.

In the end, the practical uses to which Laredo puts this memory device all rely on the fact that Laredo originally introduced the image of the jewelled city by requesting that his reader imagine his or her own soul in the middle of a plain, surrounded by crystal walls and twelve towers. The soul, in the midst of the field wherein the Christ candle with the Trinitarian flame is front and centre, understands itself in direct, even contiguous relationship to an emblem representing Christ. For that matter, the sinning soul as it purges itself becomes a higher quality of wick, and Laredo picturesquely suggests that the newly wick'd candles 'get up from the ground and enter the city.'[124] The spatial and mobile nature of the architectural mnemonic device begs for an equation between the soul of the devotee and the Son of God, while the light that reverberates translucently from the Trinitarian flame enters dynamically into relationship with Mary, the evangelists, the blessed, and so on. Perhaps most importantly, though, the wax and wick prove to be a duo that allows Laredo to proceed through a series of metaphors that coalesce the main topics of systematic theology in (and inside) one dominant image. In the *Subida*, the architectural frame of the memory device is no longer the building through which the memory wanders in order to reconstruct or create anew a meditation based on a one-to-one correspondence between objects as signs and theological concepts as the signified. Rather, the twelve-towered city walls are the bejewelled setting for the field of memory flooded with the light of God, light produced over and over again by the same sign signifying all the major topics of Godtalk. It is the candlelight, flashing off and through the walls of the image, that produces the movement of creativity and understanding, not the soul itself.

Thus Laredo's image, while rooted in medieval mnemotechnique, extends the device's efficacy by creating a thick level of signification that at once reveals the inherent unity of all aspects of God while providing separate details to mull over for many days of meditation. In this modulation of mnemotechnique, Laredo suggests images to his reader not simply in order to remind them of what is included in each day of meditations. Rather, his choice of memory devices serves to make a theological point about the unity of God, a point that in turn indicates that any memory device, to be effective within this system, must allow – or perhaps force – the reader to reverberate through a series of doctrinal points all hinged on the same visual device. The fact that the same memory device can be used to unite multiple topics, a mnemonic possibility Carruthers does not explore, provides the key to decoding one of the most difficult mnemotechnical suggestions Laredo details in his treatise. I argue that a close reading of the aquatic images (guided by the elements of a mystical mnemonics already described in this chapter) allows us to decipher the cognitive valence of Laredo's mnemotechnical mysticism.

Conclusion: Sailing into God

The use to which Laredo puts the non-architectural element (candles) of his structural mnemonic device indicates a necessary rereading of the first chapters of the *Subida*'s stage two, which are dominated by a water image that he continually modulates to apply to yet more topics of Christian doctrine. Despite his prefatory suggestion that part 2 of the *Subida* will consist only of a series of Holy Week meditations (from Gethsemane to the tomb), Laredo actually begins part 2 with an extensive discussion of Trinitarian theology (including the substance versus essence debates) and Christology concerning the Incarnation before ever getting to the Nativity, and then moves immediately to the Passion.[125] All of the topics, except that of Holy Week, are linked not by their relevance to the second Person of the Trinity but instead by an extensive, and in real life logistically impossible, aquatic image. This image's utility resides in Laredo's mystical deployment of mnemotechnique rather than simply in its metaphorical significance.

In a nearly untranslatable passage that has been taken by scholars as a reason to critique Laredo's writing style,[126] Laredo attempts to provide an analogy for the Trinity. Instead of using the wax/wick/flame metaphor typical of the Christian tradition, both mystical and theological,[127] Laredo proposes a unique image:[128]

> From the occult hiddenness and the inaccessible secret of this immense and co-eternal majesty is born *ab eterno* a fountain of living water, which goes out of paradise yet is forever within it ... The fountain is established in three rivers of eternal divinity [as follows]: the first is infinite power, the second is infinite wisdom, the third is complete and immense goodness ...

> [T]hese three rivers are established in an ocean; note that I have not said that the fountain establishes three rivers *from* it, but that it established itself *in* three rivers, because the fountain is not one and the rivers something else, rather the rivers and the fountain are one single substance. Nor, in this manner, do I say that the three rivers established an ocean from themselves, but rather that they are established in it, because the three rivers and the ocean are one single essence. Neither does the fountain have a beginning, nor do the rivers have a middle, nor does the ocean have an end. Nor does the fountain pour out [more water] than what fills the rivers, nor do the rivers have less [water] than what the fountain pours out, and this ocean has the same as the three rivers or the fountain.
>
> In this manner the fountain flows out very powerfully, and it is no other than the very fecund river running with most quiet equality, nor is it other than the deepest ocean of infinite immensity ... Neither do the rivers have banks, nor can they be forded, because their waves lap higher than the high heavens.[129] (my emphases)

Laredo goes to great pains to clarify that his mnemonic image is of a 'fountain as three rivers as ocean.' Instead of imagining them contiguously, thereby separating the unity of the three, they are meant to be envisioned contemporaneously. This rather unwieldy concretization of a Christian mystery at first glance seems only to complicate an already notably difficult point of doctrine, of no more immediate use than the baroque flourish of the soul's entrails' vein's eyes that appears later in part 2 of the *Subida* (see epigraph to the introduction). Yet in much the same way that the image of entrails' eyes usefully highlights a critical element of embodiment in Laredo's understanding of soul, the variability of Laredo's 'impossible' water image turns out to be a rich source of connection between his discussion of topics other than the Trinity throughout the entirety of part 2. A brief and paradoxical (and possibly incomprehensible) metaphor is revealed as a memory device designed to enable the reader to remember the interconnections between a variety of doctrinal topics.

To begin with, the image Laredo chooses for the Trinity is markedly different from his titular reference to the soul's attempt at union with God as a mountainous ascent. Carruthers remarks that 'spatial and directional metaphors are essential to the conception of the "way" of monastic meditation.'[130] A *camino*, or path, simply exists until someone chooses to follow it, yet paths for the most part are created by humans for their own use. In contrast, fountains and rivers are natural phenomena, defined by movement and direction whose momentum is absorbed by the ocean into which they flow. Rocks that would be obstacles on a dirt road are disdainfully ignored by flowing water.[131] Despite the intrinsic oppositions between the two metaphors of river and path, Laredo finds that a basic attribute of bodies of water will serve him better than the idea of *camino* for portraying the soul's ascent. He re-imagines the soul's journey as that of the river's incessant rushing from its origin until it 'becomes absorbed in the sea' (*engolfarse en el mar*).[132] The directionality, or *ductus*, of a river that has its source *and* its end in a body of water, unlike that of the path that goes from point A to point B, is a mnemotechnique that highlights the paradox that the soul already always has roots and finds repose in the God towards which it is ascending. Laredo's dependence on medieval memory technique proves to refashion medieval formulations of the ascent to God in a way that distinguishes *recogimiento* from other forms of mystical ascent in which God is defined as impossibly distant. He thus deploys the physicality of the visual mnemonic image to reinforce the fact that God is to be found at the centre of the embodied soul.

Laredo's fountain/river/ocean metaphor, in itself entirely original as far as I am aware,[133] was prompted by the sixteenth-century colloquial expressions in which the flow of a river in its bed is referred to as *ir en madre*, a high water level as *llenar la madre*, and a river overflowing its banks as *salir de madre* (literally, 'going into the mother,' 'filling the mother,' and 'leaving the mother,' respectively).[134] Discussing these colloquialisms directly after the fountain/river/ocean metaphor quoted above, Laredo indicates that they were not only foundational for his choice of image, but Mary as mother is implicitly incorporated in his aquatic Trinitarian mnemonic. It is precisely the multivalence of the image that makes it effective in Laredo's eyes, for he re-assigns the same metaphorical elements to different aspects of the divine when explaining the birth of the Son (the ocean as God, the river as Christ's assumed humanity, the fountain as the Virgin's womb).[135] The efficacy of this bodies-of-water metaphor is not in its utility for explaining the nature of God, but rather in its capacity to unify theological points that are of necessity discrete in scholastic *quaestiones* and the liturgies of Church feast days,[136] and even, by the nature of language, in the creedal formulations that treat the idea of the Trinity, the Incarnation, and the Nativity in successive phrases. By introducing this memory device in the first chapter of part 2 and by adapting it time and time again throughout this level, Laredo creates a singular synthesis of doctrine revolving around a picture that cannot actually exist in reality as it is imagined for the purposes of meditation.

The final application of the aquatic image signals the connection between mnemotechnique and mystical cognition. While the notion of 'absorption into God' is a common phrase for union among medieval essence mystics, for example, a secondary meaning of the Spanish verb *engolfar* is 'sailing out to sea.'[137] Laredo continues the layering of his metaphor – bodies of water as proper image for the Trinity, for Mary's role in the Nativity, for the soul, among other concepts[138] – by mutating his unique image of the soul *as* river to fit the more traditional discussion of a soul as a ship *on* the river. In this case, the soul is painted primarily in relation to its modes of cognition.

> And what does the very blessed soul have to do when it arrives thus at the river, but enter into the vessel or ship of firm hope without stopping before [reaching] the prow of faith, shutting itself up in the castle of the topsail of charity and cutting the rigging of the corporeal senses, holding onto the sails of affectivity and awakening the living winds of the most sweet desires, and ordering the breaking of the oars of the brain and the faculty of the understanding and the cutting of the anchors of natural force, and receiving the navigators of holy inclinations, ordering them to interfere with the crowd of cats and rats that are the various vacillating thoughts, and firing the quartermaster who does not fit in this ship? And the captain will be our master, Christ; and the pilot who guides us will be his [Christ's] footsteps; and in such a manner it will navigate securely to the port of love, and there it can stay without fearing need of anything.[139]

Laredo's metaphor runs away with him,[140] in a vivid passage that would be particularly appealing to the citizens of his native Seville, the largest port in Spain.[141] Seville's status as port to the New World depended on the fact that fleets of ships could sail ninety kilometres from its port down the Guadalquivir River to reach the Mediterranean Sea.[142] Thus the prosperity of the city (and of the upper-class members of society whom Laredo treated medically) depended as much on the state of the river – whether it was staying in its bed or overflowing (*ir/salir de madre*) – as it did on other natural occurrences that affected crops and other forms of livelihood. With shipping and the relation of bodies of water to one another crucial to the fame and fortune of Seville after the discovery of the New World, Laredo draws on the known material of everyday life to modulate common contemporary images of the soul, producing an insight meant to be foundational to a devout understanding of God. Yet note that this particular reuse of the aquatic image is no longer in the effort to convey God; rather, Laredo uses it to parallel the human cognitive process, beginning with the senses (the rigging) through to the powers of the soul (the oars and navigators).

In other words, intrinsic to Laredo's notion of God is a very intimate link between the soul, as a river or ship upon the river, and a God who is at once the river and the fountain and the ocean. The human soul is thus of God and lesser, painted with the same linguistic brush but with fewer levels and fewer bodies of water, from a more utilitarian view rather than as a multiplicity of metaphorical aspects that cannot physically exist in such an arrangement. By their very concreteness yet impossible interconnections, the water devices are suggestive of the essence of an indefinable God.[143]

I argue that the need for concreteness finds its roots in the medieval *habitus* of creativity based on memory devices. As Carruthers clarifies in relation to the iconoclastic controversies in the early Middle Ages, many monks relied on visual images because without being able to *see* God, they found themselves unable to *think* about God.[144] For Laredo, the technique of recollection mysticism intended to aid the soul in uniting with God must necessarily address the complicated problem of uniting with a God who is defined as existing at the centre of the soul. How could Renaissance Castilians think or meditate themselves into union with a God who is already in their entrails, especially if any human consists of the problematic continuity of body and soul? A God at the centre of our soul must be accessed through progressive awareness of exactly what constitutes a human, for only in knowing that can devotees recognize the divine at their core.

For Laredo, mystical knowing involves recognizing the human as physical body, a physicality that includes the faculty of memory localized in a brain ventricle. Indeed, this knowing, reached through meditation and thus presumably through using language in mental thought, is not simply linguistic and cognitive, for memory as the source of thought goes beyond language to depend on visual images and concrete objects and on movement through space and time for its creativity. In the stage of self-knowledge, by coming to terms with the body and activating the memory in relation to the concrete world in order to produce greater understanding of theology and thereby of God, Laredo maps out the limits of the human as the limits within which God will be found, as the centre and source of ultimate repose. The next chapter will take seriously the equation of seeing with knowing. Optics was the core metaphor for theological epistemology, and it is the continued importance of the physiology of cognition in the Castilian Renaissance that points the way to understanding Laredo's visceral deployment of Passion mnemonics as vital to the discovery of God in the entrails of the soul.

5 Optics, Pain, and Transformation into God[1]

Embodied sight and an enmattered mind are the medium of communication between self and world.

Suzannah Biernoff[2]

The most effective memory devices are those that depend on shock value or clever ornamentation. Many of the graphically violent or sexual images found in medieval literature and religious meditation were not formulated in order to appeal to the lowest common denominator; they were intended to be forceful enough to imprint on the memory like incisions on a wax tablet.[3] Authors of mnemotechnical treatises insisted that sequences of violence, whether in a historical chronicle or in depictions of the Passion, not only stayed vividly in the mind's eye but also drew the reader into visualizing the depicted scene, a necessary prerequisite to the imaginative wandering through a mnemotechnical location that created new connections between old ideas.[4] Carruthers assesses the rationale for the shock value of certain mnemonic devices: 'Without arousing emotions and so moving the will, there will be no remembering and thus no creating of thoughts.'[5] Cognition begins with sensory objects, yet the information process is more effectively remembered (and thus more useful for the subsequent creating of new ideas) if a violent experience is associated with it.

Thomas Bradwardine's late medieval treatise *On Acquiring a Trained Memory* provides a forthrightly brutal exemplar:

Suppose that someone must memorize the twelve signs of the Zodiac, that is the Ram, the Bull, etc. So he might, if he wished to, make for himself in the front of the first location a very white ram standing up and rearing on his

> hind feet, with golden horns. And he might put a very red bull to the right of the ram, kicking the ram with his rear feet; standing erect, the ram with his right foot might kick the bull in his large and super-swollen testicles, causing a copious effusion of blood. And by means of the testicles one will recall that it is a bull, not a castrated ox or a cow. In a similar manner, a woman may be placed before the bull as though laboring in birth, and in her uterus as if ripped open from her breast may be figured coming forth two most beautiful twins, playing with a horrible, intensely red crab ... To the left of the ram a dreadful lion might be placed, who with open mouth and rearing on its legs attacks a virgin, beautifully adorned, tearing her garments. With its left foot the ram might inflict a wound to the lion's head.[6]

Strongly contrasting colours, sexual imagery, fear-inducing wild animals, and above all violence characterize this schema of the heavens.[7] While many assume that such images were standard in an age marked by legal violence, scholars have recently begun to question whether public spectacles of punishment were as frequent as they have been recorded.[8] Mills, for example, suggests that the pervasive violence in medieval literature was not due to a corresponding pervasive violence in the culture itself, but rather to the memorable quality of violence in the construction of power.[9] This argument is also applicable in the era of the Inquisition, as the prospect of an *auto-da-fé* was an ever-present reminder of the consequences of heresy on a devotee's flesh.[10] Enders goes further: 'In antiquity and the Middle Ages, *memoria* was the epistemological place where the inventional materials of torture were assembled (*dispositio*) and rehearsed for performance (*actio*).'[11] The memory device was a 'virtual spectacle with brutal imaginary scenes.'[12] In the case of methods meant to train devotees to undergo a mystical experience, it is significant that the mnemonic violence of the Passion was the preliminary point of departure for most meditative methods,[13] and in the case of Laredo's *Subida*, a central concern.

How a Renaissance devotee meditatively visualized a historical event that took place fifteen hundred years previous in a foreign land at the same moment when confraternities were constantly recreating the scenes throughout the streets of his or her hometown, however, melds the visual and the visualized in ways that call for a greater understanding of the process of vision itself. Both physicians and theologians throughout the Middle Ages constructed epistemological systems on the basis of the visual sense, a theory of cognition only outmoded by the Enlightenment.[14] Some of these theories were the most successful descriptions of a body–soul continuum along cognitive lines articulated in the writings of medieval physicians and theologians.[15] In contrast to modern scholarly assumptions that Passion meditation is a form of internal imagination that is not physical but purely mental, even 'ineffable,'[16] the medieval optical theory of intromission proposes an identity between the viewer and the object of his or her knowledge in a manner that highlights the role of embodiment in the process of mental visualization. Although several scholars have explored the implications of optics for understanding Passion meditation texts,[17] particularly Suzanne Biernoff in her *Sight and Embodiment in the Middle Ages*, no scholar (as far as I am aware) addresses the epistemological implications for a mystical method that integrates Passion meditation with apophatic theology and other forms of unitive mysticism normally understood as abstract. In this chapter, I argue that Laredo's version of *recogimiento* trains the visually based cognitive process of the devotee in preparation for an experience of God.

A cognitive reading of the *Subida* reveals that Laredo articulates mnemonic violence at the heart of his mystical method in a manner that both relies on the physiology connecting externally viewed objects, the optic nerve, and the inner senses in the brain ventricles, and considers memory as equally a cognitive location and a faculty of the soul. As we saw in chapter 4, the art of memory depends on questions of space and place in which objects, agents, and images are located, and on the movement of the body and/or the mind's eye in relation to them. In turn, Laredo's mnemonic Passion device is constructed on the premise that the gaze of the devotee ought not go out of the body to Golgotha, but rather attract Golgotha into the devotee. In his method, the *sight* of the space where Christ suffered slowly but surely transforms the believer into becoming the *site* of that torture. The physical eye becomes identical with the viewed object according to intromission optics (see below), making it possible for Laredo to propose that a portion of the embodied soul can turn into an object related to Christ's torture, indeed, can be identical not only with the torture but also ultimately with the tortured Christ himself, my core argument in this chapter.[18] As a case study, his method clarifies how critical it is for historians of mysticism to reconsider mystical texts that apparently stress the fundamental opposition of body and soul, in order to determine at what level they actually depend on a cognitive continuum between the two.

When devotional attention shifted over the late Middle Ages (and post-Reconquest in Castile) towards ever-more-graphic stories concerning Jesus's torture and death, their power as mnemonic devices lay in the possibility of internalizing the stories not as a referent to someone or something else, but as part of the reader's own experience.[19] Rather than remaining as something objective and external, the internalized violence linked the tortured body of Christ and the believer's body. Despite Andrés's inclusion of Passion meditation as the second stage of recollection mysticism, repeated characterization of *recogimiento* as a 're-collecting of the outward senses to discover a God internal to the soul' defines it as a process of interiorization that surpasses external corporeal sensations and does not depend on external church ritual for access to God. This definition overlooks the role of body – in this case, the tortured body – in a method of presumably abstract interiorization. A memory device in the writings of a physician-mystic that centres on a wounded human body insists that we consider seriously the body that is the subject of violence. In Laredo's Passion meditation, a human body composed of earth and water whose blood was the result of the absorption of food during the right balance of hot and cold, dryness and moisture, ultimately endured more than 5,000 wounds' worth of torture.[20] This embodied approach is ratified by Laredo's declaration that Christ writes with his finger on the 'dusty earth' of our understanding, just as God wrote on Christ's skin on the cross.[21] Both the elemental, medical body of the human and the body in pain of the divine are united in this comment.

It is therefore not surprising that Laredo's primary concern in his Passion meditation is the construction of a method that combines the devotee's body cognitively and viscerally with Christ's body. No more than a devotee ought to forget the physiological humanity of a God made man should any mystic forget the critical role that human cognitive processes play in experiencing the divine. Before presenting a reading of Laredo's technique of Passion meditation that highlights its roots in optically based epistemology, however, it is necessary to consider medieval constructs of pain and optics, since it is the visualized image of the divine suffering body that produces knowledge of God.

Pain and the Body–Soul Construct in the Middle Ages

Recent research into the topic of pain in the Middle Ages has reframed our understanding of its relevance to medical, theological, and devotional concerns. Most potently, Donald Mowbray argues that medieval theologians created a refined medical vocabulary for pain in order to probe the relative humanity of Christ, and in doing so particularly focused on the body–soul construct.[22] Modern dichotomies between body and soul, in which pain is a bodily sensation and can be treated by medicating the body, do not map appropriately onto the body–soul continuum at the heart of medieval theology.[23] In fact, the category of pain problematizes the dualism post-Descartian thinkers ascribe to the Middle Ages, since scholastic theologians contended that physical pain felt in the body was then routed to the soul, while emotional pain felt in the soul had corporeal effects.[24] In other words, medical pain proved the theological necessity of a body–soul continuum.

These theories concerning pain's location in both the body and the soul support the intrinsic embodiment of the soul that pervades Laredo's treatise. The distinction between *dolor* (physical pain) and *tristitia* (sadness) exercised medieval theologians – did the Godman feel both as much as any human did, or did his divinity override one type of pain? The answer was typically cast in terms of which kind of external pain was most likely to affect the faculties of the soul after traversing the sensory soul's five inner senses.[25] Even those theologians who bypassed discussion of the inner senses located in the brain ventricles to examine a purely theological tripartite version of soul – sensual, lower, and superior reason – did not agree on how far the physicality of pain penetrated the soul. Emotion and *tristitia* were often considered worse than *dolor*, physical pain,[26] yet some thought that only *dolor*, not *tristitia*, could affect the superior powers. In this version, the physicality of pain could be transmitted to the soul, while emotional pain could not.[27] On the other hand, those theologians, including Aquinas, who believed that *tristitia* was worse than *dolor* suggested the following: 'The soul is moved to a greater degree by affection than by the intellect ... So the soul is dependent on a certain kind of sense perception [from affection] which will enable it to experience suffering. It is also only properly said to suffer in as far as it is part of the human composite [of body and soul].'[28] In this case, the sensation of physical pain leads to emotional pain precisely *because* a body–soul continuum exists.

Affective spirituality as a category has been periodically derided among the spiritual developments of the late Middle Ages, because it was strongly associated with women and laity who were uneducated and thus dependent on their emotions rather than theological education to express their devotion.[29] Scholars name Franciscan Passion treatises as the leading texts teaching affective spirituality to medieval devotees, suggesting that the heightened grief that dominates Franciscan works was a result of greater focus on emotions than on bodily pain. Mowbray's work complicates this assumption, since he argues persuasively that grief is a bodily experience but physical pain is experienced affectively; affective spirituality therefore concerns physiological suffering, not just emotional weeping. Another scholar examining the relationship between the senses and affective spirituality, Jill Bennett, agrees: 'Affect ... is effectively registered as corporeal sign.'[30] The inherent physicality of both pain and grief in medieval theories of the body suggests an interesting twist on Donna Trembinski's claim that Dominican theologians forefronted Christ's physical pain alone in order to distinguish his experience as more divine than that of all others, while Franciscan theologians paid close attention to both Christ's pain and grief in order to emphasize his full humanity.[31] Franciscan affective attention to both emotional and physical anguish during the Passion did not simply appeal to weepy devotees too weak-minded or uneducated to focus scholastically on the divine. Rather, it highlighted Jesus's full cognitive and embodied participation in this world.

Esther Cohen's recent examination of 'pain in late medieval culture' indicates the role cognition played in the theological discussions of pain. Referring to thirteenth- and fourteenth-century scholastics, she claims:

> The trajectory from the prefatory dread of imagination to the stick that hit the head to the mind or from the fire that burned the hand to the feeling that registered the injury, to the memory that recorded it, to the understanding that shrank from further injury and dwelt upon the former – this was what shaped human pain. And this trajectory was totally subjective and individual. The stick and the fire were unimportant. The manner in which their impact was internalized was all that mattered.[32]

Pain as an interiorizing process was key to medieval theology and devotional practice, yet no consideration of pain could avoid discussion of the body as object or the body's physiological process of cognition. This fact behooves us to take a closer look at any spiritual movement marked by a move to interiority (as traditional accounts characterize the Villacrecian Franciscan reform) if it also comes linked with an increased dissemination of Passion spirituality (as began under Isabel's reign): both the spiritual trend *and* the violence of Passion meditation travel an inward trajectory. In this view, the Passion-centred devotions so frequently assumed to be purely externally oriented because of their reliance on body and vision prove to be inwardly oriented as well.[33]

The preceding discussion of medieval theories of pain indicates the necessity of reading Laredo's Passion meditation as a mnemonic device that insists on spectacular embodiment as a method for interiorizing spirituality. My analysis of Laredo's Renaissance work is also aided at several points by Elaine Scarry's influential work *The Body in Pain*, in which she examines the universal nature of pain based on analysis of contemporary torture techniques, war, the Bible, and modern literature and philosophy. Several of her points are useful markers in any analysis of pain. (Laredo's assumptions about pain, of course, are rooted in medieval cognitive and scientific theories rather than postmodern ones.)[34] According to Scarry, pain is an overwhelming truth to the sufferer but is always doubted (as to its intensity, extension, type, and so on) by all others. Thus pain cannot be shared between two individuals; rather, it separates humans.[35] She extrapolates from this abyss between the sufferer and the spectator the notion that pain breaks down language, since no amount of vocalization or description of pain can reproduce that pain so effectively as to fully represent it to someone else.[36]

Reiterating this point, she moves quickly from the suggestion that 'there is no language for pain' to declaring that by not reaching linguistic expression, pain is thereby 'not visible,'[37] despite the fact that the person sensing the pain insists on its having temporal, thermal, and most especially spatial dimensions (for example, it may pulse over time, burn, or shoot through the body).[38] In her rendition, despite the spatial and temporal dimensions of pain felt in the body, such physicality can never be rendered 'visible' (that is, comprehensible) because of inadequate linguistic resources. We are just as likely to describe the weapon inflicting the pain ('it felt as if a nail was hammered into my foot') as we are to describe the pain itself, a metaphorical recourse that separates the pain from the body that is experiencing it and instead locates it in the inflicting object.[39] While Scarry's theories are provocative, problematizing easy interconnections or distinctions between bodily pain, language, and visibility, it is difficult to correlate her assumption that pain radically separates us from others with the dominant religious practices of the late Middle Ages, in which Christ's pain was the pre-eminent source of identification between the devotee and the divine. However, her remarks concerning the location of pain and the impossibility of communicating or 'seeing' pain are pertinent to an analysis of the locational memory and optical epistemology at the heart of Laredo's methodology.

Optical Epistemologies

This chapter takes as its point of departure that the mnemonic effectiveness of Passion meditation is due to violence. Not only is Passion meditation best contextualized in medieval pain theory, as was just discussed, but the imaginative visualization of pain depended on another cognitive theory, that of the centrality of optics to epistemology.[40] Seeing and visualizing were often intertwined at different points along the sequence of cognition – vision is one of the five senses that gathers data to activate the cognitive process; visualization is associated with imagination in the middle brain ventricle; and memories are of images, not words.[41] The spirituality of the Franciscans, the leaders of religious reform in Renaissance Castile, made constant reference to the cognitive impact of optics. Many medieval artistic representations of Francis's stigmatic experience (from Giotto onward) depicted his vision of the crucified Christ as a vision of a sculpted crucifix, thus melding a mental vision with a well-known type of devotional object (see Figure 5.1).[42] Laredo shows himself a true Franciscan when he connects exterior images with meditation, claiming at one point that Francis's visionary experience proves the need to meditate interiorly as a consequence of an exterior image's impact.[43] The easy slippage in Franciscan devotion between a physical devotional object seen with the external senses, on the one hand, and a vision seen with the mind's eye that nevertheless tore the body violently through stigmatic wounds, on the other, indicates that physicality, spirituality, and optically based cognition cannot be fully separated in any discussion of Franciscan mysticism. More broadly, according to medieval theories of cognition, sensory perception, the root of all knowledge, resulted in 'spiritual' change – even transformation – and thus any rendition of how the soul accesses God mystically must acknowledge the relevance of the senses to spiritual progress.[44]

Of all the authors in the first generation of Franciscan recollection mystics, Laredo's medical understanding of the body heightened his awareness that the spiritual could only be reached through the corporeal.[45] Medieval physicians often focused on curing disease, but pharmaceutical treatises generally provided methods to alleviate the symptoms of disease, especially pain.[46] While Laredo's comfort with the topic of pain may well stem from his role as apothecary, I argue that his interest in Passion meditation as part of a mystical method meant to transform the soul into the God found at its centre stems from assumptions about the cognitive sequence that unites vision, memory, and pain. We must turn to the field of optics in order to properly situate a mystical technique defined as a progressive re-orientation of the powers of the soul from the exterior towards the interior.

Two theories of vision dominated medieval science, extramission and intromission, as discussed briefly in the introduction.[47] Both depend on the 'corporeal and affective phenomena of sight';[48] that is, that the process of sight was understood to have an embodied emotional impact. The well-known proponents of extramission – Plato in his *Timaeus*, Augustine's

Fig 5.1 Francis receiving the stigmata from his vision of a crucifix. Frontispiece to Alfonso de Porras, *Compendium privilegiorum fratrum minorem* (Salamanca, 1532). Credit: Archivo Oronoz.

theory of vision in *De Genesi ad literam* and his theory of knowledge in *De Trinitate* – suggested that visual rays, or fire, beamed out of the eyes. These rays create a connection between the eye and the viewed object, providing the viewer with exact information on colour and then other physical details.[49] The physiology of extramission attracted a good deal of attention, and it is clear that the science of optics, now often considered a branch of physics, not biology,[50] originated from medical understandings of body. For example, Augustine deployed contemporary understandings of the medical body when he identified the liver as the source of visual fire that travels to the brain, thence through ducts to the eyes, and out from the eyes to external objects.[51] Medieval physicians later disputed some of these details, suggesting instead that visual fire originates in a *spiritus* in the heart that travels through the arteries to the brain, where it is refined before carrying the power of sight through the hollow optic nerve to the eye.[52] In other words, theological epistemologies rooted in optical theory were always based on a series of presumptions about human physiology, and thus in their historical context carried with them the implication that all knowledge is bodily.

Although Plato's theory became even more influential after the twelfth-century translation of the *Timaeus*, no scientist or theologian probed terribly deeply into the physics of how the visual firestream brought information back to the eye, or at least no suggestion won the field.[53] The notion of the eye emitting beams that touch the object, however, has gained importance in scholarly histories of Christianity because of its relevance to such practices as the reception of the Eucharist in the Middle Ages. Scholars now understand that interest in 'ocular communion' – visual observation of the raising of the host rather than actually receiving the bread – may well have been founded on the extramission theory: seeing by emitting visual fire that hit the object was tactile, not distancing.[54] Medieval laity and religious women, none of them clerics and therefore all dependent on a priest's decision to administer the Eucharist for access to the host, felt that visual access to the host was a form of touching that could substitute for ingestion. Furthermore, the apparent activity involved in emitting visual rays gave agency to those to whom full communion was prohibited.

Yet the theory of extramission never became dominant, perhaps because no one gave physical details as to *how* it worked. In contrast, the theory of intromission was more fully developed.[55] First posited by Aristotle and expanded by Alhazen (ca 965–1040),[56] it was disseminated by Roger Bacon (ca 1219–74) in the Latin West together with his own extension of the theory; followers of this view were known as the perspectivist school.[57] Bacon theorized that the *species* (form, appearance, similitude) of an object emanates from the object in such a way that its continuous regeneration creates a stream of sequential identical forms that reach from the object to the eye of the beholder.[58] Upon reaching the eye, the *species* impresses itself on the eye (or the crystalline humor in the centre of the eye)[59] in the manner of a stamp on sealing wax, notably the same example used by Bacon's contemporaries to describe the impact of visual images on the memory.[60] The sensory impression in each eye is transmitted to the 'common nerve' that joins the two optic nerves, and then to the 'common sense' in one of the front ventricles of the brain.[61] This notion is often characterized as passive reception, for although some objects appear more clearly than others, scientists assumed that the clarity comes from the angle of reception of the rays rather than any active filtering done by the eye (see Figure 5.2).[62]

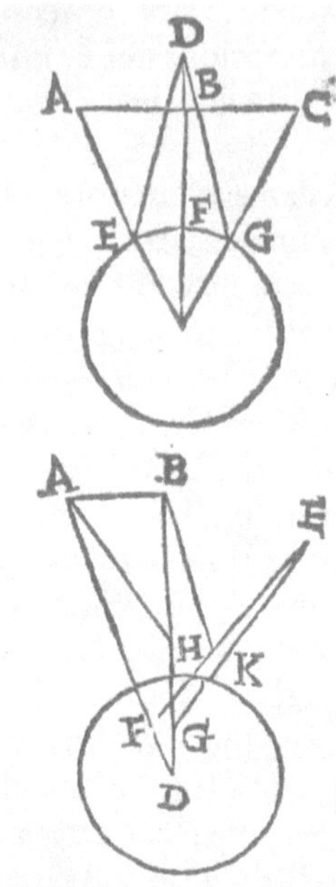

Fig 5.2 Optical diagram in a popular Spanish Renaissance mathematics text based on Roger Bacon's optics. Pedro Ciruelo, *Cursus quattor mathematicarum* (Alcalá de Henares: Arnaldus Guillelmus Brocarius, 1516), fol. b6v. Credit: Biblioteca Nacional de España, Madrid.

As the figure shows, the eye is physiologically connected with the ventricles or cells of the brain, yet for our purposes, the most important element in the theory is the relationship of the eye and the object. Scientists exploring optics frequently combined elements of both optical theories in their proposals. Even Bacon, the foremost proponent of intromission, admits that the eye itself must emit a *species* out into the world in order to itself be seen in a mirror.[63] As a result, Biernoff elucidates in her excellent application of optical theory to medieval devotional interest in the Eucharist and Passion meditation that there is a 'perceptual *relationship*, as distinct from a unidirectional act of perception.'[64] This aspect of relationship indicates that the scholarly tendency to identify extramission as active reception and intromission as passive is, in the end, simplistic. Biernoff claims: 'The eye was simultaneously receptive, passive, vulnerable to sensations; and active: roaming, grasping or piercing its objects.'[65] Since optics was the basis for theories of knowledge, it is of great interest to any mystical epistemology that both activity and passivity could be supported by the science of vision. Whether mystical experience was a passive reception of God or an active search for the divine was frequently debated throughout the Middle Ages; in Castile, it had particular relevance for the apparent distinction between *recogimiento* (active preparation for mystical union) and *dejamiento* (passive reception of God). If medieval optical theory (and therefore human epistemology) is best understood as a *combination* of activity and passivity, then those mystics who recommend rest and activity are those who are most fully aligned with the cognitive theories of their age.[66]

In my view, the optics of intromission raises the most startling possibilities for a re-consideration of mystical 'knowledge.' If the *species* is imprinted on the eye, epistemology based on intromission perforce posits an identity between the viewer and the object, since the eye of the viewer was, however briefly, transformed into the thing seen.[67] In other words, just as a drop of wax takes on the shape of the mould, so too does the organ of the eye, or perhaps even the optic nerve, take on the shape or *species* of that which it sees. The potential identity between the object and viewer is provocative in an era when devotional objects were in abundance and visual cues were meant to inspire meditation. As Biernoff notes, '[F]or Aristotle and Bacon, when we perceive something, that thing in a very real way becomes *part* of us: the essence of the thing is drawn forth from the object (or adjacent medium), and impregnates the receptive matter of our sense organs and mind.'[68] If we take medieval cognitive theory seriously, we must begin to pose new questions concerning the efficacy of pilgrimages, icons, or the Sacro Monte (in Italy, Spain, and elsewhere)[69] that provide life-size renditions of Holy Week scenes in Jerusalem for pious devotees. Is the devotee being physically changed as a result of these visual aids for meditation, if her eye is identical with what it sees?

Likewise, one must wonder about the apparent paradox that the bodily sense of sight that produces a physical identity between object and viewer is at the same time one of the five senses initiating cognition's process of progressive 'dematerialization' (according to Avicenna, see Introduction). In a continuum between body and soul, purely mental meditative processes are intrinsically connected to a bodily result; imaginative visualization, that so-called preparatory stage for mere beginners, might well create a physical identity between the devotee and a crucified Jesus.[70] If seeing is physical – if in the intromission theory of optics the viewed object actually *transforms* the eye of the beholder into the viewed object – then meditating on a crucifix leads to the crucified body existing in some sense *within* the believer.[71] Bennett elaborates: 'Viewing, on this account, is not restricted to retinal impression and interpretations; the engagement of the senses implies a transformative process through which the properties of images are transferred to the viewer. In effect, one becomes the image through an encounter with it.'[72] The processional statues found in *Semana Santa* processions thus do not simply recreate the historical scenes as an external devotion to be observed by spectators, but rather imprint the torture and death of Christ and the grief of Mary on the memory of the observers, transforming them momentarily *into* the suffering Mother and Son. The bodies of the spectators may well have been impacted more viscerally by the sight of sculptures of Christ in pain (not to mention the sight of the flagellants) than modern expectations about cognition would allow us to expect. These sculptures, once they became a standard aspect of the processions, were intentionally carved to stimulate an emotional (and therefore physical) response from the viewers, a point taught explicitly by theologians such as Juan de Avila (1500–69) who believed emotions to be embodied.[73]

As we saw in chapter 1, the authors of the Latin and Castilian *Vita Christi* treatises configured the visualization of pain – not just Christ's body but his tortured body – as the primary way for meditators to enter into full awareness of the meaning of the Crucifixion. Yet if we analyse this from a cognitive perspective, these medieval treatises asked devotees to visualize a Godman who experienced pain (*dolor*) in his body, a *passio corporalis* that altered his body's natural state and in turn conveyed pain to his soul.[74] Biernoff explains that an experience of pain followed the usual patterns accorded to optically based cognition by Bacon and others: '[P]assion – defined as any violent physical or emotional change – was a characteristic of the fleshly body. A "passion" was something one underwent or endured; a process of transformation. As such, the action of *species* [in optics] "is called 'passion' because the medium and sense, in receiving *species*, undergo a transmutation in their substance."'[75] This *double entendre* in the term *passio* – conveying both physiological and spiritual implications – is the point of connection between optical theories and Christian meditative practice. Christ's suffering proved his humanity because he endured pain as transformation; the transformation of the devotee's eye by the reception of the *species* of a viewed object provided an important analogy.

The impact of medieval optical theory on the reigning techniques of Passion meditation can be traced in Peter of Limoges's incorporation of the scientific specifics of optical theory in a highly popular collection of sermon exempla that circulated throughout Europe and Spain in manuscript translations throughout the late Middle Ages. Biernoff renders the goal of *De oculo morali*: '[W]hen the eye of the heart grasps the very essence of the crucified and redemptive body, the viewer is assimilated to Christ. Not only does the movement from bodily to interior sight follow the transformative multiplication of sensible species; the *passio* of sensation in this instance is united with the Passion of Christ.'[76] *Passio* is the central element of optics and thereby of epistemology; it is also the core of what occurred to Christ's humanity during his bodily passion. It becomes evident that transformation is the goal of Passion-centred devotions, yet Andrés, focusing only on the final stage of *recogimiento*, limits the term 'transformation' to the unitive level, as 'transformation into God through love' through apophatic theology. Most medievalists to date discuss the connection between optics and the transformation of the viewer in relation to external objects, such as a crucifix or the sculptures carried during *Semana Santa* processions. I propose that in the case of a physician mystic such as Laredo, his Passion meditation presupposes an epistemological system of optical identity that deploys the process of imaginative visualization as a method of of transformation into God's bleeding humanity.

Visualizing Mnemonic Pain

Let us turn to the mnemonic value of the violence inherent in the Passion. Providing scenes of brutality attached to characters and narrative, the *imagines agentes* in the memory device are inherently linked with violence. Beyond its emotional impact, the embodied nature of violence makes it spectacularly memorable. In one of the first articles to posit this connection, Peter Parshall points out the similarities between the description of a mnemonic figure with a crown and purple cloak provided by (Pseudo) Cicero in the *Rhetorica ad Herennium* in the first century BCE, and the figure of Christ crowned with thorns and mocked with purple robes in the Gospels in the first century CE.[77] If the Gospel sequences themselves were written with attention to the mnemonic value of details, then later practices of meditation that imaginatively lengthen the description of Christ's last days from a few pages to entire volumes were not so much changing the story as expanding its mnemonic efficacy. Authors of *Vita Christi* treatises consistently entreated their audience to add details concerning the decoration and layout of the streets and houses in which events in Jesus's life occurred, as well as to add dialogue that articulated the participants' and spectators' emotional reactions to the scenes. In other words, the narrative of Christ's life could serve as the mnemonic location through which a devotee walked, while the characters of the story functioned as *imagines agentes*.

Classical mnemotechnique's reliance on 'locative memory' did not diminish during its importation into monastic meditation in the Middle Ages; the same medieval author who provides the violent astronomical chart quoted at the beginning of this chapter also claims that '[f]or a trained memory, two things are necessary, that is, stable locations and also images for the material ... [T]he locations are permanent and fixed, whereas the images are at one moment inked on like letters and at another erased.'[78] The many medieval travelogues produced by pilgrims or the guides to Passion meditation not only brought a foreign culture or historical event alive in the mind's eye, but more importantly, they were meant to evolve into the reader's story as an experience of the place itself. For that matter, late medieval preachers often used mnemonic numbering techniques to help imprint the details of the Passion on their auditors' memories.[79]

Laredo's physiological approach to Passion meditation, in which the violated human body is put on display as a mnemonic device at the heart of a mystical treatise, must be understood in conjunction with his familiarity with the physicality of Passion devotion as practised by the new Passion confraternity members processing with sculptures of Jesus through the streets of Seville while mortifying their bodies. There is a violence to the external viewing of Passion processions that tends to root them in the memory, as a mould imprints on wax. Rather than providing a passive substitution for the mental activity of recombining stored images to construct visualizations of a historical event, I argue that these confraternal processions with statues of individuals moving along a map of Jerusalem configured onto Seville city streets re-structure 'mnemonic space.'[80] The physical actions of a ritual such as the *via crucis* are a physical enactment of the types of motion (*ductus*) required of the mental eye as it sweeps across the equine riding gear analysed in chapter 4. In this view, the *Semana Santa* processions were in essence a performative mnemotechnical device that turned an entire town into a memory castle of torture.

So far, scholars have offered only brief moments of insight into the spiritual transformation effected by these modes of mnemonic, optical cognition. Bennett suggests that the imaginative visualization of the Passion, understood mnemonically, results in a transformation of the viewer in the same way that the optical theory of intromission does, since the technique relies on visual images stored in the memory that had an emotional component in their original creation.[81] She does not follow up on this provocative possibility, however, instead returning to her analysis of a painting of Saint Francis and the likely devotional response it incurred. Likewise, Biernoff touches on the visual quality of Passion meditation as thereby drawing on optical epistemology even during imaginative meditation, but her analysis shifts without remark between imaginative visualization (images taken from storage in the memory and recombined in the faculty of the imagination during the course of cognition), visionary experience of Christ on the cross (Angela of Folingo's non-corporeal vision of a body understood to be external to her),[82] stigmatic reception during a vision (the physical effect on Francis of a non-corporeal vision of a body external to him), and paintings of the Passion (objects viewed by the eye in the first stage leading to cognition).[83] While Biernoff's conflation of all these types of devotional experiences indicates that they existed on a continuum, a critical point, their interchangeability depends on the insufficiently explored assumption that the *species* imprinted on the optical nerve is closely linked to imagination's play with images imprinted on the memory.

Let us consider this assumed connection between optical imprints and visualization in greater depth. Scholars describe mnemonic images as being 'literally re-membered' because individual memory images are recombined by the imagination, thus lending an element of embodiment to imaginative visualization that modern understandings of cognition and perception do not permit.[84] The mnemotechnical element of meditation on violence is remarked on by Bradwardine (he of the bloody constellations): '[M]emory is most powerfully affected by sensory impressions, and especially by vision; therefore something appears to your memory just as it ordinarily appears to your vision.'[85] Although Avicenna had discussed the cognitive process as a progressive dematerialization, the mental process of the image being imprinted on the optic nerve, shunted between ventricles, incised on the memory, and later 're-membered' into different forms by the imagination is not a fully abstract one (as a post-Descartian world view would assume). Parshall proposes the following: '[T]he act of calling up a memory is inherently an act of internal visualization, of image *making*' (my emphasis).[86] If thinking involves the making of visual images, then thought processes are never fully isolated from the corporeal senses. Akbari clarifies: 'Each faculty is connected with vision, for the imagination is a repository of images, impressions received from the *sensus communis* or common sense; the operation of reason or judgment is metaphorically described in terms of vision ... and memory, particularly purposeful memorization, is almost invariably constructed by means of visual images.'[87] Memory, optics and images, and violence are therefore inextricably related, yet no scholar to date has probed their interconnections for the production of mystical knowledge through Passion meditation.

Laredo's scientifically grounded mnemonics of Passion meditation provides the necessary elements to prove, not just assume, the connection between optical epistemology and imaginative visualization of the Passion, as we shall see below. In turn, his reliance on the full range of scientific information available about cognition in his time period is a clarion call to modern scholars to avoid lauding the efficacy of specific mystical methods simply because they appeal to modern assumptions about the abstract quality of mental functioning or a soul caught in a body-denying dualism. Rather, value might well lie in whether the mystical method attends to or seems to ignore the normal functioning of the human brain as understood in that era. Laredo extends the medieval method of visualization to its logical cognitive extreme by expecting that the body of the meditator can be transformed into that which he or she visualizes.

Ultimately, the optical epistemologies just reviewed – that is, *how* medieval devotees know (the world, God, and so on) – lead directly to the question as to why the bodiliness of medieval Passion spirituality appears as such a problem to medieval theologians (as it does to modern scholars of mysticism). What is it about a focus on the embodied divine, visualized imaginatively in physically transformative ways by the embodied believer, that makes such meditation a beginner's technique, if even the most speculative theologians and mystics grant that at some level all knowledge was bodily? Karnes has recently proposed that fourteenth-century texts by Bonaventure and his followers, including the *Stimulus amoris* available on the peninsula,[88] accepted the possibility of a continuum from bodily cognition to the soul's union with God. She argues, however, that at least in England, fifteenth-century translations and interpretations of these texts set firm limits on Passion meditation and thus eliminated the possibility of mystical union as a consequence of focusing on Christ's humanity.[89] In Renaissance Castile, the interest in Passion-centred devotions began so tardily as to necessitate reconsidering the question of whether an embodied Passion spirituality would actually have been seen as problematic, as the terminus ad quem given by Karnes cannot apply to a peninsular tradition begun only in the 1480s. Likewise, although a few scholars have begun probing the consequences of these cognitive theories for analysis of medieval art or Passion treatises as a particular genre, none have examined the implications for the categorization of Passion devotion as a subdiscipline distinct from that of mysticism.[90] In redressing the role of Passion spirituality in the history of mysticism, Laredo's scientific basis for a mystical method is once again an important case study. I suggest that his break with tradition can be traced most effectively by considering the visual impact of mnemonic violence, in which recognizing optics as epistemology leads to the insight that what is seen physically and imaginatively can transform the human body, indeed, its entrails and viscera, into the location of the tortured divine.

Laredo, Optics, and Pain: Becoming the Site of God

Although no previous scholar has examined mystical methods in Golden Age Spain in relation to their wider cognitive or physiological context,[91] the dominant theories of extramission and intromission were well known in the kingdom of Castile. Bacon's work was available on the peninsula,[92] both intromission and extramission theories were thoroughly explained in Bartholomeus Anglicus's encyclopedia that was available in the vernacular after 1494,[93] and John Pecham's popular *De perspectiva* (a simplification of the theory of his teacher, Bacon) was incorporated into the liberal arts curriculum at the universities of Alcalá and Salamanca in the early sixteenth century.[94] Castilians made their familiarity with optical theory evident, for the doctor chosen to accompany Columbus's second voyage references both theories in his treatise on the evil eye, including the extramissionists' assumption that a menstruating woman can turn a mirror red with the force of her gaze.[95] In turn, a Castilian friar describes the evil eye as a real danger, based on details of the extramission theory in a 1529 vernacular reference book on superstition.[96]

Perusal of Laredo's published work proves that Laredo was also fully cognizant of medieval medical discussions concerning the senses as the root of human epistemology and the two reigning optical theories.[97] For that matter, philologists note that Laredo's definition and use of the vernacular word *pupila* (pupil) was a novel extension of a recently coined term![98] Although he by no means uses optical theory as extensively as certain literary authors had in the Middle Ages, such as Jean de Meun in his allegorical *Roman de la Rose*,[99] he presupposes his audience's familiarity with the topic. In the 1538 edition of the *Subida*, he models the route to understanding God on the way humans cognitively perceive the world using an analogy linking colour as the object of eyesight and flavour as the object of taste to the mysteries of Christ as the object of faith.[100] He also deploys specific terminology from optical theory in several ways. In the 1535 edition, he uses the term 'multiplication of *species*' to indicate how sight reaches the eye, in the context of admonishing his readers that their inner eye ought to be as focused during meditation as their physical eye is when looking at the world, as both types of eyes see better the more they concentrate on one object.[101] Although in the 1538 edition he deletes the reference to *species*, he adds a metaphor from visual extramission to part 3, claiming that a lover's glance can literally pierce the beloved's heart.[102] For Laredo, this medieval commonplace from the physics of optics suggests that the inner eye of the will can pierce God directly.[103] Laredo's ease with optics as a route to understanding in general, and to devotion specifically, indicates that any reading of his method must take into account his own presuppositions about the embodied epistemology of the devotees that his book was meant to guide. In this section, I weave together both the mnemonic and the optical value of his mystical method, since close analysis of his method demonstrating its efficacy as a mnemonic device is all the more powerful when it is correlated with an epistemology of optical identity.

In the prefatory material to the *Subida del Monte Sión*, Laredo states baldly that the second level of his tripartite method consists of a week devoted to Passion meditation. He divides the days along a schema found in many Passion meditation treatises,[104] but notably mentions a beginning and end point to each day rather than a single event such as the Crucifixion on Friday, such as was typical of 'Cycle of the Passion' in contemporary Books of Hours.[105] Even the short description provided in the preface thus implies narrative movement through a historical location, already signalling its mnemonic function:

Monday	From Gethsemane to Caiaphas
Tuesday	From Caiaphas to the column
Wednesday	From the column to the *eccehomo* [Pilate's display of Jesus to the crowd]
Thursday	From the *eccehomo* to the fall with the cross
Friday	From the fall to the nailing
Saturday	From the cross to the tomb
Sunday	From the tomb to the Resurrection[106]

Various phrases indicate that Laredo understands the dependence of meditation on mnemotechnique. For example, just after the Passion narrative, he states: '[W]hat I contemplate in my memory of Christ's body on the column is not finding on him any healthy spot from the feet to the head … They hit him in the living flesh and gave it lashes like in soft wax with much blood, so many that the never-ending blows did not allow [the blood] to flow.'[107] Christ's body, a wax mnemonic in and of itself, is held in the memory as a result of violent meditation.

When Laredo first introduces the twenty chapters of Passion meditation that form the core of part 2, he includes one chapter as a methodological overview before providing multiple chapters of possible meditations. In this overview, he constructs his method of Passion spirituality in direct contrast to the custom of pilgrimages to Jerusalem, as well as to the processions recreating Jerusalem on the streets of Seville through the *via crucis*. It is noteworthy that in previous chapters, Laredo insists on an embodied version of soul in his description of God's creation of the soul in the *imago Dei*, in which he calls readers to 'open the eyes of [their] pious entrails.'[108] At first glance, his rejection of pilgrimage and processions seems critical of their physicality, valuing mental meditation over physical devotion, but note in the following quotation how quickly the term 'soul' is conflated with the organs of the body. Given that a third of Laredo's first publication, *Metaphora medicine (et chirurgia)*,[109] was devoted to a treatise on surgery, such references to bodily organs would have been more than metaphorical.

Laredo continues to forefront embodiment in his overview of his Passion-centred mystical meditation:

> Let the soul not go to see such mysteries in the place where they occurred, rather let [the soul] attract the place and the event to itself and put it [the place] in itself, receiving [*recogiéndose*] everything within it ...
>
> What I want to say here is ... reflecting on his scourging, let your heart be the column, in such a way that with each blow or resort to force, you may not feel or think about any lash or blow that does not hit you on your column [i.e., spine], and because it is of hard insensitive rock it does not know how to melt in suitable compassion ...
>
> *Item*, if you reflect on the crowning, let your heart be the throne, or even the purple [robes], and there will be no thorn at all that will not touch and wound you or drip blood in your eyes, since the sacred blood burst out of [the eyes] and the mouth and ran down the face. And if you reflect on the cross, let your heart be the stone into which it was driven and however soft and interior the hole in it may be, in this manner the blood that runs down the wood may wash your hard substance and enter into the hole of your heart and never leave it. And in this manner all [Christ's] mysteries.[110]

Laredo's development of a Passion spirituality technique, one not previously found in Latin or Castilian Passion treatises, teaches that the devotee's body can become the physical site for the torture and crucifixion of Jesus: the devotee's spine is the column to which Christ is tied, his heart is the hole in the ground that stabilizes the cross, and Christ's blood rolls down the cross into the devotee's pupils.[111] Instead of rejecting the visual mode in order to increase internal spirituality, this method in fact intensifies the visual impact of the Passion events.

In addition, the meditator must imagine him- or herself locatively, as a part of the 'where,' rather than being just another human spectator in the tradition of Bonaventure on through the Castilian *Passio duorum*: 'Look to see if this is correct and return and enter into yourself and you will bring all the mysteries to yourself and all will fit within you. And you will be the Holy Land if you know how to enclose yourself and be joyful.'[112] Bradwardine's insistence on the mnemonic twinning of location *and* images discussed earlier is more clearly at play in Laredo's method than in Latin Passion treatises that focused on the characters alone. Yet this location is not a foreign city during a historical event, but instead occurs 'within' the believer, who becomes the Holy Land. The mnemotechnique of mentally moving through a detailed visualization of a scenario filled with *imagines agentes* and violence transforms the meditator's heart into the location, into the mnemonic device itself.

Laredo's proposal that his reader transpose Calvary as a physical location to his or her own soul is no mere metaphor, therefore, but has a firm physiological basis in the multiplication of *species* posited by the perspectivist school of intromission. In intromission, a viewed object is momentarily imprinted on the devotee's optic nerve; in this view, the phrase advocating the transformation of the devotee into the Holy Land is a reality of epistemology rather than a rhetorical flight of fancy. If the meditator *is* the column receiving the whiplash from the end of the cord used to beat Jesus, or *is* the chair as it is being stained by the blood flowing from Christ's thorn-pierced brow, then the act of visualization does not involve simply imprinting the optic nerve alone but in fact converts the devotee's body into the physical backdrop for the imagined scenario. Laredo's method physiologically transforms the heart of the believer, if the entrails of the believer are made identical with the visualized events, by being turned into Calvary.

These physical results have implications for Passion meditation as a mnemonic device as well. In Laredo's approach, the outside world is no longer an external distraction, but instead is brought within by a process of interiorization that reconstitutes the devotee as the mnemonic space against which the drama of Christ's death is played. The devotee's body becoming the site of the torture of Christ radically alters the standard visualizing methods that direct the devotee to imagine entering into Christ's side wound,[113] for Christ's suffering now occurs while Christ is impaled directly onto, and into, the devotee's body. Scarry argues that many torture techniques rely on common objects, even the walls of the room where the torture takes place or the captive's own body and muscular-skeletal system, to achieve heightened pain.[114] In Laredo's version of Passion-centred mystical prayer, the devotee transforms into the space and accoutrements of Golgotha where Christ suffers, and thus is implicitly a primary source of the pain that Christ underwent. Going beyond the typical medieval spiritual rhetoric reminding the devotee that every sin contributes to the reason that Christ had to die for humanity to save it, Laredo's method turns the devotee into the torturer of Christ.

It is at this point that another suggestion by Scarry is apt. She argues that when something becomes a weapon to inflict torture, it disappears as an object and becomes understood conceptually only as a source of pain sensation.[115] In this view, the devotee's body disappears in order to reappear as one, or rather, several, of the implements that tortured the Godman. In other words, the devout human body transforms into a weapon. Recalling Scarry's theory of the separation of pain from the body, we must note that since the sufferer can only name the weapon that produces pain rather than the pain itself ('it felt like a nail was hammered into my foot'), any distinction between weapon and pain is elided. The weapon *is* (the name for) the pain. This gives insight into Laredo's Passion technique – if the devotee transforms into the space and objects that inflict pain on Christ, then the devotee *is* (the name for) the pain Christ experiences.[116] Drawing on optics and mnemotechnique, Laredo formulates what could be called a 'mnemonic identity of pain' as the formula for approaching Passion meditation. But this logical extreme is not simply a noteworthy possibility. It would be of extraordinary importance to any devotee relying on mnemotechnique to improve devotional attitudes. Becoming the objects upon which Christ's suffering occurs turns the devotee into the mnemonic space he or she needs in order to remember more effectively, a process only of mystical interest because it in turn creates new knowledge of God. It is therefore crucial to consider the specifics of the bloody narrative Laredo inserts in the middle of a mystical treatise whose third part is traditionally understood to advocate a negative theology beyond the body, based on the soul's 'transformation into God through love.'

Locative Mnemonics and Cognitive Identity

By taking the scenes created throughout the streets of Seville in the *via crucis* and applying them internally, Laredo's formula for Passion meditation cognitively creates an identity between human and divine by means of transformative, yet visceral, pain. The radical implications of turning the meditator's entrails into the site of Christ's Passion become clear when Laredo at moments elides the Passion at Golgotha and the Passion in the meditator's soul so thoroughly that it is not Christ alone who ends up crucified. In a passage that constantly switches the referents for its pronouns, the soul is directed to pray in such a way that the soul becomes identical to the bleeding Christ, not just the objects and space that wound him. Laredo's methodological overview discussed earlier indicated that the devotee becomes the torturer of Christ; I argue that in the course of the actual meditations written out in the *Subida*, the torturer also becomes the recipient of his or her own infliction of pain:

> In addition, O wounded soul of mine, would you not deserve to go about tied up and bent over with a very wounded body, outrageously shamed alongside your beloved naked Jesus? Would you not deserve to go with your most wounded Christ among such insolent and godless people? O my sweetest love, and if only I could have some part of the spittle, hissing, slaps, and the rough cruelty with which you travelled that short road from the column to your robes! If only I could see you attempt to get dressed while trembling, only to see you stripped again with dreadful fury! If only I could remove the purple cloth from that outrageous mocking! If only I could remove the blindfold from your delicate eyes! If only I could remove the throne and the reed and the insults, the saliva, the blows and the slaps! Oh, if only you could see *the thorns penetrating into my soul; the blood that runs down the brow and face, through the hair and down the throat!* O my God, if only I could receive [the blood] in my poor wounded and inflamed heart! If only I could see it begin to appear in my tear-filled eyes, or gush out the burst eardrums and nostrils and mouth, tormented to the utmost! Who will go up with You to Pilate's *Ecce homo*, before the crowd of angry townspeople! More, O my God – who will tell me if my poor mother, the mother of us all, had already come to [from her swoon], and if she had eyes with which she could see you mocked and punished or if she hears that cruel voice: 'Crucify him, crucify him'?[117] (my emphasis)

Not only is the devotee the location of Christ's torture and in some sense participates in it by being part of the *arma Christi*, the meditator actually begins to feel the physiological results of the torture. In this passage, the phrasing of 'the thorns penetrate *my* soul' makes it possible that the blood running down the face and throat slides down the meditator's face rather than Jesus's brow (an outpouring of the most important fluid of the body, medically speaking). The phrasing of the paragraph hints that the crucial image in this visual meditation is in fact the devotee crucified, not Christ.

The cognitive possibility of this provocative rhetoric is due to an identity-based optical epistemology, since the devotee's imaginative visualization of a crucified Christ, a visualization that ends up crucifying the devotee, could well have been epistemologically possible. As Biernoff states: 'The potential of sight to cause physiological change is a recurring motif in medieval theology.'[118] Any theory of vision also relates to imaginative visualization, because the original viewed object was imprinted on the memory as a stamped image, to be brought back to the middle ventricle of the imagination and recombined with other images as needed. Taking the medieval cognitive background seriously shows that Laredo's passage actually reaches a step beyond Scarry's theory: If the devotee is identical to an unsayable and invisible pain, then the devotee could end up *suffering* the pain, not just *being* the pain.

This possibility is critical to the mystical praxis taught by Laredo's *Subida*. His stratagem to turn the reader into the Holy Land in order to map a visualized Passion onto the ascending soul allows for the introduction of the torturing devotee as recipient of the blows directed at Christ. A meditator who is the column marked by the tail end of the whiplash is in fact present at the scene, or has the scene present in him, in a manner that converts the process of outward visualization to the ultimate inward trajectory. Remember, by the corporeal logic of *passio* in which the type of pain that affects either body or soul is then transmitted to the other, the thorns that penetrate Christ's body convey pain to Christ's soul. When Laredo states that the same thorns that pierced Christ's brow penetrate the devotee's soul, then the devotee's body is also in pain, based on the reverse cognitive reality that a *passio* that first affects the soul is then communicated to the body. If he or she is the recipient of each blow, the meditator/torturer is transformed into the subject of the torture inflicted on Jesus. Ultimately, Jesus's bleeding body hanging from the entrails of the devotee's soul transforms the devotee into the crucified Christ himself.

My reading is supported by Laredo's presentation of the physiological identity between the ideal spectator to the Passion, the Virgin Mary, and her son as he was crucified. Laredo devotes a full three chapters (of fifteen in total on the Passion) to her station at the foot of the cross.[119] As discussed briefly in chapter 1, the medieval theological topos designating Mary as co-redemptrix described her as suffering more than Jesus did, since his was a limited physical suffering whereas her spiritual torment began with his torture and continued for the rest of her grief-stricken life. Laredo goes further than his predecessors, presenting Mary as suffering twice as much as Jesus, because insofar as he was flesh of her flesh, she actually suffered physical torments as well as pain in her soul.[120] Note how Laredo layers the violent mnemonics of Passion meditation onto the movement of the multivalent aquatic mnemonic that bookends his Passion narrative.[121]

> And if the lance split two hearts that were in one chest only, I confess that it split them, but I cannot nor do I want to feel that [the lance] could separate them – [they were] more broken than separated. Oh, if only He who consented to break his mother's heart within His own side and with the selfsame spear thrust would deign to shatter the heart of his poorest slave with the nail in his feet! ... What more can I say, my suffering love? One soul in both bodies, two bodies and one set of entrails, if there are two sets of entrails, is there more than one heart? One heart in two chests, and in two chests one side, one heart and one lance, one joining of indivisible love that neither life nor death separated. There was only one heart between the Virgin and Christ and only one will, and of her perfect conformity we say that the soul of the Virgin and the soul of Christ, being two, are yet only one soul; because the Son never did that which his Mother did not want, not even die, and the Mother never did anything against the will of Christ, not even live.
>
> And from this conformity of the Virgin with her God was constructed the ship in which she could cross the very tempest-tossed seas of the terrible Passion of her most beloved son. It is an established thing that a pious person can think that even if she [the Virgin] will navigate such a sea in such a great ship of love, he would be shipwrecked a thousand times, not because of the very sorrowful waters, in which he could easily swim, but because of the many rocks that each pain was hiding. Who is there that could think that, with the prow of the ship of love, but without the suffering[122] boat of such conformity, he could come upon or hit the most terrible rocks of the column or the cross and have the prow or stern stay in one piece? Oh, if only there were a *calafate* (which means a carpenter or a professional who repairs boats) who could solder it? I know that this is not so; that the wood of love is incapable of splitting or cracking, for it usually lists towards the side with the heavier load, nor can it sink, on the contrary it outlasts the storm.[123]

In this excerpt from one of the final chapters of his Passion narrative, Laredo amalgamates the spiritual sufferings of the mother and the physical son in such a way that his narrative does not provide a Passion of Christ and the *com*passion of Mary, as was traditional, but instead a single Passion of both Christ and Mary.[124] Laredo's emphasis on Mary, while aimed at a Castilian audience primed by the Franciscan Passion narratives of his brethren, thus has structural implications for the unity of the whole second stage. His rendition of her physiological identification with Christ, linked immediately to the oceanic mnemonic, unites the stylistically disparate first and second section of part 2, as the soul ships out to the sea of a bloody Christ in the boat of the co-redeeming Mary. It is worth noting that Laredo refers again to the cross and the column, the moments he had originally turned to when providing examples of how to locate the soul closer to the torture of Christ and thereby transpose the Passion onto the soul itself. Doctrine, mnemonic violence, placid seas, and vivid Passions (of Christ, of Mary, of the meditating soul) eventually come together in a mnemonic description of the 'wood of love' that will transform the soul in stage three.

Conclusion

Ultimately, in Laredo's scientifically accurate version of recollection mysticism, the touted 'transformation of the soul into God' first occurs by means of mnemonic transformation of the embodied soul into the tortured Christ. This absolute identification of an embodied soul with the embodied divine paradoxically occurs even as the divine is dripping blood into the eyes of the soul's veins and is crucified in the entrails of the self-crucifying soul. Given an embodied divine whose presence at the centre of an embodied soul must be recognized in order to achieve a union always already lived out, Passion meditation turns out to be the core of a mystical method that depends on cognitive identity between a divinized human and a bleeding divine. Laredo's proposal therefore calls for a radical reconfiguration of the foundational assumptions of theories of mysticism that have served for so long to separate Passion spirituality from 'proper' or 'fully mature' mysticism. Laredo's elevation of Passion spirituality to the central stage of tripartite mystical ascent to God requires us to reconsider the value of the medical body, both visualized and visualizing, in the mnemonic Renaissance preparation for a mystical experience of God.

By not paying proper attention to Laredo's presuppositions about the cognitive and medical body of the aspiring mystic, scholars of Spanish mysticism have consistently overlooked Laredo's re-centring of Passion spirituality as pivotal to his mystic way, relegating the second stage of his tripartite method to a 'beginner' stage rather than exploring it as the central of three stages towards union with a God who can only be known through the body.[125] I suggest that is not possible to understand the origins and goals of this Galenic physician's rendition of the devotee's elemental body as the backdrop against which the drama of Christ's suffering occurs unless we examine the cognitive processes that made the mnemonic identity implicit in Passion visualization an effective method for uniting with God. For Laredo, if God who is at the core of all human souls took on the 'covering' of humanity in his incarnation,[126] then the pain inflicted on the body of God must be remembered by the embodied soul of the mystic who resonates with, even experiences, Christ's pain down to the 'pupils of the eyes of his soul.'

Conclusion: Cognition in Recollected Union

Modern scholars are unanimous in declaring the stage of recollection, termed the 'unitive way' in the 1538 edition of Laredo's *Subida del Monte Sión*,[1] to be the most important section of Laredo's prescriptive guide to the mystical ascent. Not only does Andrés choose the third level of *recogimiento* as the primary focus of his *summa* on the genre of recollection mysticism,[2] but Ros, in the sole comprehensive monograph on Laredo, turns to it with evident relief after complying with a sense of fair play that demanded at least a summary of the first two stages of the *Subida*.[3] Given that stage three was the focus of Laredo's revisions between 1535 and 1538, contains his most strenuous denials of capacity as an author because of his stated lack of unitive experience,[4] and does not conform to the proposed schema of meditations organized by days of the week, Laredo himself evidently found this section, if not the most interesting, at least the most problematic portion of his treatise.

Scholars focus on the final stage of *recogimiento* because they assume that union with an infinite God by definition must transcend the finite corporeal aspects of the self. They therefore give the apparently bodily practice of Passion meditation short shrift, presuming instead that each stage of the method outclasses the previous stage in a steady build-up to the grand finale of recollected union. Scholarship on the *Subida* frequently privileges the 1538 version of stage three over that of the 1535 version.[5] Those who do explore the transition in Laredo's thought between the two versions of stage three believe his new source texts from medieval spirituality prompted a fundamental shift in method in the 1538 edition.[6] Scholars classify Laredo's 'best' technique as a form of affective mysticism inflected by the language of negative theology. To review the differences between the two editions briefly: In 1535, Laredo advocated a threefold ecstatic union based on the method of Richard of Saint Victor,[7] usually understood to privilege the role of understanding in mystical union. Laredo's 1535 version reads: 'The first point is to enter into my heart. The second is to go above my heart. The third is to appear in the presence of my Lord, [who is] lodged in the highest heights of the soul.'[8] The 1538 edition presents Victorine ecstasy as best accomplished by the apophatic process defined by Hugh of Balma and Heinrich Herp as sudden aspirative leaps to union through a loving will. I have argued elsewhere that Laredo's preference in the revision of 1538 for the language of negative theology does not fundamentally alter his 1535 method.[9]

Here I probe the possibility that considering the *Subida* as a whole with attention to its cognitive context renders moot any simplistic distinction between the faculties of the soul, understanding, and will, a possibility that has so far escaped scholarly attention because Laredo articulates integrates the cognitive process with the faculties of the soul in part 2, which scholars ignore. In the methodological overview of his Passion meditation, he states that the meditation will be accomplished with a 'silenced understanding ... without sound and without discursiveness ... the soul being advised not to go out of itself to look for mysteries, since it will have them in itself if it considers itself in them.'[10] Laredo expands on 'silenced understanding' in the next chapters: in the ascent of the mount of contemplation, the first level of self-knowledge is achieved through the discursive work of the understanding; the second level of the mysteries of Christ through the understanding plus the receptive will; and the final level of recollection is quiet contemplation infused into the will.[11] As far as I know, Laredo is unique among mystical and meditative authors up to and including his era, both around Europe and in Spain, in assigning Passion meditation to the powers of both understanding and will rather than consigning it to the discursive scurrying of the understanding alone. His re-evaluation of how the faculty of understanding works during Passion meditation, in which it is silenced in some fashion in order to harmonize with the receptive will, eliminates the traditional gulf between the capacities of each of these two powers.[12]

Two prevailing views – the assumption by modern historians of mysticism such as McGinn that Passion meditation is always intended for beginners, and the assumption by Laredo scholars that the first two stages of his *Subida* are preliminary to the true unitive stage in part 3 – gloss over critical aspects of human epistemology's roots in the cognitive process. Leaving aside the mechanics of meditation itself, such as memory's fulcrum role as a physiological location among the inner senses and as a faculty of the soul, limits the accuracy of scholarly value judgments on the efficacy of the mystical method. Laredo's presentation of God at the centre of the soul can only be fully analysed if we understand that all information with which the soul can think (and recognize its God) comes ultimately from external senses, routed through vision above all, and processed in the brain.

In this conclusion, I highlight the cognitive continuities that link Laredo's first two stages with the third, specifically in relation to the medical body and its optical epistemology at work in the mnemonic device of Passion meditation. For example, the following passage, if read with the assumption that the third stage surpasses the other corporeal stage, seems quite standard: 'Those who contemplate God attain the greatest perfection by carefully closing the gates of the five senses and getting rid of all that is not God from the heart.'[13] I argue that it is impossible to understand this passage as a mere denigration of all that is corporeal, not after part 2's rendition of the bleeding body of Christ cognitively reconfigures the soul's entrails into the backdrop of Christ's torture, and even transforms the embodied soul of the devotee into Jesus. 'Getting rid of all that is not God from the heart' is a different kettle of fish from simply rejecting human sensory information. At this stage, the devotee's heart is *already* filled with God, albeit a crucified divine accessed by means of an interiorizing cognitive process.

The main portion of this book engaged the first two stages of Laredo's method in order to bring their relevance to his method to scholarly attention. Here, I briefly examine the cognitive and physiological elements present in both versions of his third stage of recollection. The core argument of my close scientific reading – that transformation into God (as the crucified Christ) begins in stage two as a natural extension of Galenic cognitive processes – clarifies Laredo's interventions in part 3 in the debates over the role of the faculty of understanding in meditative versus contemplative methods, and the respective role of the understanding versus the will in mystical union. I end by indicating the continuing concern with the embodied soul, not to mention the medical body, expressed by Laredo's most famous readers, Teresa of Avila and John of the Cross. The final section can do no more than point the way to future avenues of research, but it proves that ignoring embodiment by assuming the priority of the abstract in medieval, Renaissance, and Golden Age mystical texts profoundly limits scholarly efforts to explicate methods intended to achieve mystical union in a pre-modern era.

Mystical Cognition in the Recollection Method of 1535

It is my contention that Laredo never separates the physiological transformation of the soul into Jesus's humanity from the unitive process of loving transformation in either edition of the *Subida*. Throughout stage three, Laredo continues to draw on the variety of medical and cognitive assumptions previously delineated in stages one and two. In the 1535 version of the recollection stage, he mentions once again the elements, humors, and qualities of the medical body (and even the medicinal qualities of certain plants found in contemporary pharmaceuticals).[14] These Galenic details are notably brought forth in a chapter dedicated to explaining how the particularities of a human being lead to comprehending the power and wisdom of a God found at the centre of the soul.[15] In addition to these terms drawn from humoral theory, Laredo makes constant mention of the 'eyes of the soul.' While a reading of part 3 on its own could easily attribute this phrasing to the classical spiritual trope about the interior vision of God, I suggest that Laredo's use of the physiological assumptions of optics in his first reference to vision in the third stage carries through as the context for every future mention of the soul's eyes or the 'wide open eyes' of the faculty of understanding.[16]

Elsewhere, Laredo integrates mnemonic devices directly into the highest heights of the soul's union on the basis of medical and cognitive insights into how human thought processes function. In the final chapters of the treatise, he gives a spiritual reconfiguration of a medical aphorism originally coined by the ancient Greek doctor Hippocrates, mentioning that the utility of an aphorism is that its metre allows it to be retained better in the memory.[17] He then supplies forty original spiritual aphorisms concerning love's role in the pursuit of mystical union. Not only do the aphorisms serve a mnemonic function, but the role of the Passion as mnemotechnique is recapitulated in one of the forty aphorisms: 'If Christ is in the memory, victory is always gained.'[18] In fact, Laredo reproduces the list of aphorisms in the 1538 edition, indicating that one essential overlap between the two versions is the continuing place for Christ in the devotee's memory during the process of recollected transformation into God.

These uses of Galenic medicine, mnemonics, and optical epistemology all depend on Laredo's continued reliance on a theory of the soul as embodied, one still present in the unitive stage, as evidenced by such phrases as 'entrails of the rational soul,'[19] or even the 'marrow of the bones of the entrails of the soul.'[20] The final chapters of the 1535 edition prove this point, for he states in no uncertain terms that recollection is an 'interior occasion' with physical repercussions: mystical contemplation can lead to bleeding or broken bones in the course of ecstatic rapture.[21] He also warns that the devotee's ribs will feel like they are literally cracking as his or her soul expands to allow heaven to fit within it.[22] Laredo thus retains a notion of the body–soul continuum throughout the unitive stage that scholars have heretofore read as negating all that is corporeal. Moreover, this body–soul continuum never exists without its medical and cognitive framework.

Laredo's continued deployment of medical and cognitive details in his method of mystical prayer makes possible a new reading of his most extensive comments on the role of love and knowledge in recollection, a discussion found near the beginning of the 1535 third stage. Note that he is unable to address the topic of which faculty of the soul, understanding or will, helps reach union with God without reference to the mnemonics of Passion meditation; in fact, he makes it quite clear that cognitive processes continue even during 'quiet contemplation,' for memory of the Passion narrative continues 'tacitly' in the devotee throughout all the time devoted to recollection itself. I quote this passage at length to highlight Laredo's interweaving of love and knowledge with Passion meditation during his first full description of the heights of recollected union. Of particular note is his re-introduction of the ocean and ship mnemonic device from part 2:[23]

> Furthermore, love requires knowledge and knowledge begs a discourse of understanding that will seek out causes and effects and clear reason, until it ends up attaching itself to the truest truth and giving itself to the will, without which truth, reason never learns to be quiet. And it is certain that this discourse, however much it is ordered and [how much] in and of itself it is very worthwhile to those of us who are right now in our novitiates, it is most certain that it is a very great impediment to the quiet will, which asks to be quite alone to enjoy its God alone and sail out into the deeps of love, without looking for reasons for loving, all of which must already have been accomplished by proficients. But I cannot judge, nor do I want to be able to want for it to sound right to me that the contemplative soul, living in this exile, ought to leave the Passion and the high mysteries of our loving love, even for a day; and [since] walking continually in [the Passion] with all the understanding is a great obstacle to the quiet will, let this be given as a remedy: to wit, continually split the parts while leaving the time [devoted to mystical prayer] whole. I mean by this that to one part of man, which is the soul, should be given all time without time for quiet contemplation during all the moments and times that [contemplation] can be received, without working to seek it with anything more than living desires and awakened attention ... As to the other part of man, which in this division is our donkey or little ass or donkey body, put the cross on it ... Concerning that which the soul fails to contemplate in the mysteries of Christ in order to give itself over to quiet and calm prayer, it

> must beg the body ... to walk always with Christ crucified on the cross, made out of poverty and scorn and pain. And in such a way [the devotee] will rest in God and work with Christ, knowing that Christ is God, our good and our protection.
>
> [*Chapter 6*] When all our works function in the previously noted manner, the Passion of our Christ Jesus is never forgotten for a moment or even an hour, yet it occupies no time. Rather, that which used to be held in the living understanding passes to the 'tacit' [or quieted] memory, so that abstinence is never achieved without remembering for whom, though almost without looking at it ... And the soul travels by this road until it is becomes fully capable [of this method], so that the times [the devotee] lacks corporeal strength to carry the cross, [his or her] memory already possesses the passion in such a manner that [the devotee] will never let [the cross] fall, nor could it do so even if [he or she] wanted to.[24]

In the first paragraph, Laredo appears to advocate an approach originally propounded by Osuna in his *Tercer abecedario espiritual* wherein the body is meant to follow Christ's humanity and the soul his divinity,[25] a method that presupposes that meditation on or imitation of Christ is lesser and thus more appropriate for the body. In the turn to chapter 6, however, Laredo quickly reneges on this body–soul distinction, proposing that a 'tacit' memory of the Passion can continue to fortify the soul during contemplation even if the body has no more strength to imitate Christ. (Later, he will call contemplation itself 'tacit,' thus erasing any strong distinction between meditation and contemplation.)[26] By involving the more quiescent power of memory rather than the discursive and distractible understanding, Laredo here manages to stifle all the usual arguments against Passion meditation as mystical method. Memory, both a physiological location in the brain and a power of the soul, continues to link body and soul throughout the unitive stage in which contemplative exercises transform the soul into its God.

Although Laredo has not yet fully addressed recollection as union, in the quoted passage above he declares that a loving will is more necessary to union than is the faculty of the understanding. The next chapter in the *Subida* proves that he considers the two techniques of Passion meditation and recollection to be closely related. Calling once again for his reader to devote a moment every day, or at least every week, to the Passion,[27] he elaborates on the phrase concerning the 'quiet will ... sail[ing] out into the [ocean] deeps of love' in order to explain certain parallels between the activity of the understanding during Passion meditation and the quieting of the understanding during recollection:

> [S]ometimes the soul leaves the bodily mysteries that it is treating and without thinking, suddenly, it finds itself within itself without any bodiliness, it itself not knowing that it wanted to stop here where it sees itself halted in tacit love alone, without knowing how to feel that it was so in love that it could have love.
>
> Thus it must be noted that [during Passion meditation] our understanding is like a large river, which never stops running day or night, but instead sometimes runs into some very large floodgates and large caverns, which are the great desires that barely or not at all swell with the impetuous mob of surging waters that run in the whole river, that is, with the meditative discourses of the whole understanding. Instead, the water resting in that concavity forms an absorbing ocean …
>
> This ocean in the soul is the quiet will, which is here like a ship that is becalmed and stuck out to sea, which, even if it wants to, cannot tack either this way or that, but remains quiet as long as the calm, that is, the quietude, endures …
>
> In fact, when the soul can reach these gulfs full of water it ought not pass beyond there, but rather be absorbed and let itself submerge and not concern itself or weaken, not wanting to get rid of all the oars of the understanding and all five senses and everything that can be taken, which often impede greatly on such occasions. Yet when [the soul] does not reach the gulf, if it runs with … a discrete and limited understanding, it many times gains a lot and very rarely loses anything.[28]

Laredo here makes his most effective claim for the continued importance of meditation on the Passion during recollected union by asserting (with a continuation of mnemonic devices from stage two) that just as the continual flow of a river carves out caves and quiet pools in which the flowing water is subsequently caught, so discursive meditation often creates the conditions for the soul to suddenly reach a state of passive love in the quiet will.

While it is true that in the first chapters of the 1535 version of stage three, Laredo periodically dismisses the utility of meditation or information gained by the senses as distractingly corporeal, a point that previous scholars have underscored, it is also true that each time he does so, he returns in the following chapter to an emphasis on the continued value of Passion meditation and self-knowledge. Note that Figure 1.1 (reproduced in chapter 1) of a friar holding a book and a crucifix is one of the few large woodcuts in the 1535 edition – this depiction of Passion-centred devotions heads the first chapter of the supposedly non-corporeal stage three! In fact, reading against the grain that privileges his dismissal of sense-based practices, it becomes evident that Laredo makes constant reference to the first two stages in the course of the recollection stage. He mentions the soul as filth, provides yet more brief narratives of the Passion, and recalls the mnemonic image of the castle (as found in Revelation),[29] all points guaranteed to remind the devotee of the supposedly earlier or beginner stages of the mystical method. Much as the mnemonic device including the mystical saddle of recollection during the stage of self-knowledge foreshadowed the fact that the practice of recollection is not reserved for the final stage, Laredo's 1535 emphasis on self-knowledge and Passion meditation throughout stage three indicates that no part of this method is preliminary – all three stages are ongoing during the transformation into God through love.

Cognition, Embodied Soul, and Eucharistic Passion in the 1538 Unitive Way

Laredo continues to deploy his knowledge of the medical and cognitive body in his 1538 revision. This occurs most fully in the meditations that explicate a series of couplets concerning love originally proposed in the 1535 edition. Laredo analyses one couplet with reference to the function of colour in optics; in another couplet's meditation he reminds his readers that thought begins with the faculty of the memory and follows this with a verse discussing the mnemonic device of the city as provided in Revelation.[30] Traces of cognition are found elsewhere as well: he refers to the inner senses of fantasy and imagination, describes both the imagination and the faculty of the will as 'tacit,' emphasizes visual epistemology by describing two eyes as the understanding and will rather than a physical eye versus an interior eye, and quotes Herp's analogy of bees and wax for the faculty of understanding and memory.[31] Laredo's use of cognitive theory continues to inflect a concept of the embodied soul, as he describes the soul as loving with (or from) its entrails but at one and the same time physically wounded (*llagas tan sentibles*) in its most tender, interior *entrañas*.[32] In fact, Christ is still within the twisted and wounded soul even during union.[33]

Finally, even more so than in the 1535 edition, Laredo alternates between dismissing the body's role in mystical experience (in favour of the loving soul) and returning again and again to the importance of meditation on the wounds of Christ or the Crucifixion, as well as ritual.[34] It is of note that Teresa of Avila was inspired by her reading of Laredo's *Subida*, specifically his terminology of *no pensar nada* (not thinking anything) to describe the soul as resting in union with God, a fact scholars rely on in the assumption that negative theology is the key aspect of the *Subida*. However, the chapter she cites, 1538's chapter 27,[35] is followed immediately by the most direct statement in the 1538 version of part 3 that Passion meditation is the critical fulcrum point leading to contemplation.[36] One resolution to this apparent continuing contradiction may be found in Laredo's statement that mystical theology must be 'read [with a stutter] in the entrails, sensed in the soul, and planted in the heart.'[37] In this statement, apophatic theology is fully, physiologically interiorized; thus every chapter on *no pensar nada* requires pairing with a method valuing physiology.

The full import of Laredo's integration of the physiological and cognitive body into the stage of *recogimiento* emerges in relation to the single greatest structural change between the two editions. In the 1538 edition, instead of the Eucharistic treatise that had been included in 1535's part 2 after the mnemonic of the fortress, Laredo substituted a chapter on the love of God (originally composed for the end of part 3).[38] He did not delete discussion of the Eucharist from his method but instead placed a new series of chapters on the Eucharist near the end of part 3, just before several chapters on transformation into love repeated nearly verbatim from the 1535 version.[39] The second half of the new Eucharistic mini-treatise consists of an excerpt from a dialogue between the soul and God's Wisdom from Heinrich Suso's *Horologium sapientiae*.[40] Suso (d. 1366) was a German mystic whose work centres on personal experience stemming from Passion meditation. Whereas Laredo's new readings in negative theology would have made it obvious to him that many mystics did not consider the Passion an appropriate topic for union achieved abstractly through the loving will, I read his reliance on Suso (by far the longest citation found in the *Subida*) as an appeal to an authority who had not only been interested in the Passion but had even taken Jesus's sacrifice as the subject of his entire work. By this means, Laredo makes his work more palatable to those readers familiar with the medieval tradition of tripartite contemplative treatises, yet does not deviate from his own intuition, grounded in Franciscan thought and Sevillian lay tradition, that Christ's Passion is intrinsic to the union of the soul with God.

Laredo did not transfer the Eucharistic treatise to the recollection stage in order to provide advice for those readers about to receive the wafer, but rather as the culmination of the previous thirty chapters on union through love: 'The entire intent of this third book is to join the soul to its God by way of unitive love, and the most perfect union that is possible or that can exist in this harsh exile consists of the Communion of the most blessed Sacrament given in grace.'[41] His presentation of Eucharistic theology details God's love for humans in establishing this sacrament as well as human love for God shown by participating in the Eucharist as much as possible.[42] Psychologically, the process of digesting the sacramental symbol of Jesus's sacrifice is the ultimate act of confirming God's physical location at the centre of the soul. Likewise, it is illuminating that Laredo describes the reception of the Eucharist as follows: 'In this way this highest of sacraments makes a marvelous impression on the soul ... infus[ing] a ready, new and living city into the most alive, pure, and tender entrails [of the soul].'[43] Here the mnemonic device of the city creates spatial memory within the embodied soul as a result of a sacrament designated as transforming the elements of bread and wine into the very flesh and primary Galenic humor that Jesus sacrificed during Holy Week. The transposition of the Eucharistic treatise to the penultimate topic in recollection union strikes me as at least as fundamental to the radical revisions he applied to the third stage as was his desire to extend the discussion of affectivity or loving union by citing Balma's and Herp's negative theology.[44]

It is the contention of this book that the critical role of human cognitive models in understanding the mystical route to God cannot be left out of any analysis of the stage of union, for it is cognition, and the overturning of cognition after being transformed physiologically into the divine, that is core to Laredo's representation of the heights of his method. *No pensar nada* is Laredo's version of the classic 'unknowing' of negative theology, but it is in fact an 'unthinking.' Only a historically accurate understanding of 'thinking' as an epistemological sequence dependent on Galenic cognitive physiology allows us to fully engage with Laredo's method for the transformation of the embodied soul into the bleeding divine, understood biblically as so loving the world that his physical crucifixion was the ultimate act of transforming love and thereby the appropriate basis for mystical union.[45]

Cognition and Transformation through Pain in Carmelite Mysticism

Recognizing medical terminology, mnemonic devices, optics, and theories of pain as central to Laredo's formulation of a method of mystical prayer helps identify important new avenues of research for the study of Golden Age mysticism. While it is not within the scope of this project to propose new readings of any mystic besides Laredo himself, I argue that his work, both the method itself and his reliance on medieval understandings of cognition, affected Teresa of Avila and John of the Cross in far more complex ways than their simple acceptance of his term *no pensar nada.* I do not make the claim that every physiological and epistemological element of Carmelite spirituality that I highlight here has its direct source in Laredo; rather, their cognitive importance in Laredo's work suggests that they may well have played a more critical role in the works of Teresa and John than previously recognized. The leading scholarly work on cognition in the two Carmelites, Edward Howells's work on 'mystical knowing and selfhood,' is quite thorough, but does not address the physiological basis of cognition. My suggestions here draw attention to the confluence of medical, mnemonic, and/or optical points in certain passages that serve to extend or complicate Howells's insights.[46]

Teresa of Avila (1515–82), canonized in 1622 and named a doctor of the Catholic Church in 1970 (one of only four women so designated), is the most widely read of any Golden Age mystic. Her works were not published until after her death, however, held back by the Inquisition during a series of investigations. A woman from a *converso* family who spearheaded a reform of the Carmelite Order, established over twenty new Discalced houses, and wrote about her visionary experiences in the vernacular was an obvious target for inquisitorial inquiry.[47] In her famous autobiography, *Libro de la vida* (Book of Her Life), she names the *Subida* as pivotal to the start of her writing career. Required by an inquisitorial board to write about her mystical experiences in order for them to be evaluated for orthodoxy, she states:

> Looking through books to see if I could learn how to describe the prayer I had, I found in one, called *The Ascent of the Mount*, in the part which concerns the union of the soul with God, all the symptoms I had when I was unable to think of anything (*no pensar nada*). It was exactly this that I was always saying – that when I was experiencing that type of prayer I could think of nothing.[48]

I posit that Teresa's debt is more profound than this one citation and its apparent preference of the apophatic strand in the *Subida*,[49] as she proves not only to value Laredo's passion-centred method but also to draw on a wide range of elements intended to activate cognitive processes in the devotee. Maria Berbara argues cogently that Teresa's lifelong experiences of painful ailments and physical rapture led her to 'see no contradiction between bodily pain and spiritual joy.'[50] Reading Teresa in light of Laredo reveals that she drew her insights from a notion of embodied soul that goes beyond the spiritual benefits of corporeal suffering.

In her work written to guide nuns through a process of mystical prayer, *Camino de perfección* (after 1565), Teresa outlines the prayer of *recogimiento*:

> This prayer is called 'recollection' because the soul collects its faculties together and enters within itself to be with its God ... For centred there within itself, it can think about the Passion and represent the Son and offer him to the Father and not tire the intellect by going to look for him on Mount Calvary or in the garden or at the pillar.[51]

Teresa describes *recogimiento* as an interiorization of the Passion, an approach only found in Laredo.[52] Note her use of the term 'represent' (*representar*), which according to the dictionary of Spanish language released shortly after her death was defined as 'making something present with words or an image that is fixed in our imagination.'[53] She therefore does not simply assume that Passion meditation is a critical element of recollection but in fact also portrays Jesus's Crucifixion as an image fixed in the inner sense of the imagination. It is quite possible that Teresa herself was aware of definitions of the inner sense that describe images imprinted on the memory; she certainly knew enough medicine to recommend pharmaceutical remedies to her nuns.[54]

Teresa's identification of *recogimiento* with Laredo's formula continues throughout the chapter, not only because she mentions the analogy of the bee collecting honey as the collecting of the powers of the soul (in *Subida* part 3, 1538; see above),[55] but also because she revisits the two mnemonic devices that bookend Laredo's Passion meditation in *Subida* part 2. She compares the recollected to those who travel on the ocean, then suggests the image of a memory palace made of gold and jewels as a useful tool for women who have no education and must instead rely on images to aid their thought processes.[56] For that matter, earlier in the treatise, just after recommending the use of meditation guides that apportion the events of the Passion to different days of the week, she describes the soul as a wild horse that needs riding, a description that segues immediately into an aquatic metaphor.[57] The confluence of every single one of Laredo's mnemonic devices points towards the possibility that her brief deployment of the various images is not simply stylistically pleasant but deliberately evokes a method that depends on imagistic 'hooks' to be activated.

Given these allusions to Laredo's collection of memory images,[58] let us follow the memory palace mentioned briefly in the *Camino de perfección* as it becomes the organizing image for Teresa's most famous work, the

Moradas del castillo interior (known in English as *Interior Castle*). This late treatise proposes a method of mystical practice and prayer over seven stages, structured around 'a castle made entirely out of a diamond or of very clear crystal, in which there are many rooms.'[59] The crystalline castle represents the soul, yet throughout the work Teresa designates the soul as wandering through this architectural complex, circling ever nearer to God at its centre. The soul is described by, yet roams within, the mnemonic device, thereby functioning as an *imagines agente* providing the requisite movement (*ductus*) required by sophisticated mnemotechnique. Both Michael Gerli and María M. Carrión explore the link between mnemonics and Teresa's famous device, but they note the connection with mnemotechnique in general rather than Laredo as a source or model.[60] Luce López-Baralt locates the description of seven concentric castles in Sufi mystical sources but does not consider the mnemonic utility of the image in articulating Teresa's theological anthropology.[61] I suggest that comparative work on the utility of mnemotechnique for these two influential Christian authors carries with it great potential for the field. The difference between Laredo's fortress surrounding a field full of candles and Teresa's moated castle lies in Laredo's permutation of his device to describe the Trinity, Christ's nature, and Mariology, in addition to using it to portray the soul. Teresa, on the other hand, presents her image as depicting the nature and progress of the soul above all, providing a more sustained mnemonic disquisition on one theological topic than Laredo does in his continual variation of a single image to unify disparate theological topics. Laredo's manner of employing memory devices, however, signals that the various repeated elements of Teresa's castle (non-sequential rooms, poisonous beasts lurking in various corners, and so on)[62] deserve a close reading, which would reveal the subtle shifts in the mnemonic's architectural details and *imagines agentes* that may mark key moments of doctrinal elaboration previously overlooked.

Finally, in her autobiography, *Libro de la vida*, Teresa emphasizes the import of a cognitively based Passion-centred recollection to her own spiritual progress. She mentions that she tried to 'represent Christ inside herself,' not in an abstract way but rather in contemplating his suffering in Gethsemane. Not only does she fix this image inside herself, but she imagines herself interacting directly with the divine by wiping the bloody sweat of Jesus's brow, a spiritual process she takes care to describe as occurring *without* the usual discursiveness of the understanding involved in Passion meditation.[63] I argue that Teresa's intimate acquaintance with mnemonic devices as necessarily accompanying the Passion meditation is rooted in

Laredo's reconfiguration of the Passion imprinted on the entrails of the soul through the use of a silenced understanding. The critical importance of Passion meditation as a mnemonic device that leads to transformation into God, however, indicates that further studies are needed to determine the cognitive utility of other, less violent types of mnemonic devices used in mystical methods in Castile and elsewhere that either avoid mention of the Passion or do not discourse on it at length.

The mnemonic value of violence is the aspect I wish to signal in the works of Teresa's most famous friend and disciple, John of the Cross (1542–91).[64] While the direct impact of Laredo on John's writing is not acknowledged by John himself, several scholars have pointed to overarching similarities or specific metaphors, particularly given Laredo's and John's reliance on the technique of apophatic theology and the obvious parallels between the tripartite ascents in the *Subida del Monte Sión* and John's *Subida del Monte Carmelo* (John's version is accompanied in the treatise by a sketch of the mountain that cries out for extended mnemonic analysis).[65] Howells explores John's awareness of faculty psychology extensively, proposing that John separates spiritual and sensory faculties but models them as parallels to each other.[66] I suggest that it is also necessary to take into account the availability of the theory of embodied soul promulgated so provocatively by Laredo. While John does not narrate an extensive meditation on the Passion that could cue a reconsideration of the privileging of negative theology in scholarship on his mystical techniques, a brief glance at his most famous work, *La noche oscura* (usually called *The Dark Night of the Soul*) indicates his reliance on a body–soul continuum, for he describes the effects of contemplation on the soul as producing numerous forms of agony and pain.[67] An uncontextualized analysis would read these passages as concerning a form of mental grief, but consideration of physiological systems reminds us that scholastic theologians had originated the medical theory that the soul's agonies always have bodily consequences. It thus behooves modern scholars to consider the physicality of this scenario, for agonized contemplation can render the devotee equivalent to a suffering divine.

It is thus noteworthy that in John's specific citation of the phrase, *no pensar nada*, in *The Dark Night of the Soul*, the soul both suffers and endures but is warned not to attempt to accomplish anything with the inner senses – in so doing, it would lose the benefit of the good that God imprints ('engraves') on the inner senses. '[The soul] cannot do anything or think of anything [*no puede hacer ni pensar nada*] in prayer … If individuals were to desire to do something themselves with their interior faculties, they would hinder and lose the goods that God engraves on their souls through that peace and idleness.'[68] John's method thus renders God as taking over the process of cognition by imprinting images on the soul; while the soul in this case is far more passive than in Laredo's version, the need to situate a mystical method in relation to the cognitive assumptions of its era is clear. For example, John's reliance on poetry to encapsulate the core of his method, poetry he later expands on in scholastic-like commentaries, becomes recognizable as a sophisticated version of mnemotechnique, not just a contribution to the literary renaissance of Golden Age Spain.

I suggest that John of the Cross unites all of the main elements of Laredo's recollection method in several key chapters of his lengthy *Cántico espiritual* (*Spiritual Canticle*). His commentary on stanzas 12–13 of his rewriting of the biblical Song of Songs combines many of the cognitive details conjoined in Laredo's *Subida*. God creates the soul in the same way that an impression is made on wax, the soul's burning desire for God makes itself known in a faith that is compared to both a crystal and a spring of water, and the truth of faith is described as the gaze that the Beloved's eyes direct at her heart.[69] All these details reminiscent of the cognitive sequence combine into a description of the transformation of the soul into God through love,[70] a transformation that produces intense pain and torment.[71] '[T]he knowledge of God is commensurate with suffering for him.'[72] For John, as for Laredo, pain is central to transformation into God through love, a transformation accomplished through effective use of mnemonic devices and descriptions of God's impact on the soul that rely on medical norms for epistemology.

Laredo was a pivotal figure in Spanish mysticism precisely because of his grasp of the range of theories concerning the body–soul continuum that cross the spectrum of medieval science and spirituality. It was natural for him to develop a method to train devotees in the preparation for mystical union that took into account *both* the medical and religious realities of his audience. While no other mystic in the Golden Age could have profited from such a profound professional awareness of the physiological nature of cognition, Laredo's *Subida* contributed a critical confluence of spiritual and scientific postulates that influenced later mystics in their definition of human anthropology's relevance to the quest for the divine. As a consequence, our construction of the intellectual history of Spanish mysticism is impoverished if we do not take into account the contemporaneous scientific basis for the epistemology of the believer who yearned to find God at the centre of his or her embodied, cognitively constructed soul.

Notes

Introduction

1 I use Spanish names for all individuals discussed in this book, except for Teresa of Avila and John of the Cross, the only ones sufficiently discussed in English-language scholarship to be standard referents in the field. Laredo's dates cannot be fixed exactly, as the death date 1540 is based on the hagiographical tradition, yet a revised version of his pharmaceutical treatise was published in 1542 without any mention of the death of the author. See chapter 2 for the few confirmable details concerning Laredo's biography.

2 '¡Y no meresciera el pobrete pecador que fueran preciosos vasos las pupilas de los ojos de las venas que están dentro en las entrañas de mi alma, en los quales se cogiera la sacratíssima sangre que corría por el sagrado madero, sin parar hasta la tierra dende el clavo de los pies de mi amoroso Señor!' Laredo, *Subida del Monte Sión* II, chap. 22, p. 281. The modern edition of the *Subida* begins with the second version (published in 1538), with footnotes added to parts 1 and 2 indicating the small changes Laredo made to the 1535 edition. After the complete 1538 text, the editors then provide part 3 from the 1535 edition, since only a few chapters from it were retained in the 1538 version. The end of the edition includes several appendixes published in both editions: a life of Joseph, a sequence of letters (the 'Extravagante'), and a note on cycles of masses used to cure patients of a variety of illnesses. I will be quoting from the 2000 edition, as it is now easily accessible, and following the editorial decision to retain Laredo's variagated spelling but modernize the punctuation. Citations to the *Subida* note the edition date where applicable; any citation without a date indicates that the phrase appears in both 1535 and 1538 editions. All translations are my own, although I provide the page reference to *The Ascent of Mount Zion*, the English translation by Peers (referred to hereafter as 'trans. Peers') for any citation from the third part of the 1538 edition.

3 E. Allison Peers introduced Spanish mysticism to the English-speaking world and included Laredo among its masters. See Peers, *Studies of the Spanish Mystics*. Fidèle de Ros considered Laredo essential because of his influence on Teresa de Avila and wrote the only truly comprehensive monograph that exists on Laredo. Ros, *Inspirateur de Sainte Thérèse*.

4 The phrase is from the primary definition of *recogimiento*. Andrés, *Los recogidos*, 89. For a critique, see the section 'Body–Soul Dualism in the History of Christian Mysticism,' this introduction.

5 Elements of world-denying (*contemptus mundi*) texts and vice and virtue treatises are found in stage one, a 'Life of Christ' (*Vita Christi*) meditation is central to stage two, and Victorine intellectual contemplation and late medieval apophatic theology influenced two revisions of stage three. I trace the sources for Laredo's spirituality in Boon, 'Mystical Language of Recollection.' The argument of this book rests on the dissertation's conclusion concerning the centrality of Passion spirituality to Laredo's version of recollection but offers an entirely different reconstruction of it.

6 It is possible to determine Laredo's influence on later religous authors through citations in published treatises and in monastic libraries. Ros, *Inspirateur de Sainte Thérèse*, 309–35. But there is no reason to think that a widely available book would not also have been read by a lay audience, given the popularity of spiritual treatises with the sixteenth-century Spanish reading public. Griffin, *The Crombergers of Seville*, 146–8; and Nalle, 'Printing and Reading.'

7 Laredo, *Subida* III (1538), chap. 27, p. 523; trans. Peers, 172–3. Teresa of Avila emphasized that it was this phrase that caught her attention (see conclusion). Laredo's use of the term has been analysed only briefly. Andrés, *Los recogidos*, 224; Peers, Introduction, *The Ascent of Mount Zion*, 51–2; and Ros, *Inspirateur de Sainte Thérèse*, 324–8. For apophatic theology, see note 22, below, and the section 'What "Matters" in Medieval Religion' of this introduction.

8 Teresa cites the *Subida* as the immediate inspiration for the beginning of her writing career. Avila, 'Libro de la vida,' chap. 23, sections 11–12, p. 129. For further discussion, see the conclusion.

9 San Francisco del Monte in Villaverde, a village peripheral to Seville that was known as Valverde in the sixteenth century.

10 Despite their Latin titles (*Metaphora medicine con DC autoridades declaradas*, and *Modus faciendi cum ordini medicandi*), both Laredo's pharmaceutical treatises are in Castilian.

11 Gonzaga, *De ordine seraphicae*, 934. See chapter 2.

12 The internal reform of the Spanish church began with the Villacrecian movement in the mid-fifteenth century and was expanded to all religious

orders and clergy by Archbishop Cisneros at the direction of the Catholic Monarchs after 1495. See chapter 1.

13 'Entrails' as a term for 'interior man' is found in other authors of the sixteenth century, including Luther and Calvin. The framework was usually morality, not mysticism, however. Hillman, 'Visceral Knowledge,' 86.

14 In the study of the history of Christianity, 'embodied soul' is sometimes used in relation to the afterlife in terms of the resurrected body as material of the perfected soul. For example, see section heading in Zerner, 'Body and Soul,' 78.

15 For analysis, see Ros, *Inspirateur de Sainte Thérèse*, 325–34. The strongest argument for Laredo's influence on John of the Cross is found in Barroso, *La 'Subida del Monte Sión' y la 'Subida del Monte Carmelo.'*

16 Seville: Juan Cromberger, 1535 and 1538; Medina del Campo: P. de Castro, 1542; Valencia: Felipe Mey, 1590, 'corrected' by the Dominican father Geronimo Alcocer; and Alcalá: Juan Gracian, 1617. Ros, *Inspirateur de Sainte Thérèse*, 8–83. The editions are listed, with library locations and call numbers, in Rodríguez, 'Espirituales españoles,' 508. Compare the more frequently cited (in both Spanish and American scholarship) *Tercer abecedario espiritual* by Laredo's contemporary Francisco de Osuna, which reached six editions between 1527 and 1638. Ibid., 549.

17 The first bishop of Mexico used the 'Josephina,' first published as an addendum to the *Subida* and then reproduced separately, to introduce devotion to Jesus's father in the New World sometime after 1535 (and before the bishop's death in 1548). Ros, *Inspirateur de Sainte Thérèse*, 180–1. The *Subida* is listed on manifests of cargo sent by booksellers to be sold in the New World in 1597 and 1601. Leonard, *Romances of Chivalry*, 286, 297.

18 For example, Ahlgren, *Teresa of Avila*, 38. While two English-language monographs treat his contemporary and fellow founder of recollection mysticism, Francisco de Osuna, in depth (Calvert, *Francisco de Osuna*; and Bultman, *Heretical Mixtures*), none take Laredo as primary.

19 In this view, if mystical union is a foreshadowing of the beatific vision of God normally experienced only in the afterlife, then a mystical 'ascent' always involves disembodiment in order to unite with an immaterial, infinite God located 'up there' in heaven.

20 Only two studies focus on the first stage (self-knowledge) instead of the final one, but their analyses do not take Laredo's medical awareness of the body into account. One is a 1967 dissertation only published recently, the other is article-length. Hernández Moreno, *El hombre del Monte Sión*; and Chavero Blanco, 'Fray Bernardino de Laredo.'

21 Andrés and Ros, while the only scholars to devote serious attention to both versions of Laredo's part 3, consider the 1538 version's revised part 3 not only

more refined but also somehow more inherently mystical. Andrés claims the following: 'Laredo no ha alcanzado una expresión orgánica de la experiencia mística cuando escribe la primera redacción.' (Laredo had not reached an organic expression of mystical experience when he wrote the first redaction.) Andrés, *Los recogidos*, 196. Although Ros posits the provocative notion that the 1535 and 1538 versions are complementary to one another, he in effect cuts off interest in this notion by calling the second version 'more especially mystical.' In full: '[L]a deuxième [redactión], qui met davantage l'accent sur la motion divine, paraît être *plus spécialement mystique*,' and later, 'Conscient des lacunes de son premier travail, Laredo semble vouloir y remédier dans la seconde rédaction de 1538.' (Aware of lacunas in his first work, Laredo seems to have wanted to fix them in the second redaction of 1538.) Ros, *Inspirateur de Sainte Thérèse*, 135, 209. Likewise, Peers's judgment is made without apparent reference to the 1535 edition at all: 'Here it need only be said that it is this second redaction which expresses Laredo's fullest, richest and maturest thought.' Peers, Introduction, *The Ascent of Mount Zion*, 15. It is noteworthy that in the introduction to his translation of the 1538 part 3, Peers refers only briefly to Ros's description of the 1535 version, with which he was evidently unfamiliar, thus making the 1538 approach the only one known to English-language scholars. Ibid., 27, 44.

22 See the next section of this introduction ('What "Matters" in Medieval Religion') for a discussion of apophatic, or negative theology. For a new collection challenging scholars of apophaticism to engage questions of embodiment, see Boesel and Keller, *Apophatic Bodies*. The most recent summary of Laredo's theology describes both Laredo and his contemporary Osuna as advocating apophatic theology to reach 'super-essential union with a hidden God beyond knowledge.' Girón-Negrón, 'Dionysian Thought,' 166. The argument of this book is that such a description is not adequate to the cognitive complexities of Laredo's method.

23 Andrés, *Los recogidos*, 90–1.

24 Despite Pacho's critique of Andrés's valuation of *recogimiento* as the essence of Spanish mysticism, he provides much the same definition as the technical meaning of the term (Pacho, *Apogeo de la mística*, 401); see the section 'Body–Soul Dualism in the History of Christian Mysticism,' this introduction. For an overview in English of the *recogimiento* movement in the cultural context of the sixteenth century, see Rhodes, *Unrecognized Precursors*, 50–89.

25 Andrés, *Los recogidos*, 102.

26 It is customary to rely on the first Castilian dictionary, published by Covarrubias in 1611, for a view of the intended meaning of terms in Golden Age

Spanish that have since changed with usage. The third definition in his entry on *cima* is the relevant one: 'Por cuanto se forma en la parte más alta y principal del hombre, que es del celebro, trayendo origen del corazón, que por esta razón se llama alto.' (Thus it is formed in the highest and principal part of man, which is the brain, taking its origins in the heart. For this reason is it called 'high.') Covarrubias Orozco, *Tesoro*, 313.

27 Note that in Covarrubias's definition in the previous note, the brain has its 'origin in the heart'; i.e., appealing to the highest part of a human is not purely physical but also corporeal. For those modern readers inclined to take 'heart' as metaphorical as well, see the excellent argument about the double valence of the term 'heart' for Augustine. 'The [mistaken] consensus is that Augustine's "heart" is a philosophical vessel, not a bodily organ. It is both: fundamentally medical, attributively philosophical.' Boyle, 'Augustine's Heartbeat,' 24. For a discussion of the physiological heart in the later Middle Ages, see Webb, 'Catherine of Siena's Heart.'

28 A similar argument for theology rather than mysticism recently came to my attention in particular reference to Augustine. Dawson, 'Transcendence as Embodiment.'

29 Mossman's discussion of the 'theology of piety' in the late Middle Ages indicates that most authors who identify a shift from exteriority to interiority as a primary marker of the era are analysing Catholicism through the lens of the Protestant Reformation. Mossman, *Marquard von Lindau*, 34.

30 The two key shifts in the study of body in medieval religion, one to an attention to body, the second to an attention to the results of body on the mind, are catalogued by the following articles: Bynum, 'Why All the Fuss about the Body?'; and Clark, 'Why All the Fuss about the Mind?' Palgrave Macmillan's book series Cognitive Studies in Literature and Performance began publishing works in 2008. See note 112, below, for the modern cognitive models and their deployment in philosophy that began influencing the medievalist cognitive turn.

31 And perhaps also for Paul and Luther, who shared the Galenic frame of reference, though with less medical detail.

32 One of the principal interventions in gender and queer theory is Butler, *Bodies That Matter*; a fair number of studies since then have honoured her work through wordplay referents, such as Nederman, Van Deusen, and Matter, *Mind Matters*.

33 This central point in Plato's thought is usefully summarized in Coleman, *Ancient and Medieval Memories*, 5–10.

34 Ibid., 8.

35 Thus learning is intimately linked to forgetting, a point taken up not only by the medievalist Coleman but also by queer theorist Eve Kosofsky Sedgwick. Sedgwick, *Epistemology of the Closet*, 4.
36 The influence of neo-Platonism on early Christian thought has been extensively discussed, be it through reading the Gospel of John with attention to its neo-Platonic elements or examining Plotinus's impact on the early Church Fathers. Most relevant to historians of mysticism are the discussions in the first chapters of McGinn, *Foundations*; and Louth, *Origins of the Christian Mystical Tradition*.
37 Augustine, *St. Augustine on the Holy Trinity*, book 10, chap. 2, 142. For a thorough analysis, see Coleman, *Ancient and Medieval Memories*, 101–12.
38 For example, McGinn, 'Visions and Critiques of Visions,' 92; cf. Augustine, *Literal Meaning* 12.12.25.
39 Several authors have tried to recuperate a positive valuation of body in Augustine. See Miles, *Augustine on the Body*; Boyle, 'Augustine's Heartbeat'; and the dissertation by Minister, 'Critical Theories of Embodiment.' For comments on Protestant interpretations that erase body from Augustine's theology, see Dawson, 'Transcendence as Embodiment,' 19. Dawson proposes a reading of Augustine that argues that 'Jesus of Nazareth is what God is when God engages in self-determination or self-transcendence; God "becomes him or herself," so to speak, by becoming embodied.' Ibid., 22.
40 Coleman, *Ancient and Medieval Memories*, 198. For discussion of the translation, see Rorem, 'The Early Latin Dionysius.' For an edition of the thirteenth-century translation that was commonly used in university courses, see Anastatius the Librarian, *A Thirteenth-Century Textbook*.
41 Dionysius the Areopagite (Pseudo), 'Mystical Theology,' 135, 137.
42 Excellent discussions of apophatic theology in the Middle Ages are found in Sells, *Mystical Languages of Unsaying*; and Turner, *Darkness of God*. For recent discussion of the influence of Pseudo-Dionysius throughout the medieval and early modern period, see the central essays of Coakley and Stang, *Re-Thinking Dionysius the Areopagite*.
43 Peter Lombard's *Sentences* were the subject of the first lecture course taught after seven years of study at the master's level. Many theologians followed this with a commentary on the *Mystical Theology*. For discussion of the Victorine School, see Berndt, 'The School of St. Victor in Paris.'
44 For example, Michel de Certeau drew most of his discussion of *la mystique* from authors such as Teresa of Avila and John of the Cross; even though he begins his seminal work with a focus on the (abject) body, he equates 'mystical theology' with 'apophatic theology' alone in most of the text. Certeau, *The Mystic Fable*, 41, 107.

45 Bonaventure introduced this terminology in *De triplice via*. Bonaventure, 'Las tres vias,' chap. 3, p. 124. McGinn has pointed to the terminology's precedents in Origen and Pseudo-Dionysius the Areopagite, but the terminology itself is a medieval phenomenon. McGinn, *Flowering*, 102.
46 Mechtild of Hackeborn and her friend Gertrude of Helfta both received visionary information as to the number of Christ's wounds. Popularized as a vision received by an anonymous anchorite, by the fifteenth century versions of the vision attributed it to Birgitta of Sweden. It was known throughout Europe in part due to Ludolph of Saxony's inclusion of it in his *Vita Christi cartujano*. Breeze, 'The Number of Christ's Wounds.' For an overview of the violence of medieval piety, see Bynum, 'Violent Imagery.'
47 For discussion of devotees interacting with the wounds on Christ's imagined body, see Areford, 'Passion Measured'; and Hollywood, 'That Glorious Slit.'
48 Except for the 'originator,' Saint Francis, all other medieval stigmatics were women. Cohen, 'Expression of Pain,' 212.
49 Beckwith, *Christ's Body*, 1, 6.
50 Quoted in Swanson, 'Passion and Practice,' 11n25.
51 Best-sellers in terms of the number of manuscripts that have survived. Texts from the *Vita Christi* tradition and the sub-category of the *Planctus Mariae* (*Lament of Mary*) survive in greater quantities than any text but the Bible, indicating that they were probably copied more frequently than any other. Bestul, *Texts of the Passion*, 52.
52 Such as the poetic version found in the *Lignum vitae*, or *Tree of Life*. Bonaventure, 'Tree of Life,' 117–76.
53 Lengthier works include Ubertino da Casale, *Arbor vitae crucifixae Jesu*, written in 1305. The 1485 incunable is reproduced in the 1961 edition of *Arbor vitae*; also, Pseudo-Bonaventure, *Meditations on the Life of Christ*. Ludolph of Saxony's *Vita Christi cartujano* runs four volumes long in the 1502–3 Castilian translation by Ambrosio de Montesino (compared to thirty pages of Matthew's Gospel).
54 Cousins, 'Francis of Assisi,' 166–7.
55 Both theories are found in the same chapter in Pseudo-Bonaventure; *Meditations on the Life of Christ*, chap. 78, p. 334. Bestul, *Texts of the Passion*, 50, suggests that Pseudo-Bonaventure was the first to offer both versions. Compare Ludolph's meditations on the same subject in the English translation of chap. 58 of the *Vita Christi cartujano*. Ludolph of Saxony, *Hours of the Passion*, sext, p. 257ff.
56 Cohen, *Modulated Scream*, 210.
57 Dijkhuizen and Enenkel, 'Introduction: Constructions of Physical Pain,' 10.

58 Scholars of medieval English literature lead in this regard. The best-known study is Beckwith, *Christ's Body*; primary sources are provided in Bartlett and Bestul, *Cultures of Piety*. More recently, Karnes proposes a reading of Bonaventurian tradition of meditation on the life of Christ in which she argues for that tradition's ability to inculcate mystical experience, albeit of an abstract and purely intellectual kind. Karnes, *Imagination, Meditation, and Cognition*. Studies of the Passion in northern European literature and art are also frequent: see Bynum, *Wonderful Blood*; building on such as works as Marrow, *Passion Iconography*; and Hamburger, *The Visual and the Visionary*. For Latin literature, we have only two monographs: Fulton, *From Judgment to Passion*; and Bestul, *Texts of the Passion*. For the scant scholarship on the tardy appearance of such texts in Castile, see the sections 'Guides to Passion Meditation in the Cisnerian Era' and 'The Evolution of Passion Spirituality in Early Sixteenth-Century Castile,' chapter 1.

59 Unless their focus is late medieval English spirituality, in which Passion texts rather than apophatic theology predominate. See previous note.

60 The only article to seriously address Spanish mysticism and the topic of pain still presumes a disembodied abstract union to be the goal. Flynn, 'Spiritual Uses of Pain.'

61 James, *Varieties of Religious Experience*, 320–1.

62 McGinn, *Foundations*, xvii. This definition does not enter into a classification of body over soul per se, but certainly terms such as 'consciousness of' tend to invoke modern assumptions about cognition that have disassociated mind from body ever since Descartes's promulgation of 'I think, therefore I am.' See note 112, below.

63 McGinn, *Flowering*, 265–343.

64 McGinn, 'Visions and Critiques of Visions.'

65 McGinn, *Flowering*, 59.

66 In counterpoint, Denys Turner engaged the tradition of Song of Songs commentary in his work on *eros* before moving on to the apophatic tradition in another work, so his presentation of negative theology attends to some of its embodied aspects. See Turner, *Darkness of God*.

67 Oddly, Catalonian interest in mysticism and in Passion spirituality seems to have run parallel to the rest of Europe, given the influence of Ramon Llull (1232–1315) and Francesc Eiximenis (ca 1340–1409). For information on these Catalonian figures, see Hames, *Art of Conversion*; and Robinson, 'Preaching to the Converted.' For further discussion of the development of vernacular mysticism in late medieval Europe, see McGinn, *Flowering*. In contrast, scholars who work on visionaries have discussed Castilian mystical authors who wrote in the vernacular, all women, in the decades just before and after

1500. Their works rarely reached publication or wide dissemination, so their influence was mainly charismatic. See Surtz, *Writing Women*.

68 The dating on the development of *recogimiento* as a method of prayer is based on Francisco de Osuna's statements in his 1527 *Tercer abecedario espiritual* that his teacher had practised *recogimiento* for forty years. See Andrés, Introducción, *Tercer abecedario*, 32. Laredo confirms that the practice went back at least to the 1490s, since in the 1538 version of the *Subida* he mentions contemplatives who had followed the path of *recogimiento* for over forty years. Laredo, *Subida* III (1538), chap. 16, p. 483; trans. Peers, 123. Recent work has discussed mental prayer as central to Spanish religious expression in the first third of the sixteenth century but does not treat *recogimiento* as mysticism per se. Pablo Maroto, *Reformas y espirituales franciscanos*; and Pego Puigbó, *Renacimiento espiritual*.

69 'La vía completa abarca tres partes: conocimiento proprio o aniquilación; seguimiento o imitación de Cristo en cuanto hombre y en cuanto Dios; transformación del alma en Dios por amor. La presente historia se fija especialmente en esta última parte.' Andrés, *Los recogidos*, 89. (This volume was the result of a seminar, but the identification of which sections were influenced by which participants is unclear in the actual publication. The first section, including the general definitions, seems to me to be from Andrés's pen alone, as it references none of the individual figures he acknowledges to have been the subject of specific seminar participants' research.)

70 Ibid., 94.

71 López Santidrián, Introducción, *Tercer abedecario*, 38; Orella Unzué, 'Cultura religiosa,' 191; and Carrera-Marcén, *Teresa of Avila's Autobiography*, 48.

72 Pacho, *Apogeo de la mística*, 393–403.

73 '[*R*]*ecogimiento* adquiere una connotación técnica cuando se aplica en exclusiva a un tipo de contemplación que absorbe totalmente las capacidades y potencias en la experiencia de Dios presente en lo más profundo del alma.' Ibid., 401.

74 Ibid., 404.

75 Pacho therefore also does not discuss the influence of the many European works that Laredo read. For a thorough survey of the medieval spiritual treatises influential on Laredo, see Boon, 'Mystical Language of Recollection.'

76 Fernández Álvarez, *La sociedad española del Renacimiento*, 19.

77 The most recent discussion of *alumbrados* is more nuanced than previous work. Hamilton, 'The *Alumbrados*.'

78 The many studies by Ronald Surtz on the transition from the late fifteenth into the early sixteenth century avoid this valuation, but his focus on

visionaries and authority leads naturally to consideration of bodies especially in terms of gender. See comments in chapter 1.

79 Thompson, Prologue, xx. The articles in this innovative collection do not necessarily follow the view of the prologue.

80 Dangler argues that medieval notions of alterity are replaced by early modern definitions of 'other' that are more thoroughly hierarchical. She also remarks on mystical discourse, but limits her references to apophatic theology, the linguistic method of negation and silence, as discussed by scholars of the monstrous, without ever engaging actual texts from the Spanish mystical tradition. Dangler, *Making Difference*, 18–20, 144.

81 Folger, *Images in Mind*; and Folger, *Escape from the Prison of Love*.

82 Although Morales mentions Casale's *Arbor vitae crucifixae Jesu* as influential on the mystical experiences among Franciscans in the New World, he does not describe the Passion meditation itself as mystical but rather presumes the eschatological elements of the work to be most relevant. Morales, 'New World Colonial Franciscan Mystical Practice,' 96–7. Michelle Karnes's recent book is an important intervention in this regard. She modulates the assumption that Bonaventure's primary interest is in abstract contemplation (*Journey of the Soul to God*) rather than Passion meditation (found in his *Arbor vitae* and *Vitis mistica*) by examining the cognitive parallels between the different genres of treatises. Karnes, *Imagination, Meditation, and Cognition*, chaps. 2–3.

83 Bynum, *Resurrection of the Body*; for a discussion of the same point into the period of the Enlightenment, see Vidal, 'Brains, Bodies, Selves, and Science.'

84 '[S]uch desire is not only *for* bodies; it is lodged *in* bodies.' Bynum, 'Why All the Fuss about the Body?,' 26. Many excellent articles and books explore the sexuality of mystical union. Perhaps the best-known examples of this type of study are Lochrie, *Margery Kempe and Translations of the Flesh*; and Hollywood, *Sensible Ecstasy*. In her latest work, Bynum argues for a reframing of the study of body as the study of materiality (bodies relating to objects, both of which change and transform over time). Bynum, *Christian Materiality*.

85 Aristotle, *De anima* 3.7, quoted in Coleman, *Ancient and Medieval Memories*, 198.

86 See chapter 3 of this book. For a fascinating consideration of the ways that differing medical systems influence philosophic and religious ideas, see Kuriyama, *Expressiveness of the Body*. My thanks to Barbara Ambros for bringing this work to my attention.

87 Miles, 'Vision.'

88 '[According to Alhazen,] because light and colour are transmitted – Bacon would say "multiplied"– from a nearly infinite series of points on the surface

of a visible objects along rays to the eye, the latter is the recipient of "specks" of light (of varying intensity) and colour (of varying hue).' Tachau, 'What Senses and Intellect Do,' 660. Tachau goes on to point out that since light and colour do not convey depth or motion, etc., the rest of the information about the seen object is determined by the discriminative sense in the middle ventricle of the brain. For information on Alhazen and Bacon, see, among others, Lindberg, Introduction, *Roger Bacon and the Origins of 'Perspectiva,'* xxxv–xxxvii; xlvii–xlviii.

89 Siraisi, *Medieval and Early Renaissance Medicine*, 82, fig. 13; Akbari, *Seeing through the Veil*, 41; and Camille, 'Before the Gaze,' 200–1. Avicenna's description of the brain is found in his *Canon*, a core medical text for physicians throughout the West after its translation in 1187, but also well known to theologians as a description of the five internal senses that form the sensitive soul. Thoroughly reviewed in Harvey, *Inward Wits*.

90 'Operations were functions of specific organs; for example, that of the stomach was digestion. Faculties were specific abilities peculiar to various parts of the body; for example, both the nine-month gravid uterus and the intestines had an eliminitave and propulsive faculty.' Siraisi, *Medieval and Early Renaissance Medicine*, 107.

91 Or a monster more than a human. See Laredo's contemporary, Juan Luis Vives, for both examples. Vives, 'Obra psicológica,' 513.

92 Carruthers, *Book of Memory*, 21, 55.

93 Coleman, *Ancient and Medieval Memories*, 350–1.

94 Jordan is summarizing Bartholomaeus of Salerno. Jordan, 'The Construction of a Philosophical Medicine,' 58.

95 Carruthers, *Craft of Thought*, 3.

96 Coleman, *Ancient and Medieval Memories*, 200.

97 Ibid., 199.

98 Biernoff, *Sight and Embodiment*, 81.

99 The major works that reposition traditional scholarly readings of scholastic texts concerning cognition are Tachau, *Vision and Certitude*; Bynum, *Resurrection of the Body*; and Pasnau, *Theories of Cognition*, in addition to the texts on mnemotechnique cited in the main text.

100 Galen himself framed his discussion of every part of the physical body as a way of reflecting on the magnificence of a creator God who would come up with such a complex, perfect thing as a human body. For an English translation, see Galen, *On the Usefulness of the Parts of the Body*. Roger Bacon detailed his optical theories extending Alhazen's *De aspectibus* at Pope Clement IV's request. Lindberg, Introduction, *Roger Bacon and the Origins of 'Perspectiva,'* xix. Anglicus's encyclopedia (1220s) seems to have

been intended as a source not only for the uneducated, as he specifies in his preface, but also as a source of ideas for preachers. Lidaka, 'Bartholomaeus Anglicus,' 395–9; and Anglicus, *De proprietatibus rerum*.

101 See below for more details, and in full in Tachau, *Vision and Certitude*.

102 Such as Peter of Limoges's *De oculo morali*. Richard Newhauser has located four fifteenth-century manuscripts and a 1503 Latin edition printed in Logroño that prove that Limoges's collection was available in Castile. Personal communication, 21 August 2009. However, Anglicus's encyclopedia, circulated in print in the vernacular after 1494, may also have been aimed at preachers. See note 100, above.

103 The *Canon* was translated in 1187 by Gerald of Cremona, and influenced Albert the Great and others after him. Siraisi, *Medicine and the Italian Universities*, 25. It was most widely circulated in the Renaissance era in its excerpts in the *Articella*. Arrizabalaga, *The 'Articella' in the Early Press*, 5.

104 Acceptance of Aquinas's theory was certainly not general, as it was one of the condemned propositions of 1277. Bynum tracks the debate in *Resurrection of the Body*.

105 For an overview of the philosophy of hylemorphism, see Oderberg, 'Hylemorphic Dualism.' See also chapter 3 of this book.

106 Bynum, *Resurrection of the Body*, 259.

107 Mowbray, *Pain and Suffering*, 22. Hylemorphism resulted in part from a reading of a passage in Augustine's *Literal Meaning of Genesis* that states, 'The flesh does not feel, but the soul, using the body as a tool.' Quoted and analysed in Cohen, *Modulated Scream*, 201.

108 Mowbray, *Pain and Suffering*, 15.

109 Ibid., 21. This insight is also the basis for the argument in Karnes, *Imagination, Meditation, and Cognition*. As Robert Pasnau succinctly renders it in the epigraph to this book: 'Being spiritual does not entail being nonphysical.' Pasnau, *Theories of Cognition*, 69.

110 The full quotation reads: 'Las cosas espirituales son en efecto imagos de Dios, en cambio las corporales son como unos simulacros de las espirituales, de modo que no debe causar admiración que *lo espiritual se comprenda a partir de lo corporal*' (my emphasis). Vives, 'Obra psicológica,' 511.

111 For Vesalius, see Siraisi, *Medicine and the Italian Universities*, 253–86; and Kemp and Fletcher, 'Medieval Theory,' 566. Paracelsus's scorn for Galen influenced all his research; see Debus, *Chemical Philosophy*. For sixteenth-century *ars memorativa*, see Yates, *Art of Memory*.

112 A recent trend in philosophy suggests that the philosophical valuation of mind over body so acutely summarized by Descartes's 'I think, therefore I am' overlooks the fact that our bodies provide a (if not *the*) primary

limitation or constraint on how we articulate our thoughts. Linguistics professor George Lakoff and philosophy professor Mark Johnson draw on the discipline of cognitive science, especially cognitive linguistics, suggesting in two landmark works that if we can only think about what we can articulate in language, it is critical to note that much of our language seems to be based on the ways our bodies work in space. Lakoff and Johnson, *Metaphors We Live By*; Lakoff and Johnson, *Philosophy in the Flesh*; summarized in Fauconnier and Turner, *The Way We Think*. This provocative proposal takes aim at the roots of the Western philosophical tradition, defined as beginning with Descartes. Yet it is also possible to view Descartes as the endpoint of a long trend in philosophy and theology (in a line beginning with Aristotle, through medieval thinkers such as Avicenna, Albert the Great, and Roger Bacon), that theorized accounts of a physiological basis for human cognition. Descartes provided an alternative explanation after Vesalius's dissection experiments in the mid-sixteenth century proved the five-ventricle theory wrong. Kemp and Fletcher, 'Medieval Theory,' 567. The role of physiology in cognition was in fact a critical one up through the seventeenth century, and Lakoff and Turner's explorations are a return to a notion of embodied thought rather than an entirely new proposal.

113 McGinn maps the primary debates in 'Love, Knowledge, and Mystical Union.' For examples of the methodology of mysticism depending in particular on this distinction between understanding and will, see Certeau, *The Mystic Fable*, 6, 104, 126. Ros points out that this is an anachronistic question for medieval and Renaissance mystical texts. 'Avouons toutefois que ni Richard ni Laredo ne posent la question avec la clarité des théoriciens spirituels du XVIIe siècle. Le point de vue est sensiblement différent: tandis que les modernes ont particulièrement en vue la simplification des actes d'intelligence et de volonté, les anciens fondent leurs divisions sur la nature de l'object étudié: matériel ou spirituel, créé ou incréé.' (Let us admit in any case that neither Richard nor Laredo posed the question with the clarity of the theorists of spirituality of the seventeenth century. The point of view is distinctly different: while the moderns looked particularly at the simplification of the acts of understanding and or will, the earlier authors based their divisions on the nature of the object studied, material or spiritual, created or uncreated.) Ros, *Inspirateur de Sainte Thérèse*, 308. Turner's analysis of Denys the Carthusian indicates that although the Carthusian recognized the debate between the primacy of the will versus the intellect, he refused the distinction. Turner, *Darkness of God*, 220–4.

114 Laredo, *Subida* I (1535), chap. 11, p. 68; chap. 12, p. 71; and III (1535), chap. 22, p. 674.

115 Cf. Bynum, *Christian Materiality.*
116 For example, it may behoove scholars to consider why metaphors of 'ascent' are so common in medieval mysticism if theological epistemologies had depended on an internalizing process of cognition since the thirteenth century. Karnes makes a strong argument for considering Bonaventure's Passion spirituality to be an integral element of mystical union, in contrast to later authors who diminish Passion meditation to a purely beginner stage. Her work makes clear, however, that Bonaventure assumes that the spiritual is above the corporeal and that the process of union involves an ascent to the heavenly realm of the divine Christ. Karnes, *Imagination, Meditation, and Cognition*, chap. 3.
117 I offer this study as an initial response to the question recently formulated by Rachel Fulton in the afterword to a collection honouring Bynum, in which she asks whether we have drawn our scholarly boundary lines correctly ('medieval/modern; spiritual/secular; individualistic/community-oriented; body/mind; human/divine'). Fulton, 'Afterword: History in the Comic Mode,' 286.

1 Renaissance Castilian Spirituality

1 The phrase 'somatic spirituality' comes from Elliott, 'True Presence/False Christ,' 241. The bibliography is vast; see introduction.
2 Karnes, *Imagination, Meditation, and Cognition*; and Mossman, *Marquard von Lindau*, 55.
3 Robinson, 'Preaching to the Converted'; see also Robinson, *Imag(in)ing Passions.*
4 Other studies noting the importance of Passion spirituality to this era are Whinnom, 'Supposed Sources of Inspiration'; and Delbrugge, *Scholarly Edition of André de Li's 'Thesoro,'* 3–84. A study that centres on Passion spirituality in the later Golden Age is Ricard, 'Le thème de Jésus crucifié.'
5 For example, the essay on religion in the age of Charles V that accompanies a reproduction of his Book of Hours includes no discussion of Passion spirituality – despite the fact that the Hours of Mary and Cycle of the Passion are the focal point of any Book of Hours – but discusses the Protestant Reformation extensively. Edelmayer, 'Carlos V y su tiempo.' Along similar lines, Aspe's attempt to distinguish the shift in Spanish spirituality in the second half of the sixteenth century depends on a representation of the first half of the century that focuses entirely on Erasmian and Lutheran ideas; Aspe, 'Spanish Spirituality's Mid-Sixteenth-Century Change of Course,' 423–4.

6 Dana Bultman's important intervention debating the assumed omnipresence of a body–soul hierarchy in the thought of the 1520s onward is based on analysis of moral treatises and literary works, and so her insights have not yet affected studies of mysticism. For example, she focuses her chapter on Osuna on his *Norte de estados*, a work on the different forms of Christian life (clerical, married, etc). Bultman, *Heretical Mixtures*, 29–54.

7 Many scholars attribute spiritual developments in Castile in the late fifteenth century to the influence of the northern *devotio moderna*, but Whinnom effectively proves that *devotio moderna* had a relatively low impact. Whinnom, 'Supposed Sources of Inspiration,' 46–7.

8 Andrés argues that Teresa and John simply developed the Spanish tradition further, but did not initiate it. Andrés, *Los recogidos*, 40–1.

9 Gómez García's *Carro de dos vidas* and Jiménez García de Cisneros's *Ejercitatorio de la vida espiritual* represent a transitional stage between the medieval panorama and the development of a specifically Spanish spirituality, and are the first 'mystical' texts to appear in the Castilian vernacular. Neither author composed what a modern reader would consider to be an 'original' text; rather, both authors provided syntheses of earlier works, translating and organizing distinct quotations and authors into patterns for prayer and reflection. García de Cisneros's work is discussed in chapter 2 as the only precursor of Passion spirituality in Castilian mysticism to Laredo. Gómez García's treatise *Carro de dos vidas* was dedicated to a well-known local female religious. It is perhaps best thought of as a miniature vernacular *summa* of the topics relating to contemplative and active lives for all monks and nuns, from stages of contemplation through articles of faith, ending with the virtues upon which a Christian life is meant to be founded. The work, drawn primarily from Richard of Saint Victor and Thomas Aquinas, can thus be considered an encyclopedic handbook of medieval thought, well organized but not yet a prescriptive mystical method. Andrés, Introducción, *Carro de dos vidas*, 10–11, 28–9. For further discussion of García, see Boon, 'Mystical Language of Recollection,' 158–63.

10 The technical English term for *beata* is 'semi-religious woman,' but a lively audience debate at two sessions called 'Semi-Religious Women Before and After Trent' at the 2011 Sixteenth Century Studies Conference led to Jodi Bilinkoff's proposal of 'uncloistered women' as a more useful category.

11 The two main works on women religious authors in Renaissance Castile continue to be Surtz, *Writing Women*; and Muñoz Fernández, *Acciones e intenciones*. See also McKendrick and MacKay, 'Visionaries and Affective Spirituality.' Despite Surtz's and Muñoz Fernández's excellent efforts to retrieve these key religious voices and the various studies of individual *beatas*

that have followed, studies of women visionaries remain primarily the purview of women's studies rather than coming under the history of Spanish mysticism, at least among Spanish scholars. For example, the most recent extensive survey of Renaissance Castilian mysticism dedicates a mere four pages to Juana de la Cruz, an influential visionary preacher who had the ear of Cisneros and other church officials in the first two decades of the sixteenth century, in comparison to entire chapters on Osuna, Laredo, and other classically identified mystics. Pacho, *Apogeo de la mística*, 292–6. Only when Teresa of Avila appears on the scene, apparently, does it become imperative to attend to women's voices. This disparity is all the more striking given the fact that histories of religion in sixteenth-century Spain frequently feature women whose lives have been retrieved through examination of Inquisition documentation. Among the many accounts, see Giles, *Mujeres en la Inquisición*; and Vollendorf, *Lives of Women*. In my view, the study of local religion in Spain is one of the most gender-equal fields of study in contemporary academia, while the study of Spanish Christian mysticism remains mired in categorical distinctions between embodied experience (that of visionaries or Passion meditation, available to relatively uneducated women) and 'true' mystical experience to be found in abstract contemplation (usually written by and for literate men).

12 For an important article that considers the role of bodies in pain for the entire Golden Age, see Flynn, 'Spiritual Uses of Pain.' I know of no follow-through on her insights, however.

13 The literature on the definition of religion is vast, yet inconclusive. Many rely on Geertz's classic definition in Geertz, 'Religion as a Cultural System,' 90. The primary contemporary theorists include Smith, *Relating Religion*, especially chaps. 7–8; McCutcheon, *Manufactoring Religion*; and Tweed, *Crossing and Dwelling*. A recent work that attempts to use phenomenology, so often a highly abstract branch of philosophy, to construct a theory of embodied religion is Vásquez, *More Than Belief*.

14 Scholars have been arguing for the continuity between late medieval Catholic concerns and those raised by sixteenth-century reformers for some time. The point that the idea of the 'Counter-Reformation' presumes that it occurred only in response to Protestant critique rather than as a natural development within Catholic thought is made cogently by O'Malley, *Trent and All That*.

15 MacCulloch, *The Reformation*, 120–5.

16 This is the only event in Francis's life cited by Laredo. *Subida* II, chap. 13, p. 254.

17 See, for example, Bonaventure's description in the *Legenda maior.* Bonaventure, 'The Life of St. Francis,' 303–6. This vision becomes a favourite subject for painted portraits of Francis.

18 Yovel, *Other Within*, 240.

19 To provide another example, Rhodes does an excellent job of assessing various religious influences on the literary work of Montemayor in the second half of the sixteenth century, even including a description of Passion meditation as essential to his practice. However, she then identifies *recogimiento* as a method that 'exalted inner piety over ritualistic observance' and does not assess any of its three stages as mystical praxis. Rhodes, *Unrecognized Precursors*, 47–8, 57–8. Similarly, see Giordano, '"La ciudad de nuestra consciencia."'

20 Yovel, *Other Within*, 225. He defines this interiority as essential to Golden Age religion: 'But [Valdés, Vives, Teresa] were *different* Christians, expecting religion – as Marranos typically did – to express the inner self and heart rather than external worship.' Ibid., 243.

21 Bynum recently advanced this argument for all of Europe in the late Middle Ages. 'In short, interior and individualized religious response grew apace with exterior practices, partly as criticism, partly as complement.' Bynum, *Christian Materiality*, 271.

22 In Seville, for example, ten mendicant convents were founded during the first decade after its fall, an explosion of religious fervour not matched until the reform spirit swept the orders in the southern province in the late fifteenth century. García Oro, *Francisco de Asís*, 404.

23 Fremaux-Crouzet, 'Franciscanisme des villes,' 56; and García Oro, *Francisco de Asís*, 416.

24 Lejarza and Uribe, *Las reformas*, 303, gives the argument for these approximate dates. Around the same time, the Dominican Vincent Ferrer (1350–1419) began to travel around Spain preaching strongly in favour of interior spirituality among Christians. His personal interest in popular religious reform, however, inspired few others in his order to take leading roles, and it was within the Franciscan order that a widespread religious reform movement began.

25 Ibid., 307–24.

26 Herrera Casado, *Monasterios medievales de Guadalajara*, 132–9; Lejarza and Uribe, *Las reformas*, 130, 134. For information on the various houses, including charts of founders for houses, see Miura Andrades, *Frailes, monjes, y conventos*, 298–300. For discussion of the retreat houses in the early sixteenth century, see García Oro, 'Observantes, Recoletos, Descalzos.'

27 Lope de Salinas y Salazar (1393/4–1468), Villacreces's most influential disciple, wrote all the surviving works of the Villacrecian reform, collected in the 'Escritos villacrecianos' section of special issue of *Archivo Ibero-Americano* edited by Lejarza and Uribe; see following note.

28 The *Memorial de la vida y ritos de la Custodia de Santa María de los Menores*, probably written in 1461, was conceived as a rule for newer houses of recollection based on the practices of one of the original houses, Santa María. Lejarza and Uribe, *Las reformas*, 674. The list of concerns is taken from the chapter headings in Salinas y Salazar, 'Memorial de la vida,' 723–8.
29 Salinas y Salazar, 'Testamento,' 915.
30 Ibid. 'Memorial de la vida,' 723–4. Villacreces rejected the teachings of scholasticism, suggesting that if books were necessary, then believers ought to depend on such spiritual writers such as Augustine, Bonaventure, and Catherine of Siena. See also Andrés, *Teología española*, 1:94. All these writers are cited by Laredo.
31 Salinas y Salazar, 'Memorial de la vida,' 723, 728.
32 The Observant Franciscans were *idiotas*, i.e., uneducated, because they had not formally studied Scotus and other scholastics. Salinas y Salazar, 'Segundas satisfacciones,' 864.
33 Ibid., 861–7.
34 Salinas y Salazar, 'Memorial de la vida,' 727–9.
35 Andrés lists activities of mental, interiorizing prayer as well as liturgical, ritual acts in his description of the movement, but elaborates on the mental prayers as new while simply listing the exterior ones as an ongoing practice. Andrés, *Los recogidos*, 22–3.
36 Salinas y Salazar, 'Memorial de la vida,' 727.
37 Lejarza and Uribe, *Las reformas*, 650. The authors are citing Salinas y Salazar, 'Memorial de la vida,' 727. For discussion of this medieval text, see Bestul, *Texts of the Passion*, 53–4.
38 Authors throughout Europe mention having to control bodily movement during silent prayer, indicating that most practitioners did not understand private prayer as non-embodied. Saenger, 'Books of Hours,' 152.
39 Ibid., 143. Mossman describes Germany in particular when he suggests that exterior and interior practices were in 'balance' during the high Middle Ages, but interior ones became steadily more valued in the later Middle Ages. Mossman, *Marquard von Lindau*, 33.
40 'El desarrollo de la cultura de la imagen religiosa en el siglo XV es uno de los acontecimientos más extraordinarios de la evolución de la espiritualidad bajo medieval y altomoderna. Las imágenes se desplazaron desde los altares al interior de los hogares, desde los templos a las celdas, y las prácticas devocionales empezaron a conceder cada vez mayor importancia al elemento figurativo, tanto a los productos de la imaginación como a las pinturas o las esculturas que debían fomentarla.' Pereda, *Las imágenes de la discordia*, 82–3. This concluding remark is at the end of an extensive set of proofs from

Inquisition records of the role private devotional images played in allegations of judaizing. '[Carecer de imágenes religiosas] en el hogar se convertía en una prueba más de *criptojudaísmo*, nunca de forma aislada, pero sí con fuerza probatoria en casos de religiosidad dudosa.' (Not having religious images at home became yet another proof of crypto-Judaism, never on its own, but certainly providing probatory force in cases concerning doubtful religious affiliation.) Original italics retained. Ibid., 48.

41 For an example of the type of sculpture that 'left the altar for the interiors of homes,' see the small (53 cm) sculpture of the *Virgen dolorosa* dating to the first third of the sixteenth century, which might have been intended to be placed high up in a *retablo*. Moreno Mendoza, *Orto hispalensis*, 164–5.

42 For example, Wieck, *Libro de Horas*, 1:30–4.

43 Herrera García, 'Orígines,' 18.

44 Herrera García points out that most surviving *retablos* from Renaissance Castile have many nooks for religious statues that are not filled. He suggests that Tridentine limitations on images led to the removal of some images or the failure to complete the commissions. Ibid., 17. Note that Pereda's observation concerning the proliferation of private devotional images may not hold true for northern parts of Spain; see Nalle's discussion of testaments in Cuenca, in which devotional objects only began to be mentioned after 1535. Nalle, 'Private Devotion, Personal Space,' 258.

45 Christian, *Apparitions*, 206–7, 210. There were also visions that verified the miraculous nature of specific devotional images and shrines. For example, the *beaterio* Santa María de Cubas was instituted in response to a peasant girl's Marian vision in the 1460s. Christian, *Local Religion*, 57–86. Four decades later, it was saved from dissolution by the profession and leadership of Juana de la Cruz, in response to Marian visions of her own. Later, as abbess once the convent was incorporated into the Clarisan Order, Juana received visions concerning the care of the Marian imagery within the convent. See Boon, 'Mother Juana de la Cruz.' Bynum points out that these Spanish visionary experiences were validated by miraculous objects, thus materiality validates experience of the divine. Bynum, *Christian Materiality*, 110.

46 Rummel, *Jiménez de Cisneros*, 32. In 1493, the rulers of Spain had received a papal bull allowing them to name the persons in charge of the reform of each order in Spain. Cisneros was their choice for this role. Tellechea, 'La reforma religiosa,' 51. See García Oro, *El Cardenal Cisneros*, for a critical biography of Cisneros.

47 The Complutensian Polyglot Bible of 1517–20 provided the most accurate Hebrew, Greek, Latin, and Syriac texts of the two Testaments from the oldest possible manuscripts available. Rummel, *Jiménez de Cisneros*, 53–9. At the

Universidad de Alcalá, the innovative curriculum was called the *tres vías*, a method in which Thomism, Scotism, and nominalism were taught to all students as interchangeable methods rather than opposing schools of thought. Andrés, *Teología española*, 1:35.

48 The mark of Cisneros on this era is well known; see Sáinz Rodríguez, *La siembra mistica*. For a brief overview, see Tellechea, 'La reforma religiosa.'

49 For further discussion of the impact of printing on visionary spirituality, see McKendrick and MacKay, 'Visionaries and Affective Spirituality.'

50 For further information on the teachings of María de Santo Domingo, see Santo Domingo, *The Book of Prayer*, Introduction; Surtz, *Writing Women*, 85–103; and Bilinkoff, 'Establishing Authority.' For further information on Juana de la Cruz, see the discussion later in the section 'Envisioning the Passion,' this chapter. The version of Vincent Ferrer's *Tratado de la vida espiritual* that Cisneros approved for publication (Alcalá, 1510) in fact omitted the chapter containing Ferrer's famous polemic against visionaries. Sáinz Rodríguez, *La siembra mística*, 43–50.

51 For a thorough if brief survey of the plays, poetry, and translations of Latin texts under the Castilian monarchs, see Delbrugge, *Scholarly Edition of Andrés de Li's 'Thesoro,'* 33–49.

52 Most of the primary sources lack a modern edition. Recent editions that may aid the study of this genre in Castile include Román, *Coplas de la pasión*; Osuna, *Primer abecedario espiritual*; Osuna, *Abecedario espiritual, V y VI partes*; and Delbrugge, *Scholarly Edition of Andrés de Li's 'Thesoro.'*

53 Ishikawa, *The 'Retablo de Isabel,'* 26–33; and Delbrugge, *Scholarly Edition of Andrés de Li's 'Thesoro,'* 8.

54 For a discussion of this shift in the twelfth century, see the magesterial work of Fulton, *From Judgment to Passion*.

55 'Now, then, my soul, embrace that divine manger; press your lips upon and kiss the boy's feet,' and 'Become a companion of the holy kings.' Bonaventure, 'Tree of Life,' fruit 1, section 4, p. 129 (referenced by Cousins, 'Francis of Assisi,' 184); and fruit 2, section 6, p. 130. In García de Cisneros's work (discussed in chapter 2), the meditator kisses the crib itself. García de Cisneros, *Ejercitatorio de la vida espiritual*, part 4, chap. 52, p. 231; translated in García de Cisneros, *Book of Exercises*, 231.

56 The balance between imaginative meditation and the moral resonance of the scene differs in every *Vita Christi* version. Hundersmarck reads Pseudo-Bonaventure's work as more reflective of the former and Ludolph's work as more focused on the latter. Hundersmarck, 'Preaching the Passion.' Bodenstadt defines the difference as Pseudo-Bonaventure 'stressing conformity with Christ,' while Ludolph's *Vita Christi* 'stresses intimacy with Christ.' Bodenstedt, *The Vita Christi of Ludolphus*, 120n27.

57 For example, Pseudo-Bonaventure's *Meditationes Vitae Christi*, Ubertino da Casale's *Arbor vitae crucifixae*, and James of Milan's *Stimulus amoris*. Bestul encapsulates the development of the Latin *Vita Christi* genre in *Texts of the Passion*, 26–68.

58 Ludolph of Saxony, *Vita Christi cartujano*, chap. 53, fol. 130v. Also see Ludolph of Saxony, *Hours of the Passion*, sext, p. 257ff. An alternative image was also frequently provided, such that the meditator could choose between visualizing either the cross laid on the ground during the nailing, or Christ and his torturers ascending ladders to reach the already upright cross; see introduction, n55. Bestul identifies this double scenario as first being posited by Pseudo-Bonaventure. Bestul, *Texts of the Passion*, 50.

59 Ludolph of Saxony, *Vita Christi cartujano*, chap. 63, fol. 131r.

60 See Bestul, *Texts of the Passion*, 52. The *Quis dabit* was certainly in print in Spain by 1515 (possibly 1500). See the Alcalá de Henares edition listed in Norton, *Descriptive Catalogue*, no. 40, p. 19.

61 Ogier of Locedio (Pseudo-Bernard), 'Meditation by Bernard,' 169.

62 For a review of the theology of co-redemption, see Sticca, *Planctus Mariae*, 19–30. It was declared official Catholic doctrine in 1904. Flory, *Marian Representations*, 42.

63 Other spectators besides the Virgin Mary were important in this tradition. Mary Magdalene's role at the foot of the cross became ever more important throughout the sixteenth century in Spain, particularly after Tridentine directives began to reduce the number of references to the Virgin herself. See Boon, 'Full-Figured Paradox.'

64 Although I have found no indication of the presence of the *Quis dabit* on the peninsula during the thirteenth and fourteenth centuries, the fact that both Gonzalo de Berceo and Ramon Llull wrote *plancts* indicates that the genre was known. Berceo, 'El duelo de la Virgen'; and Llull, 'Plant de la verge.' Berceo's 'Duelo de la Virgen' is the best-known Castilian piece. For analysis, see Andrade de Labadía, 'Pasión de Cristo.' Francesc Eiximenis's *Vita Christi* (1398) inaugurated attention to meditation on the life of Christ in eastern Spain, heavily influencing Isabel de Villena's *Vita Christi* (1498). As Robinson points out, however, although Eiximenis's text was the most widely available teaching text for the method of meditation on Christ's life and death, his concern is not with the violence done to Christ's body. It is thus a far more spiritualizing text than its Latin equivalents. Robinson, 'Preaching to the Converted,' 125–9.

65 Mendoza, 'Coplas de Vita Christi'; Román, *Coplas de la pasión*; Pérez y Gómez, '*La pasión trobada* de Diego de San Pedro'; and Padilla, 'Retablo de la vida de Cristo.' Requena Miota's thesis is the only monograph comparing all these poetic Passions and lives of Christ (as well as Montesino's translation

of Ludolph). Requena Miota, 'La espiritualidad española.' See also Whinnom, 'El origen de las comparaciones religiosas'; and Delbrugge, *Scholarly Edition of Andrés de Li's 'Thesoro,'* 33–58.

66 Only Iñigo de Mendoza and Juan de Padilla wrote on the life of Christ (although Mendoza's version does not include the death). Religious plays, or *autos sacramentales*, however, were as likely to take the nativity or a scene from Christ's life as their focus. See the examples (Nativity, Flight to Egypt, Assumption) discussed in Surtz, 'The "Franciscan Connection."'

67 A detailed comparison of the poems with the Latin prose tradition can be found in Whinnom, 'Supposed Sources of Inspiration.'

68 Diego de San Pedro, *La pasión trobada*.

69 Ibid., fols. c2r, c4r–v.

70 The following are dated to 1494, 1499, and 1514, respectively: Juan del Encina, 'Representación a la muy bendita passión y muerte'; Alonso del Campo, 'Auto de la passión'; and Lucas Fernández, *Auto de la pasión*.

71 Torroja Menéndez and Rivas Palá, *Teatro en Toledo*, 106, 109.

72 Pérez Priego, 'Espectáculos y textos teatrales.'

73 Ishikawa, *The 'Retablo de Isabel,'* 29.

74 Ibid., 29, 31.

75 Delbrugge, *Scholarly Edition of Andrés de Li's 'Thesoro,'* 260.

76 Robinson, *Imag(in)ing Passions*, chap. 1. The first Castilian translation of Pseudo-Bonaventure's *Meditationes Vitae Christi* is found in a manuscript dated 1475–1500. Details concerning Biblioteca Nacional de Madrid Manuscript 9560 can be found at length in Philobiblon, the online collection of Iberian manuscripts, at http://sunsite.berkeley.edu/Philobiblon/BETA/2557.html; and a shorter description in Castro, *Manuscritos fransiscanos*, no. 389, pp. 421–2. It was among the first works translated and published by a printing press, issued in a bilingual version from the press of Peter Michael of Barcelona in 1493. See the *Illustrated Incunable Short-Title Catalogue*. There is some question as to whether this was a bilingual edition or appeared only in Latin, given that it is listed under both categories for the same year and publisher.

77 Whinnom, 'Supposed Sources of Inspiration,' 47. The only definitive indication of a Latin manuscript tradition of Ludolph's *Vita Christi* in medieval Iberia actually comes from a 1463 inventory of Iberian manuscripts from Majorca, which does not resolve the question of whether it would have been available in Castile. Hillgarth, *Readers and Books*, 1:169, referencing inventory no. 285 in volume 2. It has been suggested that Montesino used the 1497 Latin edition by Felicem Baligault of Paris as his source text for his 1502–3 translation of Ludolph's text, which would indicate that there was no edition available from a Spanish press. Álvarez Pellitero, *La obra lingüística*,

39. These speculations are further complicated by the fact that the author of the first Castilian treatise on Christ's life and Passion, Andrés de Li, cited Ludolph twenty-three times in his 1494 work, and his manner of narration, peppered with doctrinal tangents, is reminiscent of Ludolph. Delbrugge, *Scholarly Edition of Andrés de Li's 'Thesoro,'* 43.

78 Gorricio de Novara, *Contemplaciones sobre el Rosario*, 23–5.

79 Ludolph of Saxony, *Vita Christi cartujano*, vol. 4, chap. 58, fol. 51r. Compare the translation in Ludolph of Saxony, *Hours of the Passion*, chap. 1, p. 9.

80 Delbrugge, *Scholarly Edition of Andrés de Li's 'Thesoro,'* 92. Brought to my attention by Delbrugge, 'A Humanist's Guide to Publishing.'

81 A number of Castilian translations of Kempis's *Imitatio Christi* survive. The Sevillian translation was based on the 1488 Venetian Latin version, which attributed the work to Jean Gerson. It was reprinted a number of times, including in a 1516 edition by Laredo's publisher. Norton, *Descriptive Catalogue*, no. 896, pp. 326–7. Part 1 primarily concerns grief in the face of the misery and sinfulness of the self, part 2 touches on a variety of topics including purity, gratitude, and the pursuit of self-knowledge, and much of part 3 treats the pursuit of virtues. Kempis, 'Imitación de Cristo'; or Kempis, *Imitation of Christ*.

82 Boon, 'Agony of the Virgin,' in part reproduced in the next pages. The vernacular texts end the main narrative with Mary's movements either arriving at the sepulchre from Jerusalem (*Fasciculus Myrrhe*) or leaving the sepulchre for Jerusalem (*Passio duorum*). Interestingly, this stopping point was the norm in medieval Passion plays, but not in the medieval Latin treatises on meditation. Andrade de Labadía, 'Pasión de Cristo,' 225n20.

83 For discussion of various elements of Iberian Marian devotion, see Remensnyder, 'Colonization of Sacred Architecture,', and Boon, 'Mother Juana de la Cruz.' I am also at work on a book-length project called *Spanish Passion: Holy Week in the Castilian Religious Imagination, 1480–1560*.

84 Laredo also provided Latin titles for both of his medical books, though his project in both was to provide pharmaceutical knowledge in translation.

85 The revised edition was published by Jacobo Cromberger (Seville, 1524), with at least four subsequent editions. Andrés, *Historia de la mística*, 156. The edition accessible at the Biblioteca Nacional de Madrid is the revised edition, *Fasciculus myrrhe*, BN R-10946.

86 The original edition is *Passio duorum. Tractado de devotíssimas y muy lastimosas contemplaciones ...* (Valladolid: Nicolás Tyerri, 1526). Meseguer Fernández, 'Passio duorum,' 15. The edition accessible in the Biblioteca Nacional de Madrid is *Passio duorum* (Seville: Juan Varela de Salamanca, 1539), BN R-30651. Meseguer Fernández establishes its authorship (originally anonymous, then mis-assigned to Francisco Sánchez del Campo, and finally

traced to the friars Francisco de Tenorio and Luis de Escobar), providing a descriptive listing of the fifteen known editions and a short resumé of its contents. Meseguer Fernández, 'Passio duorum.'

87 Andrés claims, in a footnote to his fifty-page list of spiritual works published on the peninsula between 1487 and 1750, that 'Casi todas las obras anónimas son de autor franciscano. No firman por humildad.' (Nearly all the anonymous works were by Franciscan authors. They did not sign them out of humility.) Andrés, *Historia de la mística*, 156n4. Both of these tractates seem to have come from the circle of Franciscans in Valladolid. Andrés, 'En torno a la " Theologia Crucis,"' 366.

88 The treatise is dedicated to an unidentified noblewoman, referred to as 'muy illustre Señora' or 'Vuestra Señoria' throughout the preface. *Fasciculus myrrhe*, fols. 2r–5r. I do not see any indication in the preface that the material was conceptualized particularly for women – the author refers mainly to other friars as examples of devotion to the Passion – and so I take the references to this woman to be a dedication only. It is true that the most extensive elaboration of imaginative details concerns the reactions of Mary and other women to each scene, but whether this is a result of the impact of Marian devotion on Spanish religious regardless of gender or is particularly directed at women is not clear. For example, Bynum has noted that in the Middle Ages, more men devoted themselves to the Virgin and more women to Christ's humanity, a 'heterosexualization of the devotional gaze.' Bynum, *Jesus as Mother*, 140. Thus it is open to debate whether the elaboration of women's roles in the narrative is intended to support women's discovery of female role models or to focus male attention on (desirable) female exemplars.

89 *Fasciculus myrrhe*, prohemio, fol. 2v.

90 '[La Virgen], oyendo los golpes del martillo ... dava bozes diziendo "ay de mi hijo mio y mi regalo con quanta crueldad soys tratado de essos malvados. Mejor seria que essos golpes se diessen en mi cuerpo y cabeça: porque si quiera se cumpliesse mi desseo que es de morir con vos vida mia y todo mi bien." Pues tu anima ve alli y acompaña aquella triste madre y ponte junto con ella y haz apartar aquella gente porque no la enojen y aviendo della compassion la consuela y llora con ella y con las otras mugeres y las desampares.' Ibid., chap. 19, fol. 64v.

91 This led to the proscription of the *Fasciculus myrrhe* in the Index of Prohibited Works, after the Council of Trent raised concerns over the non-canonical status of the popular scenario of Mary's faints. Boon, 'Agony of the Virgin,' 11–13.

92 'Contempla anima devota como trabajava por se levantar: no hablar no podia por la gran tristeza: y levantando se de un lugar: luego por la mucha flaqueza

caya a la otra parte.' (Contemplate, devout soul, how she worked at getting up, [how] she couldn't speak for [her] great sorrow, and [even] if she rose from one place, later she fell in another due to great weakness.) *Fasciculus myrrhe*, chap. 11, fol. 43r.

93 'Ve pues y acompañalas y llora con ellas y no las desampares si quisieres alcançar alguna spiritual consolacion.' (So go and accompany them and cry with them and don't abandon them if you would like to reach some sort of spiritual consolation.) Ibid., chap. 11, fol. 43r.

94 Andrés claims that Tenerio finished the work before 1519 and that it was corrected by Escobar for publication in 1526, but does not cite proof for this dating. Andrés, 'En torno a la "Theologia Crucis,"' 367. I rely on Meseguer Fernández; see note 86, above.

95 Aldama, 'La piedad mariana,' 55. I question the contrast Aldama makes between a narrative and a book of meditative prayer – it seems to me that he misses the point of the *Vita Christi* genre as a whole when he makes this distinction.

96 Aldama provides numerous quotations from the first half of the work, before Mary's entrance as a (constantly fainting) participant. Ibid., 58–9.

97 A similar image is proposed in Berceo's 'Duelo de la Virgen' as a way to link the Passion and compassion. See the specific citations listed in Andrade de Labadía, 'Pasión de Cristo,' 222–3. Given the popularity in Spain of Saint Lawrence, whose martyrdom on a grill was often compared to cooked meat, the striking image may not have raised many eyebrows. Mills, *Suspended Animation*, 173.

98 'O mi Jesu que tanto me amas ... Que son mis servicios/para que por mi pecador te muestres a tu madre tal qual te vee: que en los pies no puedes sostenerte porque estan torcidos y presos: de las manos ayudarte tan poco puedes: ya hasta morir no esperes reposo. O matadores crueles que veda la ley/en la leche de la oveja cozer su cordero: y vosotros oveja y cordero juntos los cozeys. A el en la presencia della/y a ella en la del. O cordero sin manzilla assado en la Cruz: cozido en tu madre todo lo eres. O anima escoge como quieres celebrar la pascua del cordero/si le quieres assado: mira la Cruz: si cozido mira la madre: veras que todo se agota: la sangre del: y las lagrimas della: y que con este sacrificio a los otros no ay comparacion en ser provechoso al mundo/grato al padre/costoso al hijo/penoso a la madre.' Tenerio and Escobar, *Passio duorum*, chap. 71, fol. 117v.

99 'Longinos como era medio ciego ... sospechando que el Señor se fingia muerto ... para certificarse y no estar en dubda/llego medio atiento y con toda su fuerça por sobre la cabeça de la madre /dio al Señor a manteniente una gran lançada por el costado diestro: hazia la parte del coraçon/y tras el hierro salio

luego sangre y agua ... Lança y cuchillo todo lo eres: lança azerada al hijo: cuchillo a la madre: al uno hieres y al otro abres: a el abres el coraçon: a ella amortiguas el alma: y lo que el no siente por difuncto: ella lo siente por madre.' ([S]ince Longinus was half blind ... suspecting that the Lord was faking death, he wanted to certify it and not be in doubt. He arrived circumspectly. Over the head of the mother, he gave a great lance wound with all his might in the right rib towards the side of the heart, and after the iron was removed, blood and water came out ... You are the lance and knife: a lance of steel to the son, knife to the mother, one you wound and the other you open, you open his heart and you deaden her soul, and what he does not feel once dead, she feels as a mother.) Ibid., chap. 83, fol. 131r.

100 'O virgen crucificada que aun tu hijo no lo es y ya tu lo eres: que tu coraçon ya comiença a sentir los clavos del hijo.' (O crucified virgin, [crucified] even though your son is not, yet you already are, [for] your heart already begins to feel the nails of the son.) In the chapter detailing Mary's encounter with Christ on the road to Calvary. Ibid., chap. 63, fol. 109r. For those who do not have access to the original work, this passage is transcribed in Meseguer Fernández, 'Passio duorum,' 267.

101 Since the *Index de libros prohibidos* of 1578 had mandated the expurgation of a number of passages from the *Passio duorum*, the Mexican Inquisition required that copies found in a variety of monastic libraries and personal possessions be reviewed. For a discussion of the expurgations, see Meseguer Fernández, 'Passio duorum,' 242–4. For its presence in numerous Mexican locales, see the document 'Lista de los libros prohibidos que se han de recoger (1573?)' in Fernández del Castillo, *Libros y libreros*, 473–95.

102 Meseguer Fernández, 'Passio duorum,' 239–40.

103 Juana de la Cruz was leader of a *beaterio* named Santa María de Cubas (near Madrid), then abbess once it was incorporated into the Clarisan order. For biographical information in English and further bibliography on Juana, see Surtz, *Guitar of God*, 4–8; and Boon, 'Mother Juana de la Cruz.'

104 The dinners and gowns are included in nearly every sermon. For dancing, see, for example, Juana de la Cruz, *El Conhorte*, vol. 1, sermon 21, p. 740. For lap-sitting, see ibid., sermon 4, p. 345. The angels kiss Jesus, as well; see ibid., sermon 9, p. 461. For analysis of the scene in which God the Father fondles a partially nude Mary (and an argument for the scene as proving Mary's purity, not God's lasciviousness), see Surtz, *Writing Women*, 104–26. Further discussion of the feasts and plays described in her visions is found in *Guitar of God*. I analyse the 'shocking' type of plays for their implications for Christology in Boon, 'Christ at Heavenly Play.'

105 Juana de la Cruz, *El Conhorte*, vol. 2, sermon 27, p. 873.

106 I examine Juana's sermons for Holy Week in order to highlight the novel Christology and Marian authority that underlie her doctrinal innovations in 'Christ at Heavenly Play.'

107 According to the Gospels, of course, Jesus's body was still wounded after resurrection, since Thomas was able to insert his hand in the side wound.

108 Juana de la Cruz, *El Conhorte*, vol. 2, sermon 30, p. 902.

109 El Greco's *The Trinity* (1577).

110 Juana de la Cruz, *El Conhorte*, vol. 2, sermon 24, pp. 801, 803–6.

111 Ibid., sermon 30, p. 898.

112 Although the manuscript was read periodically by influential Franciscans throughout the sixteenth century and Juana's story was revived by several biographies and a cycle of plays by Tirso de Molina in the seventeenth century, the *sermones* were first published in 1999, in the edition cited above. The 'autobiography' (which records her funeral, so clearly is co-authored by her amanuensis, María de Evangelista) remains in manuscript. *Vida y fin de la bienabenturada virgen sancta Juana de la Cruz*, Real Biblioteca del Monasterio, El Escorial, K-III-13.

113 Cisneros wrote letters of protection for Juana. See Surtz, *Guitar of God*, 4–5; and Graña Cid, 'Terciarias franciscanas,' 609.

114 Boon, 'Mother Juana de la Cruz,' 138–42.

115 The connection between Padilla's title and Sevillian *retablos* is made explicitly by Herrera García, 'Orígines,' 16; a discussion of the *retablos* as visual Passion meditation guides is found on pp. 49–50. Note the combination of devotional practices, all embodied in some manner, found in the *retablos*: '[En las iglesias de las órdenes religiosas] no sólo se procuró disponer en un lugar idóneo la figura del santo patrón sino que, además, las advocaciones marianas predilectas de la orden, los pasajes meditativos de la vida de Cristo y la costumbre de insertar también santos de otras órdenes, como señal de reconocimiento y proximidad a las mismas, harán de los retablos piezas cada vez más dotadas de registros iconográficos y complejas en su concepción.' ([In the churches of religious orders,] not only did they attempt to place the figure of the patron saint in a suitable location, but in addition, the order's preferred Marian advocations, meditative passages on the life of Christ, and the custom of inserting the saints of other orders as a sign of recognition and proximity to them made the altarpieces into works ever-more gifted with complexly conceived iconografic registers.) Ibid., 18.

116 Ibid., 51–2.

117 Ibid., 47. More information can be found in Ferrand, *Retablo mayor*.

118 Both Juan de Avila and Francisco de Osuna came to Seville in expectation of travelling to the New World. Sala Balust and Martín Hernández, 'Biografía

del Mtro. Juan de Avila,' 1:33–4; and Giles, Introduction, *The Third Spiritual Alphabet*, 9–10. For more on Osuna, see chapter 2. Juan de Avila's focus on the Passion in his mystical guide to a female follower, *Audi, filia* (Listen, O Daughter), was highly influential but not published until the 1550s, with the definitive edition only available in 1574–5. For more information, see Gormley, Introduction, *John of Avila*.

119 Redondo, *Revistando las culturas del siglo de oro*, 84.

120 Cuevas Muñoz, *Efemérides*, 69.

121 García de la Concha Delgado, 'El via crucis,' 73. For more information on the *camino*, see Pereda, 'Measuring Jerusalem.' A chronicler of the sixteenth century suggests that the *Semana Santa* processions were already sufficiently spectacular to compete with Charles V's wedding. If this data is accurate, the ritual was already in full swing by 1526. Romero Abao, 'Las fiestas de Sevilla,' 65.

122 Webster, *Art and Ritual*, 144. The presence of sculpture in processions during Laredo's lifetime is confirmed by the fact that the Cristo de San Agustín was used for the thanksgiving procession through Sevillian streets that celebrated Charles V's victory in Tunisia on 28 August 1535. Cuevas Muñoz, *Efemérides*, 30.

123 Webster, *Art and Ritual*, 35. Also see her appendix, where she provides the processional order for the confraternities during the Holy Week of 1579 and several subsequent Holy Weeks in the seventeenth century.

124 'El cristianismo medieval fue festivo, mucho más el Sevillano.' Sánchez Herrero, *Las tres etapas de la enseñanza en Sevilla*, 24. It is of note that Rocío Romero Abao, writing on fifteenth-century feasts in Seville, relies on documents from the city of Jaen as a comparison, since there is no archival verification for such festivals as Carnival, Epiphany, or Easter, among others. Romero Abao, 'Las fiestas de Sevilla,' 66. For further discussion of 'popular religion' in late medieval Castile, see Pacho, *Apogeo de la mística*, 85–90.

125 Romero Abao, 'Las fiestas de Sevilla,' 93–4. The tradition of sacred sculpture in Seville dates back at least to the Reconquest, when King Ferdinand III entered the city in triumph in 1248, bringing with him the Virgen de los Reyes and the Virgen de las Batallas. Cuevas Muñoz, *Efemérides*, 187. A striking aspect included huge mockups of giants and dragons meant primarily for entertainment but read allegorically by the clergy (the Tarasca serpent, or dragon, as an 'effigy of sin defeated') in order to provide a reason for their incorporation into the procession. See Brooks, *The Dances of the Processions*, 54–6, 210–18.

126 Romero Abao, 'Las fiestas de Sevilla,' 111–12.

127 'Espacio sacralizado' versus 'espacio sagrado'; ibid., 87.

128 Webster, *Art and Ritual*, 15. In Spanish, the non-penitential confraternities are referred to as *cofrades de gloria*. For a more detailed study of the types of confraternities by race and social class, see Moreno, *Hermandades andaluzas*. This anthropological study draws its data from the five centuries of the tradition, not just its origins. See also Sánchez Herrero, 'La iglesia de Sevilla,' 103–6, for a list of all the Golden Age confraternities in Seville, divided by type.

129 Romero Abao, 'Las fiestas de Sevilla,' 70.

130 The first Spanish confraternities were based at Franciscan institutions, as evidenced by the fact that their founders, possibly tertiary Franciscans, adopted the knotted cord traditional to Franciscan garb as part of their uniform. Webster, *Art and Ritual*, 21–2. Webster gives 1380 as the date for the foundation of the confraternity; ibid., 22. There is no scholarly consensus on its date of origin, however. Compare Utrilla, *El Convento de San Francisco*, 94.

131 This shift was marked by the building of a special sacristy. Webster, *Art and Ritual*, 22. The focus of the Vera Cruz confraternity was not purely penitential, for members celebrated a total of fourteen festivals every year (five dedicated to Christ, two to the cross itself, another five to the Virgin Mary, and the rest to specific saints). Sánchez Herrero, *CXIX reglas de hermandades*, 46.

132 Sánchez Herrero, *CXIX reglas de hermandades*, 38.

133 Although this is not the earliest rule available for Sevillian brotherhoods as a whole, it is the earliest for a penitential confraternity. Its importance for modern historians lies not only in the early dating, but also in the fact that it was used as a guide for the many *Vera Cruz* confraternities that were quickly established in other Castilian cities. Ibid., 42–50.

134 That these processions functioned as religious spectacle is evident from the fact that the dramatic plays performed during the feast of Corpus Christi were, in contrast, not a part of the Golden Age developments of Holy Week. Webster, *Art and Ritual*, 147–52.

135 How completely women could participate is still unclear because of scarce documentation. See Sánchez Herrero, *Semana Santa de Sevilla*, 103–5.

136 Sánchez Herrero, *CXIX reglas de hermandades*, 43–4. The *de luz* level paid forty-six *reales* and the *de sangre* level paid fifteen.

137 Ibid., 47.

138 Cohen discusses 'penitential repetition' as part of a lifetime set of practices. Cohen, *Modulated Scream*, 27.

139 Sculptures of the suffering Christ are documented as the subject of devotion in Sevillian churches from the fourteenth century on, but were not carried in

the yearly procession until the 1520s. Sánchez Herrero, *Semana Santa de Sevilla*, 57–8.

140 Ibid., 22–3; my translation.

141 Much of this section is a revision of my paper, 'Towards a New Definition of *Recogimiento*,' presented at the conference '*Alumbrados* y disidencia religiosa en el mundo ibérico,' Centro de Ciencias Humanas y Sociales (CSIC), Madrid, 24–5 June 2010. My thanks to Felipe Pereda and Mercedes García-Arenal for inviting me to speak at the symposium, as well as to the participants for their enthusiastic comments.

142 Compare Pacho's chapter on spirituality during the Spanish reform, 1477–1555, in which Passion spirituality receives a few vague paragraphs. Pacho, *Apogeo de la mística*, 73–124, especially 86–7.

143 For example, an early article on the era lists only those topics. Sala Balust, 'Espiritualidad española.' Pacho's recent work critiques the emphasis on Erasmianism and Lutherans. Pacho, *Apogeo de la mística*, 342–92.

144 The influential texts that have set the parameters for the field of study are Bataillon, *Erasmo y España*; Márquez, *Los alumbrados*; and Andrés, *Los recogidos*. Ignatius of Loyola's early years also enter into the discussion, but the majority of Jesuit scholarship analyses the Society of Jesus from its formation in 1540.

145 Longhurst, *Luther's Ghost*; and Gómez Canseco, 'Poetas, humanistas, y cortesanos.'

146 An excellent recent overview is found in Hamilton, 'The *Alumbrados*.' My account depends on the classic and widely cited monographs on the subject, identified in the next note. Hamilton's article attempts to establish *dejamiento* as a mystical practice, while I am concerned in this chapter to reveal the ways that the assumed overlap between *recogimiento* and *dejamiento* has allowed scholars to misidentify elements of *recogimiento*. I thus provide the other side of the coin from Hamilton's argument.

147 Hell: accusation no.1; rejection of rituals: nos. 23, 27, 38; iconoclasm, nos. 15, 16, 18; *dejamiento*, nos. 9, 10, 32. The full edict is found in Márquez, *Los alumbrados*, 231–8; and translated in Homza, *Spanish Inquisition*, 80–92. Analysis of the accusations can be found in Márquez, *Los alumbrados*, 97–108; and Hamilton, *Heresy and Mysticism*, 29–36, 70. Other important works on *alumbrados* include Santonja, *La herejía de los alumbrados*; and Andrés, 'Los alumbrados de Toledo.'

148 The interactions of Hernández with Francisco Ortíz, an aquaintance of Osuna, are the subject of much of Selke, *El santo oficio de la Inquisición*; see also Homza, 'How to Harrass an Inquisitor-General.'

149 Osuna critiqued the *alumbrados* in Letter C of his *Tercer abecedario espiritual* (Third Spiritual Alphabet). Laredo mentions them dismissively in letter 5 in the 'Extravagante' at the end of the *Subida*, p. 790.

150 See note 148, above, for Ortíz. For Avila, see Sala Balust and Martín Hernández, 'Biografía del Mtro. Juan de Avila.'

151 Santonja, *La herejía de los alumbrados*, 105–8.

152 See, for example, the scholarship summarized in Bultman, *Heretical Mixtures*, 57n5.

153 E.g., Hamilton, *Heresy and Mysticism*, 29.

154 For one, the distinction between activity and passivity would not have been sufficient to mark a technique as heretical. Activity versus passivity during union between a finite human and an infinite God was and remains a bone of contention among mystics and scholars of mysticism, but it was an element in which a range of approaches came to be expected, including instances where both were recommended. Mystical treatises written throughout the Middle Ages demonstrate a full continuum, from the activity of bridal mysticism to the passivity of essence mysticism. Szarmach, *Introduction to the Medieval Mystics*, 13. Advocates of the combination include Bonaventure and Ruusbroec, both influential sources for 1520s mysticism. For that matter, note Ros's description of Osuna's mystical method as active, then passive, then mixed. Ros, *Un maître de Sainte Thérèse*, 525–7.

155 See remark on Hamilton in note 146, above.

156 This focus on behaviour is quite probably a result of the fact that Inquisition records are our only source for a description of the *alumbrados*, as they themselves left no writings outside their apologetics and defences during Inquisition trials. It is well known that the Inquisitorial condemnation of judaizing focused on actions such as the avoidance of pork or the lighting of Pascal candles rather than on belief in the Trinity or the dual nature of Christ, as behaviour was easier to prove than adherence to a belief system. See, for example, Alcalá, 'María de Cazalla.'

157 Andrés does repeatedly insist that body *and* soul are involved in the process of mystical union, though his interest is in elucidating the interior/soul only. 'Este hombre nuevo, reformado en su interio y exterior y con toda la fuerza integral de la unidad de su espíritu ... Este hombre nuevo, cuerpo y alma, persona y espíritu, busca y encuentra a Dios en lo más recóndito de su interior.' (This new man, reformed in his interior and exterior and with all the integral force of the unity of the spirit ... This new man, body and soul, person and spirit, seeks and encounters God in the most hidden part of his interiority.) Andrés, *Los recogidos*, 105; see also Morales Borrero, 'Beguinos, alumbrados y angelistas,' 323.

158 Andrés, *Los recogidos*, 90–1.
159 Ibid., 102, among others.
160 Ibid., 149.
161 He equates transformation into God with divinization. Ibid., 101.
162 Ibid., 13.
163 Andrés, 'Espiritualidad franciscana,' 478–9.
164 'Que el amor de Dios en el hombre *es* Dios' (my emphasis), and 'que Dios es nuestro coraçon.' See Márquez, *Los alumbrados*, 162–3.
165 'Si el amor del hombre hacia Dios es Dios, la trascendencia [de Dios] queda abolida; el hombre, deificado; el cristianismo, invertido.' Ibid., 164.
166 Even more pause is due to Márquez's scathing indictment of these heretical aspects, versus Andrés's quasi-veneration and lyrical delight in the same.
167 For example, the 1525 edict against the *alumbrados* accused them of rejecting meditation on the Passion in nos. 12, 22, and 42. Márquez, *Los alumbrados*, 232, 234, 237. Some scholars have categorized the attitudes catalogued in these accusations as a critique of the typical devotions of the church and therefore as anti-ecclesial or anti-sacramental; Márquez provides a long list of 'exterior' rites undertaken by the typical devotee, then argues that the *alumbrados* did not just reject specific sacraments but attacked the basic rationale for their existence. Márquez, *Los alumbrados*, 157–9. However, the wording of the accusation indicates that the authorities were as concerned that the *alumbrados* were rejecting Christ's humanity in forbidding Passion meditation as they were with the *alumbrados*'s dismissal of church tradition. See the translation in Homza, *Spanish Inquisition*, 90.
168 'The exaggerated spiritualism of the *alumbrados* diminishes the role of the body so much that it seems to disappear, and they do not appreciate its capacity for good or evil. They therefore fall into serious moral aberrations. The mystics do not deny the body but purify it and endow it with the greatest capacity for self-realization.' Andrés, 'Alumbrados, Erasmians, "Lutherans," and Mystics,' 480. For further discussion of the body/soul problem for the *alumbrados*, see Andrés, *Los recogidos*, 13.
169 Pacho seems inclined to accept the distinction proposed by *alumbrado* scholars Angela Selke and José Nieto of a 'double *dejamiento*' (one orthodox, one heterodox). Pacho, *Apogeo de la mística*, 355. Ultimately, this line of reasoning defines any theological or mystical (mis)interpretation leading to aberrant behaviour as the heterodox or heretical position, while orthodox Catholic behaviour and theology indicate that the devotee had accomplished the same method in an orthodox manner.

170 Andrés's proof for the recollected interest in both body and soul is grounded in Francisco de Osuna's distichs A and S in his *Tercer abecedario espiritual*: 'Let the person and spirit always walk together' (*A*nden siempre juntamente la persona y el espiritu), and 'Your body should follow Jesus and your soul his divinity' (*S*iga tu cuerpo a Jesús, y su divinidad tu anima). Close attention to those two letters shows that Osuna's topic is controlling the vacillating understanding or heart, in order to remain fixed on God. 'Doquiera que vayas lleves tu pensamiento contigo y no ande cada uno por su parte divididos; así que el cuerpo ande en una parte y el corazón en otra.' (Wherever you go, bring your understanding with you – don't let them go their own way divided, such that the body walks in one way and the heart in another.) Osuna, *Tercer abecedario espiritual*, distich A, chap. 2, p. 97. The body's role is to imitate Jesus's virtues, along the lines indicated by the tradition of *imitatio Christi*, requiring that the body seek 'a perfect imitation of the exterior Christ' ('una perfecta imitación de Cristo *exterior*'). Osuna, *Tercer abecedario espiritual*, distich S, chap. 2, p. 460. Thus body is relevant to Osuna's method not because it is integral to union in a positive way but because it needs to be brought into conformity with the rest of the person in order for union to be achieved by the soul. Osuna's point does not strike me as particularly dignifying the body more than his medieval antecedents or the *alumbrado* approach.

2 Navigating an Inquisitorial Culture

1 The literature on the Inquisition is vast, and most historians of Spanish religion depend heavily on its records for their data. A few of the foundational studies include Lea, *History of the Inquisition*; Kamen, *The Spanish Inquisition*; Pérez, *Crónica de la Inquisición en España*. Note that few such studies exist for Andalucia pre-1550, as only one *legajo* (collected file) pre-1550 is still extant from the Seville tribunal.

2 The suppression of all religious orders (exclaustration) in Spain took place in 1836. For a full account, see Revuelta González, *La exclaustración*.

3 'El otro fue fray Bernardino varon doctissimo en medicina antes de frayle, y despues muy mas docto en la sciencia de la charidad con que era enfermero de toda la prouincia.' (The other was friar Bernardino, a man highly educated in medicine before he professed, and after even more educated in the science of charity, as a result of which he was nurse to the whole [Franciscan] province.) Lisboa, *Tercera parte de las chronicas*, vol. 3, book 9, chap. 42, fol. 254v.

4 Gonzaga, *De ordine seraphicae*, 934. My thanks to Anise K. Strong for help with rare medieval terminology in the original Latin.
5 The reference to João II of Portugal (born 1455, reigned 1481–95) is a typographical error for João III of Portugal (born 1502, reigned 1521–57). Ros, *Inspirateur de Sainte Thérèse*, 44n1.
6 Wadding, *Annales minorum*, 10:254.
7 Named 'Bernardino de Alaredo' in Guadalupe, *Historia de la Santa Provincia de Los Angeles*, 322–38. A letter from the 'Extravagante' published at the end of the *Subida* in both editions is reproduced on pages 333–4. Guadalupe was not the author of the chronicle, but rather redacted the material written by Father Pedro Correa (until 1642) and Father Francisco de Yepes (until 1654), who are believed to have collected information over several decades from the archives of the convents throughout the province. Ros, *Inspirateur de Sainte Thérèse*, 17; and Zamora Jambrina, Introducción, *Historia de la Santa Provincia*.
8 Zamora Jambrina, Introducción, *Historia de la Santa Provincia*, xli–xlii.
9 Not to mention that Gaudalupe's text is adversely affected by the apologetics inherent to a chronicle written to vaunt one province over another. Ros, *Inspirateur de Sainte Thérèse*, 19. Ros even doubts the existence of the *manuscripta antiqua prov. Angelorum* referred to in a marginal notation to the first chapter.
10 Ibid., 23–4.
11 Boon, 'Mystical Language of Recollection,' chap. 1. Historians have depended on Guadalupe's chronicle as the basis for dating Laredo's life to 1482–1540, despite the misprint that puts Laredo's birth in 'mil y quinientos, y ochenta, y dos,' a full sixty years *after* the date of Laredo's first publication. It is not possible to verify the date of Laredo's death, since the death registers for the town of Villaverde del Río appear to have been housed at the other local convent, Nuestra Señora de Aguas Santas (deaths recorded only after 1633). There are no known surviving death registers of the friars at Laredo's convent, San Francisco del Monte de Villaverde del Río. See 'Guía de los archivos,' 766, 768. Given that a revised edition of one of Laredo's medical treatises appeared in 1542 with the notation that it had been newly updated and expanded by the author himself, it is evident that the date for Laredo's death is also uncertain. Laredo was put in charge of Juan Cromberger's estate upon Cromberger's death in September 1540, which indicates that there was no evidence that Laredo was close to death himself. Yet Guadalupe states that Laredo was fifty-eight when he died, which implies that he died in 1540. Guadalupe, *Historia de la Santa Provincia de Los Angeles*, 322, 339. Although a later chronicle puts Laredo's death at 1545, the first modern examination of Laredo's biography and mystical thought reverts to 1540 as the preferred date,

and nearly all scholars since have followed this lead. Foronda, 'Fray Bernardino de Laredo,' 249.

12 Not only was it customary to assign *hidalgo* status to any important figure in Spanish hagiographic literature, it is problematic that a *hidalgo* would enter the field of medicine, yet this is one of the few certain facts about Laredo's life. Statutes were passed starting in the mid-fifteenth century limiting access to political, religious, and educational institutions to those with an Old Christian heritage. Pike, *Aristocrats and Traders*, 87. In fact, there were relatively few people of *hidalgo* status in Seville, in comparison to more northern towns whose populations were sometimes primarily *hidalgo*. Domínguez Ortiz, 'La población del reino de Sevilla,' 339. Seville, as the centre of Spanish commerce in the sixteenth century, had a high rate of immigration, including former *hidalgos* throughout Spain who accepted jobs in 'vile sectors' rather than go through the difficult process of proving their Old Christian heritage. García-Baquero, *Sevilla*, 105.

13 Concerning Laredo's medical education, see chapter 3.

14 The newest literature on Laredo continues to rely on Ros's 1948 biography, in which he critiques some facts found in the hagiographical account but takes others for granted. Pacho, *Apogeo de la mística*, 486–9.

15 For a complete discussion of each detail of Guadalupe's hagiography that is historically inaccurate, updating Ros considerably, as well as for a history of the convent of San Francisco del Monte, see Boon, 'Mystical Language of Recollection,' 50–71.

16 For more information see Rubio, *La custodia franciscana de Sevilla*, 256–7, 273; Lejarza and Uribe, *Las reformas*, 132–3; Sánchez Herrero, 'La iglesia de Sevilla,' 97; and Alvarez de Sepúlveda, *Historia de la imagen de Nuestra Señora de Aguas-Santas*, 35.

17 The section 'Ésta es una entrañable devoción de ciertas missas' mentions a number of patients, as famous as Charles V's wife and as local as Sevillian merchants. The modern edition of the *Subida* includes it on pp. 892–7.

18 Laredo both gave Juan Cromberger an expensive reliquary and was executor of his will. Gestoso y Pérez, *Noticias inéditas*, 74, 78; for corrections to the transcription, see Griffin, *The Crombergers of Seville*, 110n10.

19 Those whose works were prohibited included Luis de León, Juan de Avila, and Teresa of Avila, to name just a few. For a complete list of the Golden Age mystics who were tried by the Inquisition, see the review in Gómez-Menor, 'Linaje judío.' The Indexes of Prohibited Works produced in Spain post-1559 both duplicated the Indexes published in Rome and expanded them to include more proscriptions of Castilian authors who wrote in the vernacular, including many Castilian mystics. See Bujanda, *Index des livres interdits*.

20 See Gómez-Menor, 'Linaje jodío.' For specific mystics and their heritage, frequently revealed through the inquiries of the Inquisition, see Alcalá, *Proceso inquisitorial de Fray Luis de León*, 675–99; Sala Balust and Martín Hernández, 'Biografía del Mtro. Juan de Avila,' 19; and Llamas-Martínez, *Santa Teresa de Jesús*.

21 An example of attempting to prove Kabbalistic influence on Golden Age Christian mysticism is found in Swietlicki, *Spanish Christian Cabala*.

22 Francisco de Osuna and Bernabé de Palma, immediate contemporaries of Laredo who also articulated the method of recollection mysticism, both ended up in the Indexes. Palma's *Via spiritus* was banned entirely in 1559, as was Osuna's *Gracioso convite* (Gracious Banquet). Clavería, *Arte de prohibir libros*, 52, 65. Osuna's *Primer abecedario espiritual* (First Spiritual Alphabet) was first expurgated in Soto Maios, *Novissimus librorum prohibitorum et expurgandorum index*, 862; and the *Segundo abecedario espiritual* (Second Spiritual Alphabet) in Sandoval et Roxas, *Index librorum prohibitorum et expurgatorum*, 45. See Vílchez Díaz, *Autores y anónimos españoles*, 82, for the complete list of Indexes that expurgate Osuna's works.

23 Alcalá, *Literatura y ciencia ante la Inquisitión española*, 54–5. Thanks to Sarah Bloesch for the citation count.

24 This has led some scholars to characterize part 2 as centred on 'the mysteries of Christ.' I argue that although Mariology concerns Jesus's mother and angelology addresses the distinction between human and divine natures, including these topics in the 'mysteries of Christ' produces a category so diffuse that all of theology ends up counting as the mysteries of Christ *qua* Godman. Since Laredo only maps Passion meditation onto a schema of seven days, I take it that he is insisting on Passion meditation as the core of part 2.

25 This phrase is taken from the title of a review of scholarship. Márquez Villanueva, 'The Converso Problem,' 317.

26 Many of the major works on *conversos* and on the Inquisition appear in notes below. Recent titles exploring the Jewish and *converso* experience within Spain and the diaspora produced as a result of the expulsions include Melammed, *A Question of Identity*; and Bodian, *Dying in the Law of Moses*.

27 Jewish authorities differed on the subject. Converts to Christianity were viewed on a continuum from heretic (*min*, those who if they wished to return to Judaism would have to be reinducted into the faith through ritual immersion) to unwilling apostate (*mumar*, those who had never truly left the faith), forced convert (*anus*) to true convert (*meshumad*). See Roth, *Conversos*, 4–6.

28 Starting in the late fourteenth century, Christians referred derogatorily to the *conversos* as *marranos* (term of unknown origin, often believed to be a play on the word 'swine') or as *tornizados* (renegades). See Netanyahu, *Origins of the*

Inquisition, 1134–6. Netanyahu notes that the *conversos* were not accused of judaizing until several decades had passed after the 1391 mass conversions and that the claim did not become a common one until the mid-fifteenth century. Kamen argues that it was in fact Inquisitorial pressure (and the specifics of the accusations) that led *conversos* to take up Jewish practices, rather than the reverse. Kamen, *Spanish Inquisition*, 60.

29 See Ladero Quesada, *Los Reyes Católicos*, 207; and Kamen, *Inquisition and Society*, 14.

30 See Netanyahu, *Origins of the Inquisition*, 954ff.

31 Sicroff, *Les controverses des statuts*, 89–90.

32 This was the first *limpieza* rule passed by a cathedral in Castile. At the same time, it was also one of the loosest statutes, as it only applied to the descendents of people found guilty of heresy by the Inquisition. In other words, any New Christian who had been absolved or never tried was free to take a position in the cathedral, while the Old Christian descendents condemned as any type of heretic would have been denied a job. Ibid., 91.

33 Ibid., 90–1. The prohibition on the entrance of *conversos* to the Colegio de San Ildefonso at the Universidad de Alcalá was also ratified in 1525. The Dominicans, likewise, seem to have made *limpieza* statutes official in the 1530s. Ibid., 90. It is interesting that although the Franciscans had been among the first to call for *limpieza* statutes, controversy over enacting their own divided the order. It was revoked for a short period of time in the 1560s. Ibid., 153n72.

34 Crawford, 'Honor or Financial Calculation.'

35 For a summary and assessment that problematizes the common assumptions about persecution and assimilation held by both sides of the debate, see Nirenberg, 'Enmity and Assimilation.'

36 For the crypto-Jews, see Baer, *History of the Jews*; and Beinart, *Conversos on Trial*, 286–92, where the author speaks only of the rejection of Christian theology and practice by the *conversos* in chapter 8. For the most passionate presentations of *conversos* as Christians, see Netanyahu, *The Marranos of Spain*; and Roth, *Conversos*. Netanyahu makes this argument for the first generation of children raised by converts after the 1391 pogrom: 'Intellectually, they were part of the Christian world, and saw no reason why they should not be part of the Christian society about them.' Netanyahu, *Origins of the Inquisition*, 213.

37 Starr-LeBeau, *In the Shadow of the Virgin*, 4.

38 Gitlitz, *Secrecy and Deceit*, 82–91.

39 In contrast to her important point that '[t]he experiences of *conversos* living near the Virgin's shrine in Guadalupe reveal the importance of considering to

what extent New Christians saw themselves as Christians, rather than exclusively examining connections between *conversos* and Jews,' Starr-LeBeau focuses predominately on possible Jewish practices as revealed by Inquisition documents. Starr-LeBeau, *In the Shadow of the Virgin*, 90–1. That is, immediately after mentioning that the primary focus of devotion for Old Christians in the late fifteenth century was the confraternities devoted to the Passion, Starr-LeBeau moves without transition to 'alternate religious communities' started by *conversos*, stating that '[t]he first question, for many *conversos*, was how precisely to observe Jewish law' (ibid., 83). Likewise, her interest in the Jeronymite friars is confined primarily to those identified as judaizers (ibid., 205ff). Starr-LeBeau's attention to the judaizing portion of the community may stem in part from Guadalupe's unique history as being the only town to expel its *conversos*, not just its Jewish population (ibid., 237–9). In a similar manner, Gitlitz provides his four categories of *converso* belief in chapter 3 of *Secrecy and Deceit* but throughout the rest of the book focuses on only those in the category of crypto-Jews.

40 This phrase is in direct reference to Francisco de Osuna, a presumed *converso*. Yovel, *Other Within*, 256.

41 Ibid., 225.

42 There is extensive scholarship on the political tracts of the fifteenth century by New and Old Christians that were either diatribes against *conversos* as turncoats or staunch defences of them as sincere converts. See, among others, Netanyahu, *Origins of the Inquisition*, 351–627, 814–96; Roth, *Conversos*, 157–202; and Rosenstock, *New Men*. Some *conversos* remained passionately anti-Jewish into the early part of the sixteenth century; my interest lies in *conversos* who did not explicitly align themselves as Jewish or anti-Jewish, but rather as Christian.

43 For discussion of Christian identity as racially conceived, see Buell, *Why This New Race*, 1–29.

44 These riots were local revolts against Charles V in towns across Castile, 1520–21. See Haliczer, *The Comuneros of Castile*.

45 McKendrick, 'The *Dança de la muerte* of 1520.' Interestingly enough, Varela published Laredo's first medical treatise in the year following the *comunero* uprising.

46 Any study of the origins of the *alumbrado* heresy makes it evident that every single person prosecuted in the wake of the Edict of Faith published in 1525 by the archbishop of Seville was a *converso* associated with the Franciscans, either as monk, nun, or tertiary. See Márquez, *Los alumbrados*; and Alcalá, 'María de Cazalla.'

47 At the time, a patronymic last name would have gone unremarked. Ortiz Real and Brígido Gabiola, *Historia de Laredo*, 50–4.
48 See the families of several men named 'Bernardino de Isla,' one of whom was a canon of the Seville cathedral in the 1530s and another a presbyter. Gil, *Los conversos*, 4:253–5. For the rarity of the use of the first name Bernardino, see the discussion in the section on his youth in Boon, 'Mystical Language of Recollection,' 49n79.
49 'Responde a un frayle no viejo, cuydadoso de las cosas de virtud.' Laredo, *Subida*, 'Extravagante,' letter 8, p. 798.
50 'Embiado a una monja consanguínea o sobrina del auctor, el día de su professión y velo.' Ibid., letter 7, p. 795.
51 Guadalupe, *Historia de la Santa Provincia de Los Angeles*, 333–4. It is the only quotation he provides from Laredo's published works. I assume that his identification of the recipient led to his interest in the letter.
52 Personal communication, Laureano Rodriguez Leleañez, 5 March 2004. Professor Leleañez is a faculty member of the Geography and History department of the Universidad de Sevilla, as well as the archivist of the Archivo del Monasterio de Santa Inés. I am grateful for his kindness in opening the archive during his sabbatical year when the Mother Superior fell ill and was unable to do so.
53 The only documents from the first half of the century are found in the Archivo del Monasterio de Santa Inés, *Expedientes sobre pago de dotes de religiosas, 1519–1802*, Legajo 18.
54 Primarily from the notarial protocols housed in the Archivo Histórico Provincial in Seville.
55 'A pesar de su ausencia en los padrones de habilitados, hay Laredos (los jurados y los contadores) que me parecen *conversos*.' Gil, *Los conversos*, 4:318. Gil provides specific explanations for identifying families as *conversos* in italics below the last name if the names do not appear on the *padrones*, his main source.
56 The will is found in the Archivo Histórico Provincial de Sevilla, *Sección Protocolos Notariales*, Legajo 15985 (from the year 1552), fols. 667r–669v. Gil's folio numbers are slightly faulty, and although the names he provides are correct, he missed a sixth child, Luisa de Belmañia (fol. 668v).
57 That the original number of siblings was greater than three is indicated by the fact that Juan, deceased but with children who could inherit from their uncle, is mentioned in Francisco de Laredo's will of 1556. Bernardino, who would have had no children and therefore needed no mention in a will written sixteen years after his death, could have been a fifth child. Unfortunately, as

the *legajo* in which Gaspar de Laredo's will is found is water-damaged and does not include folio numbers for the pieces of half-destroyed paper that it contains, I was unable to locate the original summarized by Gil.

58 It is entitled: 'Ésta es una entrañable devoción de ciertas missas, la qual recibió la sereníssima emperatriz en el tiempo que el turco huyó de nuestro invitíssimo emperador. Y después las han esperimentado muchas e muy notables personas, de las quales algunas nombraré aquí porque con más certidumbre se puedan saber los muchos e muy públicos mysterios que nuestro Dios y Señor ha en estas missas mostrado.' (This is an intimate [a play on words for 'entrails'] devotion [that consists] of certain masses, which the most serene empress received at the time that the Turk fled our invincible emperor. And after that, many very high-born persons have tried it, of which I will name a few here because with more certainty [on the topic], the many and very public mysteries which our God and Lord has shown in these masses will become known.) Laredo, *Subida*, back matter, p. 892. It seems likely that it was an original addition by Laredo to the sixteenth-century development of 'superstitious masses' offered in the hope of cures, escape from Purgatory, and other specific desires. See González Novalín, 'Las misas "artificiosamente ordenadas,"' for a resumé of the most popular of such masses, including the 'Amador' mass, which consisted of a cycle of thirty-three masses dedicated to a variety of saints, as well as Mary, the Passion, etc. Laredo's offering is focused entirely on the Passion and Mary, reminiscent of his twin interests in part 2 of the *Subida*.

59 Laredo's statement that he prescribed this prayer cycle with success for the empress and then for the rest of the patients listed indicates that he wrote this last section just before the publication of the work, also dated to 1535. Isabel of Portugal married Charles V in 1526 and evidently had difficulty with the birth of her children from the first child on. She would have been pregnant with her fourth child, Juana, during the emperor's battle with the Turks in Tunis, 1535. She was apparently sufficiently ill during this pregnancy to draw up a new will, which indicates that Laredo's prescription would have been in response to grave danger. Isabel died as a result of giving birth to her sixth child in 1539. Piqueras Villaldea, *Carlos V y la emperatriz Isabel*, 87, 106–15.

60 '[E]ste señor mercader se llama Juan de Espinosa [1535 edition adds: e bive a la Madalena], en esta nuestra Sevilla.' Laredo, *Subida*, back matter, p. 895, text and n106.

61 'Activísimos comerciantes.' Gil, *Los conversos*, 4:24. Gil provides genealogies both for known *converso* families and for probable ones in the case of each last name, separating the probables off by a series of arrows.

62 Or, obviously, as the nephew of his relation's spouse, if the nun were kin and not a niece.
63 The medical profession had primarily been associated with Jews before the expulsion, and a large proportion of the small number of practising doctors in the early decades of the sixteenth century were *conversos*. Rábade Obradó, 'Los judeoconversos en la corte,' 469. Certain towns in the sixteenth century even record having to choose a *converso* doctor as the official doctor of the town because no Old Christian doctors lived in the area. Pike, *Aristocrats and Traders*, 87.
64 Gracia Guillén, 'Judaism, Medicine, and the Inquisitiorial Mind,' 375, 380.
65 This fact can be proven from a comparison of his patient list (Laredo, *Subida*, 'Josephina,' pp. 892–7) with the several volumes by Juan Gil on Sevillian *conversos* (listed by last name and produced by tracking the descendents and spouses of New Christians who had been reconciled or executed in the first two decades of the Sevillian Inquisition). Gil, *Los conversos*, vols. 3–5. For further details, see Boon, 'Mystical Language of Recollection,' 96–7, and 103n252.
66 For Cromberger as a *converso*, see Gil, *Los conversos*, 3:550–1. For Laredo as executor, see the inventory of Juan Cromberger's estate, published with several faulty notations in Gestoso y Pérez, *Noticias inéditas*, 74, 78. For corrections to the relevant sections, see the comments in Griffin, *The Crombergers of Seville*, 110n15.
67 Unfortunately, we do not know the names of the theologians who approved the 1535 edition of the *Subida*. Laredo's medical works were also approved by panels of doctors, but although all but one have last names that appear in Gil's *converso* genealogies, none can be identified for certain. See the discussion in Boon, 'Mystical Language of Recollection,' 100.
68 Laredo, *Subida*, prefatory material, p. 23; on p. 25, Laredo indicates he was present at the death of the previous archbishop.
69 Laredo names the theologians Antonio del Corro and Juan Fernández Temiño in *Subida* III, chap. 1, p. 435. Both men were part of the court that tried Juan de Avila (denounced as a *converso* and an *alumbrado*, but aquitted). See the trial transcription in Sala Balust and Martín Hernández, 'Biografía del Mtro. Juan de Avila,' 51. As for the archbishops, Diego de Deza was archbishop of Seville from 1504 to 1523, and Alonso Manrique from 1523 to 1538. The archbishop was automatically a lead inquisitor.
70 The full list of Manrique's 1525 condemned *alumbrado* propositions can be found in Pérez, *Crónica de la Inquisición*, 125ff. See chapter 1 for discussion of the *alumbrados*.

71 Proof as to the *converso* heritage of the two members of the Inquisition can be found in the works that trace the original indictments of *conversos* in Seville and the records of their descendents. Corro is discussed in Guillén, 'Un padrón de conversos sevillanos,' 78. Temiño is discussed in Gil, *Los conversos*, 5:3850–6. Corro and Temiño were on the board that absolved Juan de Avila of charges of being both an *alumbrado* and a *converso*. See note 69, above. Sala Balust and Martín Hernández, 'Biografía del Mtro. Juan de Avila,' 19, 39–51. Likewise, both Archbishops Deza and Manrique were known *conversos* who extended their protection to other New Christians. See Pike, *Aristocrats and Traders*, 54.

72 Yovel offers such a study, but defines this Christianity as distinct from ordinary, embodied practice. Yovel, *Other Within*.

73 See notes 22, 107, and 127, concerning the banning and expurgation of works by the other 'founder' of recollection mysticism, Osuna. Works in the vernacular were more frequently proscribed than those in Latin, as can be seen in the fourteen standard rules accompanying the Indexes of 1583 and thereafter. For more information, see Bujanda, *Index de l'Inquisition espagnole*, 68–74.

74 Laredo, *Subida*, 'Notable,' pp. 29–30.

75 The fact that many modern scholars have presented Laredo according to the 'Notable' schema indicates that they have not actually read the entire treatise. A particularly egregious example is a relatively recent article that takes the *Subida* as part of its focus. The author seems only to have read the preface, describing the contents of the *Subida* as three separate weeks of meditation, one per stage. Mancho Duque, 'Diálogos franciscanos del quinientos,' 66. This mistake goes hand in hand with numerous others, including misidentification of the treatise as a dialogue. Pacho is the only scholar besides Ros who notes the problem of the inaccurate schematic, but he does not offer a rationale for the disjunction. Pacho, *Apogeo de la mística*, 493.

76 See Laredo, *Subida*, 'Josephina,' par. 23, p. 882.

77 For example, the fall with the cross, described in the preface as the ending point of Thursday's meditation and the beginning point on Friday, takes place in a few lines of *Subida* II, chap. 20, p. 274.

78 Ibid., chap. 22, pp. 279–82; and chap. 17, pp. 262–5.

79 For a persuasive argument that crypto-Jewish belief in the early sixteenth century featured anti-messianism above all, see Sharot, 'Millenarianism among Conversos,' 109. Since Jesus's messianic work was accomplished through his death, an emphasis on Passion spirituality would be a sure way to distinguish sincere conversion from crypto-Judaism.

80 My thanks to Jodi Bilinkoff for directing my attention to this point. For a recent synthesis of these types of accusations, see Cohen, *Christ Killers.*

81 Laredo states that the three stages are purgative, illuminative, and unitive for the first and only time in *Subida* III (1538), chap. 1, p. 435 (Spanish); trans. Peers, 63.

82 Osuna originally planned three spiritual alphabets, but ultimately wrote six between 1527–40. See bibliography for modern editions. For further information on Osuna, see Calvert, *Francisco de Osuna*; and Bultman, *Heretical Mixtures*, 29–54. In contrast, Bernabé de Palma, in his short *Via spiritus* (1532, published posthumously and banned in the 1559 Index), does not discuss the humanity of Christ at all in the four stages of his work. The only modern edition is based on the abbreviated version most commonly published in the sixteenth century. Palma, 'Via spiritus.'

83 See, for example, García, *Carro de dos vidas*, book 2, chap. 27, pp. 365–6, in which mention of the Passion is only intended as proof of Jesus's divinity, as seen in the tearing of the temple veil.

84 As cited elsewhere, neither Andrés nor Pacho include more than passing attention to mystics such as Juana de la Cruz and María de Santo Domingo, despite efforts by American scholars such as Ronald Surtz to explore their visionary works. For recent scholarship on Spanish mysticism, see the articles in Kallendorf, *New Companion to Hispanic Mysticism.*

85 Colombás, *Un reformador benedictino*, 247. Quotations and translations are from García de Cisneros, *Ejercitatorio de la vida espiritual*; and García de Cisneros, *Book of Exercises.*

86 Ignatius's work reads like a brief version of Cisneros (about 90 pages to his 300). The exact extent of the influence is debated by many scholars, including Colombás, author of the only monograph on Cisneros's work. The obvious possibility of influence, however, is evident to any casual reader who comes upon Ignatius's *Ejercicios espirituales* (*Spiritual Exercises*) after an acquaintance with Cisneros's treatise. Rotsaert, 'L'originalité des *Exercices spirituels*,' provides further discussion. Ignatius's careful attention to the role of the five senses in the crafting of effective meditation will be discussed in chapter 4.

87 Cisneros also provides an internal ordering to this tri-level scheme with a device later made famous by one of his early readers, Ignatius of Loyola, that of the daily meditation. Indicating seven different topics over the space of one week, and giving one week to each level, Cisneros sets out for his readers what Andrés terms a 'method of mental prayer.' Andrés, *Teología española*, 2:396. Various *devotio moderna* authors offered weekly meditations. Colombás, *Un reformador benedictino*, 153.

88 García de Cisneros, *Ejercitatorio de la vida espiritual*, part 3, chap. 26, p. 106; and García de Cisneros, *Book of Exercises*, 142.
89 García de Cisneros, *Ejercitatorio de la vida espiritual*, part 1, chap. 16, pp. 61–2; and García de Cisneros, *Book of Exercises*, 89.
90 Bonaventure's classical mystical works, *De triplica via* and *Itenerarium mentis deo*, do not include meditation on the humanity of Christ, but he nevertheless wrote works on Passion meditation, the *Arbor vitae* and *Vitis mistica*. Karnes provides a strong argument for the complementarity of Bonaventure's 'mysticism' with his Passion meditation technique. Karnes, *Imagination, Meditation, and Cognition*, chaps. 2–3.
91 Osuna's *Primer abecedario* on meditation on Christ's life appeared as a separate volume from the *Tercer abecedario* that addressed the final unitive stage of recollection.
92 García de Cisneros, *Book of Exercises*, 176–207. For a comprehensive survey of the medieval debate over whether the active life, the contemplative life, or a combination of the two was the ideal religious state, see Constable, 'The Interpretation of Mary and Martha.'
93 Colombás, *Un reformador benedictino*, 264. Gerard Zerbolt de Zutphen's *De spiritualibus ascensionibus* was in fact reprinted by the Montserrat press in 1499 and was one of three other texts assigned to the monks of Montserrat along with Cisneros's handbook. Ibid., 139, 194.
94 García de Cisneros, *Ejercitatorio de la vida espiritual*, part 4, chap. 49, pp. 174–8; García de Cisneros, *Book of Exercises*, 223–5.
95 '[C]a más fácil es á nosotros el conoscimiento de la humanidad así como más imprimida en nuestra mente, que el conoscimiento de la divinidad, que es muy más apartado della ... [S]i lo uno y lo otro: esto es, la divinidad y humanidad concibieres y contemplares en Cristo, gran devoción nascerá en ti, amor, confianza, temor y reverencia.' García de Cisneros, *Ejercitatorio de la vida espiritual*, part 4, chap. 49, p. 178. Compare the translation in García de Cisneros, *Book of Exercises*, 227.
96 'La tercera contemplación es: por la humanidad de Cristo al afecto espiritual levantarse contemplando: y á ese Dios por espejo y como en figura con ojos mentales mirar: y así por el conoscimiento de la humanidad al conoscimiento y amor de la divinidad venir por ayuntamiento de Dios: y por el tal miramiento de la mente, y ayuntamiento y transformación, comienza el hombre en alguna manera ser hecho un espíritu con Dios, y pasar fuera de sí mismo: y mirar esa misma verdad; y ser habilitado á la unión y ayuntamiento de Dios ... Y así mira que aqueste es el último grado de la contemplación en esta peregrinación hasta que subamos á la esencial visión de Dios.' García de Cisneros, *Ejercitatorio de la vida espiritual*, part 4, chap. 49, pp. 178–9; and

García de Cisneros, *Book of Exercises*, 227–8.

97 García de Cisneros, *Book of Exercises*, chaps. 52–3, pp. 231–9.

98 Ibid., chaps. 54–5, pp. 241–50.

99 Ibid., chaps. 56, pp. 251–4.

100 Ludolph of Saxony, *Hours of the Passion*, 23.

101 My revision of Peers's translation in García de Cisneros, *Book of Exercises*, part 4, chap. 57, p. 255. 'Acerca de la pasión del Señor, en esta manera se puede haber el varón contemplativo. Esto es, que la contemple: Primeramente, para imitar. Lo segundo, para compadescer. Lo tercero, para se maravillar. Lo cuarto, para se alegrar. Lo quinto, para se resolver. Lo sexto, para holgar.' García de Cisneros, *Ejercitatorio de la vida espiritual*, 203. Here Cisneros is quoting from the *Stimulus amoris*, attributed to Bonaventure at the time. Colombás, *Un reformador benedictino*, 265.

102 For bridal mysticism, see Newman, *From Virile Woman to WomanChrist*, 138–9; and Wiethaus, 'Christian Piety,' 49–52.

103 My revision of Peers's translation in García de Cisneros, *Book of Exercises*, part 4, chap. 57, p. 262. 'Y tanto cuanto más se allega á él, tanto más por devotísimo amor en sí desfallesce y se deshace ... y así de consuno se acrescienta el ayuntamiento de amor y devoción, hasta que toda la esposa es absorbida de aquel ardiente fuego de amor de la pasión del su amado.' García de Cisneros, *Ejercitatorio de la vida espiritual*, 210.

104 Just before his description of the three parts of what we may call his 'passionate way,' García de Cisneros quotes the Bonaventurian trope that Passion meditation is the 'door' to the contemplative life. *Ejercitatorio de la vida espiritual*, part 4, chap. 48, p. 170; and *Book of Exercises*, 222. The phrase may come from Bonaventure's *De triplice via*, in which he says, '[U] nde ipsa crux est clavis, porta, via et spendor veritatis.' Bonaventure, 'Las tres vias,' 130.

105 My revision of Peers's translation in García de Cisneros, *Book of Exercises*, part 4, chap. 49, p. 228. 'Y este tercero grado de contemplación de la vida del Señor pertenesce á los ya ejercitados, y que se acercan á la perfección.' García de Cisneros, *Ejercitatorio de la vida espiritual*, 179.

106 Portions of this section appeared in Boon, 'Agony of the Virgin,' 19–24.

107 *Primer parte del libro llamado Abecedario spiritual* (Seville: Jacobo Cromburger, 1528). Andrés lists six Golden Age editions in 'En torno a la "Theologia Crucis,"' 368n39. I will cite from the modern edition of *Primer abecedario*. In addition to the expurgation of the *Primer abecedario* (see note 127, below), one of Osuna's vernacular works, the *Gracioso convite* (1530) was banned in the 1559 Index.

108 Osuna was not brought to trial, despite his intersections with Ortíz's circle.

109 For example, Osuna's introduction to the *Segundo abecedario* describes a tripartite way to be presented in three treatises. Osuna, *Segundo abecedario*, Prologue, pp. 1–2. He wrote three more texts called 'alphabets.' While the fourth and non-alphabetic *Ley de amor* (Law of Love) addresses all three levels of recollection in one volume, and the fifth and six posthumous *Abecedarios* are parallel in subject matter to the second and first alphabets respectively, they are not of concern here, for Laredo could not have had access to them by the time he had finished the first redaction of the role of the Passion in his one-volume work.

110 It is, of course, possible that Osuna worked more quickly to publish the definitive version of the third alphabet because it was his depiction of the unitive stage of recollection that would have appeared most problematic to the Inquisition if not accurately rendered.

111 The generation of authors up through the 1560s, including Juan de Avila and others, tended to recommend the *Abecedarios* in plural, thus indicating they were at least aware of the series though without specification as to which. By the generation of Teresa of Avila, only the *Tercer abecedario* is mentioned with frequency.

112 Further discussion of Osuna's focus on Mary in his Passion meditation can be found in Boon, 'Agony of the Virgin,' 19–24.

113 '[D]espues de aver pensado entre mi mucho la sacra passion: dime a leer los libros comunes de romance que la tratan/por ver si el pueblo cristiano podia tener noticia de las cosas que yo en ella sentia: y como viesse que todos hablavan della muy humanamente como si fuesse passion de algun otro martyr: pense hazer singular offrenda al hijo de Dios.' Osuna, *Primer abecedario*, Prologue, p. 119.

114 'E no piense vuestra muy magnifica Señoria que es mi intento hablar aqui principalmente de la divinidad de Christo porque quando la esposa queria yr a contemplar la sagrada passion dezia…' (And do not think, your magnificant ladyship, that it is my intent to speak here principally of the divinity of Christ, because when the bride [in the Song of Songs] wanted to go contemplate the sacred Passion, she said …) Ibid., Prologue, p. 120.

115 Letters A, C, and T treat the reasons for the Passion, F and S Jesus's blood, L his tears, R his limbs. Osuna's other main concern is a thorough explanation of the benefits of this type of meditation for the devotee. Letters B, G, O, and Tilde (~ rather than ñ is the final letter of each of the alphabets) discuss either the benefits of the meditation or the attitude (of fervour, of imitation) that the devotee should muster.

116 The confraternity of the Cinco Llagas (Five Wounds) was possibly founded in 1507. See Sánchez del Arco, *Cruz de Guía*, 229.

117 Z, 'Zela toda la Passion: contemplando su processo,' is the penultimate treatise, followed by Tilde.
118 Osuna, *Primer abecedario*, Z, chap. 3, pp. 601–31. Bestul states that this was a typical format for medieval Latin commentaries in the high Middle Ages, but these Latin works were evidently not translated in Osuna's time. Bestul, *Texts of the Passion*, 26.
119 'E porque ay muchas personas que mas dessean ver el caso como acaecio que no vestido de glosas: y que quieren ver la verdad desnuda y sin afeyte de humana compostura.' Osuna, *Primer abecedario*, Z, chap. 1, p. 601.
120 Ibid., Z, chap. 10, p. 611.
121 '[L]a contemplacion de la passion te sirva de noche como luna: y la ymitacion della te serva de dia como sol.' Ibid., Tilde, chap. 3, p. 641.
122 Ibid., Tilde, chap. 1, p. 633.
123 Four editions within Laredo's lifetime are listed in *Catalogue of Books Printed in Spain*, 104. There are many modern editions, such as Kempis, *Imitation of Christ* (trans. Leo Sherley-Price). For my assessment of the work's irrelevance to Laredo's program, see Boon, 'Mystical Language of Recollection,' 155–6.
124 'E tú serás Tierra Sancta si te sabes encerrar e gozar.' Laredo, *Subida* II, chap. 13, p. 253. For further discussion of this and the following passage, see chapter 5.
125 Laredo, *Subida* II, chap. 13, p. 252.
126 Ibid.
127 The *Primer abecedario* was first expurgated in Soto Maios, *Novissimus librorum prohibitorum et expurgandorum index*, 862. The expurgated passages are Mary's faints, found at Osuna, *Primer abecedario*, Y, chap. 3, p. 568, and chap. 8, p. 589. Only the Castilian, not the Latin, version of García de Cisneros's *Ejercitatorio* was banned. Colombás, *Un reformador benedictino*, 448.

3 Medical Bodies, Mystical Bodies

1 Exemplary is Bynum, *Wonderful Blood*. She in turn cites a number of studies of the body in the late medieval era.
2 One older study exists, to my knowledge: Franklin, *Mystical Transformations*. Bildhauer's work on the way that blood was a term that stood in for 'body' (as the most important of the humors that regulated it) is useful in addressing this topic. In reference to Judith Butler's work on gender and other modern theories concerning race and disability, Bildhauer asserts: 'I think that bodies are defined in contrast not only to these other [gendered, abled, religiously

adherent] bodies, but also to an outside that is not other embodied people, but air, blood, matter or the world.' Bildhauer, *Medieval Blood*, 9. A few historians of science address this question; see, for example, Park, 'The Criminal and the Saintly Body.' Otherwise, attention has not centred on the living, medical body. Instead, the body in terms of its physical resurrection has been the subject of the foundational study by Bynum, *Resurrection of the Body*, and further studies such as that by Vidal, 'Brains, Bodies, Selves, and Science.' In terms of corporeality, without attention to physiology per se, neither of the following seminal studies of food (or the lack thereof) in medieval female religious experience refers to the physiological explanations of food becoming flesh in the human body: Bell, *Holy Anorexia*; and Bynum, *Holy Feast and Holy Fast*. Writers on Franciscan thinkers interpret body only in terms of sex or the body–soul dichotomy. See D'Avray, 'Some Franciscan Ideas about the Body.'

3 More work has been done on physiology in theology, as some scholars of scholastic theology have noted the important role of physiological ideas in answers to the question of the 'truth of human nature.' See especially Bynum, *Resurrection of the Body*; Reynolds, *Food and the Body*; and Ziegler, 'Medicine and Immortality.' Arnau de Villanova, a theologian and a doctor, receives excellent treatment in Ziegler, *Medicine and Religion*.

4 For an interesting discussion of body versus flesh in Christian thought (but unrelated to medical considerations), see Biernoff, *Sight and Embodiment*, 17–39.

5 Reynolds, *Food and the Body*, 87.

6 For a full discussion, see McVaugh, '"Humidum Radicale"'; and Bono, 'Medical Spirits.'

7 Bildhauer requests more attention to the medical body from modern theorists in a similar vein. Bildhauer, *Medieval Blood*, 2.

8 For the early intersection of Greek medicine and Christianity, see Temkin, *Hippocrates in a World of Pagans and Christians*.

9 Quoting from the 1512 provincial council held in Seville: '[Q]ue los médicos, lo primero y sobre todo amonesten a los enfermos que cuiden de la salud de sus almas.' (That doctors first and foremost caution the sick to look after the health of their souls.) Tejada y Ramiro, *Colección de canónes*, 71–2; summarized in Sánchez Herrero, 'La Sevilla del Renacimiento,' 150–4. This council reaffirmed the decree of the Fourth Lateran Council of 1215 and the 1311 Council of Ravenna. Similar decisions were in operation by decree of specific universities, such as Montpelier from the thirteenth century on, and medical authors included it in their directions for proper conduct. Pouchelle, *Body and Surgery*, 45–6; Archimatthaeus (Pseudo-Arnau de Villanova), 'General Instructions,' 743, col. 1.

10 Archimatthaeus (Pseudo-Arnau de Villanova), 'General Instructions,' 743, col. 1.
11 Church officials repeatedly legislated against the practice of medicine by monks (1130 Council of Clermont; 1311 Council of Ravenna), first on the basis that it was distracting them from their vocation, and second because being involved in a death, even as a doctor attempting to prevent it, would render them unclean for devotion. Pouchelle, *Body and Surgery*, 20, 45, 72–3.
12 Jacquart, 'Theory, Everyday Practice, and Three Fifteenth-Century Physicians,' 141, 146–7.
13 Chirino's work circulated extensively in manuscript and early print editions. Quoted in Solomon, *Fictions of Well-Being*, 31, 136.
14 William of Conches, for example, postulated the idea of 'elementation' to explain how earth, water, air, and fire are never present in pure form in the actual world (e.g., the largest body of water that exists, the ocean, is always salty). Laredo gives this useful example when he distinguishes between water as we are familiar with it in large bodies (such as the salty ocean) and the pure elements of which all physical bodies are composed. Laredo, *Subida* I, chap. 16, pp. 91–3. For discussion of William and the growing intersection of natural philosophy as a branch of theology informed by medicine, see McKeon, 'Medicine and Philosophy.'
15 First formulated by Bede, but traceable throughout the Middle Ages. See Gracia Guillén and Peset, 'La medicina en la Baja Edad Media Latina,' 339. This theory may also be in Laredo; see the argument proposed in Gracia Guillén, 'La fisiología escolástica,' 129–30.
16 Ziegler, '*Ut dicunt medici*,' 208, 209. For more extensive discussion, see Ziegler, 'Arnau de Vilanova.'
17 It is noteworthy that Spanish theologians schooled at major universities in the first decades of the modern era were likewise quite comfortable with the marriage of scientific knowledge and theology, for the board of theologians who approved the *Subida* for publication inserted a several-page correction at the end of the chapter on the four elements and humors. The author(s) of the correction were concerned with making a proper distinction between the four elements and 'elementation' by distinguishing between earth or water as we are familiar with it in large bodies (such as the salty ocean) and the pure elements of which all physical bodies are composed. Given that the author of the correction grounded this point on the authority of Augustine, Richard of Saint Victor, Scotus, Occam, and Biel (all referenced within the course of a single folio; *Subida* I, chap. 16, pp. 91–3), it is evident that the theory of the four elements and the consequent interpretation that connected flesh to earth/dust was a basic truth of physiology for early modern Castilian theologians.

18 García Ballester, *La búsqueda de la salud*, 297–300. Gracia Guillén gives the following analysis: 'Llevando a sus últimas consecuencias la tesis aristotélica de que la ciencia del hombre y la medicina forma parte de la filosofía de la naturaleza y han de ser expuestas en los escritos naturales o físicos, los médicos escolásticos, en el concreto tema que nos ocupa, la Fisiología, consideraron que la *physis* del hombre abarca tanto la *natura* como la *supranatura*.' 'La fisiología escolástica,' 131.

19 Further examples can be found in Cohen, *Modulated Scream*, 95.

20 '¡A hombre! ¿quién eres? Soy tierra, e aun bien astrosa. / ¿De dónde vienes? Responda: De la tierra arenosa. / ¿Por dónde has venido? Por la tierra bien fragosa. / ¿En dónde estás? En la tierra peligrosa. / ¿Adónde vas? A la tierra temerosa. / ¿Qué llevas? Una gran carga de tierra cenagosa. / E diga a sí mismo el hombre: Pues ponte del lodo, que tierra tienes harta.' Laredo, *Subida* I, chap. 10, p. 66.

21 'Tierra,' that is, land, ground, earth, dust, or homeland.

22 Here, 'contemptible' as either unfortunate or unclean.

23 'Fragosa' can mean harsh, tangled, or full of weeds and rough ground. Laredo, *Subida* I, chap. 10, p. 66n97.

24 There is no question for Sunday, because it should not be treated the same as the six days of work. Ibid. (1535), chap. 10, p. 67, n99.

25 'Ponte del lodo' again plays on the link between dirt and humiliation, literally translating as 'put on some mud.'

26 Laredo does not cite the source of the questions. This source was first identified by Ros in an appendix (Ros, *Inspirateur de Sainte Thérèse*, 345–7) and discussed with citations in full in Hernández Moreno, *El hombre del Monte Sión*, 239–45, although neither suggests how Laredo would have known of it.

27 This is the assumption of the two pieces of scholarship that focus on Laredo's stage of self-knowledge alone. See Hernandez Moreno, *El hombre del Monte Sión*; and Chavero Blanco, 'Fray Bernardino de Laredo.'

28 In the original version, the questions are followed by a straightforward discussion of God as creator and the traditional hierarchical division between body and soul.

29 Laredo cites Genesis 3:19 and Job 33:6 in the first lines of Monday's meditation. 'Sé que mi madre la Yglesia aquesto me representa diziéndome que soy polvo y he de bolver en ceniza ... Assí lo devía sentir aquel amigo de Job que le dezía: "Yo del mismo lodo soy que tú eres."' Laredo, *Subida* I, chap. 11, p. 68. The full biblical citations read: 'In the sweat of thy face shalt thou eat bread till thou return to the earth, out of which thou wast taken, for dust thou art, and into dust thou shalt return' (Genesis 3:19, Douay-Rheims translation of the Vulgate). 'Behold God hath made me as well as thee, and of the same

clay I also was formed' (Job 33:6, Douay-Rheims).

30 Thus humans, made up of the combination of dust and water, will return to dust and water in the end. See Laredo, *Subida* I, chap. 16, p. 89.
31 Also, ashes and putrefying corpses; for example, ibid., chap. 11, p. 68.
32 Rucquoi suggests that although both the Franciscans and the Dominicans focused on natural philosophy in the first centuries of their presence in Spain, by the fourteenth century the Franciscans had separated theology from higher education in natural philosophy to a considerable extent in order for theology to be accessible to all. Rucquoi, 'Contribution des *Studia Generalia*,' 756–9.
33 The meditations for Monday, Tuesday, and the second chapter on Friday.
34 See note 3.
35 Laredo, *Subida* II, chap. 22, p. 280.
36 For example, *Subida* I, chap. 11, p. 68.
37 For example, ibid., chap. 14, p. 78.
38 Ibid., chap. 15, pp. 87–91; obviously a reference to Genesis 3:19.
39 'Y tomando esto por pieças, el polvo, pura tierra es; e la sequedad de la tierra, junta a la humidad del agua, da fundamento a mi cuerpo; e agua mezclada con tierra, lodo es, o puédese llamar limo. Y aquéste es mi fundamento, porque del limo de la tierra me crio Dios en nuestro padre primero.' (And taking [Genesis's comment on dust and ashes] in parts, dust is pure earth, and the dryness of earth combined with the humidity of water gives the foundation of my body, and water mixed with earth is mud, or alternatively *limo*. And this is my foundation, because God created me [in our first father (Adam)] from the *limo* of the earth.) Ibid., chap. 11, p. 68.
40 Cohen, *Modulated Scream*, 22.
41 For example, Laredo, *Subida* I, chap. 11, p. 69; chap. 12, p. 73.
42 The term *nonada*, first introduced in *Subida* I, chap. 12, p. 71 (though the version *no nada* is mentioned in the seventeen-step ladder to God in chap. 5, p. 52) is consistently replaced by *nada* in the revised 1538 edition.
43 One of the few articles on Laredo's text that does not concentrate exclusively on the final stage of recollection attributes Laredo's anthropology in stage one of self-annihilation principally to the *contemptus mundi* tradition. Chavero Blanco, 'Fray Bernardino de Laredo.' Given Laredo's extensive reading in medieval sources and the fact that among the various vernacular mystical texts by his contemporaries, he seems only to have known Francisco de Osuna's and Bernabé de Palma's treatises, the medieval background of *contemptus mundi* more appropriately illuminates his work than does that of his Castilian comrades. In fact, Laredo's language is not directly influenced by a Castilian approach to the subject, for he never cites from his contemporaries who wrote about self-knowledge, such as Gómez García (*Carro de dos vidas*, 1500), Jiménez García de Cisneros (*Ejercitatorio de la vida espiritual*, 1500) or

Alonso de Madrid (*Arte para servir a Dios*, 1521). For a discussion of the minimal points of similarity between these Castilian authors and Laredo, see Boon, 'Mystical Language of Recollection,' 158–76.

44 For a discussion of the manuscript's dating, see Rossetti, 'Una traducción española del *De miseria humanae conditionis*,' 232–4.

45 Innocent III, *On the Misery of the Human Condition*, part 1, chap. 1, p. 6.

46 A fuller version reads: '[E]n aqueste ser, que es de cosas corruptibles e bive en corrupta subjectión y acaba en corrompimiento, se funde la fantasía d'estos nuestros muladares.' (In our being, which is [made] of corruptible things and lives in corrupt abjection and ends in corruption, is based the fantasy of these our dungheap [selves].) Laredo, *Subida*, 'Notable,' p. 39.

47 For more information on David of Augsburg, see Roest, *Franciscan Literature*, 209–13.

48 The first printed Castilian translation was David of Augsburg, *Forma de los novicios*. An earlier manuscript translation is recorded in the online BETA manuscript catalog, MANID 3479, found at http://sunsite.berkeley.edu/Philobiblon/BETA/3479.html. The Castilian translation of the *Forma noviciorum* was bound together with other treatises actually by or attributed to Bonaventure, such as the *Arbol de la vida*.

49 Augsburg, *Forma de los novicios*, part 1, chaps. 4, 15, 17, and 26, respectively.

50 Ibid., part 2, fols. 12–34.

51 Ibid., part 3, fols. 35–87.

52 I.e., according to the chapter titles, 'Se muestra el parecer convenible en las partes de corporal aspereza quanto al comer, y bever, y velar' (Here is demonstrated the appropriate advice in terms of the corporal penitence concerning eating, drinking, and vigils'), and 'Continúa la materia de la abstinencia en comunidad' (This continues the material on abstinence in community). Laredo, *Subida* I (1538), chap. 31, p. 154; and chap. 33, p. 167.

53 The actual final portion of part 1 does not mention seven rules or divide them by days. Ros attempts to apply the topics to a schema for a third week of meditation based on Laredo's comment in the prefatory material, in my opinion to little avail. See Ros, *Inspirateur de Sainte Thérèse*, 112–13; based on 'También tiene por sus días otra semana tercera donde se muestran las reglas que se deven guardar en corporal penitencia.' (There are also the days of a third week where the rules that must be followed in corporal penitence are shown.) Laredo, *Subida*, 'Notable,' p. 29. For critique of Ros's attempt to organize these chapters into a week of meditation, see Boon, 'Mystical Language of Recollection,' 193–4.

54 Ros, *Inspirateur de Sainte Thérèse*, 142n1, citing Rodolphe Hoornaert, *Sainte Thérèse écrivain*. For details on Laredo's sources, see conclusion.

55 However, it is true that the named work, Bonaventure's *Soliloquio* (quoted in Laredo, *Subida* I, chap. 5, pp. 53–4), does not seem a good source for part 1, as Bonaventure focuses on the good qualities in man that allow God to want to connect mystically with him (compare Bonaventure, 'Soliloquio,' part 1 , pp. 156–7, with *Subida* I, chap. 28, p. 141). Laredo, on the other hand, spends numerous chapters clarifying 'our annihilated littleness' (*Subida* I, chap. 7, p. 57), our 'miserable nothingness' (chap. 12, p. 71), or 'no-nothingness' (for example, chap. 11, p. 68; chap. 12, p. 71) in order to emphasize that 'quanto soy yo menos es más honrado mi Dios' (when I am less, more honour goes to my God). *Subida* I, chap. 11, p. 69.

56 The complete *Opera Bonaventurae* was available in Spain during the first half of the sixteenth century, though the date of the edition and its acquisition is unknown. See Marín, 'La biblioteca del obispo,' no. 275, p. 320. Without a definite link to Laredo, the *De perfectione vitae* can only be cited as a possible source, not a definitive one. Even if Laredo did not know the work directly, it is clear that Bonaventure, either directly or in his undoubted influence on the spirituality of the Franciscan order, is essential to Laredo's thought in the *Subida*. For a more complete discussion of Laredo's quotation of Bonaventure's *Soloquio*, and for speculation as to the possible influence of *De triplica via* on Laredo's work, see Boon, 'Mystical Language of Recollection,' 134–9.

57 My translation from the Spanish of the bilingual edition. 'El tercer sendero por el que debes caminar, si quieres llegar a la perfecta humildad, es considerar las circunstancias fundamentales de tu ser. Lo cual practicas, ¡oh carísima Madre!, cuando examinas de dónde vienes y adónde mas. Considera, pues, de dónde has venido, y conocerás que has sido hecho de la masa de perdición y del polvo y barro de la tierra ... Considera también lo segundo, adónde vas, y verás que vas a la corrupción, a convertirte en ceniza, porque *eres polvo y en polvo te has de volver.*' 'Tertia semita, per quam debes incedere, si vis ad perfectam humilitatem pervenire, est circumspectio tui. Tunc te ipsam, carissima mater, circumspicis, quando recogitas, unde veneris, aut quo vadis. —Considera ergo, unde veneris, et scias, quia de massa perditionis et de pulvere et limo terrae facta es ... Considera etiam illud, quo tendia; tendis enim ad corruptionem et incinerationem, quia *pulvis es et in pulverem reverteris.*' Bonaventure, 'Vida perfecta para religiosas,' part 2, p. 342. He even mentions the *limo terrae* that Laredo references in Saturday's meditation. *Subida* I, chap. 11, p. 68.

58 Given that Bonaventure devotes a later section of his *De perfectione vitae* to a consideration of the Passion, the topic of part 2 of the *Subida*, this work encapsulates the majority of the themes Laredo takes to heart in the first two sections of his mystical treatise. Bonaventure, 'Vida perfecta para religiosas,'

part 6, 366–76. The specific lines quoted above come in the second section on humility, but the rest of the chapter lauds humility without using the kind of language about putrefying bodies found in Innocent. Ibid., part 2, 338–45 .

59 Despite the apparent concordance between Salinas y Salazar's concerns (discussed in chapter 1) and Laredo's first stage, Laredo in fact specifically critiques the kind of humility techniques suggested by the followers of Villacreces. Salinas y Salazar describes humility as consisting of falling to one's knees in sorrow for one's many sins and recommends accepting with equanimity all sorts of discipline, both just and unjust, from the superior of the order. Salinas y Salazar, 'Memorial de la vida,' 722–3. Laredo insists that this 'ordinary manner' of indicating humility was easily feigned, proposing instead that the week of meditations based on his poem is a better method for becoming truly humble, by means of greater awareness of one's (dusty) rank in creation. *Subida* I, chap. 3, p. 46.

60 I examined all possible contemporary or recently translated sources for Laredo's approach to self-knowledge in Boon, 'Mystical Language of Recollection,' 109–200. I found no parallels, an unresolved problem in the dissertation that this book addresses by turning to the medical rather than theological context.

61 Cataphatic theology is the obverse of apophatic or negative theology. Turner, *Darkness of God*, 20.

62 'La universidad de Maesse Rodrigo.' Guadalupe, *Historia de la Santa Provincia de Los Angeles*, 323. Rodrigo de Santaella was the founder of the school and received monarchical approval for initating the University of Seville in 1502. Ortiz de Zúñiga, *Anales eclesiásticos*, 3:202.

63 There had been a 'maestro de gramática' in Seville since at least 1414, and by 1458 there are references in municipal documents to a school, which was possibly established for the youth and *bacherillatos* of the cathedral choir. Sánchez Herrero, 'Los centros de estudio,' 372–3. It is certain that by the last quarter of the fifteenth century, members of the general public and not just choir members were among the forty or so students receiving instruction each year. They were identified as *hijos de los buenos*. See Gil, 'La enseñanza del latín en Sevilla,' 270; see also Sánchez Herrero, 'La iglesia de Sevilla,' 129, for a summary of the above facts. Thus Laredo might have had access to basic education in a religious setting, though his lifelong status as a lay friar indicates that he was probably not in training as a cleric at the time of his education.

64 García Ballester, *La búsqueda de la salud*, 213. Ballester mentions Laredo's *Modus faciendi* at the end of his magnum opus on medieval Spanish medicine because it was one of the first vernacular pharmaceutical handbooks to appear on the peninsula, yet he does not provide any information on Laredo's medical

education. In contrast to his detailed discussion of the university training of Laredo's contemporaries, Ballester characterizes Laredo's educational background simply in terms of an interest in medicine arising naturally from a particularly Franciscan focus on natural philosophy. Ibid., 618–20.

65 Folch gives the entire list of authors cited in the *Modus faciendi*, including the above well-known works as well as Sarampion and Nicolas (see next note). Folch Andreu, 'El primer libro propiamente de farmacia,' 13–14. For the academic curriculum in Salamanca's school of medicine, see Amasuno Sárraga, *La escuela de medicina*, 133–41.

66 Ballester quotes the requirements for pharmacists: 'Que los boticarios examinados sean obligados a tener Mésue, e Nicolás, e Servidor, e Sarampion, e Pandetas. Los latinos en Latín e los romancistas lo que dellos se acostumbra tener e hablar en romançe.' (Let the pharmacists being tested be obliged to know Mésue, Nicolas, Servidor, Sarampion, and Pandetas. Those [who wrote] in Latin [ought to be] known in Latin and the ones in the vernacular which are usually owned and discussed in the vernacular.) García Ballester, *La búsqueda de la salud*, 625. The 1477 law built on legislation by several kings earlier in the century but was not popular among the municipalities required to enforce it, thus resulting in frequent admonishments from the Catholic Monarchs against those who delegated the examination requirements to unofficial examiners. Ibid., 529–42.

67 The *Articella* not only had several centuries of manuscript tradition but also appeared in numerous editions in the first sixty years of printing. '[The *Articella* included the] Hippocratic *Aphorismi* and *Prognostica*, Galen's *Tegni* (*Ars medica, Ars parva, Microtegni*) the *Isagoge* of Joannitius, two semiological writings (*De urinis* of Theophilus, and *De pulsibus* attributed to Philaretus) and the Hippocratic *De regimine auctorum morborum*. This core was later supplemented with a variety of works from various origins, among them other Hippocratic and Galenic writings, pieces of Avicenna's *Canon* and collections of aphorisms by Mesué, Arnau de Vilanova and others.' Arrizabalaga, *The 'Articella' in the Early Press*, 5. For the *Articella* in the sixteenth century, see Siraisi, 'Changing Fortunes of a Traditional Text.' See the next section of this chapter for more details on the basic knowledge these works would have provided.

68 The first chronicles to reference Laredo mention only that he was a lay friar as well as a doctor. His accomplishments include the *Subida*, as well as treating King João II of Portugal and gaining in return a grant of spices for his province. Gonzaga, *De ordine seraphicae*, 934; see also Ros, *Inspirateur de Sainte Thérèse*, 44n1, for accuracy as to which Portuguese king Laredo could have treated.

69 See chapter 2 for discussion of this isolated retreat house.

70 The original versions are titled as follows: *Metaphora medicine con DC autoridades declaradas, sin contar CXIV aphorismos que hazen la quarta parte, ni otros XX testos juntos que están al final de la quarta. Es, pues, nuevamente copilada por un frayle menor de la provincia de los Ángeles a gloria y honrra de Dios* (Seville: Juan de Varela, 1522); and *Modus faciendi cum ordine medicandi. A médicos, boticarios muy común y necessario. Copiado nuevamente con orden tan peregrina que no se avrá visto otra vez tan aclarada manera de platicar ni por la orden que ésta lleva. Con privilegio cesáreo* (Seville: Jacobo Cromburger, 1527). The third edition of the *Modus faciendi* was updated and enlarged by an additional short section at the end: *Modus faciendi, nueuamente por el auctor corregido: Y en esta impression tercera añedido un notable tractado de secretos cautiuos: Como al fin de la vuelta desta hoja se vera ...* (Seville: En la casa de Juan Cromburger, 1542).

71 All citations will include page numbers to the modern edition of *Modus faciendi*, ed. Milagro Laín and Doris Ruiz Otín, but since few exemplars were produced, I also include the foliation. Laredo, *Modus faciendi*, 35 [fol. 3r]; for comparison, see Joannitius (Hunain ibn Ishaq), 'Selections from *Isagogue*,' 705, col. 1. For a discussion of sixteenth-century Arabic Galenism (actually a tradition of commenting on the Latin translations of Avicenna) versus humanist Galenism (recovering Avicenna by learning the original language), see García Ballester, 'Circulation and Use of Medical Manuscripts in Arabic.'

72 Laredo's tendency to ascribe authority by citation of authors rather than by narrating specific instances of the remedy's efficacy may be associated with male rather than female textual production in this era. Cabré, 'Women or Healers?,' 49. Note that Solomon ascribes this tendency to vernacular (rather than gendered) authorship. Solomon, *Fictions of Well-Being*, 62.

73 For sixteenth-century Spanish medicine, see the many works of García Ballester cited throughout this chapter. For discussion of the impact of the New World on Iberian science, including medicine, particularly in the second half of the century, see Barrera-Osorio, *Experiencing Nature*, and Cañizares-Esguerra, 'Iberian Science in the Renaissance.' For an overview of medicine in Castile in particular, see González de Fauve and Forteza, 'Ética médica y mala praxis en Castilla.'

74 García Ballester, *La búsqueda de la salud*, 384.

75 Gracia Guillén, 'La fisiología escolástica,' 119.

76 García Ballester, *La búsqueda de la salud*, 618.

77 Temkin, *Galenism*, 118.

78 Folch Andreu, 'El primer libro propiamente de farmacia,' 13–14, lists thirty-seven authors of Greek, Arabic, Italian, and Spanish origin, among others, ranging from the earliest – Hippocrates – to Renaissance authors,

including some Franciscans. It is Folch Andreu who ascribes thirty-four remedies to Laredo himself.

79 See introduction, note 100.

80 Laredo, *Modus faciendi*, 35–6 [fol. 3v]. For the popularity of this conceit among medieval university-trained physicians, see O'Boyle, 'Medicine, God and Aristotle,' 202–8.

81 Laredo, *Modus faciendi*, 37–8 [fols. 4v–5r], 350–4 [fols. 216r–218r]. The final pages are prefaced by a Latin elegy of Mary (349–50 [fols. 215v–216r]) then continue on to one laud to Mary and two to Joseph, all in the vernacular. In contrast, the *Laus Deo, Marie et Joseph* at the end of the 'Josephina' treatise in both versions of the *Subida* is actually in Latin. See 'Josephina,' par. 26, p. 886. In the *Modus faciendi*, the laud to Mary is especially interesting, as it ends with a description of the doctrine of the Trinity, not necessarily the norm in a praise of Mary, yet indicative of Laredo's Trinitarian theology that infuses part 2 of his *Subida*. Laredo, *Modus faciendi*, 352 [fols. 217v–r].

82 Published by Juan de Varela, 1536, who had released the original 1522 edition as well.

83 See chapter 2, note 59.

84 Dangler's chapter 'The Medical Body' focuses on the continuum of gender and its relevance to coitus. Dangler, *Making Difference*, 83–110.

85 For Joannitius, for example, see Laredo, *Metaphora medicine* II, 'Extravagante,' fol. 37va. Laredo cites Avicenna constantly. Siraisi also relies on the combination of Joannitius's and Avicenna's overviews of physiology and anatomy in her overview of Renaissance medicine. Siraisi, *Medieval and Early Renaissance Medicine*, 3–7.

86 Laredo cites the *Isagoge* in his section on the non-naturals. *Metaphora medicine* II, 'Extravagante,' fol. 37vb.

87 Siraisi, *Medieval and Early Renaissance Medicine*, 101; for Iberia, see García Ballester, McVaugh, and Rubio-Vela, *Medical Licensing and Learning*, 14.

88 Siraisi, *Medieval and Early Renaissance Medicine*, 101. For a cogent discussion, see Reynolds, *Food and the Body*, 106–9, 116.

89 McVaugh discusses the common reliance of medieval medical works on the term *humidum radicale*, tracing it in Avicenna, Peter of Spain, Arnau of Villanova, etc. McVaugh, '"Humidum Radicale."' Arnau defined it more loosely than his predecessors did, as 'any moisture which is the subject of the *calor vivificus* in life.' Ibid., 280. For Avicenna's opinion about semen as the source for the passing of the radical moisture down through the generations, see Ziegler, '*Ut dicunt medici*,' 216.

90 In his pharmaceutical treatise, Laredo clarifies the need for understanding the humors when prescribing remedies. Specific medicines draw one or another

humor towards them and thus can be used to order a sick body whose humors are out of balance. Laredo, *Modus faciendi*, 36 [fol. 3v].

91 Humors are 'fluid moist bod[ies] into which our aliment is transformed.' Avicenna, 'Selections from the *Canon*,' 717, col. 2.

92 Ibid., 718, col. 1.

93 Ibid., 719, col. 2.

94 Ibid., 718, col. 1.

95 On Avicenna, see Ziegler, '*Ut dicunt medici*,' 216. For Laredo, citing Avicenna's opinion, see Laredo, *Modus faciendi*, part 3, division 1, chap. 5, p. 313 [fol. 190r].

96 McVaugh, '"Humidum Radicale,"' 260. For the application of this information in scholastic theology, see Reynolds, *Food and the Body*, 108–11. For Laredo's discussion of this as a medical process, see *Modus faciendi*, part 3, division 1, chap. 5, p. 313 [fol. 190r]. He references this physical process in particular for spiritual purposes; see *Subida* I, chap. 16, pp. 89–90; *Subida* II, chap. 17, p. 264; and discussion below.

97 The clearest description that I have read of the relationship between primary and secondary humors is found the *Metaphora medicine*'s treatise on the *humido radical*, fol. 100va. The treatise itself is found after part 3, running from folio 100rb to 110rv.

98 And thus why Laredo's mini-treatise on the *humido radical* concerns digestion and blood; see previous note.

99 Laredo includes a short treatise on phlebotomy at the end of the *Metaphora medicine* IV, fols. 106rb–111rb.

100 Joannitius (Hunain ibn Ishaq), 'Selections from *Isagogue*,' 706, col. 1.

101 Ibid., 706, col. 2.

102 Ibid. See also Laredo, *Modus faciendi*, part 3, division 1, chap. 4, 311–12 [fols. 188r–v].

103 In fact, the physicians brought another term into consideration in order to distinguish what was and was not part of their focus. A popular treatise on the process of taking the pulse (measuring the pulse and examining the urine were the two primary methods of diagnosis) explained that the soul and body could only exist in the same location because the *spiritus* connected them. Thus the physician was twice separated from direct consideration of the soul. 'Interpretation of the Pulse,' 746, col. 1.

104 Summarized in Boyle, 'Augustine's Heartbeat,' 22.

105 Ziegler, 'Arnau de Villanova,' 261. Ziegler makes the same distinction in *Medicine and Religion*, 60.

106 For a careful compilation of all the elements of Galenic medicine ever mentioned in the *Subida*, see Gracia Guillén, 'La fisiología escolástica.'

Unfortunately, he does not analyse the effect of including these materials either on the articulation of a mystical method, nor even on Laredo's theological anthropology.

107 '[N]ecessario es que en aqueste ser, que es de cosas corruptibles e bive en corrupta subjeción y acaba en corrompimiento, se funde la fantasía d'estos nuestros muladares, d'este mi cuerpo bestial, d'este elementado cieno, compuesto de agua y de tierra.' Laredo, *Subida*, prefatory material, p. 39. Note that *fantasia* is a medical term for a brain ventricle, the location of one of the inner senses. See chapter 4 of this book.

108 Laredo, *Subida* I, chap. 11, p. 68.

109 Laredo defines ash as 'dry dust' later on. Ibid., chap. 16, p. 86.

110 '[E]n mi fundamento, el ayre y el polvo están juntos, y el ayre haze al polvo que buelva a ser casi nada ... e por darme a entender que soy nada, y que soy hecho de nada ... se me dize que soy polvo.' (At my foundation, air and dust are together, and the air makes the dust turn into almost nothing ... In order to make me understand that I am nothing, and that I'm made of nothing ... it is said that I am dust.) Ibid., chap. 11, p. 68.

111 Thus playing on earth, water, and fire: '[L]uego que veys un ladrillo, sabéys que es su fundamento hecho de tierra e agua, y d'esto mismo soys Vos; lodo soys ambos a dos, e aun es el vuestro más vil y de más vil corrupción; e si se cozió con fuego, elemento es también vuestro, e tiéneos una ventaja: que aunque se quiebre, permanece en la substancia que muestra hasta que esconda su ser; e tú, al tiempo que te quiebras, passas en tal corrupción que no ay nadie que te quiera.' (Next when you see a brick, you know that its foundation is made of earth and water, and that you too are from the same [materials.] You are both mud; yours is in fact the more vile and full of filthy corruption. And if [the brick] is cooked with fire, you also are made of this element. [The brick] has the advantage that although it burns, it remains permanent in the substance that appears until it hides its substance, while you, at the moment you burn, pass into such corruption that there is nobody who will love you.) Ibid., chap. 4, p. 51.

112 Ibid., chap. 8, p. 60.

113 See note 53, above.

114 'Quando nuestro gran Dios y Señor universal crio a nuestro primero padre, la tierra de la qual su divina Magestad le plasmó era en gran pureza criada.' (When our great God and universal Lord created our first father, the earth out of which his divine majesty moulded him was created out of great purity.) Laredo, *Subida* I, chap. 28, p. 137. Cohen quotes *The Life of Adam and Eve*, an early medieval text, describing Adam's body as made out of the best quality of earth available. She has found no record of this text as a

source for late medieval texts or sermons, despite its survival in an extensive Latin and vernacular tradition, so it is unclear whether Laredo could have known of it. Cohen, *Modulated Scream*, 21–2.

115 'Toda enlodada con la compañia del cieno.' Laredo, *Subida* I, chap. 28, p. 139. The original definition of *cieno* is found in *Subida*, prefatory material, p. 39.

116 This is the version of 'radical moisture' understood to have begun with Adam and is the source of all life. It is not the Avicennean version of 'radical moisture' as the general category for types of blood. See note 89, above.

117 Ibid., chap. 16, p. 88. For medieval discussions of resurrection, see Bynum, *Resurrection of the Body*.

118 'Mas aquesto elementos, todos quatro ... y sus calidades son ya mías en mis humores, los quales, venidos en húmido radical, aun dexan de ser humores y passen en miembros particulares, para en ellos siempre mejor se conservar buscando perpetuidad.' Laredo, *Subida* I, chap. 16, pp. 89–90.

119 Gracia Guillén, 'Judaism, Medicine, and the Inquisitorial Mind,' 380. Both Christians and Jews identified different complexions as a result of humoral theory, although each seems to have associated their own group with darker complexions and the other with fair (and weak, i.e., female) complexions. Koren, 'Menstruant as "Other,"' 45n68.

120 Gracia Guillén, 'Judaism, Medicine, and the Inquisitorial Mind,' 381.

121 Laredo consistently emphasizes the nothingness of the human condition, in order to erase the human from consideration so that only God remains as a focus. This is in contrast to Bonaventure, who details the God-given human capacity to reach for God.

122 'Pues sepa este zagal presuntuoso que esta mísera materia (desnuda del espiritu de vida) es lo que tiene de sí, e allí está su presunción, porque el calor natural de mi Dios lo rescibío, e nada tiene en él, pues no sabe quándo se lo quitará e bolverá a la misma corrupción, e a la forma cenagosa aborrecible que tuviera si en su ser no recibiera de Dios el bien, que le dio de balde con el calor natural y el espíritu vidal.' (So this presumptuous adolescent is sure that this miserable material (denuded of the spirit of life) is something he has of himself, and therein lies his presumption: he received his innate heat from my God and has nothing of himself. Therefore he does not know when the [innate heat] will be taken from him and he will return to the same corruption and abhorrant muddy form which he would have if he did not receive goodness from God into himself, who gave it to him suddenly along with the innate heat and the vital spirit.) Laredo, *Subida* I, chap. 12, p. 71.

123 In his textbook, Laredo makes it clear that the innate heat brings the vital spirit along with it as it flows with the humor blood through the veins of the

body. Once this combination reaches the brain, it produces the animal spirit. Laredo, *Modus faciendi*, part 3, division 1, chap. 4, p. 311 [fol. 188v].

124 In a discussion of producing the material body from sexual union, Laredo describes the part passed on through sexual intercourse as 'putrefación más horribilidad.' *Subida* I, chap. 12, pp. 70–1.

125 Ibid. He repeats the point later in the chapter: 'Visto está ya el fundamento de aquesta nuestra miseria y que lo que le ha añadido la immensa bondad de Dios es el calor, por cuyo medio le dio espíritu de vida; y éste es su primero don sobre este mi fundamento. E sobre esto escrito está que ha formado huessos y nervios, y que de carne y de piel los cubrió y les dio vida e misericordia.' (It is seen that this is already the foundation of our misery, and what God in his great goodness has added is heat, by which means he gives the spirit of life; and this is [God's] first gift in addition to my foundation. And on this [foundation,] it is written that he formed bones and nerves, covered them with flesh and skin, and gave them life and grace.) Ibid., chap. 12, p. 72.

126 This section sets up the possibility of referencing the Fall in a later chapter, because Laredo points out that parents who give their children life are actually passing on a gift of 'vital spirit, with natural heat' which is the life-giving heat God gives humans. Ibid., chap. 12, pp. 71–2.

127 Laredo, *Subida* II, chap. 17, p. 263.

128 'E como orando se inflamasse más y más el incendio del amor, abrasó assí sus muy divinas entrañas e movió assí todo su vidal espiritu, y excitó assí todo el calor natural de su humanidad sagrada.' (And while praying, the conflagration of love is inflamed more and more, thereby burning his very divine entrails, moving all his vital spirit, and exciting all the innate heat of his sacred humanity.) Ibid.

129 Various examples provided in Bynum, 'Violence Occluded,' 101–5. Another example is found in Marquard von Lindau (d. 1392, German Franciscan), who identified fear as the reason the blood liquified, noting that 'excessive fear has the property to liquefy all the humors most aggressively and weaken the entire body.' Translated in Mossman, *Marquard von Lindau*, 64. Mossman indicates that Lindau's physiological explanation was a scientific advance on his primary source, the thirteenth-century nominalist theologian Olivi. Ibid., 79.

130 Laredo devotes an entire chapter to the subject in his mini-treatise on the *humido radical. Metaphora medicine* IV, chap. 5, fols. 102va–103rb.

131 Laredo, *Subida* II, chap. 17, p. 264.

132 Ibid. In fact, Laredo switches (without clarifying himself) to the meaning of *humido radical* as the Avicennian category of blood, rather than the 'radical

moisture' that is constituent of life since Adam – perhaps the only time in his medical discussions in the *Subida* where he could confuse his reader.

133 Note that John Pecham, well known for popularizing optical theories, as we will see in chapter 5, suggested a reading of the bloody sweat that depended on the difference between blood in the veins and blood as a humor, then examined how Christ managed to sweat a combination of the two due to his anguish, strong imagination, and complexion. Cohen, *Modulated Scream*, 203–4; and Ziegler, 'Medicine and Immortality,' 237–8.

134 Mowbray, *Pain and Suffering*; see also Cohen, *Modulated Scream*, 206–7.

135 Cohen, 'Animated Pain of the Body,' 43–4.

136 Ibid., 45–7. Modern commentators' obsession with, and disgust over, the goriness of medieval Passion-centred devotions thus overlooks the fact that Christians were supposed to feel as much empathy for his sorrow as for his physical degradation. As will be discussed in chapter 5, one scholar has suggested that Dominicans focused their Passion meditations primarily on Christ's physical pain alone, while Franciscans were concerned with both types. Trembinski, '[Pro]passio Doloris,' 656.

137 Aquinas suggested that scientific evidence revealed Christ's humanity: blood and water came from the side wound, and water is one of the elements of the human body and blood the most important humor. From his commentary on John's gospel, quoted in Bildhauer, *Medieval Blood*, 30.

138 'Estando en los lastimados braços de la ... Madre el cuerpo hecho pedaços del Hijo de Dios y suyo, ¿quál dolor se esforçava a privar más su sentido: ... ver la sagrada cabeça muy penetrada de espinas ... la boca un poco abierta como quien perdió la vida ... ¿O ver los braços caydos, los huessos descoyuntadas, ver evacuadas las venas, o los nervios contraydos ... ¿Qué aflición era mirar las descoyuntadas piernas o anbos los pies de un tal clavo penetrados que entrasse en el coraçón d'esta anima?' Laredo, *Subida* II, chap. 28, p. 295.

139 Ziegler, *Medicine and Religion*, 136–7. For hylemorphism, see Oderberg, 'Hylemorphic Dualism'; for Laredo on hylemorphism, see Gracia Guillén, 'La fisiología escolástica,' 126.

140 Laredo discusses this question in *Subida* I, chap. 16, pp. 88–9. Bynum points out that despite the theory of hylemorphic dualism, neither Aquinas nor his followers referred to it in questions of the resurrection. Instead, they discussed 'the resurrected body as reassembled by God from its own tiny bits of dust scattered throughout the universe.' Bynum, 'Material Continuity,' 258.

141 '[A]lthough after Galen ... perception and cognition were known to be seated in the brain, other influential traditions identified the heart as a seat of sensation, imagination, memory, and even the soul.' Jager, 'Book of the

Heart,' 2. Such 'influential traditions' included Aristotle as he was taken up in the scholastic theological curriculum. Ibid., 2–3.

142 For a later example, see Narveson, 'Flesh, Excrement, Humors, Nothing.'

4 Mnemotechnical Mysticism

1 Carruthers, *Book of Memory*, 54.

2 Many of the excellent articles in *History in the Comic Mode*, an homage to Caroline Walker Bynum, usefully contextualize works of theology, devotion, literature, and apocalypticism in medieval cognitive and scientific knowledge, yet none provides a reading of a mystical text per se. Fulton and Holsinger, *History in the Comic Mode.*

3 Pacho's 2008 survey of Spanish mysticism (*Apogeo de la mística*) from 1450–1650 does not take any English-language scholarship or methodology into account.

4 See chapter 3.

5 Anglicus, *De proprietatibus rerum*, book 3, chap. 10. 'On the interior senses' lists three cells: imagination, logic, memory. Numerous exemplars still exist in the Biblioteca Nacional de Madrid, so it seems to have been a popular work. Also, Laredo cites the translation. García Ballester, *La búsqueda de la salud*, 619.

6 'En el delantero es la fantasía o virtud imaginativa de lo que tomamos con la vista e con los otros sentidos; y en el ventrículo de en medio se … determina quál es lo que imaginamos y vemos si es bueno o malo, y escógose quál queremos, y éste es el libre alvedrío y el que nos causa pena o merecimiento según nos determinamos. Luego está la operación de la postrer célula o ventrículo, e allí es la servativa memoria donde se conserva o guarda lo que se le pone en cargo, de manera que lo que viene al pensamiento o fantasía se imagina con la virtud de la parte delantera del celebro e se determina en la parte de en medio y se rememora dende a un día o a muchos años en la parte o célula posterior. *Item* en el celebro nacen los nervios todos … que dan el sentido a qualquier parte del cuerpo, y principalmente nacen en su sustancia misma los siete pares de nervios que fabrican los sentidos, *scilicet, viso, audito, gusto, tacto et odorato*; e juntas estas virtudes, *scilicet* imaginativa, digestiva e memorativa, y estos comunes sentidos hazen virtud animal o animada, racional y sensitiva.' Laredo, *Modus faciendi*, part 3, division 1, chap. 4, pp. 311–12 [fol. 188r].

7 Galen and Avicenna are discussed in the introduction. Joannitius is quoted in Jordan, 'Construction of a Philosophical Medicine,' 52.

8 Note that Anglicus also had three cells (see note 5, above). For discussion and medieval images of the brain with between three and five cells,

sometimes with one faculty per cell, sometimes with two, see Clarke, Dewhurst, and Aminoff, *Illustrated History of Brain Function*, 8–13. To compare Vives's discussion of the internal senses, see 'Obra psicológica,' 511–13. For Vives, see next section of this chapter.

9 Clark, 'Optics for Preachers,' 337. See chapter 5 for further discussion of Limoges.

10 Wendy Turner suggests that a physiological location for the will might be part of a general desire in the late Middle Ages to identify a fulcrum point connecting the soul and the mind. Personal communication, 3 July 2010. Laredo returns to the question of free will just two chapters before beginning his Passion meditation in part 2. Laredo, *Subida* II, chap. 10, p. 226.

11 Archimatthaeus (twelfth century, second half) compared understanding to digestion in a commentary on Joannitius. Cited in Jordan, 'Construction of a Philosophical Medicine,' 55.

12 Coleman, *Ancient and Medieval Memories*, 361.

13 In his posthumously published commentary on Aristotle's *De anima*, Suárez rejects the theory of the inner senses. Smith, 'Getting the Big Picture,' 574n23.

14 For example, Peers, Introduction, *The Ascent of Mount Zion*, 54. For alternative views valuing Laredo's writing as inherently poetic, see Cuevas García, *La prosa métrica*; and Legarda, 'Refinamiento literario.'

15 For Carruthers's argument concerning books in general as mnemonic devices and the relevance for the practice of reading in the Middle Ages, see her 'Reading with Attitude,' 1.

16 The use of the term *recogimiento* as part of mnemotechnique is from Flor, 'La literatura espiritual,' 54. I cannot prove its usage in the era, since the mnemotechnical treatises themselves and the spiritual treatises with mnemonic images available to Laredo were in Latin. It is significant that the English word 'recollection' is often used to translate *reminiscentia*, an idea that Aristotle contrasted to simple memory. Those who simply remember are dull-witted, while those who recollect (actively think and recombine memories) are much sharper. See the discussion in Bloch, *Aristotle on Memory and Recollection*, 72–4.

17 Gerli, in his brief examination of Teresa of Avila's interior castle as a mnemonic device, suggests that she grew more organized as a writer as a result of structuring her text around the mnemonic castle. Gerli, '*El castillo interior* y el *ars memorativa*,' 154. This creates an interesting contrast to those scholars who describe Laredo as a lesser writer because his treatise, replete with mnemonics, appears unstructured.

18 Carruthers, *Book of Memory*, 50. Arnau de Villanova, a Catalan, was one of the foremost proponents of the 'somatic nature' of memory.

19 Ibid.; and Coleman, *Ancient and Medieval Memories*, 355. In some terminologies, the difference between learning new information and remembering is their location in the sensible soul and the rational soul, respectively, yet another version of the continuum between body and soul that is not purely dualist and hierarchical.
20 Bolzoni, *Gallery of Memory*, 131.
21 Ibid., 136–7.
22 Enders, 'Rhetoric, Coercion, and the Memory of Violence,' 33.
23 Carruthers, *Book of Memory*, 21, 55.
24 Ibid., 24–5.
25 Bolzoni, *Gallery of Memory*, 130.
26 Laredo, *Subida* III (1535), chap. 9, pp. 632–3.
27 Laredo indicates that the idea for the image comes from the notion of riding up Mount Zion, identifying each element of the riding kit as the virtues that a rider would need to progress up the mountain of contemplation. Here it is of note that Psalm 137 begins with a verse concerning souls who weep in order to *remember* Zion. In the context of a mystical route to union with God entitled the 'ascent of Mount Zion,' it would seem that Zion as Jerusalem, or the heavenly city, (an image Laredo will reference at length in part 2) is fundamentally connected to the faculty of memory, well as with the tears of repentance that proper self-knowledge would bring. Psalm 137 reads: 'Upon the rivers of Babylon, there we sat and wept: when we remembered Sion: On the willows in the midst thereof we hung up our instruments. For there they that led us into captivity required of us the words of songs. And they that carried us away, said: Sing ye to us a hymn of the songs of Sion. How shall we sing the song of the Lord in a strange land? If I forget thee, O Jerusalem, let my right hand be forgotten.' (Douay-Rheims, following Vulgate numbering, 136). For discussion of Psalm 137, see Carruthers, *Craft of Thought*, 67.
28 My schematization, based on the paragraph overview in Laredo, *Subida* I, chap. 18, p. 103.
29 Portions of this section were presented as 'Galloping Virtue: The Mnemotechniques of Meditative Practice in Spanish Recollection Mysticism,' at the panel 'Spaces of Vice and Virtue 1,' 43rd International Medieval Congress, Kalamazoo, MI, 11 May 2008.
30 Carruthers, *Craft of Thought*, 4. Carruthers problematizes the notion of accurate reproduction as the goal of memory. Ibid., 22, and Carruthers, *Book of Memory*, 61.
31 A first-century BCE text modelled after an earlier treatise by Cicero, the *Rhetorica ad Herennium* was the most influential source for medieval rhetoric

and mnemotechnique. Yates, *Art of Memory*, chap. 1; and Carruthers, *Book of Memory*, 145–6.

32 For a careful study of memory from the Greeks through the scholastics, see Coleman, *Ancient and Medieval Memories*. The oft-repeated example from Cicero's *Rhetorica* shows how an image's potential to combine unrelated elements can allow someone to remember the major points of a law case or political speech. First suggesting 'the scene of a sick man in his bedroom, to whom a physician, carrying a ram's testicles on his fourth finger, offers a cup,' Cicero then names how each disparate element correlates to a separate section of an overview of the case. Carruthers, *Craft of Thought*, 8.

33 Ibid., 10.

34 Ibid., 13.

35 Ibid., 12.

36 Carruthers, 'Reading with Attitude,' 7.

37 Throughout the *Book of Memory*, but summarized in Carruthers, *Craft of Thought*, 7–10. '[T]he goal of rhetorical mnemotechnical craft was not to give students a prodigious memory for all the information they might be asked to repeat in an examination, but to give an orator the means and wherewithal to invent his material, both beforehand and – crucially – on the spot ... *Memoria* is most usefully thought of as a compositional art.' Ibid., 9.

38 As Carruthers indicates, the 'inventiveness' of a particular thinker depends on the 'inventory' of knowledge upon which he or she can draw. Ibid., 11–12.

39 Ibid., 78.

40 Ibid., 73.

41 Enders, *Medieval Theater of Cruelty*, 68–9, citing *Rhetorica ad Herennium*.

42 '[Pomel] does warn against a premature identification of allegory and mnemonics. Allegorical texts are, after all, the product of multifarious and varyingly dosed traditions, of which mnemonics is only one. Moreover, they demand a hermeneutic effort on the part of the reader/listener in order to discover the meaning that the author has tried to evoke, while in the case of mnemonics the maker and the user of the images and their significance are one and the same person.' Willaert, Introduction, *Medieval Memory*, xxii.

43 Parshall, 'Art of Memory and the Passion,' 460, citing Carruthers, *Book of Memory*, 145. Carruthers expands on this: 'For the process of meaning-making to begin at all, one's memory must be "hooked up" and "hooked in" to the associational play of the mind at work. That is the essential function of any ornament, and it explains why many of the basic features of the ornaments are also elementary principles of mnemonics: surprise and strangeness

(for example, *metaphora*, metonymy, *allegoria*, oxymoron, and in art, grotesquery), exaggeration (hyperbole and litotes), orderliness and pattern (chiasmus, tropes of repetition, various rhythmic and rhyming patters) … All of these characteristics are essential for making mnemonically powerful associations. And they are all also deliberately playful and surprising, for mnemonic and recollective techniques have all relied heavily on emotion as the quickest and surest way to catch the mind's attention.' Carruthers, *Craft of Thought*, 117.

44 Coleman, *Ancient and Medieval Memories*, 148, citing Leclerq. Carruthers points out that Latin was learned through syllables rather than semantic units, making it all the more natural to associate from partial words or sound-alike words. Carruthers, *Craft of Thought*, 136, and *Book of Memory*, 90–1.

45 Akbari, *Seeing through the Veil*, 6, citing Cicero in the *Rhetorica ad Herennium* III, 17. In a primarily oral culture, writing is a visual cue to bring forth memories. Carruthers, *Craft of Thought*, 29–34, 122, 136–7. Note the contrast with her point in her earlier book that the visual images related to each like words on a page unlike the spoken, unseen word. Ultimately, the images function verbally and language visually. Carruthers, *Book of Memory*, 28, 32.

46 Discussion of Quintilian is interspersed in the section on Cicero in Coleman, *Ancient and Medieval Memories*, 39–59; and Flor, 'La literatura espiritual,' 43–9.

47 Carruthers, *Craft of Thought*, 11.

48 Written in Latin. For Eiximenis's interest in the utility of mnemonics for his audience rather than than the expositor, see Rivers, 'Memory and Medieval Preaching,' 255–62. Rivers describes Eiximenis's acquaintance with a wide range of mnemotechnique treatises, indicating his approach was part of a broad European trend. Ibid., 263.

49 'In ordinandis etiam sermonis partibus hoc unum observet: ut materie subtiliores et magis difficiles tradantur circa principium sermonis: materie aut magis practice et morales ad informationem populi facientes: versus finem, nam in principio sermonis soli ingeniosi et sapientes attenti sunt; quorum capacitati subtiliora convenient: sicut vice versa rudis populus tardius habet attentionem: cui material moralis et practice est magis conveniens et necessaria.' Sánchez Ciruelo, 'Arte memorandi,' chap. 7, fol. 274v. This was not the first mnemotechnical treatise produced by a Castilian author. That honour goes to Juan Alfonso de Benavente, *Ars et doctrina studendi et docendi* (1453). Báez Rubí, *Mnemosine novohispánica*, 59n211. Published shortly after Laredo's mystical treatises, Pedro Mexia's 1540 *Silva de varia lección* mentions the mnemotechnical arts. Discussed in Gerli, '*El castillo interior* y el *ars memorativa*,' 160.

50 Parshall, 'Art of Memory and the Passion,' 460.
51 Báez Rubí, *Mnemosine novohispánica*, 61–118.
52 Flor, *Emblemas*, 149–50, 237–8. Ignatius's brief work, in theory a systematization of his own method that brought about his famous experience of illumination in Manresa, is considered a streamlined version of García de Cisneros's *Ejercitatorio de la vida espiritual* (discussed in chapter 2 as the only text pre-Laredo to propose a tripartite mystic way yet also teach Passion meditation). The other texts formative for Ignatius's change of heart, which led him to give up being a soldier in order to be a solider for Christ, were Ludolph of Saxony's *Vita Christi cartujano* and Voragine's collection of miracle tales, the *Golden Legend.* Ignatius's conversion was thus produced by the conjunction of two texts that focused on saints' bodies and Christ's body, combined with the one mystical treatise available in Castilian that taught both abstract contemplation and Passion meditation.
53 First week, fifth exercise, in Ignatius of Loyola, *Spiritual Exercises*, 25. For a discussion of the meditations as non-corporeal despite the sensory basis, based on post-Descartian assumptions about cognition, see Nicolás, *Powers of Imagining*, 31–46.
54 Valadés, *Retórica cristiana*; and Báez Rubí, *Mnemosine novohispánica*, 119–214.
55 Flor, *Emblemas*, 251; see also Gerli, '*El castillo interior* y el *ars memorativa*'; and Carrión, 'Scent of a Mystic Woman.' Teresa's book is found in many English translations, including Teresa of Avila, *The Interior Castle Study Edition.* The sketch of Monte Carmelo is reproduced and translated in John of the Cross, *Collected Works*, 109–10.
56 Kurtz mentions the impact of mnemotechnique on the elaborate allegories written during the Spanish Renaissance, particularly that of Diego de San Pedro (see chapter 1), but does not elaborate extensively on this insight; see her 'Allegory and/of Memory.'
57 Discussed in Enders, *Medieval Theater of Cruelty*, 104–5. Excerpts of Vives's *Tratado sobre el alma y la vida* can be found in a facing-page Latin–Castilian version, translated by X. Gómez. Vives, 'Obra psicológica.' The memory texts are pp. 531–7.
58 Emblem texts imported from Germany and Italy in 1499 and 1505 were followed by the widely circulated text of Andrea Alciato, *Emblematum liber* (1531). Flor, *Emblemas*, 31. The 1499 *Poliphili hipnerotomachia* may have been the source for the decoration of the cloister at the University of Salamanca in the 1520s. Ibid., 31–2.
59 Ibid., 38–9.
60 For discussion, see Muñoz Delgado, 'Juan de Aguilera.' I do not discuss the work more fully because it could not have been directly influential on

Laredo's mnemonic devices in the 1535 edition. For translation of humanist treatises post-Laredo, see Merino Jerez, *Retórica y artes de memoria*; and López Grigera, *La retórica en la España del siglo de oro.*

61 Flor, 'La literatura espiritual,' 59.

62 It is notable that Osuna's fourth book, although bearing the name of an alphabet, does not provide twenty-two couplets like the others do. For a suggestion that there is an internal structure to Osuna's *Tercer abecedario* beyond the mnemonic itself, see Andrés, Introducción, *Tercer abecedario*, 32.

63 Flor, 'La literatura espiritual,' 39. Given the connection between the *retablos* and Passion meditation treatises I describe in chapter 1, it is not surprising that Flor connects Renaissance developments in Passion spirituality with mnemonics. Ibid., 41. See chapter 5 in this book for further discussion.

64 Ibid., 48.

65 Thus Egeria's well-known fourth-century travelogue can be understood as a memory device. Carruthers, *Craft of Thought*, 42–3.

66 See Enders's description of flagellation as 'mnemonic beating.' Enders, 'Rhetoric, Coercion, and the Memory of Violence,' 34. For discussion of the cognitive effect of such rituals in the context of late medieval England, see Stevenson, *Performance, Cognitive Theory, and Devotional Culture*.

67 Carruthers analyses Hugh of Saint Victor's mnemonics at various points, for example, in *Craft of Thought*, 243–4.

68 For an analysis of the shift in Laredo's reliance on Richard of Saint Victor in 1535 to terminology drawn from Heinrich Herp and Hugh of Balma, see Boon, 'Mystical Language of Recollection,' chap. 4.

69 'Conparación ... figura o exenplo.' Laredo, *Subida* II, chap. 51, p. 381. He uses these terms during the last chapter that describes the candles in the midst of the heavenly city in part 2. See below for analysis.

70 It is unclear from the wording whether Laredo suddenly imagined this device or believed God to have given the image to him as a gift to aid his meditation. On Tuesday of the second week of meditation, he says: 'Diolo en más breve instante que abrir y cerrar el ojo e dio en el entendimiento una cruz.' (A cross was given to the understanding in an instant shorter than the [time it takes] to open and close an eye.) Laredo, *Subida* I, chap. 20, p. 108. The description of the cross and the technique continues onto p. 109. Laredo seems to have drawn it for himself on an old scrap of paper, and was never able to reproduce it accurately again. He conserved the paper itself for several years. While I cannot trace a specific precedent for this image, a possible descendent is Nadal's pictorial elaboration on the Ignatian *Spiritual Exercises*, in which he provides images marked with letters that correspond to lists of biblical quotations, descriptive passages, and imaginative meditations. Nadal, *Annotations and Meditations on the Gospels.*

71 A process of controlling the tongue, body, and soul, followed by the three steps of *recogimiento*. Tongue: (1) never speak any word that is not entirely true; (2) never say something unclean; (3) say only good things about others; (4) never speak pointlessly; (5) never speak without benefit. Body: (6) do (or work) only what is required to be obedient (i.e., contemplate in your free time); (7) stop communicating with others, without losing charity; (8) focus on your powerlessness; (9) seek solitude; (10) have only one love. Soul: (11) have a purified conscience, be without guilt; (12) be free of temporal things, as far as possible; (13) the ordered understanding should be captive in Christ; (14) the determined will should refuse to settle for anything that is not God; (15) self-knowledge; (16) Passion meditation; (17) recollection. Summarizing Laredo, *Subida* I, chap. 5, p. 52. I have found no definite precedents for a list of seventeen (or fourteen plus three), but it is intriguing that an eighteenth-century chronicle provides tables to organize the advice of the Villacrecian writer Lope de Salinas y Salazar (discussed in chapter 1, one with fourteen steps and the other with seventeen). Hernández de Torre, *Chronica de la provincia de Burgos*, p. 322; cited in Lejarza and Uribe, *Las reformas*, 653.

72 In part 1, the first week of meditation is analogous to six workers digging the foundation for an edifice (itself a typical mnemonic device, as discussed in Carruthers, *Craft of Thought*, 17). Laredo, *Subida* I, chap. 10, p. 67. In part 2, he lists the six conditions for proper prayer: to be devout, pure, humble, violent (in order to root out your own vices), attentive (to God), and continuous (in devotion). *Subida* II, chap. 13, p. 255. Likewise, there are six stages for meditation on the Resurrection (chap. 33, p. 308). Note the slight distinction between the rhetorician's preference for the number five, the typical Christian fondness for the biblical numbers three and seven, and Laredo's choice of six. For discussion of mnemonic reliance on numbers and lists, see Flor, 'La literatura espiritual,' 46.

73 Many of the artisanal metaphors describe the soul, including God as a silversmith creating the soul. For example, Laredo, *Subida* I, chap. 7, pp. 57–8; chap. 10, p. 110; *Subida* II, chap. 9, p. 218. Discussion of human souls as soldiers can be found in *Subida* II (1535), chaps. 54–5, pp. 392–3. Military metaphors in relation to a stage of self-knowledge or awareness of vice date back to Gregory the Great's *Moralia en Job*. Carruthers, *Craft of Thought*, 148. The *Moralia* was available on the peninsula from shortly after its composition, as Gregory the Great sent a partial copy to Archbishop Leandro in Seville during his lifetime. Fernández, 'Los comienzos del cristianismo,' 20.

74 Throughout, but see Laredo, *Subida* II, chap. 9, pp. 218–22 for a lengthy one.

75 Ibid., chaps. 1–11, 28, 58.

76 Ibid., chaps. 46–54, pp. 352–92.

77 Carruthers, *Craft of Thought*, 110.

78 It is possible to understand Laredo's entire text as a text meant to be remembered, not read. Laredo himself suggests this technique in reference to the Bible, which he claims is not meant to be read from the pages of a book only, but from your heart. Laredo, *Subida* I, chap. 24, p. 126.

79 See schema provided at the end of this chapter's first section.

80 For example, in the mid-thirteenth century, William Peraldus wrote a double treatise, *Summa de vitiis* and *Summa de virtutibus*. Newhauser, *Treatise on Vices and Virtues*, 127–8. Treatises on the sins of the tongue were popular later among the mendicant orders. Ibid., 196–7. For examples, see Rivers, 'Fear of Divine Vengeance,' 88–91. These works in Latin were often translated into Iberian vernaculars throughout the Middle Ages, thanks to the prevalence of the vernacular as the official language of the courts. Newhauser, *Treatise on Vices and Virtues*, 138–9. In addition, the first translation of a collection of Bonaventurian and Pseudo-Bonaventurian treatises includes a work on vices and virtues ascribed to Isaac of Syria. Although it is not organized along the rubric typical of such treatises, it was available in Castilian bound with the works recommended for a novice entering the Franciscan life, so may well have been available to Laredo. David of Augsburg, *Forma de los novicios*, fols. 127v–162v. This interest in schematas of vices can be seen in the *Subida* in Monday's meditation, which focuses on the five sins of the tongue. Laredo, *Subida* I, chap. 19, pp. 104–5; see also Laredo's description of the seventeen steps towards God that culminate in the three stages of *recogimiento*; see note 71.

81 See chapter 1 for discussion of the Villacrecian emphasis on poverty of body and spirit, obedience, chastity, humility, simplicity, and prayer. Salinas y Salazar, 'Memorial de la vida,' chapter headings found on pp. 723–8.

82 Note the parallels with Alonso de Madrid's methodic discussion of contrition, self-disgust, ways to improve the self, prayer, humility, and patience in the second part of his 1521 *Arte para servir a Dios*. Madrid, *Arte* II, chaps. 1, 2, 3, 4, 6, 8, respectively; for analysis of the disjunction between Alonso and Laredo on the question of self-knowledge, see Boon, 'Mystical Language of Recollection,' 170–4.

83 '[L]as acciones en ella nos significan ... que siempre están en acción o en acto.' (The stirrup straps in and of themselves signify ... that they are always in action or in the act.) Laredo, *Subida* I, chap. 23, p. 121.

84 'Y aqueste querer que Dios vivo quiere amarse, porque es causa su bondad, siente el anima en quieta contemplación, que es la caridad de Dios en Dios; y el efeto del querer Dios amar siente que es amor de Dios en Dios; e, assí, dize la tal ánima que el amado y el amor y el amador en Dios que se es una cosa

misma puríssima, y no son más … Y la caridad que se conoce y se requiere en los hombres no es suya … Dios inmenso la infunde en los coraçones por su gran benignidad, que los enciende con ella, porque es encendido fuego vivo, e que d'este encendimiento – o dígase inflamación – saltan tan vivas centellas, que se encienden donde dan, y si dan en el desnudo, siéntense en el coraçón del fuego que d'él destilla, e assí lo dessea vestir como si a sí mismo fuesse, porque lo añuda en sí mismo el ñudo de las dos riendas, que el que possee el amor ya tiene la caridad, ni la caridad terná sino con el mismo amor, pues que una cosa son, añudada en solo un ñudo, y juntas en una rienda que guía sin poder falter.' Ibid., chap. 20, pp. 106–7.

85 Ibid., chap. 23, p. 122.

86 Ibid., chap. 21, p. 114.

87 Ibid.

88 'La oración segunda es incitada del demonio … saltando como urraca que no sabe pararse con la memoria, mandar con el entendimiento, ni quietar la voluntad; mas salta, e no tiene passo, y está assentado, e no tiene assiento, o posado, e sin reposo.' (The second type of prayer is incited by the devil … jumping like a magpie that does not know how to stop its memory, nor order its understanding, nor quiet the will. It jumps but has no step, is seated without a seat, and set down without repose.) Ibid., chap. 21, p. 116.

89 See chapter 1.

90 *Subida* I, chap. 22, p. 118.

91 Ibid.

92 '[L]uego se torne a la silla y le lleve su coraça levadiza … se halle en lo que primero estava, sin yrlo, a buscan de nuevo.' Ibid., chap. 22, p. 120.

93 Ibid., chap. 8, p. 60.

94 Whitehead traces two major shifts. After the Victorines, authors began to use real buildings, not biblical architectural images. Initially the buildings were churches and cloisters and then, in vernacular treatises of the thirteenth century, castles. Whitehead, *Castles of the Mind*, 51, 61, 88.

95 This extended device is foreshadowed in a brief parable about a king in a walled city, in the last day of the first stage's meditation on the riding equipment. Laredo, *Subida* I, chap. 15, p. 130.

96 See note 101 below, and conclusion.

97 Laredo, *Modus faciendi*, 36 [3v]. In addition, by continually noting that the walled city as an armed fortress would consequently need knights (mounted on horses, with riding equipment) to guard it, Laredo implicitly argues for the unity of stages one and two of the tripartite mystical technique.

98 For an interdisciplinary approach to the spatiality of mysticism based on analysis of contemporary and metaphorical architecture, see Carrión, 'Home, Sweet Home.'

99 See her discussion of the Beatus Apocalypse images. Carruthers, *Craft of Thought*, 151.

100 Starting in Laredo, *Subida* II, chap. 46, p. 352.

101 Laredo does not explicitly cite the *Homiliae*, although it was available in Latin on the peninsula by at least the fifteenth century. Álvarez Márquez, 'Las lecturas de Fray Gonzalo de Illescas,' 306. I refer to the work as an example in which the colours and materials of the city walls and towers, for instance, are set out in great detail. The English translation is found in Gregory the Great, *Homilies of Saint Gregory the Great on the Book of the Prophet Ezekiel*, book 2. Biblical commentaries on Revelation 21 would also have provided similar images. For discussion of the ubiquity of castles to describe the soul in medieval mystical treatises, see Kurtz, 'Small Castle of the Soul.'

102 '[T]ome el entendimiento un campo de ygual llaneza y de toda graciosura y tal que, puesta el ánima en medio d'él, pueda verle del todo en todas sus partes en muy quadrada ygualdad; e procure de cercarle todo de un fino cristal, que es piedra clara y preciosa. Y en cada uno de los paños o pieças de aquel quadrado se han de levantar tres torres labradas en preciosa pedrería, digo de gemmas preciosas ... De lo alto de aquestas torres, digo de cada una de ellas, han de pender quatro escudos de fino oro ...

En el medio d'este ya cercado campo ... se considere estar encendido un rico cirio pascual, cuya cera es limpidíssima, cuyo pavilo es puríssimo, obrado en tal perfeción, hecho de maestro tan sabio, que assí está el cirio encendido que en algún espacio o tiempo es impossible acabarse o diminuirse, ni faltar su claridad.'

(Let the understanding take a field equally long [on each side] and very lovely and put the soul in the middle of it, so that the soul can see it fully in all its very rectilinear parts. Try to encircle it entirely with a fine crystal made of clear and precious stone. And in each of the panels or pieces of this square must be raised three towers worked out of precious stones, I mean precious gems ... From the top of these towers, I mean from each one of them, four shields of fine gold must be hung ...

In the middle of this surrounded field ... a rich Paschal candle must be considered to be lit, whose wax is most pure, whose wick is pure, worked in such perfection, made by a master so wise, that in the way the candle is lit, at all points in time it is impossible [for it] to die out or diminish or lose clarity.) Laredo, *Subida* II, chap. 46, pp. 352–3.

103 '[L]a cera es el sacratíssimo cuerpo de Christo; el pavilo, su ánima felicíssima y de su lumbre perfectamente encendida podéys ... alçar el entendimiento a la sancta Trinidad en una sola e puríssima substancia. De manera que en la essencia de la lumbre se contemple la persona paternal, por el resplandor

levantad la ánima al Hijo, e por la luz, que es claridad, podéys llevar el espíritu al Espíritu Paráclito.' Ibid., chap. 46, p. 353.

104 Davlin, *Place of God*, 99.

105 Jordan, 'Construction of a Philosophical Medicine,' 59. Citing Bartholomaeus (fl. 1150–80).

106 'De la claridad del cirio tienen tanta claridad el oro, cristal y gemmas, e los muros e las torres; y el cirio tan lleno está como antes que oviesse cristal, ni oviesse torres, ni cerca a quien se comunicar, que es el tesoro de Dios el fuego de aqueste cirio.' (From the clarity of the candle, the gold, crystal, and gems receive great clarity, and [so do] the walls and towers. And the candle is so full that it is [the same] as it was before there was crystal or towers or someone near to communicate [its light] to, because the flame of this candle is the treasure of God.) Laredo, *Subida* II, chap. 46, p. 354.

107 'Encendido consideramos el cirio, cuya pureza, cuya perfeción y grandeza da de sí tan grande lumbre y de tanta claridad, que quiere passar el muro y se lança en el cristal ... [E]l muy bivo resplandor, que ya está dentro y fuera de cada una de las piedras, reciproca y pássase en el jocundo cristal, y rebervera la claridad del cristal en cada una de las piedras; y las piedras y el cristal en los escudos o clípeos lançan su reberverança ... y el oro de las piedras e cristal recibe refulgente resplandor e ni por sólo un momento cessan de reciprocar, que es passar de unas en otras e tornar a repassar esse mismo resplandor.' Ibid., chap. 46, p. 353.

108 'Repassa la claridad y resplandor reberverante en las gemmas y en el oro y lo demás, porque assí se comunican los bienes de nuestro Dios en los bienaventurados.' (Review the clarity and reverberating resplendance in the gems and the gold and all the rest, because it is in this way that the good things of our God are communicated to the blessed.) Ibid., chap. 46, pp. 354–5.

109 Carruthers makes her point in reference to Hugh of Saint Victor's mystical ark. '[T]he details of the model are after all incoherent, impossible to graph completely ... because they shift and change – indeed, this "picture" only works as a mental encyclopedia whose lineaments can merge and separate and shuffle about in the way that mental images do, but two-dimensional ones fixed on a page cannot.' Carruthers, *Book of Memory*, 232.

110 Laredo, *Subida* II, chap. 46, p. 355.

111 Mary is the opening by which Christ came into the world, and in reverse, Mary as mediator is the means by which to attract God's attention. Saint Ildefonsus (d. 667), a Spanish author and early defender of Mary's immaculacy, describes her virginity as closing the gates to God. Discussed in Roth, *Jews, Visigoths, and Muslims*, 20.

112 Whitehead, *Castles of the Mind*, 92. The scholastic theologian and scientist Robert Grosseteste (ca 1170–1253) had even written an entire treatise on Mary as a fortified castle. Ibid., 93–4.

113 'Esposa de Dios Hijo.' Laredo, *Subida* II, chap. 46, p. 355.

114 '[E]sta torre de Sión, este omenaje de Dios, esta nuestra fortaleza, esta mi muy gran Señora, nuestra reyna universal de todo quanto no es Dios, es la torre principal de la cibdad soberana.' Ibid., chap. 46, pp. 355–6. It is of note that Grosseteste (see n112) provides an example of a rainbow in the midst of a discussion of refraction in his treatise *De luce* (Of Light), in which the rainbow is described as arching over a castle that is identified as the Virgin Mary. Described in Akbari, *Seeing through the Veil*, 43.

115 Laredo claims that this city was constructed before all time, thus affirming Mary's role in salvation history as preceding the world's creation, not to mention preceding the Nativity itself. *Subida* II, chap. 46, p. 356. This is a gesture of support for the immaculist position common to Franciscans, a stance he advocates more clearly elsewhere. *Subida* I, chap. 28, p. 138.

116 '[Q]uanto es piedra más preciosa y de mayor claridad y está al cirio más cercana, tanto resplandesce más y tanto más rebervera con muy mayor claridad que todos … E la gloria que ella tiene e toda su claridad, toda su reberverancia e todo su resplandor, todo lo toma del cirio de donde lo toman todos.' Laredo, *Subida* II, chap. 46, p. 356.

117 Ibid., chap. 49, p. 367.

118 Ibid., chap. 51, p. 376.

119 Ibid., chap. 52, p. 379.

120 The burning of a candle accompanied by odours of vinegar and salt might have appealed to the olfactory sense in addition to the visual sense, à la the Ignatian composition of place mentioned earlier this chapter. My thanks to Quincy Newell for raising this point.

121 See González Novalín, 'Las misas "artificiosamente ordenadas."'

122 Sánchez Herrero, 'La iglesia de Sevilla,' 115.

123 Laredo, *Subida* II, chap. 50, pp. 371–5.

124 '[E]stas candelas tienen ya muy buen pavilo … se levantarán de tierra y entrarán en la cibdad.' Ibid., chap. 52, p. 381.

125 For analysis of Laredo's Nativity sermon, see Boon, 'Glory of the Virgin.'

126 Ros refers to the beginning of part 2 as 'alambiqué' (convoluted). Ros, *Inspirateur de Sainte Thérèse*, 114.

127 For examples, see the various Trinitarian similes in the 'Vision of the Trinity' described by the twelfth-century Benedictine Hildegard of Bingen, including the human body, breath, and eyesight. Hildegard of Bingen, *Scivias*, 416–19. Given that Hildegard's visions include an extensive set of

architectural images and that her Trinitarian examples are all drawn from the physiology of the body, it would be interesting to compare her with Laredo, despite their separation by century, language, and mystical genre.

128 Although Gregory of Nazianzus mentions a version of the Trinity in which the Father is the centre of a spring, the Son is a fountain, and the Holy Spirit is a river, he does not expand on it, nor does his version emphasize the three-in-one in the way that Laredo's fountain becoming three rivers ending in an ocean does. Gregory of Nazianzus, *On God and Christ*, Oration 31, chap. 31, p. 141. My thanks to Meredith Minister for bringing this to my attention.

129 'Del escondimiento oculto, del secreto inacessible d'esta inmensa y coeterna magestad nace *ab eterno* una fuente de agua biva, la qual sale del parayso e siempre está dentro en él ... Establécese en tres ríos de eterna divinidad: el primero es de infinita potencia, el segundo de sabiduría infinita, el tercero es un todo en bondad imensa ...

Estos tres divinos ríos se establecen en un piélago; notando que yo no he dicho que la fuente establece de sí tres ríos, sino que ella se establece en tres ríos; porque no es una cosa la fuente y otra los ríos, antes los ríos e la fuente son una sustancia misma. E, assí, ni tampoco digo que los ríos establescen de sí el piélago, mas que se establecen en él; porque los tres ríos y el piélago se son una essencia misma; ni la fuente tiene principio, ni tienen medio sus ríos, ni el piélago tiene fin. Ni la fuente mana más de lo que caben los ríos, ni los ríos tienen menos de lo que mana la fuente; y el piélago aquesso tiene que los tres ríos o la fuente.

De manera que una es la fuente potentíssima en manar, e no otra cosa el río fecundíssimo en correr con quietíssima ygualdad, ni otra el piélago profundíssimo de infinita immensidad ... Ni los ríos tienen ribera, ni se pueden vadear, porque levantan sus ondas más altas que al alto cielo.' Laredo, *Subida* II, chap. 1, pp. 189–91.

130 Carruthers, *Craft of Thought*, 80.

131 'Y el río quando passa sobre barrancos o piedras parece que el agua se ríe, casi como haziendo burla de quien la quiso estorvar.' (And when the river passes over gullies or rocks, it appears to laugh, almost as though it were making a mockery of anything in its way.) Laredo, *Subida* II, chap. 10, p. 225.

132 Ibid.

133 Francisco de Osuna is the only contemporary author we know Laredo to have read. Ros, *Inspirateur de Sainte Thérèse*, 137. Osuna does use both oceans and rivers as metaphors for God and for Christ in his *Tercer abecedario* but does not describe a series of linked bodies of water. Osuna, *Tercer*

abecedario, B, chap. 1, p. 115, and chap. 5, p. 126; translated in Osuna, *Third Spiritual Alphabet*, 69, 81.

134 'El río se dize yr en madre quando va por la canal que suele yr, e quando por su gran llenedubre toma más de lo que antes ocupava, quedando llena la madre, se dize salir de madre.' Laredo, *Subida* II, chap. 1, p. 191.

135 'Mas si queremos pensar que sea el piélago infinito la immensidad de mi Dios, el río sentiremos que sea su sagrada humanidad, e la fuente de la gracia, las entrañas puríssimas de la Madre virginal.' (In addition, if we want to think of the infinite ocean as the immensity of God, we will feel that the river should be his sacred humanity, and the foundation [will be] grace [and] the most pure entrails of his virginal mother.) Ibid., chap. 2, p. 194. This phrase indicates that his plan to discuss the Incarnation presupposed a definition of the Trinity.

136 E.g., Trinity Sunday versus Christmas.

137 *Engolfar* can also mean 'entering a gulf or bay,' which indicates that God is a metaphorical safe harbour.

138 He also applies the metaphor to the Holy Spirit (chapter 4) and the twofold nature of Christ (chapters 5 and 6) in part 2 of the *Subida*.

139 'Y qué ha de hazer el ánima muy dichosa que assí llegare a la mar; sino entrarse en la nave o navío de firme esperança, sin parar hasta la proa de la fe, y encastillarse en la gavia de la caridad, e cortar la xarcia de los corporales sentidos, tendiendo las velas de la afeción y despertando los vientos bivos de los muy suaves desseos, e mandar quebrar los remos del seso y entendimiento, e cortar las áncoras de la fuerça natural, y recebir navegantes de sanctas inclinaciones e mandarles que estorven el tropel de los gatos e ratones de diversos vacilables pensamientos, y despedir el contramaestre que no quepa en esta nave? Y el maestre será nuestro maestro, Christo; y el piloto que nos guíe, sus pisadas lo serán; e assí navegue con seguridad hasta el puerto del amor, e allí se puede quedar sin temer necessidad.' Laredo, *Subida* II, chap. 10, p. 227.

140 Laredo may very well have drawn on this metaphor as it is found in Ludolph of Saxony's *Vita Christi cartujano*, though given the parallels between the Spanish Franciscan author Francisco de Osuna's use of the ship to describe the soul in his *Tercer abecedario*, it seems most likely that Laredo is revising his contemporary's image of the soul to address the intersection of the soul and God. Although the idea of a ship as metaphor for the soul is a common medieval trope (Whinnom, 'El origen de las comparaciones religiosas,' 267), both Ludolph and Osuna present it in a version similar to Laredo's. For example, Bodenstadt's description reads as follows: 'Ludolphus gives a detailed explanation as to who is the pilot of the ship,

how the ship is entered, the signification of the winds and billows, of the lee of Christ, and the calming of the sea … another tropological or moral explanation sees in the ship the faithful soul, in the sea, the body.' Bodenstedt, *The Vita Christi of Ludolphus*, 99; referencing Ludolph's *Vita Christi cartujano*, part 1, chap. 46. Osuna's version is found in Osuna, *Tercer abecedario*, E, chap. 2, p. 182; translated in Osuna, *Third Spiritual Alphabet*, 140–1.

141 It is also reminiscent of the *Narrenschiff* tradition of Sebastian Brant, in print in a Latin edition translated by Jacobo Locher Philomuso since 1497 (Basil: Johannes Bergmann). Although this incunable now exists in the Colombina library in Seville, there is no record of when it was acquired. Castro, *Catálogo general de incunables en bibliotecas españolas*, no. 1168.

142 See the description of Seville's physical and agricultural features in Chaunu, *Seville et l'Amérique*, 19–50. Or, for a multi-volume economic study, see Chaunu and Chaunu, *Seville et l'Atlantique*.

143 Gerson (French theologian and ecclesiastic, 1363–1429), one of Laredo's sources, presents a version of this metaphor as applied to all three stages in the ascent to God. In his case, the image is of a dangerous ocean full of ships, with one tall rock in a harbour whose top provides safety. The rock has three levels, which Gerson describes as the three stages. Gerson, 'The Mountain of Contemplation,' paragraph 44, p. 122.

144 Carruthers, *Craft of Thought*, 73.

5 Optics, Pain, and Transformation into God

1 My thanks to the excellent session 'Cognitive Theory and Medieval Performance' at the 44th International Medieval Congress, Kalamazoo, MI, 8 May 2009, for bringing optics in particular and cognitive theory as a general field to my attention, thus entirely changing the argument of this chapter.

2 Biernoff, *Sight and Embodiment*, 102.

3 This is the argument of Enders's entire book; see her *Medieval Theater of Cruelty*, 16. See also Carruthers, *Craft of Thought*, 146–8.

4 Enders, *Medieval Theater of Cruelty*, 19, 77. For the application of Carruthers's work to medieval Passion treatises, see Parshall, 'Art of Memory and the Passion.'

5 Carruthers, *Craft of Thought*, 100. This point was made by some of the monastic authors Carruthers analyses, as Cohen points out: 'Memory, for Hugh [of Saint Victor], was the recollection of pain and fear of pain.' Cohen, *Modulated Scream*, 38. She then analyses a similar connection between pain and memory in Richard of Saint Victor's *Benjamin minor*, highly influential

on Laredo. Ibid. For discussion of Richard's influence on Laredo, see Boon, 'Mystical Language of Recollection,' 324–40.

6 Bradwardine, 'On Acquiring a Trained Memory,' 209–10. For discussions of Bradwardine, see Enders, 'Rhetoric, Coercion, and the Memory of Violence,' 34–6; and Enders, *Medieval Theater of Cruelty*, 82–91. I use this quotation as an example of a late medieval memory text. While only three versions of this short text exist in manuscript, none from Spain, Bradwardine's astronomical and geometrical treatises were known on the peninsula, as evidenced by Pedro Ciruelo's editing of Bradwardine's Latin texts for a French press; see Bradwardine, *Geometria speculatiua*.

7 Other scholars have focused on the sexuality inherent to violent images in the Middle Ages. Hollywood, 'That Glorious Slit'; Mills, *Suspended Animation*. The scholarly 'fun' of analysing sex and violence frequently reduces analysis of the 'body' in pain to its sexuality or its gender; in the interests of focusing on the medical body, I do not explore sexuality per se in this chapter. For that matter, Laredo's interest in location, also promoted by Bradwardine, far outstrips any potential sexualized reading of his Passion meditation.

8 Mills, *Suspended Animation*, 14–15. Mills's assertion is intended to contradict the presumption that scenes of Calvary were modelled on modes of punishing criminals and therefore would have been highly familiar to the artists' audience. See Merback, *The Thief, the Cross, and the Wheel*, 69–125.

9 Mills, *Suspended Animation*, 15–17.

10 Flynn, 'Mimesis of the Last Judgment.'

11 Enders, *Medieval Theater of Cruelty*, 61.

12 Ibid., 66.

13 For overviews of Passion meditation as mnemotechnique, see Parshall, 'Art of Memory and the Passion'; Villalobos Hennessy, 'Passion Devotion, Penitential Reading, and the Manuscript Page'; and Arvay, 'Private Passions,' 28–82.

14 Sensory information imprinted on the optic nerve was transferred to and collated in the common sense of the front ventricle, recombined and re-imagined in the estimative and imaginative faculties in the middle ventricle of the brain, and stored as images in the memory in the rear ventricle of the brain. See introduction and chapter 4.

15 Biernoff, *Sight and Embodiment*, 81.

16 For the continuing presumption that imagination and internal pictures are 'ineffable,' see Krüger, 'Authenticity and Fiction,' 37–69.

17 For a cogent discussion of the medievalist turn to 'visual studies' in relation to questions of gender, see Watson, 'Methods and Objectives.'

18 A point Laredo himself makes when using the term 'multiplication of *species*' in the 1535 version of the *Subida*. See note 101, below.

19 Carruthers, *Book of Memory*, 169; Carruthers, *Craft of Thought*, 43.
20 'Cinco mil y tantos golpes de açotes' (Five thousand and then some blows of the whip). Laredo, *Subida* II, chap. 19, p. 268.
21 Laredo, *Subida* I, chap. 26, p. 132.
22 Mowbray, *Pain and Suffering*. The new scholastic theories replaced Augustine's theory of pain, which had been dominant until then. Cohen, *Modulated Scream*, 183.
23 See Mowbray, *Pain and Suffering*; see also Cohen, 'Animated Pain of the Body.' Note Cohen's recent argument that pain was considered an interior sensation, and indeed, was 'the central factor in sensation.' Cohen, *Modulated Scream*, 258. For that matter, twentieth-century developments in pain management have criticized the medical assumption that pain is only of the body. See Morris, *Culture of Pain*, 1–8.
24 Mowbray, *Pain and Suffering*, 22.
25 For a careful review of texts concerning Christ's pain from the Gospels through the scholastics, see Trembinski, '[Pro]passio Doloris.' Eventually, theologians divorced pain entirely from the body: 'By the mid-fourteenth century, pain was credited with a purely metaphysical ancestry. It was born of cognition, memory, imagination – anything but stones and blows.' Cohen, *Modulated Scream*, 174. Laredo's medical training would have made such an approach impossible.
26 Thus leading, in some medieval texts, to more concern for Mary's grief than for Christ's physical suffering. Bestul, *Texts of the Passion*, 124.
27 Mowbray, *Pain and Suffering*, 37–8.
28 Ibid., 21.
29 See Karnes's critique of this proposal by Ewert Cousins and Emile Mâle. Karnes, *Imagination, Meditation, and Cognition*, chap. 5.
30 Bennett is describing both Francis's reception of stigmata and his way of memorizing texts. Bennett, 'Stigmata and Sense Memory,' 7.
31 Trembinski, '[Pro]passio Doloris,' 649–56.
32 Cohen, *Modulated Scream*, 175. She returns to the topic in her conclusion. Ibid., 258.
33 Flynn's article on the role of pain in Golden Age mysticism endorses the opposite view: '[M]ost Spanish mystics ... came to view the entire created world, including their bodies and minds, as barriers to God's disembodied, eternal form.' Flynn, 'Spiritual Use of Pain,' 267. Her analysis centres on the later Golden Age authors, Juan de los Angeles and John of the Cross. By skipping the recollection mystics, she loses the body's value as articulated by Laredo.
34 For a critique of Scarry's conclusions, see Glucklich, 'Sacred Pain.'

35 Scarry, *Body in Pain*, 3–4.
36 Ibid., 4–5, 49.
37 Ibid., 12.
38 Ibid., 7–8.
39 Ibid., 13–17.
40 In the 1980s and 1990s, the historian of science David Lindberg focused scholarly attention on the primacy of optics in medieval epistemological systems with his translations and analyses of medieval optical treatises; soon thereafter Tachau and Pasnau traced the medieval scholastic discourse that resulted from the use of optics in theological discussions of cognition. Lindberg, *Theories of Vision*; Lindberg, Introduction, *Roger Bacon and the Origins of 'Perspectiva'*; Tachau, *Vision and Certitude*; and Pasnau, *Theories of Cognition*. For alternative views on medieval epistemology that forefront the senses of taste or touch over vision, see Rudy, *Mystical Language of Sensation*; and Coolman, *Knowing God by Experience*. Since the turn of the millennium, this interdisciplinary work, the relationship of natural theology (modern 'science') with what has come to be taken as traditional topics in theology and faith, has been taken further as Denery explores the application of optical theory in mendicant training and preaching, Akbari examines its relevance to medieval allegoresis in the *Roman de la rose* and the *Divine Comedy*, and Biernoff traces the influence of optic's relationship to knowledge in a variety of forms of medieval religious practice, including texts of Passion devotion. Denery, *Seeing and Being Seen*; Akbari, *Seeing through the Veil*; and Biernoff, *Sight and Embodiment*.
41 The direct connection of the eye to the brain was affirmed in influential medical works by Constantinus the African, Alhazen, and Avicenna. Lindberg, Introduction, *Roger Bacon and the Origins of 'Perspectiva,'* lxxi. Augustine privileges sight, as did all those who read him. Biernoff, *Sight and Embodiment*, 74.
42 My thanks to Pamela Patton and Eric White for aid in locating the earliest images of this vision. See Cook, 'Giotto and the Figure of Saint Francis.' Early hagiographers of Francis, including Thomas of Celano and Bonaventure, pointed to the physical and emotional impact of the experiences as their primary point of interest, rather than providing extended consideration of the objective visual content of the experiences. Bennett, 'Stigmata and Sense Memory,' 6–7.
43 Citing the miracle at Saint Damian; see Laredo, *Subida* II, chap. 13, p. 254.
44 According to Aquinas. Bennett, 'Stigmata and Sense Memory,' 6, citing Carruthers's discussion in *Book of Memory*, 54.
45 As his compatriot Juan Luis Vives had said; see introduction, note 110.

46 Cohen, *Modulated Scream*, 95–101.

47 A concise history of the development of both theories is found in Akbari, *Seeing through the Veil*, 21–44. A third theory was much less common, in which the vital spirit beams out of the eye into the air, which has been impressed by the form of the seen object. The air then changes the spirit, which returns into the optic nerve. This theory is found in the Digby commentary on Joannitius; later discussions by Bartholomaeus use candles as an analogy. Jordan, 'Construction of a Philosophical Medicine,' 51, 59. For discussion of these theories in the Renaissance, see Spruit, 'Renaissance Views of Active Perception.'

48 Biernoff, *Sight and Embodiment*, 64.

49 Also described as a kind of motion that communicated information back to the eye. Lindberg, *Theories of Vision*, 5–6; and Lindberg, Introduction, *Roger Bacon and the Origins of 'Perspectiva,'* xxx. See also Miles, 'Vision.'

50 And therefore part of the discipline of the history of science, not medicine, in modern scholarship. As a result, scholars who note the optical basis of medieval epistemology continue to ignore the medical body, while those who address body directly rarely connect it to epistemological concerns. Recent excellent work on vision and embodiment, while wide-ranging and highly perceptive, nevertheless frequently treats body in terms of gender rather than physiology – for example, the focus on optical desire throughout Biernoff, *Sight and Embodiment*.

51 In Augustine, *De Genesi* 7.13.20; cited in Lindberg, Introduction, *Roger Bacon and the Origins of 'Perspectiva,'* xxix.

52 Siraisi, *Medieval and Early Renaissance Medicine*, 108.

53 Various theories were proposed but none became primary. For example, Adelard of Bath (fl. ca 1110–50) updated Plato's idea by positing that a 'fiery virtue' comes from the brain through the eye to pass out to objects in the world, where the object's form is impressed on it so that the fiery virtue returns to the brain and introduces the form into the eye. Lindberg, Introduction, *Roger Bacon and the Origins of 'Perspectiva,'* xxx; and Lindberg, *Theories of Vision*, 90–4.

54 For the tactile results, see Rubin, *Corpus Christi*, 63; Miles, *Image as Insight*, 96–7; and Biernoff, *Sight and Embodiment*, 141–4. Camille describes it as distancing. Camille, *Gothic Idol*, 217. Biernoff provides a reading to show how intromission, as opposed to extramission, *could* be interpreted as distancing, but outlines the possibility only in order to counteract it. Biernoff, *Sight and Embodiment*, 85–103.

55 An overview can be found in Smith, 'Getting the Big Picture.'

56 Lindberg, *Theories of Vision*, 6–9, 58–86. Note that Lindberg problematizes an easy distinction between Platonic extramission and Aristotelian intromission on pp. 4–9. For Alhazen's influence on Bacon, see the discussion in Tachau, *Vision and Certitude*, 4–26.

57 Bacon's works such as *De multiplicatione specierum* and *De perspectiva* were commissioned by Pope Clement IV. Bacon's theory (especially its roots in Alhazen) was supported and popularized by scientists such as John Pecham (ca 1235–92) and Witelo (d. after 1281), incorporated by scholastics such as John Duns Scotus (ca 1266–1308) and Petrus Olivi (1248–98), critiqued by Ockham (1288–1348), yet not surpassed until Kepler (1571–1630). Tachau's work in *Vision and Certitude* is critical in tracing the interpretative changes proposed to Bacon's optics by major voices among the scholastic theologans.

58 '[A] visible object generates, or "multiplies" species of light and color in the adjacent, transparent medium. These species ... generate further species in the medium contiguous to them, which results in a continuous multiplication of species along rays ... These visible species convey the object's accidents through the intervening medium ... to the eye of the viewer, upon which they are, loosely speaking, "impressed" ... Once received in the sense organ, each species continues to be multiplied along the optic nerves into the cavities of the brain housing the internal senses.' Tachau, *Vision and Certitude*, 8. For other renditions, see Biernoff, *Sight and Embodiment*, 74–5; and Lindberg, Introduction, *Roger Bacon and the Origins of 'Perspectiva,'* lxix. Bacon borrows the term *species* from Grosseteste, who believed that all objects release emanations of themselves. Lindberg, Introduction, *John Pecham and the Science of Optics*, 35–6.

59 Lindberg, *Theories of Vision*, 54–6.

60 Biernoff, *Sight and Embodiment*, 75; and Carruthers, *Craft of Thought*, 27.

61 Denery, *Seeing and Being Seen*, 106–7. Some scientists posited a special visual sense that led into the common sense. Smith, 'Getting the Big Picture,' 584n51.

62 The notion of stamping an image on the eye obviously brings with it complications when more than one object is in view. The perspectivists offered theories as to how the *species* in the eye could be overlapping or partial. The *species* was believed to consist of multiple rays that came out of every iota of the object, emanating in all directions; if the eye processed some of the rays, not all, it would see part of the object at a time. Authors such as Pecham, following Alhazen, relied on the notion that any given ray can only intersect with the eye at one given point on the spherical surface without ending up refracted (the ray was received by the glacial humor on the tunic of the eye, and in turn passed through to other humors and then to the optic nerve).

Other rays hitting the same point would end up slightly or greatly refracted, therefore weakened. The strongest ray leaves the strongest impression, so that which is directly in front of the eye is seen with greatest clarity. Lindberg, Introduction, *John Pecham and the Science of Optics*, 37–8.

63 Thus the fact that Laredo cites both theories is not a scientific error but a theological commonplace. For example, a menstruating woman can turn a mirror red by the force of her gaze. See note 95, and Lindberg, *Theories of Vision*, 138.

64 Biernoff, *Sight and Embodiment*, 86. Original emphasis retained.

65 Ibid., 3.

66 For example, Jan van Ruusbroec, one of the medieval Flemish mystics most influential on sixteenth-century Spanish mysticism, proposed a constant cycle between rest and activity during mystical union; he also made direct reference to optical theories. Rather than treating Ruusbroec in the history of speculative mysticism or Trinitarian theology, scholars might equally fruitfully consider the optical epistemological basis for his method. Rothstein, 'Vision, Cognition, and Self-Reflection,' 45; Boon, 'Trinitarian Love Mysticism,' 496–8, Hatzfeld, 'Influencia de Raimundo Lulio y Jan van Rusybroeck,' 103–14; and Martín, 'Los místicos alemanes,' 118–22.

67 Pasnau, *Theories of Cognition*, 95–6. For her presentation at the session mentioned in note 1, above, Marla Carlson created a composite image of a standard crucifix *inside* each brain ventricle of the diagram provided in this book's introduction; this image and her proposals concerning its relevance to assessment of Passion spirituality provided the inspiration for this chapter. Carlson, 'Pain and the Brain'; see also her *Performing Bodies in Pain*.

68 Biernoff, *Sight and Embodiment*, 100. A new study that appeared in print too late to be fully integrated into my argument examines the frequent medieval combination of optics and poetry into a love trope about the lovesickness that can result from the lover gazing at the beloved. The trope is dependent on the intromission theory and details the physiological transformation of the optic nerve into the beloved. See Singer, *Blindness and Therapy*, esp. chap. 1.

69 For more information on the Sacro Monte, see Hood, 'Sacro Monte of Varallo'; Freedberg, *Power of Images*, 192–201; and Merback, *The Thief, the Cross, and the Wheel*, 41–8. For the late sixteenth-century adaptation in Granada, see Harris, *From Muslim to Christian Granada*.

70 'The hypersensitivity of the perceiving subject to every bleeding gash and open orifice in God's broken body was built on a radical openness to exterior sensations and became crucial to forms of mystical devotion. In earlier medieval image making and in the extramission theory of their apperception, the notion of likeness (similitude) was not strong because the object was always to some extent produced by the gaze. But the intromission model took

the emphasis away from vision and onto the power of images themselves, whose eyes, as in cult statues and devotional images, could stare back.' Camille, 'Before the Gaze,' 207.

71 Late medieval theologians critiqued the most literal version of identity in epistemological intromission: if I see a stone, a stone does not pass through the ventricles of my brain. Pasnau, *Theories of Cognition*, 67. It is the idea of 'transformation into' rather than 'continued existence as' that will prove key to understanding this epistemology.

72 Bennett, 'Stigmata and Sense Memory,' 6.

73 As mentioned in his *Audi, filia* (written 1533, first published 1554). Juan would have seen some of the early processions during his stay in Seville from 1526–34. Webster, *Art and Ritual*, 27, 173. The majority of Webster's book is devoted to analysing the role of these sculptures in Golden Age lay piety.

74 Mowbray, *Pain and Suffering*, 22.

75 Biernoff, *Sight and Embodiment*, 96; quoting Bacon, *De multiplicatione specierum*, chap. 7 (1.1).

76 Biernoff, *Sight and Embodiment*, 123–4. She cites Limoges: 'Anyone can enter into the interior of his conscience and meditate in his mind's eye on Christ's wound, so that he conforms to Christ's sufferings through his model,' drawing the citation from Clark, 'Optics for Preachers,' 338.

77 Parshall, 'Art of Memory and the Passion,' 457–9.

78 Bradwardine, 'On Acquiring a Trained Memory,' 207.

79 Cohen, *Modulated Scream*, 214–15.

80 Bennett, 'Stigmata and Sense Memory,' 4.

81 Ibid., 3–6.

82 Note Cohen's remark: 'For the visionaries, seeing pain was akin to sensing it.' Cohen, *Modulated Scream*, 220.

83 Biernoff, *Sight and Embodiment*, 137–40.

84 Smith, 'Getting the Big Picture,' 572; Carruthers, *Craft of Thought*, 58, 159.

85 Bradwardine, 'On Acquiring a Trained Memory,' 207.

86 Parshall, 'Art of Memory and the Passion,' 466.

87 Akbari, *Seeing through the Veil*, 4. For that matter, Vincent of Beauvais, an encyclopedist, renamed 'reason' with the term 'internal vision.' Ibid., 41.

88 The transmission of the *Stimulus Amoris* is discussed in Robinson, *Imag(in)-ing Passions*, chap. 2.

89 Karnes, *Imagination, Meditation, and Cognition*, chap. 6.

90 Bennett does provide an extensive discussion of Pseudo-Bonaventure's *Meditatitiones Vitae Christi*, but her reading is in support of a larger argument about spectatorship rather than about meditation or contemplation. Bennett, 'Stigmata and Sense Memory.' Biernoff examines a range of

texts, but focuses on the specific image of the Man of Sorrows rather than a single, entire Passion meditation text. Biernoff, *Sight and Embodiment*, 133–65.

91 Pereda contextualizes devotion to Marian icons with reference to optical treatises available on the peninsula, an important contribution to the discussion that gave many leads to the evidence I rehearse below. Pereda, *Las imágenes de la discordia*, 249–54.

92 *Perspectiva fratris Rogerii Bacum*, one of several scientific treatises with marginal diagrams collected in Biblioteca Nacional de Madrid, MSS 10112, is dated to the fourteenth century. See bibliographic information in *Inventario general de manuscritos de la Biblioteca Nacional*, 14:342–3.

93 Anglicus, *De proprietatibus rerum*, book 3, chap. 17, fol. c8r–v. For discussion of Anglicus, see introduction to this book; and Akbari, *Seeing through the Veil*, 38–9, 41.

94 Lindberg points out that Pecham's work exists in so many manuscripts and early printed editions (in comparison to Bacon's or Witelo's writings) that it was likely the standard university textbook on optics. Its influence in Castile came as a result of Pedro Ciruelo's paraphrase in his *Cursus quatuor mathematicarium artium liberalium*, published by presses in Alcalá four times between 1516 and 1528 and used at the University of Paris as well as at Alcalá and Salamanca. Lindberg, Introduction, *John Pecham and the Science of Optics*, 29–30. In addition, the region of Valencia produced a fifteenth-century manuscript and a 1503 printed edition. Ibid., 56–7.

95 Diego Alvarez Chanca mentions both the passive reception of species and visual fire in his discussion of the 'plague' of *mal de ojo*, which afflicted the sailors on one of the voyages of discovery to the New World. Chanca, 'Tratado del ojo 1495,' 175–7. (In this study, the original text is both reproduced as a fascimile and transcribed after the 'estudio preliminar,' although the original had no publication data or folio numbers.) Chanca depended on the extramission theory to prove the possibility of the reality of the evil eye, and had recourse to the Aristotelian point that menstruating women looking at a mirror can cloud it red. Lindberg, *Theories of Vision*, 138; and Bildhauer, *Medieval Blood*, 100–1, 111–12. This point was often associated with the myth that a basilisk can kill with its eyes, a myth known throughout the Golden Age, as evidenced by John of the Cross's reference in his analysis of stanza ten in the *Canticos espirituales*. John of the Cross, *Collected Works*, 512.

96 Martin de Castañega, *Tratado … de las supersticiones y hechizerias …* (Logroño: Miguel de Eguia, 1529), fol. 23v, transcribed in Castañega, *Tratado de las supersticiones y hechicerias*. He used the same argument as Chanca; see previous note. Several of Laredo's sources in spirituality also had an interest

in vision, at least tangentially. Heinrich Herp was a follower and compiler of Jan van Ruusbroec, whom one scholar suggests was influenced by theories of optics. See note 66, above. Jean Gerson dealt with vision, as Rothstein points out in 'Vision, Cognition, and Self-Reflection,' 42n18; see Gerson, 'On Distinguishing True from False Revelations,' 334–64. Juan Luis Vives described the senses receiving an impression like a ring makes on sealing wax. Vives, 'Obra psicológica,' 509.

97 Spanish Renaissance texts addressing the anatomy of the eye began to appear shortly after Laredo's death. For the visual function in discussions of eye anatomy during the Renaissance, see Hernández Benito, *Saber oftalmologico*, 171–80. However, the topic had clearly been popular on the peninsula in the Middle Ages, as the only Spaniard to become pope, Petrus Hispanus, wrote a book on the eye in the thirteenth century. Daly and Yee, 'Eye Book of Master Peter.'

98 Herrero and Mancho, 'Neología' 129.

99 Discussed extensively in Akbari, *Seeing through the Veil*, 88–96.

100 'E dezir que la Encarnación es objeto de la fe es assí como dezir que el color es la cosa en quien se determina la vista. Porque, assí como la vista de nuestros ojos se emplea y se satisfaze y determina en las colores y cosas corpóreas, bien assí la vista de nuestra fe vee y se emplea y se determina en la creencia de las cosas invisibles inteletuales; de manera que dezimos los colores ser objeto de la vista y los sabores objeto del gusto y d'esta manera se dize que las cosas que creemos, como la Encarnación y misterios de Christo, son objeto de la fe, porque a esta dición "objeto" no se le puede dar más claro romance que por estos circonloquios o palabras rodeadas.' (And to say that the Incarnation is an object of faith is like saying that colour is the thing that guides vision. Because, just as the vision of our eyes is employed and satisfies itself and is determined by colours and corporeal things, it is this way that the vision of our faith is employed and determined by belief in invisible intellectual things. In the same manner that we say that colours are the object of vision and flavours the object of taste, in this same manner it is said that the things that we believe in, like the Incarnation and the mysteries of Christ, are objects of faith, because in this terminology 'object' cannot be said more clearly in the vernacular than by these circumlocutions or roundabout wordings.) Laredo, *Subida* II (1538), chap. 5, p. 206.

101 'Y devéys considerar que el bien que ay en la lición no está en el leer demasiado, sino en sentir bien lo leydo. E para bien lo sentir no ha de ser larga lición. E también devéys pensar que la vista corporal no sale fuera de sí a mirar lo que ver quiere, sino ello viene a su potencia, *multiplicando su especie* e dándose a conocer; e quanto menos se distrae, tanto vee mucho mejor e más

y en más perfeción. Este aviso ha de tener nuestra vista inteletual, porque no deve de aver otra tan gran libertad debaxo de todo el cielo como saberse absconder el alma dentro en sí misma.' (And you should consider that the benefit that comes from reading is not from reading too much, but in understanding the reading well. And it need not be a long reading in order to understand it well. And also you ought to think that corporeal sight does not go out of itself in order to look at what it wants to see, but it comes to the power [inner sense], *multiplying its species* and giving itself to be known. The less it is distracted, the better it is seen and in more and more perfection. This advice is for our intellectual sight, because it is impossible that there is any other equally great liberty under the sun as that which comes from knowing how to hide the soul within itself.) Laredo, *Subida* II (1535), chap. 53, p. 391, my emphasis. Note the use of intromission in a Eucharistic treatise, in reverse of the usual scholarly association of optical reception with extramission.

102 '[Y] este ojo [de la voluntad] nunca mira atentamente a su amado sin penetrar el coraçón con el rayo del amor que sale de su esplendor interior.' (And this eye [of the will] never looks attentively at its beloved without penetrating his heart with a ray of love that issues out of its interior splendour.) Laredo, *Subida* III (1538), chap. 12, p. 472. Laredo also refers to the eye as the receptor for colour, so clearly understands the physiology of the eye. Laredo, *Subida* II (1538), chap. 5, p. 206. See conclusion.

103 A version of extramission, in which the lover's glance penetrates the beloved's eyes and is carried with the bodily humors down to the heart. Akbari, *Seeing through the Veil*, 67.

104 Andrés, 'En torno a la "Theologia Crucis,"' 370.

105 'Matins: Agony of Jesus. Lauds: Betrayal of Judas. Primes: Christ before Pilate. Terce: Flagellation. Sext: Christ carrying the cross. Nones: Crucifixion. Vespers: Descent from the cross. Compline: Entombment.' Wieck, *Libro de Horas de Carlos I*, 36; my translation.

106 Laredo, *Subida*, 'Notable,' p. 30. For a discussion of the rhetorical intent of this misleading schema for part 2 of his treatise, see chapter 2.

107 'Lo que yo para mí tengo e mi memoria contempla del cuerpo de Christo a la columna, no hallo en él cosa sana desde los pies hasta la cabeça … Ya dava en la viva carne y se pegavan ya en ella los açotes como en cera blanda con la mucha sangre; e aun más, que los golpes sin parar no la dexavan correr.' Laredo, *Subida* II, chap. 32, p. 306.

108 '[A]brir los ojos de las piadosas entrañas.' Ibid., chap. 9, p. 222. Laredo then uses the term 'entrails of the soul' several times throughout the extended chapter on the Nativity just before beginning the Passion meditation section. Ibid., chap. 12, pp. 235, 247, 249.

109 The first chapters of the surgical section define different types of wounds, particularly interesting given Laredo's later interest in the medical aspects of Christ's bloody sweat, as discussed in chapter 3.

110 '[Q]ue no vaya el ánima a ver aquestos misterios al lugar adonde acaescieron, mas que el lugar y el misterio lo atrayga y lo meta en sí misma, recogiéndose toda dentro en sí ...

De manera que quiere dezir aquí que ... pensando en sus açotes sea tu coraçón columna; de manera que de golpe o recudida no puedas sentir ni pensar en algún açote o golpe que no toque en tu columna, e porque es de piedra dura insensible no se sabe deshazer en tan digna compassión.

Iten, si piensas en la coronación, sea tu coraçón la silla, o sea la púrpura, e no aya alguna espina que no toque e lastime o te ensangriente los ojos, pues que la sangre sagrada aun por ellos e la boca rebentava e por el rostro corría. E si piensas en la cruz, sea tu coraçón la piedra en que fue hincada e aun lo más tierno e interior sea el agujero de ella, de manera que la sangre que corre por el madero lave tu dura substancia y se entre en el cordial agujero e nunca salga de allí. E assí en todos los misterios.' Laredo, *Subida* II, chap. 13, p. 252.

111 Ibid., chap. 13, p. 252; and chap. 22, p. 281.

112 'Véase si esto está en razón y buelve y éntrate en ti e a ti traerás los misterios e todos cabrán en ti. E tú serás Tierra Sancta si te sabes encerrar e gozar.' Ibid., chap. 13, p. 253.

113 See introduction, note 47.

114 Scarry discusses how the doors, wall, or objects left in a room can contribute to mental and physical torture, and also details the types of torture that involve turning the body against itself (through cramps, etc.). Scarry, *Body in Pain*, 41–8. For intriguing reflections on the medieval classroom as a nmnemonic torture device, see Enders, *Medieval Theater of Cruelty*, 93.

115 Scarry, *Body in Pain*, 41.

116 The thirteen chapters of part 2 of the *Subida* that narrate Christ's Passion read quite differently in light of these mnemotechnical and cognitive assumptions. Throughout the individual scenes, Laredo centres his readers' attention on the objects in order that they imagine themselves as the location of the events rather than as spectators. Rather than explicating the prayer in the Garden at any great length, Laredo begins his narrative by enumerating the *arma Christi*, thus foreshadowing the events of the days to come. This popular medieval devotion, also a quintessential mnemonic device, allows him to interweave object-based meditation (Christ's blood, limbs, among others) with the chronological narrative. *Subida* II, chap. 17, p. 262. He then names the rope, robes, blindfold, crown of thorns, nails, lance, and other objects that would be used to inflict pain and humiliation on Jesus in the

course of the Passion. All of these objects were well known from popular images of the *arma Christi* so frequently used in woodblocks to decorate printed books and pamphlets, especially the frontispieces. The focus on the *arma Christi* thus links Laredo's interest in basing his transformation of the devotee into the objects adjacent to the Passion – the column, the chair, even the base of the cross – with a traditional image from the artistic tradition that would have been familiar to his readers. Griffin provides a lengthy discussion of early modern Spanish woodcut techniques, including ones with the *arma Christi.* He emphasizes the fact that the designs were not only generally derivative, but that Cromburger's press in fact copied medieval prints as precisely as possible. Griffin, *The Crombergers of Seville*, 183–9.

117 'Mas ¡o, anima mía lastimada! ¿Y no merescieras yr con tu amoroso Jesú desnudo, con ultrage avergonçado, atado e inclinado todo el muy llagado cuerpo? ¿Y no merescieras yr con tu muy llagado Christo entre gente tan desmedida y profana? ¡O, mi dulcíssimo amor, e quién me diera la parte de las salivas, los silvos y bofetadas y el tumultuoso rigor con que passastes aquella breve jornada de la colunna hasta vuestras vestiduras! ¡Quién os viera quereros vestir temblando y con espantosa furia tornaros a desnudar! ¡Quién os quitara la púrpura de vuestro ultrajable escarnio! ¡Quién os tomara la venda de los delicados ojos!, ¡quién os tomara la silla e la caña e los pujeses, las salivas, los golpes y bofetadas! ¡O, si viera las espinas en mi ánima penetradas. E la sangre que corría por la frente, y por el rostro, por el cabello y garganta! ¡O, mi Dios, quién la cogiera en el pobre lastimado e abrasado coraçón! ¡O, quién la viera apuntar a los lacrimables ojos o rebentar por los oydos, por las narizes y boca, en lo último atormentada. E quién subiera con Vos al *Ecce homo* de Pilato, a la presencia del pueblo y gente desesperada! Mas, ¡Dios mío!, ¿quién me dirá si mi lastimada madre, nuestra universal Señora, si avía ya tornado en sí e si tuvo ojos con que os viesse escarnecido y penado o si oya aquella cruel boz: "*Crucifige, crucifige*"?' Laredo, *Subida* II, chap. 19, pp. 270–1, but changing some punctuation based on comparison with the 1538 edition.

118 Biernoff, *Sight and Embodiment*, 96. Later she writes: 'Vision, in the medieval world, did not leave the viewer untouched or unchanged.' Ibid., 137.

119 Laredo, *Subida* II, chaps. 28–30, pp. 295–301.

120 Mary's grief lasted longer than Christ's did, but she suffered in her entrails as badly as he did. Ibid., chap. 28, p. 297.

121 Ibid., chap. 22, p. 281. I should note that in the Latin Passion narratives, Mary's suffering is deemed extraordinary, but only on a mental and emotional level. See Bestul, *Texts of the Passion*, 124ff.

122 'Lastimada' has the dual sense of 'wounded' or 'moved to compassion,' so both a physical and an emotional reading is possible.

123 'E si la lança partió dos coraçones en no más que un solo pecho, confiesso que los partió, pero no puedo ni quiero poder sentir que pudo en nada apartarlos, sino partidos mas no apartados. ¡O si tuviesse por bien el que consintió partir el coraçón de su madre dentro en su proprio costado y con su misma lançada que se pudiesse romper el coraçón de su pobrezillo esclavo con el clavo de sus pies! ... Mas ¿qué digo?, ¡o, mi lastimado amor! Una ánima en ambos cuerpos, dos cuerpos e unas entrañas, e si son dos las entrañas, ¿no es más de uno el coraçón? Un coraçón en dos pechos, y en dos pechos un costado, un coraçón e una lança, un juntamiento de amor indivisible en la vida ni la muerte le apartó, que un solo coraçón fue entre la Virgen e Christo e una sola voluntad, con cuya perfecta conformidad dezimos que la ánima de la Virgen e la ánima de Christo, siendo dos, son sola una ánima; porque nunca el Hijo hizo lo que no quiso su Madre, ni aun morir, pues nunca la Madre quiso contra voluntad de Christo ni aun bivir.

Y d'esta conformidad de la Virgen con su Dios fue fabricada la nave en la qual pudo passar el muy tempestuoso mar de la terrible Passión de su amantíssimo hijo; pues que es cosa averiguada en el piadoso pensar que, si en tal mar navegara en gran carraca de amor, que mil vezes naufragara, no por falta de las tristíssimas aguas, que bien pudiera nadar, pues avía tanta abundancia, pero por las muchas rocas que escondía cada dolor. ¿Quién ay que pueda pensar que si con la proa de la carraca de amor, sin la lastimada nave de aquella conformidad, pudiera dar o topar en las muy terribles rocas de la columna o la cruz si quedara la proa o la popa sana? ¿O si oviera calafate (que quiere dezir carpintero o oficial de adobar navíos) que la pudiera soldar? Sé que no: que la madera de amor no sabe hender ni raja, antes se suele acostar a la parte a la cual va más cargada; ni se sabe sumergir, antes sobrepuja las tempestades y el agua.' Laredo, *Subida* II, chap. 28, pp. 296–7.

124 Contrast the chapter of Osuna's Passion meditation treatise, in which he provides an entire Passion of Mary separately from the narrative of Christ's last days. Osuna, *Primer abecedario*, Y; analysed in Boon, 'Agony of the Virgin,' 19–24. One scholar has collected all of Laredo's references to Mary together in one article (though he provides little analysis). Calvo Moralejo, 'La compasión corredentora.'

125 Pacho in fact summarizes Laredo's entire Passion sequence in a single page. Pacho, *Apogeo de la mística*, 524.

126 Laredo, *Subida* II, chap. 12, p. 238. For this version of Christology, known as *habitus*, see Mowbray, *Pain and Suffering*, 28–9; and Trembinski, '[Pro] passio Doloris,' 638–9.

Conclusion

1 Laredo, *Subida* III (1538), chap. 1, p. 435; trans. Peers, 63. This is the only time he uses the terminology of purgative/illuminative/unitive. Laredo emphasizes the term 'union' in the second version, although he speaks of 'contemplation' in both. See the *via contemplativa* referred to in the 'Notable,' p. 33.

2 Andrés, *Los recogidos*, 89; also see the introduction, note 69.

3 Ros states: '[L]e moment est venu d'aborder la partie la plus importante du *Mont Sion*, c'est-à-dire le livre III.' (The time is come to tackle the most important part of *Mount Zion*, that is to say, the third book.) Ros, *Inspirateur de Sainte Thérèse*, 120.

4 Laredo classifies himself with those who talk too much but do not take action, and thus he is not 'proficient with experience.' *Subida* II (1535), chap. 54, p. 392. For example, Laredo states specifically that he has never experienced complete rapture. *Subida* III (1535), chap. 33, p. 726; reprinted in 1538, chap. 41, p. 599; trans. Peers, 262.

5 Pacho's recent discussion centres on the 1538 edition. Pacho, *Apogeo de la mística*, 500–4, 526–56. Peers did not translate anything but part 3 of the 1538 edition. The 1948 edition of the *Subida* in the *Místicos Franciscanos españoles* volumes in the *Biblioteca de Autores Cristianos* series, edited by Juan Bautista Gomis, only reproduces the 1538 version, which means that the majority of Spanish scholarship on Laredo published between 1948 and the appearance of the critical edition in 2000 refers only to the second edition. For example, Aramendia, 'Las oraciones afectivas,' draws on a reprint of the 1538 edition.

6 Only Andrés and Ros present serious attempts at comparing the two versions, although all discussions of Laredo refer to Laredo's new sources. Andrés, *Los recogidos*, 193–232; and Ros, *Inspirateur de Sainte Thérèse*, 120–35, 255–93. In the 1535 edition, Laredo cites Richard of Saint Victor ten times, Gregory the Great sixteen, and Bonaventure only five. In the 1538 version, he cites Richard fifteen times, Heinrich Herp sixteen times, Gregory the Great nineteen times, and Bonaventure only two.

7 'Enlarging of the mind [*dilatatio mentis*] is when the sharp point of the soul is expanded more widely and is sharpened more intensely; yet this in no way goes beyond the mode of human activity. Raising up of the mind [*sublevatio/elevatio mentis*] is when the vivacity of the understanding, being divinely irradiated, transcends the bound of human activity; nevertheless it does not pass over into alienation of mind, so that what it sees is above it, and yet it does not withdraw even a little from accustomed things. Alienation of mind [*alienatio/excessus mentis*] is when the memory of present things is forgotten by the mind, and by a transfiguration from divine working the mind goes over

to a state of soul both alien and inaccessible to human activity. Those who are worthy to be raised up to the supreme stronghold of such grace experience these three kinds of contemplation. The first rises up from human activity; the third from divine grace alone; the middle one from the combination of both.' Richard of Saint Victor, 'The Mystical Ark,' part 5, chap. 2, p. 310; Latin from Chatillon, 'Les trois modes,' 4.

8 'El punto primero es entrar en mi coraçón. El segundo subirme sobre él. El tercero parescer en la presencia de mi Señor, aposentado en lo muy más alto del ánima.' Laredo, *Subida* III (1535), chap. 12, p. 639. This is the primary version. Laredo also speaks of it in the following way: 'Y el ánima que assí se puede quietar se dirá estar dentro en sí; e si no cobdicia nada de todo lo que no es Dios, passa adelante de sí; e quando todo lo olvida se sube sobre sí misma, llegándose más a Dios.' (And the soul that can quiet itself in this way is said to be within itself, and if it lusts after nothing that is not God, it will pass in front of itself, and when it forgets all it will rise above itself, arriving closer to God.) Ibid., chap. 4, p. 618.

9 Boon, 'Mystical Language of Recollection,' 314–83.

10 '[C]on tassado entendimiento ... sin ruydo e sin discurso ... [T]eniendo siempre aviso de no yr fuera de sí misma la ánima a buscar misterios, pues que ella los terná en sí, si se tuviere a sí en ellos.' Laredo, *Subida* II, chap. 13, p. 253.

11 Ibid., chap. 14, p. 256. Note that Laredo actually refers to the second stage as involving contemplation, despite the fact that chronological narratives of Christ were always assigned to meditation alone in the Middle Ages. For a brief overview of *recogimiento* in general that does not delve in depth but also does not entirely exclude the body from stage three, see Mark, *Mysticism and Cognition*, 99–100.

12 Stating that the stage of self-knowledge involves the external senses in a manner that stays external, Laredo characterizes imaginative visualization of the Passion as a process of 'searching exteriorly, while remaining interior' (Buscar también en lo exterior, y ha de permanecer dentro), a distinction he had also used when discussing devotion using icons and images. *Subida* II, chap. 13, p. 254, and chap. 14, p. 256. This description of stage two is only comprehensible if we take into account the cognitive process that transfers sensory information to the mind and soul, where it is imprinted as images that can then be manipulated by the inner sense of the imagination. This Galenic cognition sequence renders it possible for exterior senses to have interior effects. Laredo later equates desire with eyeglasses, stating that desire, i.e., the loving will, allows the intellectual sight (understanding) to focus on the higher mysteries: 'Y los antojos de la vista intelectual son los muy bivos e caríssimos

desseos de la libre voluntad.' (The eyeglasses of intellectual sight are the most lively and clear desires of the free will.) Ibid., chap. 36, p. 323. Thus cognitive theories and the theological faculties of the soul again overlap extensively.

13 '[L]a mayor perfeción de los que en su Dios contemplan está en cerrar bien las puertas de todos cinco sentidos y en quitar del coraçón toda cosa que no es Dios.' Laredo, *Subida* III (1535), chap. 4, p. 618.

14 For discussion of Laredo's contribution to the science of botany, see Laín, 'Los inicios de la terminología botánica.'

15 Laredo, *Subida* III (1535), chap. 28, pp. 697–700.

16 Laredo describes eyesight in relation to seeing with clarity (a term frequently used in optical treatises) in ibid., chap. 18, p. 659. He refers to interior eyes or the eyes of the soul in chap. 21, p. 670; chap. 24, p. 685; chap. 26, p. 690; chap. 29, p. 706; and chap. 31, p. 711. All should be read with an awareness that visual cognition is a 'hook' that such references could easily stimulate.

17 Ibid., chap. 37, pp. 746–7. As discussed in chapter 4, Carruthers suggests that language-based mnemonics are retained as imprinted images of words on a page. For discussion of Laredo's use of Hippocrates, see Santander Rodríguez, *Hipócrates en España*, 9–17.

18 'Si Christo está en la memoria, siempre se gana vitoria.' Laredo, *Subida* III (1535), chap. 37, p. 749; (1538), chap. 50, p. 592.

19 'Las entrañas del ánima racional.' Ibid. (1535), chap. 14, p. 646.

20 'Medula de los huessos de las entrañas de la ánima.' Laredo, *Subida* III (1535), chap. 33, p. 721; and (1538), chap. 41, p. 594. Note that the chapter was moved to the penultimate location in the 1538 edition.

21 Laredo, *Subida* III (1535), chap. 33, p. 728.

22 Ibid.

23 Laredo had connected his oceanic mnemonic to the Passion in part 2 primarily by using it to link disparate discussions concerning the Trinity, the soul, and Mary together as framework for a Passion narrative that does not itself involve any aquatic references. In part 3, he finally applies the ocean metaphor to the Passion itself, but notably to the Passion only as technique in the ascent to recollected union, not to a new narrative example of meditation.

24 'Mas el amor requiere concocimiento y el conocimiento pide discurso de entendimiento que busque causas y efectos e la patente razon, hasta dar para afixarse en la verdad verdadera e darse a la voluntad, sin la qual verdad nunca se sabe quietar. Y es cierto que este discurso, quanto quiera sea ordenado y es en sí muy provechoso a los que aora nos estamos dentro en nuestro noviciado, certíssima cosa está que es muy grande impedimento a la quieta voluntad, que pide muy a sus solas gustar sola a su Dios y engolfarse dende luego en el piélago de amor, sin buscar causas de amar, que aquesto ya ha de estar hecho en los bien

aprovechados. Pero porque no puedo sentir, ni quiero poder querer que me pueda sonar bien, que la ánima contemplativa, estando en este destierro, deve ningún día dexar la Passión e altos misterios de nuestro amoroso amor, e andar de contino en ella con todo el entendimiento es un estorvo muy grande a la quieta voluntad, dase aquesto por remedio, es a saber, partir continuo las partes dexándose entero el tiempo. Quiero dezir que a la una parte del hombre, que es el ánima, se le da todo el tiempo sin tiempo para la quieta contemplación todas las vezes y tiempos que la pueda recebir, sin trabajar en buscarla con más que bivos desseos y con despierta atención ... E a la otra parte del hombre, que en este repartimiento es nuestro asnillo o sardesco o corpazo azemilar, ponerle a cuestas la cruz ... Assí lo que el ánima falta de contemplar en los misterios de Christo por darse a quieta y remansada oración, halo de suplir el cuerpo ... andando siempre con Christo crucificado en la cruz, fabricada de pobreza y menosprecio e dolor, e assí descansará en Dios e trabajará con Christo, sabiendo que Christo es Dios, nuestro bien e amparo nuestro.

[Capítulo VI] Quando todas nuestras obras andan por el notado tenor, no se olvida ni aun una hora ni un momento la Passión de nuestro Christo Jesús sin ocupar ningún tiempo; mas passa a la tácita memoria lo que se solía tener en el bivo entendimiento e nunca haze abstinencia sin acordarse por quién, casi sin mirar en ello... E por este tal camino viene el ánima hasta ser assí capaz, que las vezes que le falta fortaleza corporeal para traer la cruz a cuestas, ya la memoria possee la passión en tal manera que nunca la dexa caer y que, aunque quiera, no pueda.' Laredo, *Subida* III (1535), chaps. 5–6, pp. 621–3.

25 Osuna, *Tercer abecedario*, S, 457–80; translated in *Third Spiritual Alphabet*, S, 449–74; as discussed in Ros, *Inspirateur de Sainte Thérèse*, 140.

26 Laredo, *Subida* III (1535), chap. 35, p. 738. For that matter, he also refers to Passion meditation as 'la contemplación callada de la sacra humanidad' (quieted contemplation of the sacred humanity). Ibid., chap. 5, p. 620.

27 Ibid., chap. 7, p. 624. See also the 'Notable' in both editions, in which Laredo suggests that every time the hour strikes, the soul should think of Christ (*Subida*, p. 32). The recommendation for daily remembrance was common among those who wrote guides to Passion meditation. The anonymous author of the *Fasciculus myrrhe*, for example, recommends an hour of Passion meditation per day. See citation in Andrés, 'En torno a la "Theologia Crucis,"' 366.

28 '[A]lgunas vezes dexa el ánima los misterios corpulentos de que trata e sin pensar, súbitamente, se halla dentro en sí sin alguna corpulencia, ella misma no sabiendo que quería parar allí donde se vee estar parada en solo tácito amor, sin saber ella sentir que era muy enamorada hasta tener el amor.

Por lo qual se ha de notar que nuestro entendimiento es assí como río de muchas aguas, que de noche ni de día nunca dexa su correr, mas algunas vezes halla unos tablazos muy grandes e grandes concavidades, que son los grandes desseos que apenas o no se hinchen con el tropel impetuoso de las muy onduosas aguas que corren en todo el río, esto es, con los meditables discursos de todo el entendimiento; mas, reparándose el agua en la tal concavidad, haze piélago engolfado ...

Este pielago, en el ánima, es la quieta voluntad, que es assí como nave que está en calma e muy metida en el mar, que, aunque ella quiera, no puede un poquito declinar acá ni allá, mas permanece en quietud mientra le dura la calma, es a saber, la quietud ...

Mas quando el ánima puede llegar a estos golfos de mucha agua no deve passar de allí, sino engolfarse y dexarse sumergir e no curarse de sí y quebrar, no querer y desechar los remos de todo el entendimiento y de todos cinco sentidos y toda cosa tomable, que suele mucho impedir en aquestos tiempos tales. Mas, quando no llega a golfo, en correr con discreción el discreto e tassado entendimiento muchas vezes gana mucho y muy pocas pierde nada.' Laredo, *Subida* III (1535), chap. 7, pp. 625–6.

29 Ibid., chap. 24, p. 686; chap. 20, p. 666; and chap. 9, p. 632, respectively.

30 Laredo, *Subida* III (1538), chap. 40, pp. 577 and 587; trans. Peers, pp. 237 and 247. Note that the translations continue to be my own, but I provide the citations to Peers's (loose) translation for reference.

31 Ibid., chap. 10, p. 469 (Peers, 106); chap. 7, p. 460 (not translated literally in Peers); chap. 12, p. 472 (Peers, 110); and the bee/wax figure in both chap. 12, p. 473 (Peers, 111), and chap. 20, p. 495 (Peers, 139). This image is one of the few analogies given by Herp in an otherwise fairly abstract treatise rooted in Ruusbroec's writings. Herp, *Directorio de contemplativos*, part 2, p. 434.

32 Laredo, *Subida* III (1538), chap. 10, p. 468; trans. Peers, 104.

33 In this case, twisted and wounded by harm from neighbours, at which point the soul calms itself by seeing in the mirror that Christ is at its centre. Laredo, *Subida* III (1538), chap. 31, p. 541; trans. Peers, 194, though he translates 'wounds' as 'grief.'

34 The chapters that appear contradictory include Laredo, *Subida* III (1538), chap. 23, p. 508 (Peers, 154) versus chap. 24, pp. 510–11 (Peers, 157–8); and chap. 28, p. 528 (Peers, 178) versus chap. 29, p. 531 (Peers, 182).

35 'Assí que, si la perfeción de todo contemplativo consiste en el amor de nuestro Christo Jesús, en el qual los pensamientos impiden, necessario es que sintamos que entendió lo que dezía el que dixo que es mejor en quieta contemplación *no pensar nada*. E por esso dize la auctoridad que se levante nuestro coraçón de noche, porque, assí como la noche quita de nuestra vista corporal todo lo que con la claridad podemos ver, bien assí el muy súbito alçamiento de

nuestra afectiva esconde de la vista intellectual todo lo que Dios crio y quédase sólo en él.' (Thus, if the perfection of each contemplative consists in loving our Jesus Christ, which thoughts would impede, it is necessary that we feel that he, who said that it is better *not to think anything* during quiet contemplation, was making sense. And for this reason the authority [Jeremiah] says that our heart should be lifted at night, because just as the night takes away from our corporeal sight all that we can see when it is light, so the very sudden ascent of our affection hides from intellectual sight all that God created and rests in Him alone.) Laredo, *Subida* III (1538), chap. 27, p. 523; trans. Peers, 172–3; my emphasis.

36 Laredo, *Subida* III (1538), chap. 28, p. 526; trans. Peers, 176.

37 The term 'mystical theology' is found in the previous sentence. Laredo says that it speaks stammeringly (*tartamudeando*) and thus one can 'leerla en las entrañas, darala a sentir en el ánima, plantarla en el coraçón.' Laredo, *Subida* III (1538), chap. 15, p. 481; trans. Peers, 122.

38 Laredo, *Subida* III (1535), chap. 38, pp. 750–6, revised in *Subida* II (1538), chap. 53, pp. 383–9. Perhaps because Laredo considered that his new discussion of love at the end of part 2 on the Passion would serve to integrate the Passion into the beginning of the third level, he deleted the first dozen chapters, which were on the incorporation of the Passion into the third level of part 3.

39 Laredo, *Subida* III (1538), chaps. 32–9, pp. 546–67; trans. Peers, 200–7.

40 Chapters 35–8 are taken from Suso, *Horologium sapientiae*, chap. 23, according to Peers, Introduction, *The Ascent of Mount Sion*, 21n1. See the English translation of the German original in Suso, 'The Little Book of Eternal Wisdom,' 276–86.

41 'Porque todo el intento de aqueste tercero libro es juntar la ánima a su Dios por vía de amor unitivo, e la más perfecta unión que es possible o puede ser en este duro destierro consiste en la agraciada Comunión del Sacramento Sanctíssimo.' Laredo, *Subida* III (1538), chap. 31, p. 545; trans. Peers, 199.

42 For example, Laredo, *Subida* III (1538), chap. 32, pp. 546–7; trans. Peers, 201.

43 'Siendo assí que este Sacramento altíssimo haze maravillosa impressión en el ánima ... e assí infunde en lo más bivo, más puro e más tierno de las entrañas una prontíssima y nueva y biva ciudad.' Laredo, *Subida* III (1538), chap. 32, p. 547; trans. Peers, 201–2, yet note Peers's refusal to translate 'city' as a concrete place, much less as a locative mnemonic device.

44 Scholars interested in Laredo's language of negative theology have consistently overlooked this return to Christ and to devotional practices at the height of the unitive stage. Andrés not only states that he will look only at the two versions of part 3 but also implies that the chapters on the Eucharist in both editions are separate from the main work, despite their integration

within the body of the text in each case. 'Dejo a un lado las obras de medicina, *Josefina* y los opúsculos eucarísticos.' (I leave to one side the medical works, the treatise on Joseph, and the Eucharistic treatises.) Andrés, *Los recogidos*, 195. Ros does discuss the Eucharistic treatises, but by putting them in a separate and very brief chapter, he in effect treats them as unrelated to the main content of the *Subida*. Ros, *Inspirateur de Sainte Thérèse*, 156–64. Those who advocate a fundamental difference between the two versions of stage three fail to note that the remaining chapters after the Eucharistic treatise in the 1538 part 3 are revised versions of chapters from the 1535 edition.

45 This is a Johannine point, rather than one derived from the synoptic gospels.

46 Howells, *John of the Cross and Teresa of Avila*. For further comparison of Teresa and John, see Howe, *Mystical Imagery*.

47 Biographies of Teresa include Medwick, *Teresa of Avila: The Progress of a Soul*; a social history of Avila as context for Teresa's work is found in Bilinkoff, *The Avila of Saint Teresa*; leading analyses of her texts include Weber, *Teresa of Avila and the Rhetoric of Femininity*; Carrión, *Arquitectura y cuerpo*; Ahlgren, *Teresa of Avila and the Politics of Sanctity*; and Carrera-Marcén, *Teresa of Avila's Autobiography*. Recent work on her method of prayer is found in López, 'Oralidad, misticismo y espiritualidad.'

48 'Mirando libros para ver si sabría decir la oración que tenía, hallé en uno que llaman *Subida del Monte*, en lo que toca a unión del alma con Dios, todas las señales que yo tenía en aquel no pensar nada, que esto era lo que yo más decía: que no podía pensar nada cuando tenía aquella oración.' Teresa of Avila, 'Libro de la vida,' chap. 23, sections 11–12, p. 129; my revision of the translation in Teresa of Avila, *Life*, 225.

49 Ros's rationale for writing a monograph on Laredo was his role in 'inspiring' Teresa. It is interesting that Ros only has a handful of pages examining actual points of continuity. Ros, *Inspirateur de Sainte Thérèse*, 324–34.

50 Berbara, '"Este pena tan sanbrosa,"' 295. Berbara cites information regarding Teresa's lifelong pain at pp. 268–72.

51 Teresa of Avila, 'Way of Perfection,' chap. 28, p. 141. 'Llámase recogimiento, porque recoge el alma todas las potencias y se entra dentro de sí con su Dios ... Porque allí metida consigo mesma, puede pensar toda la Pasión y representar allí al Hijo y ofrecerle a el Padre y no cansar el entendimiento, andándole buscando en el monte Calvario, y al Huerto, y a la Coluna.' Teresa of Avila, 'Camino de perfección,' chap. 28, p. 351.

52 Teresa also knew Francisco de Osuna's writings, but primarily the *Tercer abecedario espiritual*, not the first alphabet that is his treatise on the Passion. See chapter 2 for a discussion of the differences between Laredo's and Osuna's valuation of the Passion.

53 'Representar: hazernos presente alguna cosa con palabras, o figuras que se fixen en nuestra imaginacion.' Covarrubias Orozco, *Tesoro*, fol. 160r.
54 Mujica, '*Corpus sanus*,' 14.
55 Teresa of Avila, 'Way of Perfection,' chap. 28, p. 143; and 'Camino de perfección,' chap. 28, p. 352.
56 Teresa of Avila, 'Way of Perfection,' chap. 28, pp. 143–4; and 'Camino de perfección,' chap. 28, pp. 352–3.
57 Teresa of Avila, 'Way of Perfection,' chap. 19, p. 107; and 'Camino de perfección,' chap. 9, p. 311.
58 Chorpenning suggests that such images 'reverberate' throughout her work. Chorpenning, 'The Monastery, Paradise, and the Castle.'
59 Teresa of Avila, 'Interior Castle,' chap. 1, p. 283. '[U]n castillo todo de un diamante u muy claro cristal, adonde hay muchos aposentos.' Teresa of Avila, 'Moradas del castillo interior,' chap. 1, p. 472.
60 Gerli, '*El castillo interior* y el *ars memorativa*'; and Carrión, *Arquitectura y cuerpo*, 173–88, 249–57.
61 López-Baralt, 'Teresa of Jesus and Islam.'
62 See the useful chart of repeated elements found in the appendix to Teresa of Avila, *Collected Works*, 2:544–52. Analysis of the architectural impact of the interior castle is found in Carrión, 'Home, Sweet Home.'
63 Teresa of Avila, 'Libro de la vida,' chap. 9, p. 64.
64 For a cogent description of the encounters between Teresa and John, see Howells, *John of the Cross and Teresa of Avila*, 65–9. Studies of John of the Cross include Ubarri, *Las categorías de espacio y tiempo*; and Thompson, *St. John of the Cross: Songs in the Night*. The intriguing title of Mark's work is misleading, as she explores how John of the Cross's experiences map onto modern theories of cognition, not Renaissance ones. Mark, *Mysticism and Cognition*.
65 Barroso, *La 'Subida del Monte Sión' y la 'Subida del Monte Carmelo'*; Ricard, '*La fonte* de San Juan de la Cruz'; and Ros, *Inspirateur de Sainte Thérèse*, 322–4. For a brief analysis of John's sketch of Mount Carmel, see Flor, *Emblemas*, 251–2.
66 Howells, *John of the Cross and Teresa of Avila*, 34–9.
67 John of the Cross, *Collected Works*, 2nd night, chaps. 5–6, pp. 403–4; and *Obras completas*, 2nd night, chaps. 5–6, pp. 480–2.
68 John of the Cross, *Collected Works*, 1st night, chap. 10, p. 382. 'En la oración *no puede hacer ni pensar nada* … porque, si de suyo quiere algo obrar con las potencias interiores, será estorbar y perder los bienes que Dios por medio de aquella paz y ocio del alma está asentando e imprimiendo en ella,' *Obras completas*, 1st night, chap. 10, p. 456, my emphasis.

69 John of the Cross, *Collected Works*, stanza 12, sections 1–2, 515–16; and *Obras completas*, 622–3.
70 John of the Cross, *Collected Works*, stanza 12, section 8, 518; and *Obras completas*, 625.
71 John of the Cross, *Collected Works*, stanza 13, section 1, 519; and *Obras completas*, 626–7.
72 John of the Cross, *Collected Works*, stanza 12, section 9, 519. '[C]onocimiento de él es la pena por él.' *Obras completas*, 626.

Bibliography

Ahlgren, Gillian T.W. *Teresa of Avila and the Politics of Sanctity*. Ithaca, NY: Cornell University Press, 1996.

Akbari, Suzanne Conklin. *Seeing through the Veil: Optical Theory and Medieval Allegory*. Toronto: University of Toronto Press, 2004.

Alcalá, Ángel. *Literatura y ciencia ante la Inquisitión española*. Madrid: Ediciones del Laberinto, 2001.

– 'María de Cazalla: The Grievous Price of Victory.' In *Women in the Inquisition: Spain and the New World*, edited by Mary E. Giles, 98–118. Baltimore: Johns Hopkins University Press, 1999.

– *Proceso inquisitorial de Fray Luis de León*. Salamanca: Junta de Castilla y León, 1991.

Aldama, J.A. de. 'La piedad mariana en el tratado *Passio Duorum*.' *Estudios Marianos* 44 (1979): 53–72.

Alvarez de Sepúlveda, Juan. *Historia de la imagen de Nuestra Señora de Aguas-Santas: Patrona de Villaverde del Río*. Seville: Adalid Seráfico, 1970.

Álvarez Márquez, María Carmen. 'Las lecturas de Fray Gonzalo de Illescas, Obispo de Córdoba (1454–1464).' In *Las fiestas de Sevilla en el siglo XV: Otros estudios*, 289–328. Madrid: Editorial DEIMOS, S.A., 1991.

Álvarez Pellitero, Ana María. *La obra lingüística y literaria de Fray Ambrosio de Montesino*. Valladolid: Universidad de Valladolid, Departamiento de lengua y literatura española, 1976.

Amasuno Sárraga, Marcelino V. *La escuela de medicina del estudio salmantino (siglos XIII–XV)*. Salamanca: Ediciones Universidad de Salamanca, 1990.

Anastatius the Librarian. *A Thirteenth-Century Textbook of Mystical Theology at the University of Paris*. Edited by L. Michael Harrington. Paris: Peeters, 2004.

Andrade de Labadía, Gabriela. 'La pasión de Cristo como "gesta" en *El duelo de la Virgen*, de Gonzalo de Berceo.' *Revista Chilena de Literatura* 16–17 (1980–1): 215–28.

Andrés, Melquíades. 'Alumbrados, Erasmians, "Lutherans," and Mystics: The Risk of a More "Intimate" Spirituality.' In *The Spanish Inquisition and the Inquisitorial Mind*, edited by Angel Alcalá, 457–95. New York: Columbia University Press, 1987.
– 'En torno a la "Theologia Crucis" en la espiritualidad española (1450–1559).' *Dialógo Ecuménico* 6 (1971): 359–90.
– *Historia de la mística de la Edad de Oro en España y América*. Madrid: Biblioteca de Autores Cristianos, 1994.
– Introducción to *Carro de dos vidas*, by Gómez García, 9–90. Madrid: Fundacion Universitaria Española, 1988.
– Introducción to *Tercer abecedario espiritual*, by Francisco de Osuna, 3–120. Madrid: Biblioteca de Autores Cristianos, 1972.
– 'La espiritualidad franciscana en España en tiempos de las Observancias (1380–1517).' *Studia Histórica: Historia Moderna* 6 (1988): 465–79.
– *La teología española en el siglo XVI*. 2 vols. Madrid: Biblioteca de Autores Cristianos, 1977.
– 'Los alumbrados de Toledo en el *Cuarto abecedario espiritual*, o *Ley de amor*, de Francisco de Osuna (1530).' *Archivo Ibero-Americano* 41 (1981): 459–80.
– *Los recogidos: Nueva visión de la mística española 1500–1700*. Madrid: Fundación Universitaria Española, 1976.
Anglicus, Bartolomeus. *De proprietatibus rerum. Español*. Translated by Vicente de Burgos. Toulouse: Enrique Meyer, 1494.
Aramendia, Julio. 'Las oraciones afectivas y los grandes maestros espirituales de nuestro siglo de oro: La escuela franciscana.' *El Monte Carmelo* 36 (1935): 387–95, 435–42.
Archimatthaeus (Pseudo-Arnau de Villanova). 'General Instructions for the Practitioner (*De Cautelis medicorum*).' In *A Source Book of Medieval Science*, edited by Edward Grant, 742–5. Cambridge, MA: Harvard University Press, 1974.
Areford, David S. 'The Passion Measured: A Late-Medieval Diagram of the Body of Christ.' In *The Broken Body: Passion Devotion in Late-Medieval Culture*, edited by A.A. MacDonald, H.N.B. Ridderbos, and R.M. Schlusemann, 211–38. Groningen: Egbert Forsten, 1998.
Arrizabalaga, Jon. *The 'Articella' in the Early Press: c. 1476–1534*. Cambridge: Cambridge University Press, 1998.
Arvay, Susan. 'Private Passions: The Contemplation of Suffering in Medieval Affective Devotions.' PhD diss., Rutgers University, 2008.
Aspe, María-Paz. 'Spanish Spirituality's Mid-Sixteenth-Century Change of Course.' In *The Spanish Inquisition and the Inquisitorial Mind*, edited by Ángel Alcalá, 421–30. Boulder, CO: Social Science Monographs, 1987.
Augsburg, David of. *Forma de los novicios*. Seville: Ungut and Polono, 1497.

Augustine. *The Literal Meaning of Genesis.* Translated by John Hammond Taylor. New York: Newman Press, 1982.

– *St. Augustine on the Holy Trinity, Doctrinal Treatises and Moral Treatises: Nicene and Post-Nicene Fathers*, translated by Arthur West Haddan, 1887. Reprint, Kila, MT: Kessinger Publishing, 2004.

Avicenna. 'Selections from the *Canon.*' In *A Source Book of Medieval Science*, edited by Edward Grant, 715–22. Cambridge, MA: Harvard University Press, 1974.

Avila, Teresa of. 'Camino de perfección.' In *Obras completas*, edited by Efrén de la Madre de Dios and Otger Steggink, 236–420. Madrid: Biblioteca de Autores Cristianos, 2003.

– *The Collected Works of St. Teresa of Avila.* Translated by Kieran Kavanaugh and Otilio Rodriguez. Vol. 2. Washington, DC: ICS Publications, 1980.

– 'Interior Castle.' In *The Collected Works of St. Teresa of Avila,* translated by Kieran Kavanaugh and Otilio Rodriguez, 2:281–452. Washington, DC: ICS Publications, 1980.

– *The Interior Castle Study Edition.* Translated by Kieran Kavanaugh and Otilio Rodriguez. Edited by Kieran Kavanaugh and Carol Lisi. Washington, DC: Institute of Carmelite Studies, 2010.

– 'Libro de la vida.' In *Obras completas*, edited by Efrén de la Madre de Dios and Otger Steggink, 31–232. Madrid: Biblioteca de Autores Cristianos, 2003.

– *The Life of Saint Teresa of Jesus: The Autobiography of Teresa of Avila.* Translated by E. Allison Peers. New York: Image Books, 1991.

– 'Moradas del castillo interior.' In *Obras completas*, edited by Efrén de la Madre de Dios and Otger Steggink, 469–583. Madrid: Biblioteca de Autores Cristianos, 2003.

– 'The Way of Perfection.' In *The Collected Works of St. Teresa of Avila*, edited by Kieran Kavanaugh and Otilio Rodriguez, 2:39–206. Washington, DC: ICS Publications, 1980.

Baer, Yitzhak. *A History of the Jews in Christian Spain.* 2 vols. Philadelphia: The Jewish Publication Society of America, 1978.

Báez Rubí, Linda. *Mnemosine novohispánica: Retórica e imágenes en el siglo XVI.* Mexico City: Universidad Nacional Autónoma de México, 2005.

Barrera-Osorio, Antonio. *Experiencing Nature: The Spanish American Empire and the Early Scientific Revolution.* Austin: University of Texas Press, 2006.

Barroso, Santiago. *La 'Subida del Monte Sión' y la 'Subida del Monte Carmelo': (Dos sendas parallelas).* Murcia, Spain: Pontificia Studiorum Universitas AS Thomas Aquinas in Urbe, 1970.

Bartlett, Anne Clark, and Thomas H. Bestul, eds. *Cultures of Piety: Medieval English Devotional Texts in Translation.* Ithaca, NY: Cornell University Press, 1999.

Bataillon, Marcel. *Erasmo y España: Estudios sobre la historia espiritual del siglo XVI*. Translated by A. Alatorre. 2 vols. 2nd rev. ed. Mexico: Fondo de Cultura Económica, 1950.
Beckwith, Sarah. *Christ's Body: Identity, Culture and Society in Late Medieval Writings*. London: Routledge, 1993.
Beinart, Heim. *Conversos on Trial: The Inquisition in Cuidad Real*. Jerusalem: Magnes Press, 1981.
Bell, Rudolph M. *Holy Anorexia*. Chicago: University of Chicago Press, 1985.
Bennett, Jill. 'Stigmata and Sense Memory: St. Francis and the Affective Image.' *Art History* 24, no. 1 (2001): 1–16.
Berbara, Maria. '"Este pena tan sabrosa": Teresa of Avila and the Figurative Arts in Early Modern Europe.' In *The Sense of Suffering: Constructions of Physical Pain in Early Modern Culture*, edited by Jan Frans van Dijkhuizen and Karl A.E. Enenkel, 267–98. Leiden: Brill, 2009.
Berceo, Gonzalo de. 'El duelo de la Virgen.' In *Obras completas III*, edited by Brian Dutton, 17–51. London: Tamesis Books, 1975.
Berndt, Rainer. 'The School of St. Victor in Paris.' In *Hebrew Bible / Old Testament: The History of Its Interpretation*, edited by Magne Saebo, vol. 1, *The Middle Ages*, 467–95. Göttingen: Vandenhoeck & Ruprecht, 2000.
Bestul, Thomas H. *Texts of the Passion: Latin Devotional Literature and Medieval Society*. Philadelphia: University of Pennsylvania Press, 1996.
Biernoff, Suzannah. *Sight and Embodiment in the Middle Ages*. New York: Palgrave MacMillan, 2002.
Bildhauer, Bettina. *Medieval Blood*. Cardiff: University of Wales Press, 2006.
Bilinkoff, Jodi. *The Avila of Saint Teresa: Religious Reform in a Sixteenth-Century City*. Ithaca, NY: Cornell University Press, 1989.
– 'Establishing Authority: A Peasant Visionary and Her Audience in Early Sixteenth-Century Spain.' *Studia Mystica* 18 (1997): 36–59.
Bloch, David. *Aristotle on Memory and Recollection: Text, Translation, Interpretation, and Reception in Western Scholasticism*. Leiden: Brill, 2007.
Bodenstedt, Sister Mary Immaculate. *The Vita Christi of Ludolphus the Carthusian: A Dissertation*. Washington, DC: The Catholic University of America Press, 1944.
Bodian, Miriam. *Dying in the Law of Moses: Crypto-Jewish Martyrdom in the Iberian World*. Bloomington: Indiana University Press, 2007.
Boesel, Chris, and Catherine Keller. *Apophatic Bodies: Negative Theology, Incarnation, and Relationality*. New York: Fordham University Press, 2009.
Bolzoni, Lina. *The Gallery of Memory: Literary and Iconographic Models in the Age of the Printing Press*. Toronto: University of Toronto Press, 2001.

Bonaventure. 'Las tres vias o incendio de amor.' In *Obras de San Buenaventura: Edición bilingüe*, vol. 4, edited by Bernardo Aperribay, Miguel Oromi, and Miguel Oltra, 4:102–40. Madrid: Biblioteca de Autores Cristianos, 1963.

– 'The Life of St. Francis.' In *The Soul's Journey into God; The Tree of Life; The Life of St. Francis*, translated by Ewert H. Cousins. 177–328. Mahweh, NJ: Paulist Press, 1978.

– 'Soliloquio.' In *Obras de San Buenaventura: Edición bilingüe,* vol. 4, edited by Bernardo Aperribay, Miguel Oromi, and Miguel Oltra, 147–245. Madrid: Biblioteca de Autores Cristianos, 1963.

– *The Soul's Journey into God; The Tree of Life; The Life of St. Francis.* Translated by Ewert H. Cousins. Mahweh, NJ: Paulist Press, 1978.

– 'Tree of Life.' In *The Soul's Journey Into God; The Tree of Life; The Life of St. Francis*, translated by Ewert H. Cousins, 117–76. Mahweh, NJ: Paulist Press, 1978.

– 'Vida perfecta para religiosas.' In *Obras de San Buenaventura: Edicion bilingüe,* vol. 4, edited by Bernardo Aperribay, Miguel Oromi, and Miguel Oltra, 331–85. Madrid: Biblioteca de Autores Cristianos, 1963.

Bono, James J. 'Medical Spirits and the Medieval Language of Life.' *Traditio* 40 (1984): 91–130.

Boon, Jessica A. 'The Agony of the Virgin: The Swoons and Crucifixion of Mary in Sixteenth Century Castilian Passion Treatises.' *Sixteenth Century Journal* 38, no. 1 (2007): 3–26.

– 'Christ at Heavenly Play: Christology through Mary's Eyes in the Sermons of Juana de la Cruz (1481–1534).' *Archiv für Reformationsgeschichte* 102 (2011): 243–66.

– 'A Full-Figured Paradox: Mary Magdalene as Prostitute, Apostle, Virgin, Ascetic, and Contemplative.' In *The Prado at the Meadows*, vol. 2, *Jusepe de Ribera's Mary Magdalene in a New Context*, edited by Robert R. Belanger, 91–101. Dallas: Meadows Museum, Southern Methodist University, 2011.

– 'The Glory of the Virgin: The Mariology of the Incarnation in Early Modern Castilian Mystical Sermons.' *La Corónica*, forthcoming.

– 'Medical Bodies, Mystical Bodies: Medieval Physiological Theory in the Recollection Mysticism of Bernardino de Laredo.' *Viator* 39, no. 2 (2008): 245–68.

– 'Mother Juana de la Cruz: Marian Visions and Female Preaching.' In *A New Companion to Hispanic Mysticism*, edited by Hilaire Kallendorf, 127–48. Leiden: Brill, 2010.

– 'A Mystic in the Age of the Inquisition: Bernardino de Laredo's *Converso* Environment and Christological Spirituality.' *Medieval Encounters* 12, no. 2 (2006): 133–52.

– 'The Mystical Language of Recollection: Bernardino de Laredo and the *Subida del Monte Sión*.' PhD diss., University of Pennsylvania, 2004.
– 'Trinitarian Love Mysticism: Hadewijch, Ruusbroec, and the Gendered Experience of the Divine.' *Church History* 72 (2003): 484–503.
Boyle, Marjorie O'Rourke. 'Augustine's Heartbeat: From Time to Eternity.' *Viator* 38, no. 1 (2007): 19–43.
Bradwardine, Thomas. *Geometria speculatiua Thome brauardini: Recoligens omnes conclusiones geometricas studentibus artium & philosophie aristotelis valde necessarias simul cum quodam tractatu de quadratura circuli nouiter edito*. Edited by Pedro Ciruelo. Paris: Jean Marchant, 1511.
– 'On Acquiring a Trained Memory.' In *The Medieval Craft of Memory: An Anthology of Texts and Pictures*, edited by Mary Carruthers and Jan M. Ziolkowski, 205–14. Philadelphia: University of Pennsylvania Press, 2002.
Breeze, Andrew. 'The Number of Christ's Wounds.' *The Bulletin of the Board of Celtic Studies* 32 (1985): 84–91.
Brooks, Lynn Matluck. *The Dances of the Processions of Seville in Spain's Golden Age*. Kassel, Germany: Edition Reichenberger, 1988.
Buell, Denise Kimber. *Why This New Race: Ethnic Reasoning in Early Christianity*. New York: Columbia University Press, 2005.
Bujanda, J.M. de. *Index de l'Inquisition espagnole, 1583, 1584*. Geneva: Droz, 1993.
– ed. *Index des livres interdits*. 11 vols. Geneva: Droz, 1984–2002.
Bultman, Dana. *Heretical Mixtures: Feminine and Poetic Opposition to Matter-Spirit Dualism in Spain, 1531–1631*. Valencia: Albatros-Hispanófilia Siglo XXI, 2007.
Butler, Judith. *Bodies That Matter: On the Discursive Limits of 'Sex.'* New York: Routledge, 1993.
Bynum, Caroline Walker. *Christian Materiality: An Essay on Religion in Late Medieval Europe*. New York: Zone Books, 2011.
– *Holy Feast and Holy Fast : The Religious Significance of Food to Medieval Women*. Berkeley: University of California Press, 1987.
– *Jesus as Mother: Studies in the Spirituality of the High Middle Ages*. Berkeley: University of California Press, 1982.
– 'Material Continuity, Personal Survival, and the Resurrection of the Body: A Scholastic Discussion in Its Medieval and Modern Contexts.' In *Fragmentation and Redemption: Essays on Gender and the Human Body in Medieval Religion*, 239–98. New York: Zone Books, 1992.
– *The Resurrection of the Body in Western Christianity, 200–1336*. New York: Columbia University Press, 1995.
– 'Violence Occluded: The Wound in Christ's Side in Late Medieval Devotion.' In *Feud, Violence and Practice: Essays in Medieval Studies in Honor of Stephen*

D. White, edited by Belle S. Tuten and Tracey L. Billado, 95–118. Burlington, VT: Ashgate, 2010.

– 'Violent Imagery in Late Medieval Piety.' *GHI Bulletin* 30 (2002): 1–34.

– 'Why All the Fuss about the Body? A Medievalist's Perspective.' *Critical Inquiry* 22 (1995): 1–33.

– *Wonderful Blood: Theology and Practice in Late Medieval Northern Germany and Beyond*. Philadelphia: University of Pennsylvania Press, 2007.

Cabré, Montserrat. 'Women or Healers? Household Practices and the Categories of Health Care in Late Medieval Iberia.' *Bulletin of the History of Medicine* 82, no. 1 (2008): 18–51.

Calvert, Laura. *Francisco de Osuna and the Spirit of the Letter*. Chapel Hill: University of North Carolina Department of Romance Languages, 1973.

Calvo Moralejo, Gaspar. 'La compasión corredentora de María en fray Bernardino de Laredo.' *Estudios Marianos* 48 (1983): 421–41.

Camille, Michael. 'Before the Gaze: The Internal Senses and Late Medieval Practices of Seeing.' In *Visuality Before and Beyond the Renaissance: Seeing as Others Saw*, edited by Robert S. Nelson, 197–223. Cambridge: Cambridge University Press, 2000.

– *The Gothic Idol: Ideology and Image-Making in Medieval Art*. Cambridge: Cambridge University Press, 1989.

Campo, Alonso del. 'Auto de la passión.' In *Teatro medieval*, edited by Ana Maria Álvarez Pellitero, 183–207. Madrid: Espasa-Calpe, 1990.

Cañizares-Esguerra, Jorge. 'Iberian Science in the Renaissance: Ignored How Much Longer?' *Perspectives on Science* 12, no. 1 (2004): 86–124.

Carlson, Marla. 'Pain and the Brain: Comparing Contemporary and Medieval Neuroscience as Explanations for Spectator Response to Torture.' Paper presented at the International Medieval Congress, Kalamazoo, MI, May 7–10, 2009.

– *Performing Bodies in Pain: Medieval and Post-Modern Martyrs, Mystics, and Artists*. New York: Palgrave MacMillan, 2010.

Carrera-Marcén, Elena. *Teresa of Avila's Autobiography: Authority, Power, and the Self in Mid-Sixteenth-Century Spain*. London: MHRA, 2005.

Carrión, María M. *Arquitectura y cuerpo en la figura autorial de Teresa de Jesús*. Barcelona: Anthropos, 1994.

– 'Home, Sweet Home: Teresa de Jesús, Mudéjar Architecture, and the Place of Mysticism in Early Modern Spain.' In *A New Companion to Hispanic Mysticism*, edited by Hilaire Kallendorf, 343–66. Leiden: Brill, 2010.

– 'Scent of a Mystic Woman: Teresa de Jesús and the Interior Castle.' *Medieval Encounters* 15, no. 1 (2009): 130–56.

Carruthers, Mary. *The Book of Memory: A Study of Memory in Medieval Culture*. Cambridge: Cambridge University Press, 1990.

– *The Craft of Thought: Meditation, Rhetoric, and the Making of Images, 400–1200*. Cambridge: Cambridge University Press, 1998.

– 'Reading with Attitude, Remembering the Book.' In *The Book and the Body*, edited by Dolores Warwick Frese and Katherine O'Brien O'Keeffe, 1–33. Notre Dame, IN: University of Notre Dame Press, 1997.

Castañega, Martin de. *Tratado de las supersticiones y hechicerias*. Edited by Agustín G. de Amezúa. Madrid: Sociedad de Bibliófilos Españoles, 1946.

Castro, Manuel de. *Catálogo general de incunables en bibliotecas españolas*. 2 vols. Madrid: Biblioteca Nacional, 1990.

– *Manuscritos franciscanos de la Biblioteca Nacional de Madrid*. Madrid: Servicio de Publicaciones del Ministerio de Educación y Ciencia, 1973.

Catalogue of Books Printed in Spain and of Spanish Books Printed Elsewhere in Europe before 1601 Now in the British Library. London: The British Library, 1989.

Certeau, Michel de. *The Mystic Fable*. Vol. 1, *The Sixteenth and Seventeenth Centuries*. Translated by Michael B. Smith. Chicago: University of Chicago Press, 1992.

Chanca, Diego Alvarez. 'Tratado del ojo/Tractatus de fascinatione, 1495.' In *Tratado de la fascinación*, edited by Fernando Pagés Larraya, Julieta María Consigli, and Estela María Astrada, 166–206. Córdoba, Argentina: Prosopis Editoral, 1998.

Chatillon, Jean. 'Les trois modes de la contemplation selon Richard de Saint-Victor.' *Bulletin de littérature ecclésiastique* 41 (1940): 3–26.

Chaunu, Pierre. *Seville et l'Amérique: XVIe–XVIIe siècles*. Paris: Flammarion, 1977.

Chaunu, Pierre, and Huguette Chaunu. *Seville et l'Atlantique (1504–1650)*. 8 vols. Paris: Armand Colin, 1955–6.

Chavero Blanco, Francisco de Ásis. 'Fray Bernardino de Laredo y su *Subida del Monte Sión*: Una visión cristiana del hombre.' In *IV Curso de Verano: El franciscanismo en Andalucía: San Francisco en la cultura andaluza e hispanoamericana*, edited by Manuel Peláez del Rosal, 585–618. Córdoba: CajaSur, 2000.

Chorpenning, Joseph F. 'The Monastery, Paradise, and the Castle: Literary Images and Spiritual Development in St. Teresa of Ávila.' *Bulletin of Hispanic Studies* 62 (1985): 245–57.

Christian, William A., Jr. *Apparitions in Late Medieval and Renaissance Spain*. Princeton, NJ: Princeton University Press, 1981.

– *Local Religion in Sixteenth-Century Spain*. Princeton, NJ: Princeton University Press, 1981.

Clark, Anne L. 'Why All the Fuss About the Mind?: A Medievalist's Perspective on Cognitive Theory.' In *History in the Comic Mode: Medieval Communities and the Matter of Person*, edited by Rachel Fulton and Bruce W. Holsinger, 170–81. New York: Columbia University Press, 2007.

Clark, David L. 'Optics for Preachers: The *De oculo morali* by Peter of Limoges.' *Michigan Academician* 9 (1977): 329–43.

Clarke, Edwin, Kenneth Dewhurst, and Michael Jeffrey Aminoff. *An Illustrated History of Brain Function: Imaging the Brain from Antiquity to the Present.* 2nd ed. San Francisco: Norman Publishing, 1996.

Clavería, Carlos, ed. *Arte de prohibir libros: Indice de libros prohibidos 1559.* Barcelona: Delstres, 2001.

Coakley, Sarah, and Charles M. Stang. *Re-Thinking Dionysius the Areopagite.* Malden, MA: Wiley-Blackwell, 2009.

Cohen, Esther. 'The Animated Pain of the Body.' *The American Historical Review* 105, no. 1 (2000): 36–68.

– 'The Expression of Pain in the Later Middle Ages: Deliverance, Acceptance and Infamy.' In *Bodily Extremities: Preoccupations with the Human Body in Early Modern European Culture*, edited by Florike Egmond and Robert Zwijnenberg, 195–219. Burlington, VT: Ashgate, 2003.

– *The Modulated Scream: Pain in Late Medieval Culture*. Chicago: University of Chicago Press, 2010.

Cohen, Jeremy. *Christ Killers: The Jews and the Passion from the Bible to the Big Screen*. Oxford: Oxford University Press, 2007.

Coleman, Janet. *Ancient and Medieval Memories: Studies in the Reconstruction of the Past*. Cambridge: Cambridge University Press, 1992.

Colombás, García M. *Un reformador benedictino en tiempo de los Reyes Católicos: García Jiménez de Cisneros, abad de Montserrat*. Montserrat, Spain: Abadía de Montserrat, 1955.

Constable, Giles. 'The Interpretation of Mary and Martha.' In *Three Studies in Medieval Religious and Social Thought*, 1–141. Cambridge: Cambridge University Press, 1995.

Cook, William. 'Giotto and the Figure of Saint Francis.' In *The Cambridge Companion to Giotto*, edited by Anne Derbes and Mark Sandona, 135–56. Cambridge: University of Cambridge, 2004.

Coolman, Boyd Taylor. *Knowing God by Experience: The Spiritual Senses in the Theology of William of Auxerre*. Washington, DC: The Catholic University of America Press, 2004.

Cousins, Ewert H. 'Francis of Assisi: Christian Mysticism at the Crossroads.' In *Mysticism and Religious Traditions*, edited by Steven T. Katz, 163–90. Oxford: Oxford University Press, 1983.

Covarrubias Orozco, Sebastián de. *Parte primera del Tesoro de la lengua castellana*. Madrid: Melchor Sánchez: 1674. Alicante: Biblioteca Virtual Miguel de Cervantes, 2006.

– *Tesoro de la lengua castellana o española (1611)*. Edited by Felipe C.E. Maldonado and Manuel Camarero. 2nd rev. ed. Madrid: Editorial Castalia, 1995.

Crawford, Michael. 'Honor or Financial Calculation: The Desire for *Hidalgo* Status in Sixteenth-Century Castile.' Paper presented at the Society for Spanish and Portuguese Historical Studies, Madrid, 4 July 2003.

Cuevas García, Cristóbal. *La prosa métrica: Teoría: Fay (sic) Bernardino de Laredo: Estructuración y relaciones con el verso*. Granada: Universidad de Granada, 1972.

Cuevas Muñoz, Juan Antonio. *Efemérides de las hermandades y cofradías de Sevilla*. Alicante: Fundación Cofrade, 2002.

Daly, Walter J., and Robert D. Yee. 'The Eye Book of Master Peter of Spain: A Glimpse of Diagnosis and Treatment of Eye Disease in the Middle Ages.' *Documenta Ophthalmologica* 103 (2001): 119–53.

Dangler, Jean. *Making Difference in Medieval and Early Modern Iberia*. Notre Dame, IN: University of Notre Dame Press, 2005.

Davlin, Mary Clemente. *The Place of God in Piers Plowman and Medieval Art*. Burlington, VT: Ashgate, 2001.

D'Avray, David L. 'Some Franciscan Ideas about the Body.' *Archivum Franciscanum Historicum* 84 (1991): 343–63.

Dawson, David. 'Transcendence as Embodiment: Augustine's Domestication of Gnosis.' *Modern Theology* 10, no. 1 (1994): 1–26.

Debus, Allen G. *The Chemical Philosophy: Paracelsian Science and Medicine in the Sixteenth and Seventeenth Centuries*. New York: Science History Publications, 1977.

Delbrugge, Laura. 'A Humanist's Guide to Publishing: Issues of Marketing and Faith in the *Thesoro de la passion* (Hurus: Zaragoza, 1494).' Paper presented at the International Medieval Congress, Kalamazoo, MI, 16 May 2010.

– *A Scholarly Edition of Andrés de Li's 'Thesoro de la passion' (1494)*. Leiden: Brill, 2011.

Denery, Dallas G., II. *Seeing and Being Seen in the Later Medieval World: Optics, Theology, and Religious Life*. Cambridge: Cambridge University Press, 2005.

Diego de San Pedro. *La pasión trobada* (facsimile of Salamanca, 1494–5 edition). In *Tercera floresta de incunables*, edited by Antonío Pérez y Gómez. Valencia: Talleres de Típografia Moderna, 1959.

Dijkhuizen, Jan Frans van, and Karl A.E. Enenkel. 'Introduction: Constructions of Physical Pain in Early Modern Culture.' In *The Sense of Suffering: Constructions of Physical Pain in Early Modern Culture*, edited by Jan Frans van Dijkhuizen and Karl A.E. Enenkel, 1–18. Leiden: Brill, 2009.

Dionysius the Areopagite (Pseudo). 'Mystical Theology.' In *Complete Works*, 135–41. New York: Paulist Press, 1987.

Domínguez Ortiz, Antonio. 'La población del reino de Sevilla en 1534.' In *Andalucía, de la Edad Media a la Moderna*, 337–55. Madrid: Instituto Jerónimo Zurita, CSIC, 1977.

Edelmayer, Frederich. 'Carlos V y su tiempo.' In *Libro de Horas de Carlos I, Emperador Carlos V: Ms. 411 de la Beinecke Library*, edited by Roger S. Wieck, 53–136. Madrid: Edilán-Ars Libris, 2000.

Elliott, Dyan. 'True Presence/False Christ: The Antinomies of Embodiment in Medieval Spirituality.' *Mediaeval Studies* 64 (2002): 241–65.

Encina, Juan del. 'Representación a la muy bendita passión y muerte de nuestro precioso Redentor.' In *Juan del Encina: Obras completas IV: Teatro*, edited by Ana María Rambaldo, 19–31. Madrid: Espasa-Calpe, 1983.

Enders, Jody. *The Medieval Theater of Cruelty: Rhetoric, Memory, Violence.* Ithaca, NY: Cornell University Press, 1999.

– 'Rhetoric, Coercion, and the Memory of Violence.' In *Criticism and Dissent in the Middle Ages*, edited by Rita Copeland, 24–55. Cambridge: Cambridge University Press, 1996.

Fasciculus myrrhe: El qual trata de la passion de nuestro redemptor Jesu Christo Seville: Juan Varela de Salamanca, 1524.

Fauconnier, Gilles, and Mark Turner. *The Way We Think: Conceptual Blending and the Mind's Hidden Complexities.* New York: Basic Books, 2002.

Fernández, Juan Gil. 'Los comienzos del cristianismo en Sevilla.' In *Iglesías de Sevilla, Huelva, Jedrez y Cádiz y Ceuta*, edited by José Sánchez Herrero, 1–58. Madrid: Biblioteca de Autores Cristianos, 2002.

Fernández, Lucas. *Auto de la pasión.* Edited by Marciano Cuesta Polo. Segovia: Caja de Ahorros de Segovia, 1995.

Fernández Álvarez, Manuel. *La sociedad española del Renacimiento.* 2nd rev. ed. Madrid: Ediciones Cátedra, 1974.

Fernández del Castillo, Francisco. *Libros y libreros en el siglo XVI.* Mexico: Fondo de Cultura Económica, 1982.

Ferrand, Manuel. *El retablo mayor de la Catedral de Sevilla: Estudios e investigaciones realizadas con motivo de su restauración.* Seville: Monte de Piedad y Caja de Ahorros, 1981.

Flor, Fernando R. de la. *Emblemas: Lecturas de la imagen simbólica.* Madrid: Alianza Editorial, 1995.

– 'La literatura espiritual del siglo de oro y la organización retórica de la memoria.' *Revista de literatura* 45, no. 90 (1983): 39–85.

Flory, David A. *Marian Representations in the Miracle Tales of Thirteenth-Century Spain and France.* Washington, DC: The Catholic University of America Press, 2000.

Flynn, Maureen. 'Mimesis of the Last Judgment: The Spanish *Auto de fe*.' *Sixteenth Century Journal* 22 (1991): 218–97.

– 'The Spiritual Uses of Pain in Spanish Mysticism.' *Journal of the American Academy of Religion* 62, no. 2 (1996): 257–78.

Folch Andreu, Rafael. 'El primer libro propiamente de farmacia escrito en castellano.' *Anales de la Universidad de Madrid* 2, nos. 2–3 (1933): 1–53.

Folger, Rober. *Escape from the Prison of Love: Caloric Identities and Writing Subjects in Fifteenth Century Spain*. Chapel Hill: University of North Carolina Press, 2009.

– *Images in Mind: Lovesickness, Spanish Sentimental Fiction and 'Don Quijote.'* Chapel Hill: University of North Carolina Press, 2002.

Foronda, Bienvenido. 'Fray Bernardino de Laredo, su vida, sus escritos, y su doctrina ascética-mística.' *Archivo Ibero-Americano* 33 (1930): 213–50, 497–526.

Franklin, James C. *Mystical Transformations: The Imagery of Liquids in the Work of Mechthild von Magdeburg*. Madison, NJ: Fairleigh Dickinson University Press, 1978.

Freedberg, David. *The Power of Images: Studies in the History and Theory of Response*. Chicago: University of Chicago Press, 1989.

Fremaux-Crouzet, Annie. 'Franciscanisme des villes et franciscanisme des champs dans l'Espagne du Bas Moyen Âge.' *Annales de la Faculté des Lettres et Sciences Humaines de Nice* 46 (1983): 53–65.

Fulton, Rachel. 'Afterword: History in the Comic Mode.' In *History in the Comic Mode: Medieval Communities and the Matter of Person*, edited by Rachel Fulton and Bruce W. Holsinger, 279–92. New York: Columbia University Press, 2007.

– *From Judgment to Passion: Devotion to Christ and the Virgin Mary, 800–1200*. New York: Columbia University Press, 2002.

Fulton, Rachel, and Bruce W. Holsinger, eds. *History in the Comic Mode: Medieval Communities and the Matter of Person*. New York: Columbia University Press, 2007.

Galen. *On the Usefulness of the Parts of the Body*. Translated by Margaret Tallmadge May. Ithaca, NY: Cornell University Press, 1968.

García, Gómez. *Carro de dos vidas*. Edited by Melquíades Andrés. Madrid: Fundación Universitaria Española, 1988.

García Ballester, Luis. 'The Circulation and Use of Medical Manuscripts in Arabic in Sixteenth-Century Spain.' *Journal for the History of Arabic Science* 3 (1979): 183–99.

– *La búsqueda de la salud: Sanadores y enfermos en la España medieval*. Barcelona: Ediciones Península, 2001.

García Ballester, Luis, Michael R. McVaugh, and Agustín Rubio-Vela. *Medical Licensing and Learning in Fourteenth-Century Valencia*. Philadelphia: The American Philosophical Society, 1989.

García-Baquero, Antonio, ed. *Sevilla*. Madrid: Editorial MAPFRE, 1992.

García de Cisneros, Jiménez. *Book of Exercises for the Spiritual Life*. Translated by E. Allison Peers. Montserrat, Spain: Abadía de Montserrat, 1929.

– *Ejercitatorio de la vida espiritual*. Edited by R.P. Fausto Curiel. Barcelona: Luis Gili, 1912.

García de la Concha Delgado, Federico. 'El vía crucis a la cruz del campo: Origen y desarrollo histórico.' In *El Humilladero de la Cruz del Campo y la religiosidad sevillana*, edited by José Roda Peña, Manuel García Fernández, and Federico García de la Concha Delgado, 63–84. Seville: Fundación Cruzcampo, 1999.

García Oro, José. *El Cardenal Cisneros: Vida y empresas*. 2 vols. Madrid: Biblioteca de Autores Cristianos, 1992.

– *Francisco de Asís en la España medieval*. Santiago de Compostela: Consejo Superior de Investigaciones Cientificas, Liceo Franciscano, 1988.

– 'Observantes, Recoletos, Descalzos: La monarquía católica y el reformismo religioso del siglo XVI.' In *Actas del congreso internacional sanjuanista*, 2:53–98. Valladolid: Junta de Castilla y León, 1993.

Geertz, Clifford. 'Religion as a Cultural System.' 1966. In *The Interpretation of Cultures: Selected Essays*, 87–125. New York: Basic Books, 1973.

Gerli, E. Michael. '*El castillo interior* y el *ars memorativa*.' *Bulletin Hispanique* 86, nos. 1–2 (1984): 154–63.

Gerson, Jean. 'The Mountain of Contemplation.' In *Early Works*, edited by Brian Patrick McGuire, 75–127. New York: Paulist Press, 1998.

– 'On Distinguishing True from False Revelations.' In *Early Works*, edited by Brian Patrick McGuire, 334–64. New York: Paulist Press, 1998.

Gestoso y Pérez, José. *Noticias inéditas de impresores sevillanos*. Seville: Gomez Hermanos, 1924.

Gil, Juan. 'La enseñanza del latín en Sevilla en la época del descubrimiento.' *Excerpta Philologica* 1, no. 1 (1991): 259–80.

– *Los conversos y la Inquisición sevillana*. 8 vols. Seville: Universidad de Sevilla, Fundación El Monte, 2000–3.

Giles, Mary E. Introduction to *The Third Spiritual Alphabet*, by Francisco de Osuna, 1–34. New York: Paulist Press, 1981.

– ed. *Mujeres en la Inquisición: La persecución del Santo Oficio y el Nuevo Mundo*. Barcelona: Editorial Martínez Roca, 2000.

Giordano, María Laura. '"La ciudad de nuestra conciencia": Los conversos y la construcción de la identidad judeocristiana (1449–1556).' *Hispania Sacra* 57 (2010): 43–91.

Girón-Negrón, Luis M. 'Dionysian Thought in Sixteenth-Century Spanish Mystical Theology.' In *Re-Thinking Dionysius the Areopagite*, edited by Sarah Coakley and Charles M. Stang, 163–76. Malden, MA: Wiley-Blackwell, 2009.

Gitlitz, David M. *Secrecy and Deceit: The Religion of the Crypto-Jews*. Philadelphia: The Jewish Publication Society, 1996.

Glucklich, Ariel. 'Sacred Pain and the Phenomenal Self.' *Harvard Theological Review* 91, no. 4 (1998): 389–412.

Gómez Canseco, Luis. 'Poetas, humanistas, y cortesanos en la Sevilla del Emperador.' In *Orto hispalensis: Arte y cultura en la Sevilla del emperador*, edited by Arsenio Moreno Mendoza, 105–12. Seville: Patronato del Real Alcázar, 2001.

Gómez-Menor, José-Carlos. 'Linaje judío de escritores religiosos y místicos españoles del siglo XVI.' In *Judíos, Sefarditas, Conversos: La expulsión de 1492 y sus consecuencias*, edited by Angel Alcalá, 587–600. Valladolid: Ámbito, 1995.

Gonzaga, Francisco. *De ordine seraphicae religionis franciscanae eiusque progressibus*. Rome, 1587.

González de Fauve, María Estela, and Patricia de Forteza. 'Ética médica y mala praxis en Castilla: Una visión realista del quehacer profesional (siglos XIV–XVI).' In *Ciencia, poder e ideología: El saber y el hacer en la evolución de la medicina española (siglos XIV–XVIII)*, edited by María Estela González de Fauve, 13–60. Buenos Aires: Universidad de Buenos Aires, 2001.

González Novalín, José Luis. 'Las misas "artificiosamente ordenadas" en los misales e escritos renacentistas.' In *Doce consideraciones sobre el mundo hispano-italiano en tiempos de Alfonso y Juan de Valdés*, 281–96. Rome: Instituto Español de Lengua y Literatura de Roma, 1979.

Gormley, Joan Frances. Introduction to *John of Avila: Listen, O Daughter*, edited by Joan Frances Gormley, 1–33. New York: Paulist Press, 2006.

Gorricio de Novara, Dom Gaspar. *Contemplaciones sobre el Rosario de Nuestra Señora historiadas: Un incunable sevillano*. Edited by Santiago Cantera Montenegro and Almudena Torrego Casado. Salzburg: Universität Salzburg, 2002.

Gracia Guillén, Diego. 'Judaism, Medicine, and the Inquisitorial Mind in Sixteenth-Century Spain.' In *The Spanish Inquisition and the Inquisitorial Mind*, edited by Ángel Alcalá, 375–400. Boulder, CO: Social Science Monographs, 1987.

– 'La fisiología escolástica de Fray Bernardino de Laredo.' *Cuadernos de Historia de la Medicina Española* 12 (1973): 125–92.

Gracia Guillén, Diego, and José Luis Peset. 'La medicina en la Baja Edad Media Latina (siglos XIV y XV).' In *Historia universal de la medicina III*, edited by Pedro Lain Entralgo, 338–49. Barcelona: Salvat, 1972.

Graña Cid, María del Mar. 'Terciarias franciscanas, apostolado y ministerios: Juana de la Cruz y el sacerdocio femenino.' In *El Franciscanismo en la península ibérica: Balance y perspectivas. I Congreso Internacional, Madrid, September 22–27, 2003*, edited by María del Mar Graña Cid, 601–22. Barcelona: Asociación Hispánica de Estudios Franciscanos, 2005.

Gregory of Nazianzus. *On God and Christ*. Crestwood, NY: St. Vladimir's Press, 2002.

Gregory the Great. *The Homilies of Saint Gregory the Great on the Book of the Prophet Ezekiel.* Translated by Theodosia Gray. Edited by Juliana Cownie. Etna, CA: Center for Traditionalist Orthodox Studies, 1990.

Griffin, Clive. *The Crombergers of Seville: The History of a Printing and Merchant Dynasty.* Oxford: Clarendon Press, 1988.

Guadalupe, Andrés de. *Historia de la Santa Provincia de Los Angeles.* Edited by Antolín Abad Pérez. Cronicas Franciscanas de España 9. Madrid: Mateo Fernández, 1622. Reprint, Madrid: Editorial Cisneros, 1994.

Guía de los archivos de la iglésia en España. Available at http://perso.club-internet.fr/punsola/punsola/menu/Sevilla.pdf.

Guillén, Claudio. 'Un padrón de conversos sevillanos (1510).' *Bulletin Hispanique* 65 (1963): 48–98.

Haliczer, Stephen H. *The Comuneros of Castile: The Forging of a Revolution, 1475–1521.* Madison: University of Wisconsin Press, 1981.

Hamburger, Jeffrey F. *The Visual and the Visionary: Art and Female Spirituality in Late Medieval Germany.* New York: Zone Books, 1998.

Hames, Harvey J. *Art of Conversion: Christianity and Kabbalah in the Thirteenth Century.* Leiden: Brill, 2000.

Hamilton, Alastair. 'The *Alumbrados*: *Dejamiento* and Its Practitioners.' In *A New Companion to Hispanic Mysticism*, edited by Hilaire Kallendorf, 103–26. Leiden: Brill, 2010.

– *Heresy and Mysticism in Sixteenth-Century Spain: The Alumbrados.* Cambridge: James Clarke, 1992.

Harris, A. Katie. *From Muslim to Christian Granada: Inventing a City's Past in Early Modern Spain.* Baltimore: Johns Hopkins University Press, 2007.

Harvey, E. Ruth. *The Inward Wits: Psychological Theory in the Middle Ages and the Renaissance.* London: Warburg Institute, 1975.

Hatzfeld, Helmut. 'Influencia de Raimundo Lulio y Jan van Rusybroeck en el lenguaje de los místicos españoles.' In *Estudios literarios sobre mística española*, 35–115. Madrid: Editorial Gredos, 1968.

Hernández Benito, Emiliano. *El saber oftalmologico en la medicina renacentista española.* Salamanca: Universidad de Salamanca, 1957.

Hernández Moreno, Roberto. *El hombre del Monte Sión: Antropología religiosa de Fr. B. de Laredo, ofm.* Paris, 1967. Reprint, Mexico: R. Hernández Moreno, 2000.

Herp (Harphius), Enrique (Hendrik). *Directorio de contemplativos.* Translated from the Latin by Juan Martin Kelly. Madrid: Fundación Universitaria Española, 1974.

Herrera Casado, Antonio. *Monasterios medievales de Guadalajara.* Guadalajara: Aache, 1997.

Herrera García, Francisco Javier. 'Los orígenes de una afortunada creación artística: El retablo gótico en Sevilla.' In *El retablo sevillano: Desde sus orígenes a la actualidad*, edited by Fátima Halcon, Francisco Javier Herrera García, and Álvaro Recio, 15–68. Seville: Fundación Cajasol, 2009.

Herrero, J.L., and M.J. Mancho. 'La neología en la mística española temprana: La *Subida del Monte Sión* de Bernardino de Laredo.' *Voces* 7 (1996): 123–58.

Hildegard of Bingen. *Scivias*. Translated by Columba Hart and Jane Bishop. New York: Paulist Press, 1990.

Hillgarth, J.N. *Readers and Books in Majorca, 1229–1550*. Paris: Centre National de la Recherche Scientifique, 1991.

Hillman, David. 'Visceral Knowledge.' In *The Body in Parts: Fantasies of Corporeality in Early Modern Europe*, edited by David Hillman and Carla Mazzio, 81–106. New York: Routledge, 1997.

Hollywood, Amy. *Sensible Ecstasy: Mysticism, Sexual Difference, and the Demands of History*. Chicago: University of Chicago Press, 2002.

– 'That Glorious Slit: Irigaray and the Medieval Devotion to Christ's Side Wound.' In *Luce Irigaray and Premodern Culture: Thresholds of History*, edited by Theresa Krier and Elizabeth D. Harvey, 105–25. New York: Routledge, 2005.

Homza, Lu Ann. 'Conocimiento contra instituciones: La disidencia de Francisco Ortiz, preso del tribunal de Toledo (1529–1532).' Paper presented at the CSIC conference, 'Alumbrados y disidencia religiosa en el mundo ibérico,' Madrid, 24–5 June 2010.

– 'How to Harass an Inquisitor-General: The Polyphonic Law of Friar Francisco Ortíz.' In *A Renaissance of Conflicts: Visions and Revisions of Law and Society in Italy and Spain*, edited by John A. Marino and Thomas Kuehn, 299–336. Toronto: Center for Reformation and Renaissance Studies, University of Toronto, 2004.

– ed. *The Spanish Inquisition, 1478–1614: An Anthology of Sources*. Indianapolis: Hackett Publishing, 2006.

Hood, William. 'The Sacro Monte of Varallo: Renaissance Art and Popular Religion.' In *Monasticism and the Arts*, edited by Timothy Verdon, 291–311. Syracuse, NY: University of Syracuse, 1984.

Hoornaert, Rodolphe. *Sainte Thérèse écrivain: son milieu, ses facultés, son oeuvre*. Paris: Desclée, 1922.

Howe, Elizabeth Teresa. *Mystical Imagery: Santa Teresa de Jesús and San Juan de la Cruz*. New York: Peter Lang, 1988.

Howells, Edward. *John of the Cross and Teresa of Avila: Mystical Knowing and Selfhood*. New York: Crossroad Publishing Company, 2002.

Hundersmarck, Lawrence F. 'Preaching the Passion: Late Medieval *Lives of Christ* as Sermon Vehicles.' In *De Ore Domini: Preacher and Word in the Middle Ages*, edited by Thomas L. Amos, Eugene E. Green, and Beverly Mayne Kienzie, 147–67. Kalamazoo, MI: Medieval Institute Publications, 1989.

Ignatius of Loyola. *The Spiritual Exercises of Ignatius of Loyola*. Translated by Elder Mullan. Available at http://www.ccel.org/ccel/ignatius/exercises.html.

The Illustrated Incunable Short-Title Catalogue on CD-ROM. 2nd ed. Reading: England: Primary Source Media, British Library, 1996.

Innocent III. *On the Misery of the Human Condition (De miseria humane conditionis)*. Translated by Margaret Mary Dietz. Edited by Donald R. Howard. Indianapolis: Bobbs-Merrill, 1969.

'Interpretation of the Pulse.' In *A Source Book of Medieval Science*, edited by Edward Grant, 745–8. Cambridge, MA: Harvard University Press, 1974.

Inventario general de manuscritos de la Biblioteca Nacional. Vol. 14. Madrid: Ministerio de Educación Nacional, Dirección General de Archivos y Bibliotecas, Servicio de Publicaciones, 2000.

Ishikawa, Chiyo. *The 'Retablo de Isabel la Catolica' by Juan de Flandes and Michel Sittow*. Turnhout, Belgium: Brepols, 2004.

Jacquart, Danielle. 'Theory, Everyday Practice, and Three Fifteenth-Century Physicians.' *Osiris* 6 (1990): 140–60.

Jager, Eric. 'The Book of the Heart: Reading and Writing the Medieval Subject.' *Speculum* 71, no. 1 (1996): 1–26.

James, William. *Varieties of Religious Experience*. Edited by Peter J. Gomes. New York: Signet Classic, 2003.

Joannitius (Hunain ibn Ishaq). 'Selections from *Isagogue*.' In *A Source Book of Medieval Science*, edited by Edward Grant, 705–15. Cambridge, MA: Harvard University Press, 1974.

John of the Cross. *The Collected Works of St. John of the Cross*. Translated by Kieran Kavanaugh and Otilio Rodriguez. Washington, DC: Institute of Carmelite Studies, 1991.

– *Obras completas*. Edited by Maximiliano Herráiz. 2nd ed. Salamanca: Ediciones Sígueme, 1992.

Jordan, Mark D. 'The Construction of a Philosophical Medicine: Exegesis and Argument in Salernitan Teaching on the Soul.' *Osiris* 6 (1990): 42–61.

Juan de Avila. *Epistolario espiritual*. Edited by Vicente García de Diego. Madrid: Espasa-Calpe, S.A., 1962.

Juana de la Cruz. *El Conhorte: Sermones de una mujer. La Santa Juana (1481–1534)*. Edited by Inocente García de Andrés. 2 vols. Madrid: Fundación Universitaria Española, 1999.

Kallendorf, Hilaire, ed. *A New Companion to Hispanic Mysticism*. Leiden: Brill, 2010.

Kamen, Henry. *Inquisition and Society in Spain in the Sixteenth and Seventeenth Centuries*. London: Weidenfeld and Nicolson, 1985.

– *The Spanish Inquisition: A Historical Revision*. New Haven, CT: Yale University Press, 1997.

Karnes, Michelle. *Imagination, Meditation, and Cognition in the Middle Ages*. Chicago: University of Chicago Press, 2011.

Kemp, Simon, and Garth J.O. Fletcher. 'The Medieval Theory of the Inner Senses.' *The American Journal of Psychology* 106, no. 4 (1993): 559–76.

Kempis, Thomas à. 'Imitación de Cristo.' In *Imitación de Cristo por Tomas de Kempis y Devocionario por Andrés Pardo*, edited by Francisco Martín Hernandez, 6–248. Madrid: Biblioteca de Autores Cristianos, 1975.

– *The Imitation of Christ*. Translated by Leo Sherley-Price. London: Penguin Books, 1952.

Koren, Sharon Faye. 'The Menstruant as "Other" in Medieval Judaism and Christianity.' *NASHIM: A Journal of Jewish Women's Studies and Gender Issues* 17 (2009): 33–59.

Krüger, Klaus. 'Authenticity and Fiction: On the Pictorial Construction of Inner Presence in Early Modern Italy.' In *Image and Imagination of the Religious Self in Late Medieval and Early Modern Europe*, edited by Reindert Falkenburg, Walter S. Melion, and Todd M. Richardson, 37–69. Turnhout, Belgium: Brepols, 2007.

Kuriyama, Shigehisa. *The Expressiveness of the Body and the Divergence of Greek and Chinese Medicine*. New York: Zone Books, 1999.

Kurtz, Barbara E. 'Allegory and/of Memory: Allegories of Amorous Imprisonment in Medieval Spanish Literature.' *Medievalia et Humanistica*, n.s., 16 (1988): 133–51.

– 'The Small Castle of the Soul: Mysticism and Metaphor in the European Middle Ages.' *Studia Mystica* 15 (1992): 28–35.

Ladero Quesada, Miguel Ángel. *Los Reyes Católicos: La corona y la unidad de España*. Valencia: Asociación Francisco Lopéz de Gómara, 1989.

Laín, Milagro. 'Los inicios de la terminología botánica en castellano: Bernardino de Laredo (1482–1548).' In *Actas del V congreso internacional de historia de la lengua española*, edited by María Teresa Echenique Elizondo and Juan Sánchez Méndez, 2157–72. Madrid: Editorial Gredos, 2002.

Lakoff, George, and Mark Johnson. *Metaphors We Live By*. Chicago: University of Chicago Press, 1980.

– *Philosophy in the Flesh: The Embodied Mind and Its Challenge to Western Thought*. New York: Basic Books, 1999.

Laredo, Bernardino de. *The Ascent of Mount Sion: Being the Third Book of the Treatise of That Name*. Translated by E. Allison Peers. London: Faber and Faber, 1952.

– *Metaphora medicine con DC autoridades declaradas …* Seville: Juan de Varela, 1522.

– *Modus faciendi cum ordine medicandi*. Seville: Juan Cromberger, 1527.

– *Modus faciendi cum ordine medicandi, 1527*. Edited by Milagro Laín and Doris Ruiz Otín: Fundación de Ciencias de la Salud, D.L., 2001.

– *Subida del Monte Sión*. Edited by Juan Bautista Gomis. In *Misticos franciscanos españoles*, vol. 1. Madrid: Biblioteca de Autores Cristianos, 1948.

– *Subida del Monte Sión*. Edited by Alegría Alonso González, Mercedes García Trascasas, and Bertha Gutiérrez. Madrid: Fundación Universitaria Española, 2000.

Lea, Henry Charles. *A History of the Inquisition of Spain*. 4 vols. New York: MacMillan, 1906.

Legarda, Anselmo de. 'Refinamiento literario de la *Subida del Monte Sión*.' *Verdad y Vida* 45 (1987): 83–99.

Lejarza, Fidel (de), and Angel Uribe, eds. *Las reformas en los siglos XIV y XV: Introducción a los orígenes de la Observancia en España*. Special issue, *Archivo Ibero-Americano* 17 (1957).

Leonard, Irving A. *Romances of Chivalry in the Spanish Indies: With Some 'Registros' of Shipments of Books to the Spanish Colonies*. Berkeley: University of California Press, 1933.

Lidaka, Juris G. 'Bartholomaeus Anglicus in the Thirteenth Century.' In *Pre-Modern Encyclopaedic Texts: Proceedings of the Second COMERS Congress, Groningen, 1–4 July 1996*, edited by Peter Binkley, 393–406. Leiden: Brill, 1997.

Lindberg, David C. Introduction to *John Pecham and the Science of Optics: 'Perspectiva communis,'* edited by David C. Lindberg, 3–58. Madison: University of Wisconsin Press, 1970.

– Introduction to *Roger Bacon and the Origins of 'Perspectiva' in the Middle Ages: A Critical Edition and English Translation of Bacon's 'Perspectiva,'* edited by David C. Lindberg, xvii–cxi. Oxford: Oxford University Press, 1996.

– *Theories of Vision from Al-Kindi to Kepler*. Chicago: University of Chicago Press, 1996.

Lisboa, Marcos de. *Tercera parte de las chronicas de la orden de los frayles menores del seraphico padre Sant Francisco …* Salamanca: Alexandro de Canova, 1570.

Llamas-Martínez, Enrique. *Santa Teresa de Jesús y la Inquisición española*. Madrid: Academía de Doctores de Madrid, 1970.

Llull, Ramon. 'Plant de la verge.' In *Obras literarias*, edited by Miguel Batllori and Miguel Caldentey, 1070–93. Madrid: Biblioteca de Autores Cristianos, 1948.

Lochrie, Karma. *Margery Kempe and Translations of the Flesh*. Philadelphia: University of Pennsylvania Press, 1991.

Longhurst, John Edward. *Luther's Ghost in Spain (1517–1546)*. Lawrence, KS: Coronado Press, 1969.

López, Josefina C. 'Oralidad, misticismo y espiritualidad en Santa Teresa de Jesús.' In *Los cinco sentidos del convento: Europa y el Nuevo Mundo*, edited by Josefina C. López, 41–74. Caracas: Universidad Católica Andrés Bello, 2010.

López-Baralt, Luce. 'Teresa of Jesus and Islam: The Simile of the Seven Concentric Castles of the Soul.' In *A New Companion to Hispanic Mysticism*, edited by Hilaire Kallendorf, 175–99. Leiden: Brill, 2010.

López Grigera, Luisa. *La retórica en la España del siglo de oro: Teoría y práctica*. Salamanca: Universidad de Salamanca, 1994.

López Santidrián, Saturnino. Introducción to *Tercer abecedario espiritual*, by Francisco de Osuna, 5–84. Madrid: Biblioteca de Autores Cristianos, 1998.

Louth, Andrew. *The Origins of the Christian Mystical Tradition: From Plato to Denys*. Oxford: Clarendon Press, 1981.

Ludolph of Saxony. *The Hours of the Passion: Taken from The Life of Christ by Ludolph the Saxon*. Translated by Henry James Coleridge. Quarterly Series 59. London: Burns and Oates, 1887.

– *Vita Christi cartujano*. Translated by Ambrosio de Montesino. Alcalá de Henares: Stanislau de Polonia, 1502–3.

MacCulloch, Diarmaid. *The Reformation: A History*. New York: Penguin Books, 2003.

MacDonald, A.A., H.N.B. Ridderbos, and R.M. Schlusemann, eds. *The Broken Body: Passion Devotion in Late-Medieval Culture*. Groningen: Egbert Forsten, 1998.

Madrid, Alonso de. *Arte para servir a Dios*. Edited by Luis Cortest. Madrid: Editorial Playor, 1989.

Mancho Duque, María Jesús. 'Diálogos franciscanos del quinientos: El deslizamiento al tratado.' *Analecta Malacitana* 23 (2000): 57–84.

Marín, Tomás. 'La biblioteca del obispo Juan Bernal Díaz de Luco (1495–1556), I.' *Hispania Sacra* 5 (1952): 263–326.

Mark, Birgitta. *Mysticism and Cognition: The Cognitive Development of John of the Cross as Revealed in His Works*. Aarhus, Denmark: Aarhus University Press, 2000.

Márquez, Antonio. *Los alumbrados: Orígenes y filosofía (1525–1559)*. 2nd ed. Madrid: Taurus, 1980.

Márquez Villanueva, Francisco. 'The Converso Problem: An Assessment.' In *Collected Studies in Honour of Américo Castro's Eightieth Year*, edited by Marcel P. Hornik, 317–33. Oxford: Lincombe Lodge Research Library, 1965.

Marrow, James H. *Passion Iconography in Northern European Art of the Late Middle Ages and Early Renaissance: A Study of the Transformation of Sacred Metaphor into Descriptive Narrative*. Kortrijk, Belgium: Van Ghemmert Publishing Company, 1979.

Martín, Teodoro H. 'Los místicos alemanes en la España del XVI y XVII.' *Revista de Espiritualidad* 48 (1989): 111–28.

McCutcheon, Russell T. *Manufacturing Religion: The Discourse on Sui Generis Religion and the Politics of Nostalgia*. Oxford: Oxford University Press, 2003.

McGinn, Bernard. *The Flowering of Mysticism: Men and Women in the New Mysticism, 1200–1350*. Vol. 3 of *The Presence of God: A History of Western Christian Mysticism*. New York: Crossroads, 1998.

– *The Foundations of Mysticism*. Vol. 1 of *The Presence of God: A History of Western Christian Mysticism*. New York: Crossroads, 1991.

– 'Love, Knowledge, and Mystical Union in Western Christianity: Twelfth to Sixteenth Centuries.' *Church History* 56, no. 1 (1987): 7–24.

– *The Presence of God: A History of Western Christian Mysticism*. 4 vols. New York: Crossroads, 1991–2005.

– 'Visions and Critiques of Visions in Thirteenth-Century Mysticism.' In *Rending the Veil: Concealment and Secrecy in the History of Religions*, edited by Elliot R. Wolfson, 87–113. New York: Seven Bridges Press, 1999.

McKendrick, Geraldine. 'The *Dança de la muerte* of 1520 and Social Unrest in Seville.' *Journal of Hispanic Philology* 3 (1979): 239–60.

McKendrick, Geraldine, and Angus MacKay. 'Visionaries and Affective Spirituality in the First Half of the Sixteenth Century.' In *Cultural Encounters: The Impact of the Inquisition in Spain and the New World*, edited by Mary Elizabeth Perry and Anne J. Cruz, 93–104. Los Angeles: University of California Press, 1991.

McKeon, Richard P. 'Medicine and Philosophy in the Eleventh and Twelfth Centuries: The Problem of Elements.' *The Thomist* 24 (1961): 211–56.

McVaugh, Michael R. 'The "Humidum Radicale" in Thirteenth-Century Medicine.' *Traditio* 30 (1974): 259–83.

Medwick, Cathleen. *Teresa of Avila: The Progress of a Soul*. New York: Doubleday, 1999.

Melammed, Renée Levine. *A Question of Identity: Iberian Conversos in Historical Perspective*. Oxford: Oxford University Press, 2004.

Mendoza, Fray Iñigo de. 'Coplas de Vita Christi.' In *Fray Iñigo de Mendoza y sus 'Coplas de Vita Christi,'* edited by Julio Rodríguez Puértolas, 291–513. Madrid: Editorial Gredos, 1968.

Merback, Mitchell B. *The Thief, the Cross, and the Wheel: Pain and the Spectacle of Punishment in Medieval and Renaissance Europe*. London: Reaktion, 1999.

Merino Jerez, Luis. *Retórica y artes de memoria en el humanismo renacentista: Jorge de Trebisonda, Pedro de Ravena, y Francisco Sánchez de las Brozas*. Cáceres, Spain: Universidad de Extremadura, 2007.

Meseguer Fernández, Juan. 'Passio duorum: Autores-ediciones-La obra.' *Archivo Ibero-Americano* 29 (1969): 217–68.

Miles, Margaret. *Augustine on the Body*. Missoula, MO: Scholars Press, 1979.

– *Image as Insight: Visual Understanding in Western Christianity and Secular Culture*. Boston: Beacon Press, 1985.

– 'Vision: The Eye of the Body and the Eye of the Mind in Saint Augustine's *De trinitate* and *Confessions*.' *The Journal of Religion* 63, no. 2 (1983): 125–42.

Mills, Robert. *Suspended Animation: Pain, Pleasure and Punishment in Medieval Culture*. London: Reaktion Books, 2005.

Minister, Meredith. 'Critical Theories of Embodiment and Trinitarian Theologies: Mapping a Trajectory for Theological Responsibility in the Quest for Embodied Justice.' PhD diss., Southern Methodist University, 2011.

Miura Andrades, José María. *Frailes, monjes, y conventos: Las órdenes mendicantes y la sociedad sevillana bajomedieval*. Seville: Diputación de Sevilla, 1998.

Morales, Francisco. 'New World Colonial Franciscan Mystical Practice.' In *A New Companion to Hispanic Mysticism*, edited by Hilaire Kallendorf, 71–101. Leiden: Brill, 2010.

Morales Borrero, Manuel. 'Beguinos, alumbrados y angelistas: Gloria y tragedia de Fray Francisco de la Cruz.' *Boletín del Instituto de Estudios Giennenses* 145, no. 145 (1992): 319–43.

Moreno, Isidoro. *Las hermandades andaluzas: Una aproximación desde la antropología*. 2nd ed. Seville: Universidad de Sevilla, Secretariado de Publicaciones, 1999.

Moreno Mendoza, Arsenio, ed. *Orto hispalensis: Arte y cultura en la Sevilla del emperador*. Seville: Patronato del Real Alcázar, 2001.

Morris, David B. *The Culture of Pain*. Los Angeles: University of California Press, 1993.

Mossman, Stephen. *Marquard von Lindau and the Challenges of Religious Life in Late Medieval Germany: The Passion, The Eucharist, The Virgin Mary*. Oxford: Oxford University Press, 2010.

Mowbray, Donald. *Pain and Suffering in Medieval Theology: Academic Debates at the University of Paris in the Thirteenth Century*. Woodbridge, England: Boydell Press, 2009.

Mujica, Bárbara. '*Corpus sanus, mens sana, spiritus sanus*: Cuerpo, mente y espíritu en las cartas de Teresa de Jesús.' In *Los cinco sentidos del convento: Europa y el Nuevo Mundo*, edited by Josefina C. López, 13–24. Caracas: Universidad Católica Andrés Bello, 2010.

Muñoz Delgado, Vicente. 'Juan de Aguilera (d. 1560/1) y su *Ars memorativa* (1536).' *Cuadernos de Historia de la Medicina Española* 14 (1975): 175–89.

Muñoz Fernández, Angela. *Acciones e intenciones de mujeres en la vida religiosa de los siglos XV y XVI*. Madrid: Horas y Horas, 1995.

Nadal, Jerome. *Annotations and Meditations on the Gospels*. Translated by Frederick A. Homann. Edited by Frederick A. Homann and Walter S. Melion. 3 vols. Philadelphia: St. Joseph's University Press, 2003.

Nalle, Sara T. 'Printing and Reading Popular Religious Texts in Sixteenth-Century Spain.' In *Culture and the State in Spain, 1550–1850*, edited by Tom Lewis and Francisco J. Sánchez, 126–56. New York: Garland, 1999.

– 'Private Devotion, Personal Space: Religious Images in Domestic Context.' In *La imagen religiosa en la monarquía hispánica: Usos y espacios*, edited by María Cruz de Carlos, Pierre Civil, Felipe Pereda, and Cécile Vincent-Cassy, 255–72. Madrid: Casa de Velásquez, 2008.

Narveson, Kate. 'Flesh, Excrement, Humors, Nothing: The Body in Early Stuart Devotional Discourse.' *Studies in Philology* 96, no. 3 (1999): 313–33.

Nederman, Cary J., Nancy Van Deusen, and E. Ann Matter, eds. *Mind Matters: Studies of Medieval and Early Modern Intellectual History in Honour of Marcia Colish*. Turnhout, Belgium: Brepols, 2009.

Netanyahu, Benzion. *The Marranos of Spain from the Late 14th to the Early 16th Century: According to Contemporary Hebrew Sources*. 3rd ed. Ithaca, NY: Cornell University Press, 1999.

– *The Origins of the Inquisition in Fifteenth Century Spain*. 2nd ed. New York: New York Review of Books, 2001.

Newhauser, Richard. *The Treatise on Vices and Virtues in Latin and the Vernacular*. Turnhout, Belgium: Brepols, 1993.

Newman, Barbara. *From Virile Woman to WomanChrist: Studies in Medieval Religion and Literature*. Philadelphia: University of Pennsylvania Press, 1995.

Nicolás, Antonio T. de. *Ignatius of Loyola, Powers of Imagining: A Philosophical Hermeneutics of Imagining through the Collected Works of Ignatius of Loyola with a Translation of Those Works*. Albany, NY: State University of New York Press, 1986.

Nirenberg, David. 'Enmity and Assimilation: Jews, Christians, and Converts in Medieval Spain.' *Common Knowledge* 9, no. 1 (2003): 137–55.

Norton, F.J. *A Descriptive Catalogue of Printing in Spain and Portugal, 1501–20*. London: Cambridge University Press, 1978.

O'Boyle, Cornelius. 'Medicine, God and Aristotle in the Early Universities: Prefatory Prayers in Late Medieval Medical Commentaries.' *Bulletin of the History of Medicine* 66 (1992): 185–209.

Oderberg, David S. 'Hylemorphic Dualism.' *Social Philosophy and Policy* 22 (2005): 70–99.

Ogier of Locedio (Pseudo-Bernard). 'Meditation by Bernard on the Lamentation of the Blessed Virgin (Meditacio Bernardi de lamentacione beate virginis).' In

Texts of the Passion: Latin Devotional Literature and Medieval Society, edited by Thomas Bestul, 165–85. Philadelphia: University of Pennsylvania, 1996.

O'Malley, John W. *Trent and All That: Renaming Catholicism in the Early Modern Era*. Cambridge, MA: Harvard University Press, 2000.

Orella Unzué, José Luis. 'La cultura religiosa y la revolución de las ideas.' In *La cultura del Renacimiento (1480–1580)*, edited by Víctor García de la Concha, 179–212. Madrid: Espasa Calpe, S.A., 1999.

Ortiz de Zúñiga, Diego. *Anales eclesiásticos de la muy noble y muy leal ciudad de Sevilla.* 8 vols. Madrid: Imprenta Real, 1796.

Ortiz Real, Javier, and Baldomero Brígido Gabiola. *Historia de Laredo*. Laredo, Spain: Ayuntamiento de Laredo, 1999.

Osuna, Francisco de. *Abecedario espiritual, V y VI partes*. Edited by Mariano Quirós García. 2 vols. Madrid: Fundación Universitaria Española, 2002.

– 'Ley de Amor.' In *Místicos Franciscanos Españoles I*, 221–700. Madrid: Biblioteca de Autores Cristianos, 1948.

– *Primer abecedario espiritual.* Edited by José Juan Morcillo Pérez. Madrid: Editorial Cisneros, 2004.

– *Segundo abecedario espiritual.* Edited by José Juan Morcillo Pérez. Madrid: Editorial Cisneros, 2004.

– *Tercer abecedario espiritual de Francisco de Osuna*. Edited by Saturnino López Santidrián. Madrid: Biblioteca de Autores Cristianos, 1998.

– *The Third Spiritual Alphabet*. Translated by Mary E. Giles. New York: Paulist Press, 1981.

Pablo Maroto, Daniel de. *Reformas y espirituales franciscanos en el Renacimiento*. Salamanca: Universidad Pontificia de Salamanca, 2003.

Pacho, Eulogio. *Apogeo de la mística cristiana: Historia de la espiritualidad clásica española 1450–1650*. Burgos, Spain: Monte Carmelo, 2008.

Padilla, Juan de. 'Retablo de la vida de Cristo.' In *Cancionero castellano del siglo XV*, edited by Foulché-Delbosc, 423–49. Madrid: Casa Editorial Bailly-Baillière, 1912.

Palma, Bernabé de. 'Via spiritus.' In *Via spiritus, Subida del Monte Sión*, edited by Teodoro H. Martín, 1–146. Madrid: Biblioteca de Autores Cristianos, 1998.

Park, Katharine. 'The Criminal and the Saintly Body: Autopsy and Dissection in Renaissance Italy.' *Renaissance Quarterly* 47, no. 1 (1994): 1–33.

Parshall, Peter. 'The Art of Memory and the Passion.' *The Art Bulletin* 81, no. 3 (1999): 456–72.

Pasnau, Robert. *Theories of Cognition in the Later Middle Ages*. Cambridge: Cambridge University Press, 1997.

Peers, E. Allison. Introduction to *The Ascent of Mount Sion: Being the Third Book of the Treatise of that Name*, by Bernardino de Laredo, 11–58. London: Faber and Faber, 1952.

– *Studies of the Spanish Mystics*. 2 vols. London: Sheldon Press, 1927/1930.

Pego Puigbó, Armando. *El Renacimiento espiritual: Introducción literaria a los tratados de oración españoles (1520–1566)*. Madrid: Consejo Superior de Investigaciones Científicas, 2004.

Pereda, Felipe. *Las imágenes de la discordia: Política y poética de la imagen sagrada en la España del 400*. Madrid: Marcel Pons, 2007.

– 'Measuring Jerusalem: The Marquis of Tarifa's Pilgrimage in 1520 and Its Consequences.' Città e Storia (forthcoming).

Pérez, Joseph. *Crónica de la Inquisición en España*. Barcelona: Ediciones Martínez, 2002.

Pérez Priego, Miguel Angel. 'Espectáculos y textos teatrales en Castilla a fines de la Edad Media.' *Revista de filología* 5 (1989): 141–64.

Pérez y Gómez, Antonio. '*La pasión trobada* de Diego de San Pedro.' *Revista de Literatura* 1 (1952): 147–82.

Pike, Ruth. *Aristocrats and Traders: Sevillian Society in the Sixteenth Century*. Ithaca, NY, and London: Cornell University Press, 1972.

Piqueras Villaldea, María Isabel. *Carlos V y la emperatriz Isabel*. Madrid: Actas Editorial, 2000.

Pouchelle, Marie-Christine. *The Body and Surgery in the Middle Ages*. Translated by Rosemary Morris. Cambridge: Polity Press, 1990.

Pseudo-Bonaventure. *Meditations on the Life of Christ: An Illustrated Manuscript of the Fourteenth Century*. Translated by Isa Ragusa. Edited by Isa Ragusa and Rosalie B. Green. Princeton, NJ: Princeton University Press, 1961.

Rábade Obradó, María del Pilar. 'Los judeoconversos en la corte y en la epoca de los Reyes Catolicos.' PhD diss., Universidad Complutense de Madrid, 1990.

Redondo, Agustin. *Revistando las culturas del siglo de oro: Mentalidades, tradiciones culturales, creaciones paraliterarias y literarias*. Salamanca: Ediciones Universidad de Salamanca, 2007.

Remensnyder, Amy G. 'The Colonization of Sacred Architecture: The Virgin Mary, Mosques, and Temples in Medieval Spain and Early Sixteenth-Century Mexico.' In *Monks and Nuns, Saints and Outcasts: Religion in Medieval Society: Essays in Honor of Lester K. Little*, edited by Sharon Farmer and Barbara Rosenwein, 189–219. Ithaca, NY: Cornell University Press, 2000.

Requena Miota, Juan Carlos. 'La espiritualidad española de los siglos XV–XVII a través de las *Vita Christi*.' PhD diss., Universidad de Barcelona, 1997.

Revuelta González, Manuel. *La exclaustración (1833–1840)*. Madrid: Biblioteca de Autores Cristianos, 1976.

Reynolds, Philip Lyndon. *Food and the Body: Some Peculiar Questions in High Medieval Theology*. Leiden: Brill, 1999.

Rhodes, Elizabeth. *The Unrecognized Precursors of Montemayor's 'Diana.'* Columbia: University of Missouri Press, 1992.

Ricard, Robert. 'La fonte de San Juan de la Cruz y un capitulo de Laredo.' In *Estudios de literatura religiosa española*, edited by Robert Ricard, 181–93. Madrid: Editorial Gredos, 1964.

– 'Le thème de Jésus crucifié chez quelques auteurs espagnols du XVIe et du XVIIe siècles.' *Bulletin Hispanique* 57 (1955): 45–55.

Richard of Saint Victor. 'The Mystical Ark.' In *The Twelve Patriarchs; The Mystical Ark; Book Three of the Trinity*, translated by Grover A. Zinn, 149–370. New York: Paulist Press, 1979.

– *The Twelve Patriarchs; The Mystical Ark; Book Three of the Trinity*. Translated by Grover A. Zinn. New York: Paulist Press, 1979.

Rivers, Kimberly. 'The Fear of Divine Vengeance: Mnemonic Images as a Guide to Conscience in the Late Middle Ages.' In *Fear and Its Representations in the Middle Ages and Renaissance*, edited by Anne Scott and Cynthia Kosso, 66–91. Turnhout, Belgium: Brepols, 2002.

– 'Memory and Medieval Preaching: Mnemonic Advice in the *Ars praedicandi* of Francesc Eiximenis (ca. 1327–1409).' *Viator* 30 (1999): 253–84.

Robinson, Cynthia. *Imag(in)ing Passions: Christ, the Virgin, Images, and Devotion in a Multi-Confessional Castile (14th–15th c)*. University Park, PA: Pennsylvania State Press, forthcoming.

– 'Preaching to the Converted: Valladolid's *Cristianos nuevos* and the *Retablo de don Sancho de Rojas* (1415).' *Speculum* 83 (2008): 112–63.

Rodríguez, Isaías. 'Espirituales españoles (1500–1570).' In *Repertorio de historia de las ciencias eclesiasticas en España (RHCEE) III*, 407–625. Salamanca: Instituto de Historia de la Teología Española, 1971.

Roest, Bert. *Franciscan Literature of Religious Instruction before the Council of Trent*. Leiden: Brill, 2004.

Román, Comendador. *Coplas de la pasión con la resurrección*. Edited by Giuseppe Mazzocchi. Florence: La Nuova Italia, 1990.

Romero Abao, Rocío. 'Las fiestas de Sevilla en el siglo XV.' In *Las fiestas de Sevilla en el siglo XV: Otros estudios*, 12–180. Madrid: Editorial DEIMOS, S.A., 1991.

Rorem, Paul. 'The Early Latin Dionysius: Eriugena and Hugh of Saint Victor.' In *Re-Thinking Dionysius the Areopagite*, edited by Sarah Coakley and Charles M. Stang, 71–84. Malden, MA: Wiley-Blackwell, 2009.

Ros, Fidèle de. *Un inspirateur de Sainte Thérèse: Le frère Bernardin de Laredo*. Paris: Librairie Philosophique J. Vrin, 1948.

– *Un maître de Sainte Thérèse: Le père François de Osuna: Sa vie, son oeuvre, sa doctrine spirituelle*. Paris: Gabriel Beauchesne, 1936.

Rosenstock, Bruce. *New Men: Conversos, Christian Theology, and Society in Fifteenth-Century Castile*. London: Department of Hispanic Studies, Queen Mary, University of London, 2002.

Rossetti, Laura. 'Una traducción española del *De miseria humanae conditionis: El libro de la vileza de la humana condiçión*.' *Carte Romanze*, serie 1 (1995): 227–44.

Roth, Norman. *Conversos, Inquisition, and the Expulsion of the Jews from Spain*. Madison: University of Wisconsin, 1995.

– *Jews, Visigoths, and Muslims in Medieval Spain: Cooperation and Conflict*. Leiden: Brill, 1994.

Rothstein, Bret. 'Vision, Cognition, and Self-Reflection in Rogier van der Weyden's Bladelin Triptych.' *Zeitschrift für Kunstgeschichte* 64 (2001): 37–55.

Rotsaert, Mark. 'L'originalité des *Exercices spirituels* d'Ignace de Loyola sur l'arrière-fond des renouveaux spirituels en Castille au début du seizième siècle.' In *Ignacio de Loyola y su tiempo: Congreso internacional de historia*, edited by Juan Plazaola, 329–40. Bilbao: Mensagero, Universidad de Deusto, 1992.

Rubin, Miri. *Corpus Christi: The Eucharist in Late Medieval Culture*. Cambridge: Cambridge University Press, 1991.

Rubio, Germán. *La custodia franciscana de Sevilla: Ensayo histórico sobre sus orígenes, progresos y vicisitudes (1220–1499)*. Seville: Editorial San Antonio, 1953.

Rucquoi, Adeline. 'Contribution des *Studia Generalia* à la pensée hispanique médiévale.' In *Pensamiento medieval hispano: Homenaje a Horacio Santiago-Otero*, 2:737–70. Madrid: CSIC, 1998.

Rudy, Gordon. *Mystical Language of Sensation in the Later Middle Ages*. New York: Routledge, 2002.

Rummel, Erika. *Jiménez de Cisneros: On the Threshold of Spain's Golden Age*. Tempe: Arizona Center for Medieval and Renaissance Studies, 1999.

Saenger, Paul. 'Books of Hours and the Reading Habits of the Later Middle Ages.' In *The Culture of Print: Power and the Uses of Print in Early Modern Europe*, edited by Roger Chartier, 141–73. Cambridge: Polity Press, 1989.

Sáinz Rodríguez, Pedro. *La siembra mística del Cardenal Cisneros y las reformas en la iglesia*. Madrid: Universidad Pontificia de Salamanca, 1979.

Sala Balust, Luis. 'La espiritualidad española en la primera mitad del siglo XVI.' *Cuadernos de historia* 1 (1967): 169–87.

Sala Balust, Luis, and Francisco Martín Hernández. 'Biografía del Mtro. Juan de Avila.' In *Obras completas del santo maestro Juan de Avila: Edición critica*, 1:3–392. Madrid: Biblioteca de Autores Cristianos, 1970.

Salinas y Salazar, Lope de. 'Memorial de la vida y ritos de la Custodia de Santa María de los Menores.' In *Las reformas en los siglos XIV y XV: Introducción a*

los orígenes de la Observancia en España, edited by Fidel (de) Lejarza and Angel Uribe, special issue, *Archivo Ibero-Americano* 17 (1957): 714–76.
– 'Segundas satisfacciones.' In *Las reformas en los siglos XIV y XV: Introducción a los orígenes de la Observancia en España*, edited by Fidel (de) Lejarza and Angel Uribe, special issue, *Archivo Ibero-Americano* 17 (1957): 852–96.
– 'Testamento …' In *Las reformas en los siglos XIV y XV: Introducción a los orígenes de la Observancia en España*, edited by Fidel (de) Lejarza and Angel Uribe, special issue, *Archivo Ibero-Americano* 17 (1957): 897–925.
Sánchez Ciruelo, Pedro. 'Arte memorandi.' In *Expositio libri missalis*, fols. 270r–276v. Alcalá de Henares, 1528.
Sánchez del Arco, Manuel. *Cruz de Guía: Exégesis profana de la Semana Santa en Sevilla*. Seville: Ediciones Espuela de Plata, 2003.
Sánchez Herrero, José, ed. *CXIX reglas de hermandades y cofradías andaluzas: Siglos XIV, XV, y XVI*. Huelva, Spain: Universidad de Huelva, 2002.
– 'La iglesia de Sevilla durante los siglos bajomedievales (1248–1474).' In *Historia de las diócesis españolas*, vol. 10, *Iglesias de Sevilla, Huelva, Jerez y Cádiz y Ceuta*, 59–130. Madrid: Biblioteca de Autores Cristianos, 2002.
– 'La Sevilla del Renacimiento (1474–1581).' In *Historia de las diócesis españolas*, vol. 10, *Iglesias de Sevilla, Huelva, Jerez y Cádiz y Ceuta*, 131–87. Madrid: Biblioteca de Autores Cristianos, 2002.
– *Las tres etapas de la enseñanza en Sevilla a finales del siglo XV y comienzos del XVI*. Seville: Universidad de Sevilla, 2007.
– 'Los centros de estudio y la enseñanza en Sevilla durante el siglo XV.' In *La ciudad hispánica durante los siglos XIII al XVI*, 367–92. Madrid: Universidad Complutense, 1987.
– *Semana Santa de Sevilla*. Madrid: Sílex, 2003.
Sandoval et Roxas, Bernardi de. *Index librorum prohibitorum et expurgatorum*. Madrid: Ludovicum Sanchez, 1612.
Santander Rodríguez, Teresa. *Hipócrates en España (siglo XVI)*. Madrid: Direccíon General de Archivos y Bibliotecas, 1971.
Santo Domingo, María de. *The Book of Prayer of Sor Maria of Santo Domingo: A Study and Translation*. Translated by Mary E. Giles. Albany, NY: State University of New York Press, 1990.
Santonja, Pedro. *La herejía de los alumbrados y la espiritualidad en la España del siglo XVI: Inquisión y sociedad*. Valencia: Biblioteca Valenciana, 2001.
Scarry, Elaine. *The Body in Pain: The Making and Unmaking of the World*. Oxford: Oxford University Press, 1985.
Sedgwick, Eve Kosofsky. *Epistemology of the Closet*. Berkeley: University of California Press, 1990.

Selke, Angela. *El santo oficio de la Inquisición: Proceso de Fr. Francisco Ortiz (1529–1532)*. Madrid: Ediciones Guadarama, 1968.

Sells, Michael A. *Mystical Languages of Unsaying*. Chicago: University of Chicago Press, 1994.

Sharot, Stephen. 'Millenarianism among Conversos (New Christians) and Former Conversos (Returnees to Judaism).' In *Comparative Perspectives on Judaisms and Jewish Identities*, 105–22. Detroit: Wayne State University Press, 2010.

Sicroff, Albert A. *Les controverses des statuts de 'pureté de sang' en Espagne du XVe au XVIIe siècle*. Paris: Librairie Marcel Didier, 1960.

Singer, Julie. *Blindness and Therapy in Late Medieval French and Italian Poetry*. Woodbridge, Suffolk: D.S. Brewer, 2011.

Siraisi, Nancy. 'The Changing Fortunes of a Traditional Text: Goals and Strategies in Sixteenth-Century Latin Editions of the *Canon* of Avicenna.' In *The Medical Renaissance of the Sixteenth Century*, edited by A. Wear, R.K. French and I.M. Lonie, 16–41. Cambridge: Cambridge University Press, 1985.

– *Medicine and the Italian Universities*. Leiden: Brill, 2001.

– *Medieval and Early Renaissance Medicine: An Introduction to Knowledge and Practice*. Chicago: University of Chicago Press, 1990.

Smith, A. Mark. 'Getting the Big Picture in Perspectivist Optics.' *Isis* 72, no. 4 (1981): 568–89.

Smith, Jonathan Z. *Relating Religion: Essays in the Study of Religion*. Chicago: University of Chicago Press, 2004.

Solomon, Michael. *Fictions of Well-Being: Sickly Readers and Vernacular Medical Writing in Late Medieval and Early Modern Spain*. Philadelphia: University of Pennsylvania Press, 2010.

Soto Maios, Antonii a. *Novissimus librorum prohibitorum et expurgandorum index pro Catholicus Hispaniarum Regnis, Philippi IV*. Madrid: Didacus Diaz, 1640.

Spruit, Leen. 'Renaissance Views of Active Perception.' In *Theories of Perception in Medieval and Early Modern Philosophy*, edited by Simo Knuuttila and Pekka Kärkkäinen, 203–24. New York: Springer, 2008.

Starr-LeBeau, Gretchen D. *In the Shadow of the Virgin: Inquisitors, Friars, and 'Conversos' in Guadalupe, Spain*. Princeton, NJ: Princeton University Press, 2003.

Stevenson, Jill. *Performance, Cognitive Theory, and Devotional Culture: Sensual Piety in Late Medieval York*. New York: Palgrave Macmillan, 2010.

Sticca, Sandro. *The Planctus Mariae in the Dramatic Tradition of the Middle Ages*. Translated by Joseph R. Berrigan. Athens, GA, and London: University of Georgia Press, 1988.

Surtz, Ronald E. 'The "Franciscan Connection" in the Early Castilian Theater.' *Bulletin of the Comediantes* 35 (1983): 141–52.

– *The Guitar of God: Gender, Power, and Authority in the Visionary World of Mother Juana de la Cruz (1481–1534)*. Philadelphia: University of Pennsylvania Press, 1990.

– *Writing Women in Late Medieval and Early Modern Spain: The Mothers of Saint Teresa of Avila*. Philadelphia: University of Pennsylvania Press, 1995.

Suso, Heinrich. 'The Little Book of Eternal Wisdom.' In *Henry Suso: The Exemplar, with Two German Sermons*, translated and edited by Frank Tobin, 205–304. New York: Paulist Press, 1989.

Swanson, R.N. 'Passion and Practice: The Social and Ecclesiastical Implications of Passion Devotion in the Late Middle Ages.' In *The Broken Body: Passion Devotion in Late-Medieval Culture*, edited by A.A. MacDonald, H.N.B. Ridderbos, and R.M. Schlusemann, 1–30. Groningen: Egbert Forsten, 1998.

Swietlicki, Catherine. *Spanish Christian Cabala: The Works of Luis de León, Santa Teresa de Jesús, and San Juan de la Cruz*. Columbia: University of Missouri Press, 1986.

Szarmach, Paul. *An Introduction to the Medieval Mystics of Europe: Fourteen Original Essays*. Albany, NY: State University of New York Press, 1984.

Tachau, Katherine H. *Vision and Certitude in the Age of Ockham: Optics, Epistemology, and the Foundations of Semantics, 1250–1345*. Leiden: Brill, 1988.

– 'What Senses and Intellect Do: Argument and Judgment in Late Medieval Theories of Knowledge.' In *Argumentationstheorie: Scholastische Forschungen zu den logischen und semantischen Regeln korrekten Folgerns*, edited by Klaus Jacobi, 653–70. Leiden: Brill, 1993.

Tejada y Ramiro, Juan. *Colección de canónes y de todos los concilios de la iglesía española, traducida al castellano*. Vol. 5. Madrid: Pedro Montero, 1855.

Tellechea, José-Ignacio. 'La reforma religiosa.' In *La hora de Cisneros*, edited by Joseph F. Perez, 43–56. Madrid: Editorial Complutense, 1995.

Temkin, Owsei. *Galenism: Rise and Decline of a Medical Philosophy*. Ithaca, NY, and London: Cornell University Press, 1973.

– *Hippocrates in a World of Pagans and Christians*. Baltimore: The Johns Hopkins University Press, 1991.

Tenerio, Francisco de, and Luis Escobar. *Passio duorum*. Seville: Juan Varela de Salamanca, 1539.

Thompson, Colin. Prologue to *A New Companion to Hispanic Mysticism*, edited by Hilaire Kallendorf, xix–xxii. Leiden: Brill, 2010.

– *St. John of the Cross: Songs in the Night*. Washington, DC: The Catholic University of America Press, 2003.

Torroja Menéndez, Carmen, and María Rivas Palá. *Teatro en Toledo en el siglo XV: 'Auto de la Pasión' de Alonso del Campo*. Madrid: Real Academia Española, 1977.

Trembinski, Donna. '[Pro]passio Doloris: Early Dominican Conceptions of Christ's Physical Pain.' *Journal of Ecclesiastical History* 59, no. 4 (2008): 630–56.

Turner, Denys. *The Darkness of God: Negativity in Christian Mysticism*. Cambridge: Cambridge University Press, 1995.

Tweed, Thomas A. *Crossing and Dwelling: A Theory of Religion*. Cambridge, MA: Harvard University Press, 2008.

Ubarri, Miguel Norbert. *Las categorías de espacio y tiempo en San Juan de la Cruz*. Madrid: Editorial de Espiritualidad, 2001.

Ubertino da Casale. *Arbor vitae crucifixae Jesu*. Edited by Charles T. Davis. Torino: Bottega d'Erasmo, 1961.

Utrilla, María José del Castillo. *El Convento de San Francisco, Casa Grande de Sevilla*. Seville: Diputación Provincial, Sevilla, 1988.

Valadés, Diego. *Retórica cristiana*. Edited by Tarsicio Herrera Zapin. 2 vols. Mexico City: Fondo de Cultura Economica, 1989.

Vásquez, Manuel A. *More Than Belief: A Materialist Theory of Religion*. Oxford: Oxford University Press, 2010.

Vidal, Fernando. 'Brains, Bodies, Selves, and Science: Anthropologies of Identity and the Resurrection of the Body.' *Critical Inquiry* 28 (2002): 930–74.

Vílchez Díaz, Alfredo. *Autores y anónimos españoles en los indices inquisitoriales*. Madrid: Universidad Complutense, 1986.

Villalobos Hennessy, Marlene. 'Passion Devotion, Penitential Reading, and the Manuscript Page: "The Hours of the Cross" in London, British Library Additional 37049.' *Mediaeval Studies* 66 (2004): 213–52.

Vives, Juan Luis. 'Obra psicológica.' In *Antología de textos de Juan Luis Vives*, edited by F. Jordi Pérez i Durà, 498–581. Valencia: Universitat de València, 1992.

Vollendorf, Lisa. *The Lives of Women: A New History of Inquisitorial Spain*. Nashville: Vanderbilt University Press, 2005.

Wadding, Lucas. *Annales minorum seu trium ordinum a S. Francisco Institutorum*. Edited by Joseph María Fonseca ab Ebora. 32 vols. 1625. Reprint, Florence: Ad Claras Aquas, Quaracchi, 1932.

Watson, Nicholas. 'The Methods and Objectives of Thirteenth-Century Anchoritic Devotion.' In *The Medieval Mystical Tradition in England: Exeter Symposium IV: Papers Read at Dartington Hall, July 1987*, edited by Marion Glasscoe, 132–53. Cambridge: D.S. Brewer, 1987.

Webb, Heather. 'Catherine of Siena's Heart.' *Speculum* 80 (2005): 802–17.

Weber, Alison. *Teresa of Avila and the Rhetoric of Femininity*. Princeton, NJ: Princeton University Press, 1990.

Webster, Susan Verdi. *Art and Ritual in Golden-Age Spain: Sevillian Confraternities and the Processional Sculpture of Holy Week*. Princeton, NJ: Princeton University Press, 1998.

Whinnom, Keith. 'El origen de las comparaciones religiosas del siglo de oro: Mendoza, Montesino y Román.' *Revista de Filología Española* 46 (1963): 263–85.

– 'The Supposed Sources of Inspiration of Spanish Fifteenth-Century Narrative Religious Verse.' *Medieval and Renaissance Spanish Literature* 17 (1994): 46–70.

Whitehead, Christiania. *Castles of the Mind: A Study of Medieval Architectural Allegory*. Cardiff: University of Wales Press, 2003.

Wieck, Roger S. *Libro de Horas de Carlos I, Emperador Carlos V: Ms. 411 de la Beinecke Library*. 2 vols. Madrid: Edilán-Ars Libris, 2000.

Wiethaus, Ulrike. 'Christian Piety and the Legacy of Medieval Masculinity.' In *Redeeming Men: Religion and Masculinities*, edited by Stephen Blake Boyd, W. Merle Longwood, and Mark William Muesse, 48–61. Louisville, KY: Westminister John Knox Press, 1996.

Willaert, Frank. Introduction to *Medieval Memory: Image and Text*, edited by Frank Willaert et al., ix–xxv. Turnhout, Belgium: Brepols, 2004.

Yates, Frances A. *The Art of Memory*. Chicago: Chicago University Press, 1966.

Yovel, Yirmiyahu. *The Other Within: The Marranos: Split Identity and Emerging Modernity*. Princeton, NJ, and Oxford: Princeton University Press, 2009.

Zamora Jambrina, Hermenegildo. Introducción to *Historia de la Santa Provincia de Los Angeles*, by Andrés de Guadalupe, i–xliii. Madrid: Editorial Cisneros, 1994.

Zerner, Catherine Wilkinson. 'Body and Soul in the Basilica of the Escorial.' In *The Word Made Image: Religion, Art and Architecture in Spain and Spanish America, 1500–1600*, edited by Jonathan Brown, 66–90. Boston: Isabella Stewart Gardner Musem, 1998.

Ziegler, Joseph. 'Arnau de Vilanova: A Case-Study of a Theologizing Physician.' *Arxiu de Textos Catalans Antics* 14 (1995): 249–303.

– 'Medicine and Immortality in Terrestrial Paradise.' In *Religion and Medicine in the Middle Ages*, edited by Peter Biller and Joseph Ziegler, 201–42. York: University of York Press, 2001.

– *Medicine and Religion c. 1300: The Case of Arnau de Vilanova*. Oxford: Clarendon Press, 1998.

– '*Ut dicunt medici*: Medical Knowledge and Theological Debates in the Second Half of the Thirteenth Century.' *Bulletin of the History of Medicine* 73, no. 2 (1999): 208–37.

Index

TORONTO IBERIC

1 Anthony J. Cascardi, *Cervantes, Literature, and the Discourse of Politics*

2 Jessica A. Boon, *The Mystical Science of the Soul: Medieval Cognition in Bernardino de Laredo's Recollection Method*

www.ingramcontent.com/pod-product-compliance
Lightning Source LLC
LaVergne TN
LVHW040152080826
844660LV00014B/936/J

* 9 7 8 1 4 4 2 6 4 4 2 8 1 *